DATE DUE

SEP 6 1976			
NOV 3 1977			
MAY 11 1983			
MAY 13 1985			
APR 24 1987			
NOV 24 1988			
OCT 16 1989			
JAN 2 1990			
MAY 5 1994			
MAY 24 1994			
MAR 28 1995			
APR 1 2000			

DEMCO NO. 38-298

PUBLIC OPINION
AND
RESPONSIBLE DEMOCRACY

Dennis S. Ippolito
Emory University

Thomas G. Walker
Emory University

Kenneth L. Kolson
Hiram College

PRENTICE-HALL, INC., *Englewood Cliffs, New Jersey*

Library of Congress Cataloging in Publication Data

Ippolito, Dennis S.
  Public opinion and responsible democracy.

  Bibliography: p. 314
  Includes index.
    1. Public opinion—United States. 2. Political
participation—United States. 3. United States—
Politics and government. I. Walker, Thomas G., joint
author. II. Kolson, Kenneth L., joint author.
III. Title.
HN90.P8I66   301.15′43′329   75-26852
ISBN 0-13-737833-5

PRENTICE-HALL INTERNATIONAL, INC., *London*
PRENTICE-HALL OF AUSTRALIA PTY. LTD., *Sydney*
PRENTICE-HALL OF CANADA, LTD., *Toronto*
PRENTICE-HALL OF INDIA PRIVATE LIMITED, *New Delhi*
PRENTICE-HALL OF JAPAN, INC., *Tokyo*
PRENTICE-HALL OF SOUTHEAST ASIA (PTE.) LTD., *Singapore*

CONTENTS

PREFACE *v*

1 THE INFLUENCE OF PUBLIC OPINION *1*

*Masses, elites, and democracy / Direct influence / Group influence
Indirect influence / Summary*

Part one   Mass opinion

2 THE ANALYSIS OF POLITICAL ATTITUDES *19*

*The status of attitude as a concept / Collecting and analyzing attitudinal data
Attitude measurement / Attitudes—basic concepts / Summary*

3 POLITICAL SOCIALIZATION: THE FORMATION OF ATTITUDES *42*

*Political socialization and the political system
The learning of basic political orientations
Agents in the political socialization process
Discontinuities and differential political socialization / Summary*

**4 GROUP DIFFERENCES:
PARTY IDENTIFICATION AND ISSUE OPINIONS** *72*

Party identification / Issues and ideology / Summary

**5 THE AMERICAN POLITICAL CULTURE:
ATTITUDES ABOUT DEMOCRACY** *102*

*Direct democracy / Representative democracy / Citizen roles
The American participant / Summary*

Part two   Elite opinion

6   POLITICAL ELITES, LEADERSHIP, AND AMERICAN DEMOCRACY *121*

Political elites and democratic government
Political leadership: Responsiveness, responsibility, and accountability
Recruiting political elites / Summary

**7   ELITE OPINION AND POLITICAL DECISION MAKING:
INDIVIDUAL FACTORS** *145*

Social background factors / Personality factors / Attitudinal factors
Summary

**8   ELITE OPINION AND POLITICAL DECISION MAKING:
INSTITUTIONAL FACTORS** *175*

Institutional roles / Institutional norms
Collective behavior in political institutions / Summary

Part three   Opinion and government

9   OPINION INFLUENCE: ELECTIONS AND DIRECT ACTION *211*

Elections / Direct action / Summary

**10   OPINION INFLUENCE:
POLITICAL PARTIES AND INTEREST GROUPS** *241*

Political parties / Interest groups / Summary

11   OPINION INFLUENCE: REPRESENTATIVE INSTITUTIONS *268*

The presidency / Congress / Summary

Part four   Overview

12   PUBLIC OPINION AND RESPONSIBLE DEMOCRACY *301*

The people and their political leaders
Responsiveness and governmental institutions / Summary

BIBLIOGRAPHY *314*

INDEX *321*

PREFACE

The study of public opinion can be approached from a variety of perspectives. The emphasis in this book is upon the political consequences and effects of public opinion with respect to American national politics, and this emphasis has led us to consider not only mass opinion but also elite opinion and the institutional linkages between the public and political elites. In adopting this perspective, we have attempted to heed the advice of the late Professor V. O. Key, Jr. In *Public Opinion and American Democracy,* Professor Key suggested that the relationship between public opinion and democratic government could be understood only partially by analyzing mass opinion. A "missing piece of the puzzle," according to Key, was the elite element of the opinion system. Without making any pretense of solving the puzzle of how democratic regimes function, we have organized previous research so as to indicate the important characteristics of mass opinion and elite opinion and have attempted to delineate the primary types of interaction between them. There are accordingly three major divisions in the book.

Part One. Chapters Two through Five examine the characteristics and distribution of mass opinion. Chapter Two deals with the relationship between political attitudes and public opinion—the concept and measurement of attitudes, and what is meant by "public opinion." Chapter Three discusses political socialization—how attitudes are formed and influenced, how the citizen is assimilated into the political system, what values the citizen acquires about political life. Chapter Four surveys the differences between groups with respect to party identification and issue opinions. Chapter Five interprets the content of attitudes toward the American political culture—that is, how the public feels about democracy.

Part Two. Chapters Six through Eight analyze political elites. Chapter Six defines political elites in terms of their functions in a democracy and suggests factors that contribute to the development of effective leadership. Chapter Seven examines the personal characteristics, such as social background and personality, which affect elite decision making. Chapter Eight discusses the context of elite decision making—how perceptions of roles and norms relating to the conduct of politics and how the interaction among elite groups affect elite decision making.

Part Three. Chapters Nine through Eleven are devoted to institutional linkages between the public and political elites with a focus on national politics. Chapter Nine analyzes opinion influence transmitted through elections and direct action. Chapter Ten deals with group linkages— political parties and interest groups. Chapter Eleven assesses the linkage provided by representative institutions—the Presidency and Congress.

Dennis S. Ippolito
Thomas G. Walker
Kenneth L. Kolson

THE INFLUENCE OF
PUBLIC OPINION

1

Among Americans, there is considerable dissatisfaction with politics. Trust and confidence in the federal government have deteriorated, and many citizens believe that political leaders and political institutions are not sufficiently responsive to their needs and interests.[1] It is doubtless correct that the public's cynicism about politics can be attributed to a variety of factors—dissatisfaction with policies, negative reactions to political leaders, or unfavorable evaluations of political institutions. But what ties these factors together is the widespread belief that the governmental system is falling short of democratic goals. Thus, reforms in the election system, in the party system, or in the relations between the President and Congress are perceived as necessary to increase popular control and governmental responsiveness.[2] What the public is concerned about, in sum, reflects a classic concern of democratic politics—the relationship between public opinion and government.

This book examines public opinion and government in the United States by focusing upon three broad areas of inquiry: (1) the characteristics and distribution of opinions among the general public—what is generally termed mass opinion; (2) the characteristics and distribution of opinions among political leaders and political activists—that is, elite opinion; and (3) the institutional linkages—such as elections, political parties and interest groups, and representative institutions—which structure the interaction between the masses and the elites. The purpose of this book is to "prove" neither that the public is incompetent nor that public opinion is always characterized by wisdom and common sense but rather to provide a reasoːably accurate portrayal of the various ways in which government and public opinion interact and to identify the major strengths and weaknesses in that interaction.

Masses, elites, and democracy

The numerous studies of political attitudes and political behavior that have been conducted over the past several decades reflect both a popular and a scholarly fascination with what the American public is like politically. On many major and even a good many minor issues, the media feature polls about what the public thinks, and the implication is clear—what the public thinks is important. Specifically, what the public thinks directly concerns those who have the power and responsibility to make decisions about governmental policy. The President, members of Congress, cabinet members, and even Supreme Court justices—to say nothing of their elected and appointed counterparts at the state and local level—are presumably very much interested in what the public thinks about impeachment, or busing, or taxes, or crime.

The assumption that political leaders should be sincerely interested in what the public thinks is a distinguishing feature of democratic politics. The legitimacy of democratic regimes is based upon popular consent, a consent which applies not only to the choice of leaders but which also guides leaders once they are chosen. The division of society into the few who make important decisions, and consequently exercise great power, and the many who exercise little direct control over what the government does is not uncharacteristic of democracies, but democratic theory proposes that it is necessary and proper that the few, the elites, pay heed to the opinions of the many, the masses, if they are to govern rightly.

Expectations notwithstanding, there is considerable disagreement about the public's actual influence upon government. One interpretation, by two well-known political analysts, holds that this influence is substantial.

For the voters are very important people. Among other things, and despite what one may read about back-room political machinations, it is the voters who in large measure shape the men they elect and, in shaping the men, shape ultimately the politics of the nation. Political leaders are leaders only insofar as they can lead voters. The leaders are in office only insofar as they can win elections. These are elementary truths. . . .[3]

But a popular and influential textbook on American politics states that the "truths" are quite different.

Elites, not masses, govern America. . . . Elites may be responsive to the demands of the masses and influenced by the outcome of elections, or they may be unresponsive to mass movements and unaffected by elections. . . . Elites must govern wisely if government "by the people" is to survive. If the survival of the American system depended upon an active, informed, and enlightened citizenry, then democracy in America would have disappeared long ago. . . .[4]

It is not always popular to be realistic or analytical about politics, and, as the quotations above indicate, even the "realists" can adopt quite different perspectives. What is clear, however, is that normative theorizing about the public's role must be informed by empirical evidence regarding the public's interest in and capacity for political participation, by accurate appraisals of how political leaders evaluate and respond to public opinion, and by realistic assessments of the effects of particular institutions upon the interaction between the public and political leaders.

Analysis of each of these points is necessary for an accurate portrayal of the role that public opinion can and should play in governmental decision making. But in order to place such analysis in perspective, it is necessary to examine the various "models" of representation that symbolize the relationships between political leaders, or representatives, and the public. Basic to representative government is the idea that the public chooses representatives—executives and legislators—to act in its behalf and that these representatives will take into account the public's needs and opinions in making their decisions. The types of influence available to the public are: (1) direct constituent influence upon representatives through the use of rewards and sanctions—votes, campaign assistance, various forms of pressure; (2) constituent influence upon representatives through membership in or support for mediating groups, such as interest groups or political parties (again, similar rewards and sanctions can be utilized by groups against candidates or representatives); and (3) indirect constituent influence, which results when representatives act in accordance with constituent preferences because (a) they share such preferences or (b) they believe such preferences should prevail over their own judgments or preferences. Each of these models of representation symbolizes a political "linkage," an institutionalized factor that structures the interaction between the public and its leaders.[5] In examining them, we must recognize that American politics cannot be interpreted by relying exclusively on any single model. There is an obvious interdependence among these models; the effectiveness of the electoral linkage, for example, is significantly related to group linkages and to representative linkages.

Each of these models, then, reflects a different focal point in interpreting governmental responsiveness. Each involves certain assumptions about the nature of masses and elites and about the relations between them. In the following sections, we will point out the major assumptions underlying each model of representation and indicate some of the important studies that have examined these assumptions. In addition, we provide three case

studies to illustrate the direct, group, and indirect models. The school busing, gun control, and SST cases are not, of course, "pure" examples. Like
most issues, these are too complex for such a purpose. However, each has
characteristics that are especially appropriate for illustrating the relevance
of models of representation for political decision making.

Direct influence

In American national politics, the public cannot decide directly issues of
public policy. Nonetheless, the public does choose members of Congress
and the head of the executive branch. Elections provide not only the constitutional legitimacy for governmental action but also the potential for
popular influence on that action.

The model of representation which stresses direct constituent influence assumes that elected officials will act in accordance with public preferences in order to gain reelection. This in turn necessitates that the voters
be aware of policy issues, be informed about the differences between
candidates in terms of issues, and render their judgments based upon this
information. Direct constituent influence depends, in other words, upon
candidates or elected officials confronting an active, informed, and rational
electorate.

In addition to the rewards and sanctions relating to electoral support,
direct constituent influence can also be realized through forms of citizen
action aimed at officials already in office. Direct action—writing or petitioning officials, organizing ad hoc groups on policy issues, or engaging in
protest politics, such as marches or demonstrations—represents a second
mechanism for communicating with or pressuring officials.

Those who stress effectiveness of this type of linkage make certain
assumptions about elites and the mass public. According to this view, the
public has both the capacity and the inclination for informed, continuous,
and rational political participation. Citizens pay attention to campaigns,
listen to speeches, read platforms, and compare the candidates' positions.
Moreover, they remain vigilant between campaigns and stand ready to
inform officials about their views on new issues and to protest when their
opinions are disregarded.

Elites, on the other hand, recognize that they are dealing with an
active and informed public. Recognizing the ethical imperative to govern
in accordance with the public's consent and the pragmatic imperative to
remain in office, elites will keep informed about public opinion as far as
possible and will attempt to anticipate public opinion when it is not discernible.

Empirical evidence about the public's political participation and about the factors affecting elite decision making has considerably modified the assumptions concerning direct constituent influence. In particular, numerous studies have indicated that voters are not usually aware of policy issues and do not generally reward or punish representatives on the basis of their legislative records. Equally damaging, elites do not have accurate perceptions of voter preferences on many issues.[6]

This does not mean that the direct influence model is inapplicable in all cases. Upon occasion, the public may indeed have intense and stable opinions. Leaders, in turn, may have accurate perceptions about the public's attitudes and believe that ignoring those attitudes could lead to electoral reprisals. One policy area in which the direct influence model frequently operates is civil rights. Representatives tend to have relatively accurate perceptions of public attitudes in this area, and their legislative records on civil rights appear to be influenced by these perceptions.[7] Thus in order to illustrate how the direct influence model works, we can examine legislative attempts to curb school busing, one of the most controversial civil rights issues of recent years.

SCHOOL BUSING:
A CASE OF DIRECT INFLUENCE

The use of busing as a device to combat racial segregation in the public schools was first applied in southern states where dual school systems had been mandated by law. Between 1968 and 1970, federal court orders and pressure from administrative agencies, most notably the Department of Health, Education and Welfare (HEW), achieved considerable success in the South. Indeed, according to statistics provided by HEW, public school desegregation in the South had progressed considerably beyond that in the rest of the country by 1970.[8]

As desegregation proceeded in the South, however, attention shifted to the rest of the nation. In February 1970, a major desegregation order requiring substantial busing was issued against the Los Angeles school system. Over the next 18 months, similar orders were handed down against numerous urban and suburban school districts, including a metropolitan area-wide desegregation order in Detroit.[9] When the public schools opened in the fall of 1971, several hundred thousand students were being bused under desegregation orders written by the courts or by HEW. In many school districts, no serious disruptions ensued. But there was occasional violence, temporary boycotts were instituted in some cities, and reaction against busing was being translated into constituent pressure.

Public opinion was clearly opposed to interdistrict busing. In March 1970, the Gallup organization reported that only 14 percent of a national sample supported busing. In October 1971, 77 percent opposed busing, while only 17 percent supported it. Even among blacks, support of and opposition to busing were about equal.[10] In October 1971, antibusing groups from 47 cities met in Washington, D.C. to lobby for a constitutional amendment prohibiting busing. The Nixon administration, which had frequently stated its opposition to what it termed "massive busing," stepped up its campaign in 1971. Then, in March 1972, the President delivered a major speech attacking busing and outlining his legislative proposals to combat it. It appeared that busing would be a major issue in the 1972 campaign.

Caught in the cross-fire were many northern legislators who had traditionally opposed legislative attempts to curb busing. This was especially true of northern Democrats in the House. In 1968, 1969, and 1970, the House had ultimately rejected an antibusing provision known as the Whitten amendment, and northern Democrats had voted against the provision by margins of 96–12, 216–17, and 110–26.[11] In April 1971, the Whitten amendment was again rejected, with northern Democrats voting against it 108–23. In September, a federal judge handed down the Detroit desegregation plan. James G. O'Hara, a Democratic Representative from a suburban working-class district in the Detroit area and for years a leader in the floor fights against the Whitten amendment, signaled the change. He responded to the court order by declaring himself ready "to do whatever is necessary by way of further legislation or a constitutional amendment to prevent implementation of the . . . decision by cross-district busing." [12] On November 4, 1971, the House adopted two strong antibusing amendments to the Higher Education Act of 1971 by margins of 235–125 and 233–124. Northern Democrats opposed both provisions but by relatively small margins—90–56 and 94–50. O'Hara and his fellow Representatives from Michigan, however, supported the antibusing provisions overwhelmingly. And similar shifts occurred in delegations from other states where busing orders had been issued or were being considered, such as Illinois, Indiana, New York, Connecticut, and Pennsylvania. Even stronger antibusing legislation was passed by the House following Nixon's speech in March 1972, but the legislation was successfully filibustered in the Senate. Finally, the Senate and House agreed to compromise versions of the amendments passed by the House the previous November, but even the compromises represented the strongest antibusing language ever passed by Congress.

It seems clear that many Representatives were forced to change or at least to modify their positions on busing as a result of constituent opposition to busing. That the upcoming campaign—and the Nixon administration's stated intention to make busing a campaign issue—had something to do with this turnabout appears equally clear. In 1973, busing was not a major congressional issue; whatever attention there was focused on a proposed and unsuccessful constitutional amendment. And in July 1974, the Supreme Court reversed the district court order for Detroit and held that cross-district busing could not be utilized unless it could be shown that all the districts involved had engaged in racial discrimination. While this decision alleviated the busing controversy, it did not eliminate it. The disturbances in Boston in 1974 again showed the emotional and sometimes violent public reaction to busing.

Group influence

Models of representation based upon group influence focus upon the activities of political parties and interest groups. These are sometimes termed intermediate institutions—devices for aggregating the interests and opinions of numerous individuals and for influencing decisions of governmental officials in accordance with these interests and opinions.

RESPONSIBLE PARTIES

The transmission of public preferences through political parties depends upon an active and informed citizenry and upon parties which are "responsible"—that is, able to commit their officeholders to the support of common programs. Under the responsible party model, the voter directs his attention to the legislative records and proposed programs of the competing parties and selects candidates on the basis of national party programs. The voter in effect seeks correspondence between personal views of what government should or should not be doing and the positions represented by the competing parties.

The political party, in turn, presents candidates who appeal to the electorate on the basis of a common program. If the party gains a popular majority and hence control of government, it proceeds to enact its program. The minority party is responsible for monitoring and criticizing the majority party's performance and for presenting the voters with alternatives at the next election.

The requirements of the responsible parties model—that the voters grant or withhold their electoral support based upon party programs and performance, that the parties present the electorate with clear-cut policy alternatives, and that party candidates be committed to a common program —have not been typical of American party politics. Neither voter awareness nor party control has generally been sufficient to accomplish these ends. Yet the responsible parties model remains an important theoretical concern, and there is evidence to suggest that the model has applicability in certain policy areas, notably on social welfare issues.[13]

INTEREST GROUPS

Interest groups bring together individuals with common policy interests and concerns. While there are extreme variations in the size, activities, and effectiveness of interest groups, the assumption is that the leaders of interest groups will convey the views and interests of their members to governmental officials. This can be done directly, by lobbying in Congress or exerting pressure on the executive branch for example, or indirectly through involvement with political parties. From this perspective, the public depends on its group ties.

The membership of interest groups (the organized segment of the public) controls its own leadership by the rewards and sanctions it can employ within the group. Continued membership, selection of group leaders, and willingness to act in support of group positions (by, for example, voting or petitioning) represent means by which the membership can insure that the group's leadership accurately represents its preferences.

Externally, the group's influence is based upon the rewards and sanctions it, and its members, can employ against the parties, candidates, or officeholders. For large groups, this might include votes and various forms of campaign assistance; for smaller groups, campaign funds or publicity.

There is no question that interest groups are a major element in the political process and that some interest groups have established effective connections with political parties and with government. The legitimacy of this activity is based upon First Amendment guarantees of free speech and of the people's right "to petition the Government for a redress of grievances." But despite the extensive and legitimate involvement of interest groups in politics, this model has serious limitations. First, many important interests and many segments of the public are not organized. The interest group model can obviously work only for organized segments of society. Second, it appears that certain groups do not accurately represent the views or opinions of their members.[14] Indeed, some groups are characterized by clear differences between leaders and the membership in terms of opinions about issues and political tactics and strategy. And third, it is important to recognize that group leaders may have the same difficulty in assessing and evaluating member preferences as governmental representatives have in dealing with the mass public.

One can illustrate the interest group model with a variety of major issues. In fact, it is difficult to find issue controversies in which interest groups have not been involved. One example of the potency of interest group activity, illustrative of a long-standing battle between tenacious interest groups and majority public opinion, is the issue of gun control.

GUN CONTROL:
A CASE OF GROUP INFLUENCE

For more than three decades, the American public has consistently favored legislative restrictions on the purchase of firearms. During the past 15 years, majorities ranging from two-thirds to three-fourths of the adult public have supported requirements for police permits as a condition for purchasing a gun. There have been, of course, variations in support among certain groups. Support for controls has been higher in the East than in the South and West. Women have been more likely to support controls than men. And gunowners have been less enthusiastic about controls than those not owning guns. But even in this last case, a majority of the gunowners (61 percent) favored controls according to recent surveys.[15]

During the 1960s, increases in violent crimes along with the fatal shootings of President John F. Kennedy in 1963 and of Martin Luther King and Senator Robert Kennedy in 1968 sparked public campaigns for federal controls on the sale and registration of firearms. But each of these campaigns was countered and at least partially defeated by lobbying campaigns waged by hunting groups, by rifle and gun associations, most notably the National Rifle Association (NRA), by some wildlife and conservation organizations, and by firearms and ammunition manufacturers organizations, such as the National Shooting Sports Foundation and the Sporting Arms and Ammunition Manufacturers Institute. The NRA is generally conceded to be the most powerful opponent of strict controls. Its membership during the 1960s was more than 900,000, and its secretary estimated that NRA appeals could generate letters from more than half its members.[16] In 1968, the only organization primarily concerned with supporting strict controls was the Council for a Responsible Firearms Policy. While prominent individuals were on its board of directors, the Council had about 75 members, no full-time staff, and little money.[17]

Between 1963 and 1968, the Johnson administration continually requested control legislation, but Congress failed to enact limits on the sale and importation of firearms, to say nothing of licensing and registration. In 1968, however, the King and Kennedy killings prompted public pressure on Congress to enact strict controls. After Robert Kennedy's death on June 6, members of Congress reported receiving huge amounts of pro-control mail. But within two weeks, the NRA and its allies had swung into action, and congressional mail and petitions were soon running against controls.

The lobbying campaign against controls was not entirely successful. As part of the Omnibus Crime Control and Safe Streets Act, Congress did prohibit interstate sale or shipment to individuals of handguns, rifles, shotguns, and ammunition. This was a slightly expanded version of legislation introduced five years earlier. But the NRA and its allies did succeed on the more important point of blocking congressional approval of the Johnson administration's request for owner licensing and gun registration. The public responded to Congress' record on gun control accordingly. In January 1968, the Harris poll reported that 48 percent of the public rated Congress negatively and 28 percent positively on its gun control record. One year later, the negative rating had increased to 59 percent and the positive rating to 34 percent.[18] Public support for licensing and registration requirements has persisted in recent years, but significant governmental action has not been forthcoming.

The gun control controversy illustrates that well-organized interest groups with significant resources and staffs, and with active memberships, can counter public opinion. Even when public opinion becomes intense, as it did after the assassinations, this intensity tends to be relatively short-lived. Thus the potential rewards and sanctions perceived by many legislators on gun control issues are those associated with stable organizations and their members.

Indirect influence

In the absence of constituent or group influences aimed directly at officials, representatives may still act in accordance with the public's preferences. One way in which this can occur is when the legislator accepts that style of representation known as Instructed Delegate. Whether or not his own judgment corresponds with that of his constituents, the Instructed Delegate accepts it as his duty to act upon his constituents' views. Of course, it is often difficult to differentiate between representatives who bow to their constituents' demands because of principle and those who do so for pragmatic reasons. But it is clear that many legislators do believe that their proper role is that of Instructed Delegate.[19] One of the obvious requirements of this model of representation, however, is that the representatives have reasonably accurate perceptions of constituency attitudes, and this has been found lacking in many policy areas.[20] Thus the difficulty of ascertaining "true" constituency attitudes on the large number of issues with which a representative is confronted imposes a severe practical limit on this form of representation.

A second avenue of influence emerges when the representative shares his constituency's views. By voting his own preferences, he votes theirs as well. The model of representation based upon shared attitudes assumes that the representative and his constituency, through their common backgrounds and experiences, form common attitudes and beliefs about politics which are then translated into similar views about specific issues.

A major problem with this model is that numerous studies have indicated that masses and elites generally have quite different attitudes about politics and hold different issue positions.[21] It would be foolish, however, to assume that this model has no relevance for actual representative behavior, although the extent of shared attitudes might vary significantly depending upon the policy area. It is also possible that issues will occasionally emerge about which representatives and their constituents will develop similar positions.

One of the problems in attempting to illustrate this phenomenon is the lack of evidence about representatives' attitudes and constituency attitudes on specific issues. It is possible, for example, that many members of Congress and their constituents came to hold similar views about impeachment between the summer of 1973 and the summer of 1974. With little public or congressional support in early 1973, the gradual uncovering of evidence, the firing of the special prosecutor, the release of transcripts, and the Judiciary Committee hearings resulted in public support for impeachment, and estimates of congressional sentiment were that the House would vote to impeach even prior to the release of the final tapes which led to Richard Nixon's resignation.

Recognizing the degree of speculation and inference necessary, it is possible that certain other issues might fit the shared attitude model of representation. One case that presents such a possibility is that of the SST —or supersonic transport—which Congress voted down in 1971.

THE SST:
A CASE OF INDIRECT INFLUENCE

Beginning in 1959, the federal government and private contractors had commenced a program for development of a supersonic transport plane. Unsuccessful efforts to halt the project had surfaced in the House in 1964 and in the Senate in 1966. By 1970, questions about the economic viability and environmental effects of the plane received considerable publicity, and funding for the project was jeopardized. Finally, in March 1971, Congress terminated federal financial participation. Later attempts to reverse the vote during that session were unsuccessful, and for all practical purposes, the SST was finished, since adequate private funding was unlikely.

The lobbying campaign against the SST was extensive. A coalition of environmental and taxpayer groups had worked throughout 1970 to influence public and congressional opinion. But the pro-SST lobby was also substantial. Backed by the Nixon administration, labor unions and industry formed two groups—the National ·Committee for the SST, and Industry and Labor for the SST—which utilized existing legislative liaison staffs in Washington to work with members of Congress and also mounted extensive public campaigns to encourage support of the SST. A major argument of the labor and industry lobby was that termination of the project would eliminate 50,000 jobs and adversely affect the U.S. balance of payments.

During 1970, opposition to the SST focused upon potential environmental damage, especially noise pollution and atmospheric contamination. The former objection was partially undercut when the Nixon administration agreed in late 1970 to rule out SST flights over land at supersonic speeds. In 1971, the debate shifted partially to economics. Against administration arguments relating to economic dislocations, U.S. superiority in air technology and marketing, and balance of payments effects, SST opponents focused on the economic viability of the plane. Continued uncertainty about the project's ultimate cost to the government and about the potential market for the aircraft marked the debate.

The termination vote in March was close in both houses. In the Senate, the vote was 51–46. In the House, the vote was 217–204. Moreover, party and ideological lines were blurred, as might be expected given the types of groups supporting and opposing the plane. In the House, for example, a slight majority of Democrats voted against the SST while Republicans barely voted for it, 90–85.

Some members of Congress suggested that the SST vote reflected constituency influence. As one indication of this, surveys were conducted in ten House districts, including the constituencies of the Democratic and Republican leadership. In every district, public opinion was clearly opposed to continued funding of the SST, yet Representatives from eight of these districts voted to continue the SST program.[22] This suggests that, at least for some members of Congress, constituency preferences were not determinative, and electoral reprisals seemed unlikely.

Furthermore, the major interest groups involved were unable to exert compelling pressure. The more intensive and best financed effort, after all, was by the pro-SST groups allied with the administration. Why did the major lobbying campaign on this issue fail? Apparently the public and members of Congress had become increasingly sensitive to environmental problems. Louis Harris (director of the Harris poll) has suggested that the underlying issue in the public's opposition to the SST was the possibility of environmental damage and that ecological questions had become important political concerns by the late 1960s.[23] It certainly appears that new members of Congress were aware of this aspect, since freshmen Senators and Representatives voted against the SST by almost 2–1. It may be, then, that the environmental and economic issues raised by the SST project produced a similar reaction within the public and Congress. Acting from shared concerns, legislators and their constituents may have formed shared attitudes albeit with little direct communication between them. Thus the SST issue may represent a case in which many legislators voted in accordance with their constituents' views because they shared those views.

Summary

The influence of public opinion upon government is a persistent problem of democratic politics. Democratic theory holds that elites should be responsive to the interests and preferences of the masses and, consequently, that mass opinion should have a clear bearing upon the decision making process in government. Analyses of American politics, however, evidence considerable disagreement about the actual impact of public opinion upon government.

The interaction between public opinion and government is structured by linkages. These include such elements as elections and direct action, political parties and interest groups, and representative institutions. One can categorize these linkages according to types of influence. The direct influence model focuses upon representation which results from citizen participation in elections and in various forms of direct action. Logically, representatives should take constituent preferences into account because of the rewards and sanctions citizens can employ against them. The group influence model involves intermediate institutions, political parties and interest groups, whose function it is to bring together citizens with common interests and preferences and to transmit these interests and preferences to political leaders. Here again, political leaders are forced to pay attention because of the sanctions these groups can employ against them. A third model of representation is based upon indirect citizen influence resulting from the types of political leaders chosen. This model presupposes that political leaders act in accordance with the public's preferences because they share those preferences, or because they feel obligated to give those preferences primacy over their own judgments.

Each of these models has theoretical and practical limitations. Therefore, in order to evaluate the quality of mass-elite interaction in any given model, we must examine our assumptions about masses, elites, and institutions in terms of empirical evidence. The remainder of this book attempts to do just that.

NOTES

1 Arthur H. Miller, "Political Issues and Trust in Government; 1964–1970," *American Political Science Review*, 68 (September 1974), 951–72; see also Philip E. Converse, "Change in the American Electorate," in *The Human Meaning of Social Change*, ed. Angus Campbell and Philip E. Converse (New York: Russell Sage Foundation, 1972).

2 Arthur H. Miller, "Rejoinder to 'Comment' by Jack Citrin: Political Discontent or Ritualism?" *American Political Science Review*, 68 (September 1974), 992.

3 Richard M. Scammon and Ben J. Wattenberg, *The Real Majority* (New York: Coward, McCann & Geoghegan, Inc., 1971), pp. 15–16.

4 Thomas R. Dye and L. Harmon Zeigler, *The Irony of Democracy*, 2d ed. rev. (Belmont, Calif.: Wadsworth Publishing Co., Inc., 1972), pp. 3–4.

5 The concept of linkages as applied to the interaction between public opinion and government was developed by V. O. Key, Jr., *Public Opinion and American Democracy* (New York: Knopf, 1965), pp. 411–531. An excellent examination of models of political linkage is provided by Norman R. Luttbeg, ed., *Public Opinion and Public Policy*, rev. ed. (Homewood, Ill.: Dorsey Press, 1974).

6 Donald E. Stokes and Warren E. Miller, "Party Government and the Saliency of Congress," *Public Opinion Quarterly*, 26 (Winter 1962), 531–46; Warren E. Miller and Donald E. Stokes, "Constituency Influence in Congress," *American Political Science Review*, 57 (March 1963), 45–56.

7 Miller and Stokes, "Constituency Influence in Congress." Also, in a study of public opinion and public policy within states, public preferences and state policy on civil rights coincided in 46 of 50 states. The congruence between opinion and policy was greater for civil rights than for any of the other policies studied—gun control, lotteries, capital punishment, or right-to-work laws. Frank J. Munger, "Opinion, Elections, Parties, and Policies: A Cross-State Analysis," unpublished paper delivered at the American Political Science Association Meeting, 1969.

8 *Congressional Quarterly Almanac*, Vol. 27, 92d Congress, 1st Session (Washington, D.C.: Congressional Quarterly Service, 1972), p. 602.

9 The Supreme Court reversed the Detroit order on July 25, 1974. *Milliken* v. *Bradley*, 94 S.Ct. 3112 (1974). Busing remained an available remedy, but interdistrict busing was prohibited unless all districts affected had engaged in racial discrimination.

10 *Gallup Opinion Index*, Report No. 58 (April 1970), p. 9; *Gallup Opinion Index*, Report No. 77 (November 1971), p. 24. An August 1973 poll found that busing was the least favored method of eliminating segregation in the schools, with only 5 percent supporting busing, as opposed to 27 percent favoring changes in district boundaries and 22 percent favoring creating housing to change residential segregation. *Gallup Opinion Index*, Report No. 100 (October 1973), p. 18.

11 This provision was authored by Jamie L. Whitten (D. Miss). It prohibited HEW from withholding federal funds from school districts in order to require further school desegregation, by busing or other means.

12 *Congressional Quarterly Weekly Report*, 29, No. 50 (December 11, 1971), 2559.

13 Miller and Stokes, "Constituency Influence in Congress."

14 Norman R. Luttbeg and L. Harmon Zeigler, "Attitude Consensus and Conflict in an Interest Group: An Assessment of Cohesion," *American Political Science Review*, 60 (September 1966), 655–66.

15 Hazel Erskine, "The Polls: Gun Control," *Public Opinion Quarterly,* 36 (Fall 1972), 455–69.

16 *Legislators and the Lobbyists,* 2d ed. (Washington, D.C.: Congressional Quarterly Service, 1968), p. 86.

17 Ibid., p. 87.

18 Erskine, "The Polls: Gun Control," 469.

19 See Roger H. Davidson, *The Role of the Congressman* (New York: Pegasus, 1969), pp. 110–42.

20 Miller and Stokes, "Constituency Influence in Congress."

21 Philip E. Converse, "The Nature of Belief Systems in Mass Publics," in *Ideology and Discontent,* ed. David Apter (New York: The Free Press, 1964), pp. 206–61. See also John L. Sullivan and Robert E. O'Connor, "Electoral Choice and Popular Control of Public Policy," *American Political Science Review,* 66 (December 1972).

22 *The New York Times,* August 22, 1971, p. 19.

23 Louis Harris, *The Anguish of Change* (New York: W. W. Norton & Company, Inc., 1973), pp. 111, 116.

Part one
Mass opinion

THE ANALYSIS OF
POLITICAL ATTITUDES

2

There is probably no good purpose to be served by endeavoring too strenuously to define precisely what we mean by "attitude," as opposed to "opinion" or "belief." No doubt some heuristic purpose is sometimes served by rigorous formal definitions, but for the most part this effort is not very rewarding, and can even lead to a false sense of self-confidence. We shall, then, make it a practice to use the terms as though they were synonymous. Berelson and Steiner, in their important integrating volume, *Human Behavior: An Inventory of Scientific Findings,*[1] solved the problem by referring to "OAB's," and although we shall not follow this practice, it does seem to us that Berelson and Steiner were right in not becoming obsessed with distinguishing among these very similar terms. Despite this disclaimer, we do have a preference for "attitude," since this is the term that is employed by those social psychologists who have contributed to the development of "attitude theory."

This book is not concerned with *all* attitudes (or opinions, or beliefs) that can be identified in society; we are interested in *political* attitudes. For our purposes any attitude found within the political community which has some bearing on the operation of the political system, at any level, will be considered a political attitude. We are aware of the fact that many private attitudes, or attitudes which are not overtly political, often have a way of intruding into the political realm. Once present, we shall acknowledge them as "political attitudes." That an individual's attitude, if he has one, about the SST, or civil rights, is political in nature is so obvious as to need no further elaboration.

The status of attitude
as a concept

Attitudes cannot be observed in a direct and unambiguous way. "Attitude" is a *concept,* and as such it must be given what is called an *operational definition.* This manner of definition allows us to employ certain specified (and preferably unambiguous) operations in order to "observe" the thing in question. This method of definition is quite obviously scientific. The scientific method requires that the operations can be, at least in principle, replicated by anyone. The procedures employed should not be idiosyncratic, intuitive, or subjective.

The existence of an attitude must always be inferred since attitudes cannot be observed directly. It is *behavior* that we observe, and from which we infer the presence of attitudes. It is for this reason that some behavioral scientists, most notably B. F. Skinner,[2] condemn the use of "attitude" as being unscientific.

These critics emphasize three valid points. First, attitudes cannot be directly observed, they must be inferred. Second, attitudes can be misleading. There is no question about this; very often people say they believe something but their actions would appear to deny it. This is frustrating, to be sure, but what it really means is that we must conduct our research with care because unraveling the fabric of human behavior is a very difficult task. Third, attitudes are learned; they are not inherited genetically. It cannot be denied that most, if not all, political attitudes are learned. Perhaps attitudes should thus be thought of as "intervening variables"—standing between learning experiences on the one hand and political behavior on the other. Since the environment is so complex that we could never hope to enumerate all of the learning experiences of an individual (not to mention of the electorate), it is efficient to study these experiences *as they have been internalized by the individual.* If it is the case that attitudes "sum up" the learning experiences of an individual, and if it is true that behavior is learned, then studying attitudes allows us better to understand how the environment "shapes" an individual's behavior.

Let us turn to the political realm to illustrate the points that have been made about the status of attitude as a concept. Visualize the following hypothetical exchange taking place on an American doorstep:

Interviewer: For whom did you vote in the presidential election of 1972?
Respondent: Nixon.
Interviewer: Why?
Respondent: I like him. For one thing I'm a Republican. And I liked what he said about law and order.

Are we to conclude that nothing has been explained by the respondent? That may be true in a sense, since his or her "likes and dislikes" are the products of prior learning experiences, which are the "true causes" of the voting behavior. We are nonetheless very interested in this person's attitudes. A number of political objects (stimuli, if you prefer) have been identified. These objects are linked together and have positive connotations for the respondent. Even though it may be that the preference expressed for the Republican party has not been "explained," that is of no real concern. What is important is that we have learned something about the manner in which this person has organized the political world, and this organization has an evaluative component. Any behavior must surely be regarded as a manifestation of these attitudes—even if attitude is only an intervening variable—despite the fact that the origin of these attitudes and the manner in which attitudes and their outward manifestations are related to one another remain obscure.

More relevant from our point of view is that the concept "attitude" helps us to piece together complex political events in the real world. How, for example, can the presidential election of 1972 be best understood? What is the "meaning" of that election? Perhaps it would be possible to concoct an explanation that makes no reference to attitudes, opinions, beliefs, values, or ideologies, but it is difficult to conceive how this might be done. Was the 1972 election an endorsement of Richard Nixon or a rejection of George McGovern? Was it a rejection of the Democratic party, or an endorsement of the Republican party? Surely an investigation of attitudes would help us to answer these questions. Individual attitudes "uncovered" through the method of survey research can be pieced together into a mosaic we can properly term "public opinion." Since the methods employed in the construction of this mosaic can be replicated, hypotheses can be re-tested, refined, supported, or rejected. Fortunately, we do not have to depend on intuitive processes in order to be enlightened about politics.

Collecting and analyzing attitudinal data

Now that we have introduced attitude as a concept, we shall investigate the methods by which attitudinal data may be collected. Essentially there are two distinct approaches, each of which is appropriate to certain kinds of research interests, and both of which are quite legitimate. The first is a rather indirect method of analysis which employs what are termed aggregate data. The more customary and direct method is survey research.

AGGREGATE ANALYSIS

Data that come in aggregate form are familiar to us all. The median income of persons living in New York, the percentage of blacks residing in Los Angeles, the number of tractors per farm in Kansas, the number of votes cast in Cleveland precincts—these are examples of aggregate data. These data were collected by aggregating, or combining, data from smaller units into larger units.

How does one work with data in the aggregate form? How does one "do" aggregate analysis? The procedures are rather well known, since very often certain types of data, such as election results, come in this form. Electoral data come to us in aggregate form—by precinct, ward, county, state, and so on. Of course we are all familiar with the election analysts on television who tell us such things as "Nixon has a comfortable lead in southern California because of all the conservatives in Orange County." Such a statement is an inference about the attitudes of individual voters based on their behavior in the aggregate. This is how public opinion is reconstructed using aggregate data.

What one usually does is to compare election returns with other data for the same geographical units in order to see if any patterns emerge. "The vote" is a variable—it is not uniform from state to state, from county to county, or from precinct to precinct. The fluctuation, or variation of the vote can be compared with the variation of other factors—social, economic, or political. In Table 2.1, we have hypothetical data from the election of 1960. In the first column is "Percentage Catholic," and in the second column is "Percentage voting for Kennedy." The reason that we wish to compare the configurations of these two variables is that we have presumably posited a hypothesis concerning religion and voting.

With aggregate data, using the appropriate analytical and statistical techniques, we can come to some conclusion as to whether or not our

Table 2.1
Religion and Voting Behavior in a Hypothetical State, by County, 1960

COUNTY	PERCENTAGE CATHOLIC	PERCENTAGE VOTING FOR KENNEDY
A	22.1	22.1
B	59.3	59.3
C	76.4	76.4
D	40.3	40.3

hypothesis is confirmed by our "observations." In the case presented in Table 2.1, we would treat Catholicism as the *independent* variable, and voting for Kennedy as the *dependent* variable. Presumably, our hypothesis suggests that the vote is, in part at least, dependent upon one's religious affiliation, and not vice versa.

Table 2.1 presents hypothetical data, of course, and it illustrates a perfect correlation. Statistics which can be computed to summarize the relationship between two variables such as those in Table 2.1 are called "measures of association." Inasmuch as they tell us something about the correlation of two variables, they are sometimes called "coefficients of correlation."

The meaning of a measure of association is not self-evident. Meaning must be attributed to statistics, and the variables being studied must be taken into account. This is especially true regarding interpretations of causation. Can we infer from the high correlation between numbers of tractors per county and Republicanism in Kansas that owning tractors "causes" counties to vote Republican? Hardly. Nor can we say that the percentage of blacks in a precinct "causes" that precinct to vote for or against a black candidate. What we can say is that the variables are associated; that race accounts for some of the variation in voting at the precinct level. We may even develop a theory that seeks to explain the election in terms of race; but we cannot say that the correlation between race and voting behavior demonstrates that the former "causes" the latter.

Along these lines, we should also consider the concept of *spuriousness.* In our example about the correlation between tractors and Republicans in Kansas, it can be seen that attributing causation in this case would be absurd. But what if we in fact did find that the two variables were positively related? How would we interpret this finding? How would we account for a strong relationship between these two variables? Actually, we should not be at all surprised to find that the two variables were related, and this is of course due to the fact that each is positively correlated with a third factor—income. In a rural state such as Kansas, we would expect that income is positively associated with owning tractors on the one hand, and with Republicanism on the other. The original relationship is therefore "spurious"; it is a statistical artifact resulting from the correlation between income and the other two variables. To use a more familiar, and delicate, example of the same thing, the relationship between race and crime rates in the United States is no doubt spurious. To say that blacks are somehow inherently prone to crime, or that they are the "cause" of crime is to ignore the fact that blacks are more frequently subject to social, economic, and cultural circumstances that promote crime among people of all races. Borrowing an example from Buchanan,[3] to cite race as the "cause" of crime would be about as fallacious as identifying swamps, rather than mosquitoes (or more properly, the agents carried by mosquitoes), as the cause of malaria.

Another danger inherent in aggregate analysis was alluded to earlier —the so-called ecological fallacy.[4] When working with aggregate data, it is essential that the researcher not forget the nature of his data. In the examples used in this chapter our data have been aggregated by geographical units—states, counties, precincts. This means that any inferences we may wish to draw from our data must relate to these geographical units, and we must be careful not to transcend the limits of our data. Look again at Table 2.1. The fact is that we have no data here bearing on individuals, and to conclude from Table 2.1 that "Catholics voted for Kennedy" would be to fall victim to the ecological fallacy. Table 2.1 does not tell us anything about the behavior of *Catholics*—it tells us something about *counties*. This may at first blush seem trivial, especially since there is no particular reason why we should be interested in a county, since a county is only an aggregative unit. Nevertheless, even though it is the behavior of the *parts* that interests us, and even though the relationship in Table 2.1 seems unambiguous, a valid generalization can only extend to counties, not to individuals. The fact is that Table 2.1 does *not* demonstrate that "Catholics voted for Kennedy." It is possible, for example, that every single Catholic in County D voted for Nixon. We just do not know. To commit the ecological fallacy, then, is to attribute to individuals the characteristics of their milieu, in this case the characteristics of counties; just because Catholic counties supported Kennedy does not mean that Catholics did.

Given all of the caveats that have been entered regarding aggregate analysis, the reader must by now think that this is not a very good way of studying political attitudes. This is not true. In fact there are some research purposes for which aggregate analysis is especially well suited.

In the first place aggregate data can be used in the study of political history. For example, the presidential election of 1896 has often been referred to as a "critical" election, and it occupies an important place in American electoral history. But some nagging questions remain. The electorate of 1896 cannot be resurrected to answer the questions that we might wish to put to it directly, but fortunately this public has left a record of itself, from which its attitudes might fairly be reconstructed. Census data, election returns, and other data in aggregate form can be used to indicate in a rough way the state of public opinion during that campaign. Walter Dean Burnham's analysis of critical elections using aggregate data is a particularly impressive example of how the electorates of the past may be brought back to life.[5]

There is another great advantage that the aggregate data approach has over survey research. That is simply that it is cheap and readily accessible. Since public libraries are filled with data, and since voting data can be collected in the county courthouse, one can easily undertake this kind of research.

SURVEY RESEARCH

We have all become accustomed to survey research, yet this method of research—commonly referred to as "opinion polling"—is quite new. Survey research is the most direct, and therefore the best, way of collecting data pertinent to the study of political attitudes. In this section we shall examine the historical and theoretical roots of survey research, paying special attention to sampling.

Historically, survey research has roots in market research, which began to serve American business during the 1920s. In fact, many of the pioneers of survey research were not social scientists at all, but came out of business or advertising fields. We have in the United States today a number of large polling organizations—the Roper poll, the Harris poll, the American Institute of Public Opinion, and the National Opinion Research Center, to name just a few—but it took some time for the idea of survey research to spread to the realm of politics.

Early efforts to measure public opinion were rather quaint, to say the least. The classic example of how *not* to conduct survey research remains the *Literary Digest* poll of 1936, which predicted a victory for Alf Landon in the presidential election of that year. As we know, Franklin D. Roosevelt won that election with one of the biggest landslides in American history. What went wrong? The *Digest,* which was not unlike *Time* or *Newsweek,* had used a sample drawn from its own subscribers, from lists of automobile owners, from telephone books, and the like. Despite the fact that it con- tacted literally millions of voters that year, and that it tried to balance the geographical representation of its sample, its disastrous prediction was in- evitable. The country was in the midst of the Great Depression in 1936, but the sample the *Digest* drew did not take cognizance of that fact. It was hopelessly skewed toward the well-to-do element of American society—an element that was not only overwhelmingly Republican but also looked upon Roosevelt as being a "traitor to his class," or worse. Moreover, those who chose to fill out and return cards on their own (the method the *Digest* used to conduct its "straw poll") were of course persons who held the most intense opinions. Thus a serious *sampling error* resulted in a totally un- representative survey. Within a matter of months after the 1936 election the *Literary Digest* was defunct.

The basic idea underlying survey research is *sampling.* The owner of a factory, for example, wants to make sure that his product meets some self-determined standard of quality. One way for him to do this is to "test" every item as it comes off the assembly line. Since this is not feasible, he must learn to live with a certain element of doubt. On the other hand, if he sampled only one item per day, he would be living with a great deal of doubt indeed. He must reach a compromise that will reduce his doubt to a personally acceptable level and at the same time establish a feasible limit for "testing."

In survey research the problems are similar. The large polling organization that wishes to predict the outcome of a presidential election attempts to make a generalization about the millions of American voters (in survey terminology, the "population," or "universe"). But of course the entire population of American voters cannot be surveyed. The polling organizations, then, need to draw from the population under investigation a *representative* sample, and this sample must be of a size small enough to be surveyed feasibly, but large enough to reduce the doubt about its representativeness to an "acceptable" level. It is now possible for polling organizations to predict presidential elections with considerable accuracy using samples of between 1,500 and 3,000 people.

There are some obvious problems involved in conducting survey research for the purpose of predicting, for example, the outcome of a presidential election. In the first place, note that the relevant universe here is not the American population, but the American *electorate*. It is necessary therefore to exclude from the sample people who might be representative of the former but not the latter—seventeen year olds, for instance. The universe must be precisely defined. Second, it would be prohibitively expensive to send interviewers all over the country to track down 1,500 or 3,000 people whose names had been randomly selected from some mythical list of all eligible voters. Therefore, interviewers are assigned to specific election precincts and draw their respondents from certain blocks or houses, selected randomly. Third, samples of the American electorate are always stratified so as to guarantee that members of certain identifiable subgroups are not excluded. Finally, the sample must be of a size sufficient to minimize the risk to an acceptable level, but not unnecessarily large.

The great disadvantage of survey research is that it is costly—in terms of resources, time, and manpower. The great advantage that survey research has over aggregate analysis is that it enables us to measure attitudes directly. Perhaps we can infer from aggregate data that in 1972 Richard Nixon was perceived more positively by the American electorate than was George McGovern. After all, he did win a majority of the votes in forty-nine of the states. If we were to study the election returns at the county or precinct level, using the techniques of aggregate analysis, we might be able to say much more about the way in which Nixon was perceived by the American electorate in 1972. But we could never in this manner match the information which survey research can provide. See, for example, Table 2.2. Such information can be acquired only through survey research.

Louis Harris' reaction to Table 2.2 is as follows:

Richard Nixon, two weeks away from a landslide victory, received negative marks from the American people. Had he been running on the issue of his own personal confidence alone, he would have held no more than a slim 48% to 44% lead. But it was obvious that the Nixon magic lay in his ability to say in nearly every speech and point up in nearly every TV commercial that he had moved the world closer to peace by his dramatic trips to Peking and Moscow. When the people were asked who could "best negotiate with the Russians and Chinese," Nixon swamped McGovern by a 70% to a 14% margin. Nixon gained his basic credibility as a candidate on the peace issue, and that was the main reason, by 56% to 26%, most Americans in the fall of 1972 felt that he, rather than McGovern, could best "inspire confidence in the White House." In turn, this was reflected in the massive 61% to 37% victory margin of the president on election day.[6]

Imagine how a study of the 1972 presidential election based on aggregate data alone would compare with Harris' description. The point should be clear: survey research is an effective method for studying mass political attitudes.

Table 2.2
Nixon Ratings by Voters, Mid-October 1972

	POSITIVE	NEGATIVE	NOT SURE
Overall rating	59%	40%	1%
His trip to China	75%	20%	5%
His handling of relations with Russia	73	22	5
His Russian summit trip	72	22	6
Working for peace in the world	67	31	2
Handling relations with China	66	26	8
Inspiring confidence personally	48	44	8
Handling war in Vietnam	46	52	2
Stand on busing for racial balance	42	45	13
Handling race problems	43	52	5
Helping curb drug abuse	43	49	8
Handling air and water pollution	39	49	12
Negotiating final Vietnam settlement	39	53	8
Helping keep economy healthy	38	57	5
Handling crime, law and order	38	57	5
Keeping unemployment down	34	61	5
Keeping effective controls on wages and prices	33	63	4
Handling taxes and spending	32	63	5
Handling corruption in government	32	55	13
Keeping down cost of living	22	76	2

Source: Louis Harris, *The Anguish of Change* (New York: W. W. Norton & Company, Inc., 1973), p. 256.

Attitude measurement

Survey research is the best available method for providing evidence about mass attitudes. This, however, does not mean that there is no controversy about its widespread use. There is considerable concern, for example, about the effects of polls upon the democratic process. Some critics charge that polls result in "packaged candidates," encourage manipulative efforts by politicians and their advisers, and even create a "bandwagon psychology" among the electorate, with voters casting their ballots for the candidate reported ahead in the polls in order to be on the winning side.[7] While these types of questions are certainly important, our concern at this point is with the accuracy of survey research in "measuring" attitudes rather than with the desirability of its use by candidates, campaign consultants, or the media.

Whether or not a survey provides us with accurate evidence about individual attitudes and hence about public opinion depends upon a number of factors, none of which can be assessed with absolute certainty. As we noted earlier, for example, accuracy is dependent first upon the utilization of proper sampling procedures. In dealing with data reported by the major survey research organizations—such as the American Institute of Public Opinion (the Gallup poll), the Survey Research Center at the University of Michigan, the National Opinion Research Center, the Harris poll, and so on—sampling questions are not especially troublesome. These organizations have achieved an impressive level of sophistication in sampling, and this gives us considerable assurance about the representativeness of their samples. It is important to remember, however, that even with proper procedures in sampling and adequately sized samples, there is a range of sampling error which must be taken into account. This is especially true of election polls, where the typical maximum range of error at ± 3 percent is sufficiently large as to give us little certainty about which candidate is ahead in a close race. Of course, what a poll does tell us under such circumstances is that there is indeed a close race.

In addition to the general problem of sampling, there are potential weaknesses in any survey which relate to such factors as question wording, types of attitude measures, and problems of "response set" (in which the respondent tends to react to attitude statements for reasons other than the content of those statements). A brief discussion of each of these might indicate the caution which is necessary in interpreting public opinion.

QUESTION WORDING

Problems of question wording go beyond the questionnaire item which is obviously biased or "loaded" to elicit a desired response. Even in simple, carefully written, and supposedly neutral questions, the presence of certain cue words or the tone of the language employed can affect the respondent's reactions.[8] Mueller's study of public opinion about the wars in Korea and Vietnam found that responses were affected by the word "communist" used in some questions. Support for the Korean intervention, for example, was higher in questions which contained references to a "Communist invasion of South Korea," than in questions which simply asked whether or not the United States did the right thing in getting involved in Korea.[9]

Controversial issues are especially susceptible to cue words and language tone problems. Issues such as abortion, school busing, gun control, and foreign policy issues such as the Vietnam war generate strong feelings among many people, and this fact means that we should be aware of the possible effects that question wording can have on responses. One type of check is to compare the questions used on the same issue by different polling organizations. If we find wording differences along with different results, we might expect that the question stimulus is providing much of the variation. Mueller's conclusion about the question wording problem is a useful reminder. *"The polls,"* he suggests, *"are simply incapable of answering a large number of the questions to which they have been applied."* [10]

ATTITUDE MEASURES

The types of attitude measures utilized in survey research range from the simple type of closed-ended, dichotomous response question ("Do you approve or disapprove of the way that Gerald Ford is handling his job as President?") to rather involved types of attitudes scales that seek to measure liberalism–conservatism, racial prejudice, internationalism, and similarly complex phenomena.

Much of the data reported by the media tends to be of the closed-ended, dichotomous response variety. The polling organizations find these kinds of data easy to accumulate, and the media find them easy to report. And for certain purposes, this elementary form of attitude measure is quite appropriate. During election campaigns, for example, the percentage favoring Candidate A and the percentage favoring Candidate B give us useful and generally accurate approximations of public opinion. Such responses do not tell us anything about the potential voter's interest in the campaign, information about politics, or rationality in assessing the candidates. But the primary purpose of the pre-election poll is to give us an idea about candidate strength. Thus we can expect voter preferences to be translated into votes, and the process by which the voter attains his preferences are less important than the fact that he will usually vote in accordance with those preferences.

A somewhat more complicated form of attitude measurement is provided by questions which allow us to gather information about intensity or degree. The "yes" vs. "no" or the "approve" vs. 'disapprove" question provides evidence about the *direction* of public opinion. But in some cases, we are also interested in additional information. A measure of party identification which breaks the population down into Democrats, Republicans, and Independents is useful. But it is even more useful if we can measure strength of identification—whether an individual considers himself to be a "strong Democrat" or a "weak Democrat," for example. We are aware that strong identifiers differ from weak identifiers in several important respects. The strong identifier is more likely to be interested and knowledgeable about politics and is also more likely to support consistently his party's candidates. The weak identifier, while less politically aware, is more likely to desert his party in response to short-term forces such as candidate personalities and issues.

The same logic about the importance of degree or intensity can also be applied to attitudes on issues. As we suggested in Chapter One, public opinion on gun control is characterized by a relatively passive majority which favors controls and an unusually active minority which opposes controls. Questions which are confined only to the direction of opinion— that is, the percentages supporting and opposing controls—are not nearly as useful in estimating the potential impact of public opinion as are questions which measure direction and intensity. We would expect, for example, that individuals who have intense opinions about an issue are more likely to act as a consequence of those opinions (voting for candidates who agree with them on that specific issue, or writing letters to public officials, or even participating in protest demonstrations) than are individuals whose opinions are lukewarm. Thus we might find that public opinion on gun control is characterized by two distinct groups: (a) an apathetic majority supporting controls which is unlikely under normal circumstances to take any action on the basis of its opinion on the issue; and (b) an intense minority which opposes controls and which is likely to act on the basis of its opinion. Accordingly, we should not be surprised to find public officials more concerned about the latter group.

Where possible, then, we usually prefer to have attitudinal measures which allow us to make estimates about direction and intensity. These measures are not precise. We do not know, for example, the amount of difference between a "strong Democrat" and a "weak Democrat." But these measures do provide us with useful information about the possible political consequences of public opinion.

Single-item indicators of opinion are appropriate for the uses described above, but in certain instances we might wish to utilize an index or a scale which consists of several items which are related. For example, an index of liberalism–conservatism might consist of a series of questions dealing with domestic policy. Usually these questions will be in the form which measures direction and intensity:

Congress is currently debating legislation which would establish a guaranteed annual income. How do you feel about such a program—do you strongly favor it, favor it, oppose it, or strongly oppose it?

In constructing such an index, we might ask a series of perhaps six domestic policy questions which are phrased like the one on a guaranteed national income and which tap liberal–conservative differences. For each question, we would assign a score or value to each response. For the above questions, the most liberal response (strongly favor) might receive a value of +2, the approve response a +1, the oppose response a −1, and the most conservative response (strongly oppose), a −2. We could then score a respondent's answer to each of the questions in the index. Finally, respondents could be categorized on the basis of their scores. For example, all those whose combined scores were in the +9 through +12 range might be classified as "strong liberals." By similar classification, we would be able to estimate the proportion of liberals, conservatives, and strong conservatives. It should be clear that if the index items actually measure the attitudes we are interested in (whether they meet the requirement of validity) and if the items consistently measure the same attitudes with similar results (whether they meet the requirement of reliability), we are able to measure attitudes much more meaningfully and effectively than we can with a single-item question. The index provides us with a single value which conveniently summarizes the responses that have been given to each of the items.

We can, of course, utilize an index to measure other politically relevant factors, such as participatory behavior. The Woodward and Roper Political Activity Index shown below contains items which cover a wide range of political actions. These range from the least demanding (and most frequent) types of activity—such as voting or talking about politics occasionally with friends—to the more demanding types—such as working in campaigns or writing to public officials. Thus we have activities which are characteristic of the passive spectator and those which define the activist. Moreover, we find that political participation tends to be cumulative: the activists who engage in the most demanding forms of participation are very likely to engage also in the least demanding forms. An individual who goes to political meetings, works in campaigns, and contributes money to candidates will usually vote. On the other hand, many persons who vote do not engage in other activities beyond voting.

Political activity index

1. Do you happen to belong to any organizations that sometimes take a stand on housing, better government, school problems, or other public issues? (If "yes") What organizations?
2a. When you get together with your friends would you say that you discuss public issues like government regulation of business, labor unions, taxes, and farm programs frequently, occasionally, or never?

2b. (If "frequently" or "occasionally") Which of the statements on this card best describes the part you yourself take in these discussions with your friends?

    (1) Even though I have my own opinions, I usually just listen.

    (2) Mostly I listen, but once in a while I express my opinions.

    (3) I take an equal share in the conversation.

    (4) I do more than just hold up my end in the conversation; I usually try to convince others that I am right.

3. Have you ever written or talked to your Congressman or Senator or other public officials to let them know what you would like them to do on a public issue you were interested in?

4. In the last four years have you worked for the election of any political candidate by doing things like distributing circulars or leaflets, making speeches, or calling on voters?

5. Have you attended any meetings in the last four years at which political speeches were made?

6. In the last four years have you contributed money to a political party or to a candidate for a political office?

7. Probably you can't remember exactly, but about how many times do you think you have gone to the polls and voted during the last four years? [11]

In the liberalism–conservatism index discussed above, each respondent was given a score which allowed us to classify him in terms of ideological position. Except for those respondents with the highest or lowest possible scores ($+12$ or -12), however, there is no way of knowing from the respondent's total score which particular items he favored or opposed. For example, one respondent might take the liberal position on the first three items and a conservative position on the second three items and receive an index score of 0. A second respondent might do the reverse— that is, take the conservative position on the first three items and the liberal position on the second three items. But the index score in both instances would be the same.

A more sophisticated method of attitude measurement, the cumulative or Guttman scale, also provides us with scores for a respondent, but in addition it enables us to determine from the score which items the respondent has endorsed or opposed.[12] The cumulative scale, in other words, presents a series of items which are ordered according to some dimension and which are also cumulative. The concept is illustrated by one of the early attempts at such scaling, a social-distance attitude scale, which measured attitudes toward certain ethnic groups.[13] A number of categories ordered along the dimension of social-distance were provided. The first involved allowing members of the ethnic group in question into this country. These progressed upward to allowing citizenship, employment in the respondent's occupation, residence on the respondent's street, membership in the respondent's club, and finally kinship to the respondent through marriage. Each respondent was asked to indicate which of these statuses he would be willing to allow for members of each ethnic group. The logic involved here should be apparent. A respondent who was willing to have a member of an ethnic group as a relative or fellow club-member would presumably favor allowing members of that group into the country, and each respondent's score would show which items he had approved.

A number of these cumulative scales have achieved widespread scholarly use and are quite helpful in measuring complex attitudes. There are, of course, standards which a scale must satisfy in order to be acceptable, including the tests of reliability and validity mentioned earlier. Thus both the construction and use of these types of attitude measurements are considerably more difficult than the closed-ended, dichotomous response questions. We are unlikely, therefore, to find the commercial polling organizations making extensive use of sophisticated attitude scales. In sum, much of the data we are likely to see are generated by the simpler forms of attitude measurement, and it is important to keep in mind that attitudinal data generated by the more complex methods of attitude measurement also have important, albeit somewhat different, limitations.

RESPONSE SET

In asking respondents attitude questions, we are interested in responses to the content of the question. In using agree-disagree and yes-no items, however, researchers have emphasized the importance of avoiding response set—that is, indiscriminate agreement (or disagreement) with the questions. The causes for this are several.[14] First, if the respondent finds the interview boring or unpleasant, he may try to finish as quickly as possible. This might result in unthinking responses. For example, on a series of agree-disagree items, he would agree to all of them. Second, there is the problem of acquiescence in which the respondents answer "agree" or "yes" consistently, simply because they are unwilling to oppose anything that sounds reasonable. The third problem is somewhat similar in its effect. The problem of social desirability results when respondents try to make a good impression by "agreeing" to questionnaire items. Each of these problems is especially relevant in scale construction, and it should be recognized by those who are attempting to interpret (as well as by those who gather) attitudinal data.

Response set bias is an important example of spurious response. Respondents have been known to answer factual questions incorrectly even when responses could easily be checked. In post-election polls, there appears to be some inflation of the winner's support; apparently some individuals report having voted for the winner when they did not. Since the ballot is secret, there is no way of checking who is "misrepresenting" the facts. That some respondents provide rather useless or even misleading responses is not surprising. But it should caution us against treating survey data as absolutely accurate. The difficulties which we have noted in the collection of survey data do not present insuperable obstacles, but they do require that students of public opinion very carefully examine these data and be aware of the kinds of problems which can contaminate these data.

Attitudes—basic concepts [15]

We have chosen to use the term "attitude" rather than "opinion," "belief," or similar terms in this chapter primarily because social psychologists have tended to prefer this term. In order to talk meaningfully about attitudes we must begin with the ideas of perception and cognition. *Perception* is the process of screening, or filtering, the multitudinous stimuli by which we *might be* bombarded all the time. We say "might be" because it is perception that prevents us from being overwhelmed by our environment. This device enables us to "see" certain things and to "miss" others; if we "tuned in" to every available stimulus in our environment we would incapacitate ourselves, since we would be distracted by every one of our senses. Fortunately, perception allows us to filter out those stimuli which are not "relevant," and to allow in all those which we deem important. The process of *selective perception,* then, causes us to "be responsive" to different things in our environment.

Related very closely to perception is the concept of *cognition.* Cognition occurs after information has been received through the senses from the outside world. Cognition is the process of categorization, or classification. Our eye receives the sensory stimulus, we sort out the images, perceiving some and not perceiving others, then we make sense of these images by "filing them" into unique "cognitive categories" for future reference. Verbal labels are attached to these "filing cabinets" and language itself has a bearing on how the information is stored.

Cognition is a remarkable facility. Without cognition, we would be incapable of *learning* in any but the most primitive sense. As it is, we have an amazing talent for putting this chaotic world of ours into order through the process of cognition, and each person's cognitive world (perception, categorization, and verbalization) is unique.

So far we have received stimuli from our environment, sorted them out, decoded and stored them in our cognitive categories. Next comes an evaluation process: what we do is simply attach a valence to our cognitive category according to whether we are positively or negatively "inclined" toward it. Now we have an *attitude,* defined simply as a "valenced cognition." [16]

Of course the elaborate distinctions we have made among perception, cognition, and attitude are somewhat artificial. It certainly would be difficult to differentiate them in a practical application. Certainly the attitudes that we already have determine to a large extent what stimuli we expose ourselves to, how we perceive the outside world, and how we organize it. Thus we should not be surprised to learn that during the television debates of 1960 liberal Democrats were more attentive to what John F. Kennedy said than to his rival. Moreover, Democrats were more likely to claim their man as the "winner" of the debates.[17] We would not even be surprised if Democrats were significantly more likely to have noticed Nixon's "five o'clock shadow," due to the device of selective perception.

It remains now for us to investigate several related questions: What properties do attitudes have? How are attitude systems organized? How do attitudes change?

THE PROPERTIES OF ATTITUDES

Direction.   In our discussion of attitude measurement, we observed that attitudes have the property of "direction," and this is sensible if one thinks of attitudes as "valenced cognitions." Newcomb, Turner, and Converse think of the direction of an attitude as being synonymous with the valence, or positive or negative sign, that is attached to a cognition. "Yes," "no," "agree," "disagree"; each tells us the direction of an attitude. The fundamental property of an attitude, then, is its positive or negative valence. As Newcomb et al. have said, "Positive attitudes predispose the person to some kind of approach toward the object; negative attitudes predispose to some kind of avoidance of the object." [18]

Intensity.   But we know that attitudes, while having direction, vary in the *degree* to which they possess positive or negative qualities. In other words, I may be negatively inclined toward a political party, but I may be *very* negatively inclined toward its particular candidate. This is obvious, and it follows directly from our discussion of attitude scales that attitudes have the property of intensity. The manner in which Newcomb et al. depict an "attitude continuum" is shown in Figure 2.1.

An attitude may be located at any point along the continuum, with the sign (+ or −) indicating direction, and the degree of intensity (or "degree of feeling ") being indicated by the degree of emphasis given to the sign (+, ++, or +++). Newcomb and his collaborators contend that "the two key properties—direction and degree of feeling—can be economically expressed in terms of this single dimension." [19] Most social psychologists would agree that direction and intensity can be thought of as being exclusively cognitive and that therefore attitudes are qualitatively different from pure emotional or affective states.

Figure 2.1
Representation of an Attitude Continuum

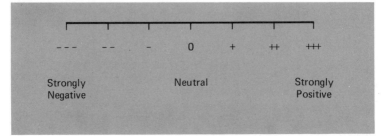

Source: Theodore M. Newcomb, Ralph H. Turner, and Philip E. Converse, *Social Psychology* (New York: Holt, Rinehart & Winston, Inc., 1965), p. 50.

Inclusiveness.   The concept of inclusiveness is derived from the notion that "attitude objects" may be linked together or isolated from one another. Inclusiveness indicates the degree to which an attitude object is grouped, or clustered, with others. Attitude objects, to begin with, vary in the extent to which they are broad and diffuse on the one hand, or narrow and specific on the other. As Newcomb and his associates point out, "America," a much more inclusive attitude object than "this apple," is bound to consist of many more component parts.[20] In addition, since we all have idiosyncratic ways of clustering attitude objects, "America" means something a little different to each of us.

Inclusiveness, in large part simply a matter of relevance, can be spotted at the level of public opinion in any of the recent presidential election campaigns. The presidential candidate wishes, of course, to be "identified" with attitude objects that are viewed positively by most voters. This is, however, often difficult. It would be impossible for us to think about Hubert Humphrey in 1968, for example, without thinking of certain attitude objects from which, despite dogged efforts, he failed to dissociate himself. Many voters in 1968 associated Hubert Humphrey with the following: the Johnson administration, the Vietnam war, the violence at the Democratic convention. Many probably also in some vague way associated him with what Scammon and Wattenberg have called the "Social Issue," which identified him with "the young, the poor, and the black."[21]

At both the micro (individual attitudes) and the macro (public opinion) levels, then, inclusiveness is an important concept since attitude objects tend to "rub off" on one another. We will examine several interpretations of how this occurs in the next section on attitude change. For the moment, simply note that the phenomenon of inclusiveness aids us in understanding why political candidates like to be seen kissing babies, eating pizzas and bagels, milking cows in Wisconsin, and sporting American flag pins on their lapels. It also explains why politicians prefer to have their expletives deleted from the public record.

Centrality. Most of us no doubt share negative attitudes toward war. Nevertheless, for many of us the subject is fairly remote from our daily lives. And yet the subject of war is probably a fairly central political object. Since war, or the threat of it, seems to be a permanent ingredient of international politics, it is a subject that will not "go away." This attitude object is said to have centrality because it is important and it persists over time.

Occasionally the subject of war does loom large in our daily lives— during the days immediately following the Cuban missile crisis, for example. At such times war is said to be not only central, but *salient.* Newcomb and his co-workers say that "salience is a short-term phenomenon that is a function of the immediate situation; centrality refers to a much more durable interest on the part of the individual in certain objects or kinds of objects, with these objects remaining important for him through many differing specific situations." [22] Thus the centrality and inclusiveness of attitude objects depend on a number of factors—the amount of information that we possess about an object, our own interests and motivations, and the state of our environment.[23]

A good example of salience can be drawn from the 1964 presidential election campaign. During that campaign Barry Goldwater tried to convince American voters that they should be concerned with "the level of public morality." Surveys taken at various times during the campaign show that he was making considerable headway with this issue when, in the middle of October, events conspired against him. Premier Khrushchev was ousted in the Soviet Union, a Labour government was elected in Great Britain, and China exploded her first nuclear device. Suddenly the morality issue was dead and foreign affairs became highly salient. This was unfortunate for Goldwater, since his "shoot from the hip" reputation made voters skeptical about his foreign policy leadership.[24]

It is probably safe to say that the direction of a highly central attitude is likely to be quite stable, and that a very central attitude will probably be held with some intensity. Highly central attitudes lie at the core of other peripheral, or derivative attitudes, and constitute the keystones of a person's attitude system.

ATTITUDE SYSTEMS
AND ATTITUDE CHANGE

For the most part attitudes once formed tend to be highly resistant to change. This is true because attitudes are combined with one another in highly complex systems, and systems tend to be adaptive to potentially disruptive forces. Systems have a way of maintaining themselves by reverting, as much as possible, to a prior state of balance, or equilibrium. A good example of systematic adaptation is provided by the events following the Legislative Reorganization Act of 1946, which abolished a number of standing committees in Congress. Since this Act disturbed the "balance of power" on Capitol Hill, the congressional system responded by increasing the number of congressional subcommittees, hence retaining the same number of chairmanships. Despite the formal "streamlining" of Congress, then, the proliferation of subcommittees enabled the system to maintain the equilibrium that had prevailed prior to the Act.

Attitude systems are thought to behave in a similar fashion. For the present we should be content with documenting the fact that attitudes tend to be stable and that attitude systems are characterized by their stability, not change.

Studies of individuals whose attitudes systems can be reconstructed from their private papers and public utterances confirms this fact. One such study is Ole Holsti's psychological analysis of John Foster Dulles.[25] Dulles, Secretary of State under Dwight Eisenhower, had a strongly negative view of the Soviet Union, and this attitude was highly central and held with great intensity. Holsti shows that despite repeated evidence that contradicted his attitudes, Dulles was able to maintain to the end his belief that the Soviet Union was on the verge of economic collapse. Information to the contrary was "defused" by Dulles; in fact he even was able at times to twist it so as to bolster his belief. At first glance the Dulles case seems quite remarkable, but actually all of us have the capacity to live with contradictions and ambiguity and to maintain our attitudes in the face of incompatible or incongruous evidence.

At the macro level, public opinion once formed also has a tendency to remain stable. Like individual attitudes, public opinion does change, and can even change dramatically. But the tendency is for public opinion to do the same thing that individuals do, i.e., to respond to contradictory or disruptive stimuli by forcing them to conform to a pre-existing attitude system. Ralph K. White, for example, has shown that for a considerable period American attitudes about the Vietnam war constituted an almost "airtight" system that defied alteration.[26] However, public opinion often does change. Racial attitudes in the United States have changed markedly in the past two decades. Granting that attitudes tend to remain stable and more or less inflexible, how can we account for the fact that attitudes do change?

Although social psychologists have done a great deal of research on the subject of attitude change, the complex dynamics of this process remain only partially elucidated. One concept that underlies much of the research however is that of "balance." The idea of balance is especially useful in accounting for attitude change when new information is added to an existing and stable attitude system. For example, a person who was anti-Semitic would find himself stunned at suddenly finding out that a good friend was Jewish. This situation would create pressure and would lead to change. One of these attitudes—the positive attitudes toward the friend, or the negative attitude toward Jews, or both—would tend to be revised in such a way as to make them compatible. Social psychology has produced a number of different theories that attempt to explain and predict the outcome of this situation, and while these theories are very different, they all stress the movement of attitude objects within a person's attitude system to positions resolving the imbalance, or incongruity.

In the past two decades, racial attitudes in America have changed quite dramatically. This is due to the fact that white Americans have had to revise their attitudes in response to new information about blacks. When nearly all whites were totally ignorant of African history and of the contributions of American blacks to our own culture, it was much easier to justify, or at least to ignore, the separate and unequal status of American blacks. New information forced many whites to recognize that racial discrimination could not be defended. In effect, the new information caused imbalance and thus created a pressure toward change.

This theory of attitude change assumes that changes in attitudes result in behavioral changes. It also makes sense, though, to think of behavior itself as being sometimes involved in attitude change. Much of the legislation coming out of the civil rights movement, for example, was aimed at curtailing certain racially discriminatory practices on the part of whites. Everyone knows that statutes and court decisions did not eliminate bigotry overnight, but they did alter behavior, and this may gradually have had the effect of changing atttiudes. A bigot who is barred by law from practicing racial discrimination may over time find the discrepancy between his attitudes and his behavior so serious that his attitudes must be revised. Since he cannot reinforce his attitudes through action, the attitudes may atrophy in the course of time.

As implied above, attitude change depends in large part on the nature of the attitude in question—not only its direction but also its intensity, centrality, and inclusiveness. It should not be surprising that public opinion can change very quickly when the original attitude is not strong or central, or when the attitude object is not particularly salient for most people. No doubt the public's opinion about our foreign policy toward Iceland is more amenable to change than, say, the public's view of the Soviet Union. Similarly, the public's view of particular political leaders is more changeable than is party identification. The Democratic party has been nominating presidential candidates who are not particularly attractive to Southerners since the nomination of Al Smith in 1928, and yet partisan realignment has occurred only very gradually in the South. To sum up, individual attitudes may change even though attitude systems tend to remain relatively stable. The degree to which attitudes are resistant to change depends on the properties that characterize them, and although social psychologists do not speak with one voice on the subject of the dynamics involved in attitude change, the literature suggests that attitude systems tend to strive toward balance, or equilibrium. Factors which upset the equilibrium, such as new information or altered behavior patterns, are forces which make attitudes more conducive to change.

Summary

Individual attitudes, like public opinion, cannot be "seen" directly. We can make inferences about public opinion when we observe the behavior of the American electorate in the nation's voting booths, and we can make inferences about public opinion based on the behavior of respondents in opinion polls.

Most of what we know about American public opinion has been the product of survey research, especially that research conducted by the nation's large polling organizations. Attitudes are measured in the interview situation by the administration of questions which range from the fixed-alternative question to the open-ended question. These measurement devices also range from the single-item, closed-ended, dichotomous response measure to the series of items that comprise a cumulative scale.

Attitude systems are extremely complex, and we have limited information on the way in which attitudes or attitude objects are related to one another. We do know that attitudes differ in the degree to which they are central and inclusive, but the investigation of these matters is difficult. We know too that attitudes, once formed, are not easily changed, and the prognosis for attitude change depends in large part on the direction, intensity, inclusiveness, and centrality of the attitude. The receipt of new information, however, is very often the catalyst for attitude change, but our understanding of the "mechanics" of this process is somewhat incomplete.

This chapter has of necessity emphasized individual attitude formation, but we shall gradually move toward the macro level in the succeeding chapters. Chapter Three continues the discussion of attitude formation and the political socialization process. Chapter Four describes the distribution of political attitudes in the American population, and Chapter Five focuses on the American political culture.

NOTES

[1] Bernard Berelson and Gary A. Steiner, *Human Behavior: An Inventory of Scientific Findings* (New York: Harcourt Brace Jovanovich, 1964).

[2] B. F. Skinner, *Beyond Freedom and Dignity* (New York: Knopf, 1971).

[3] William Buchanan, *Understanding Political Variables* (New York: Charles Scribner's Sons, 1969), ch. 8.

[4] See W. S. Robinson, "Ecological Correlations and the Behavior of Individuals," *American Sociological Review,* 15 (June 1950), 351–57.

[5] Walter Dean Burnham, *Critical Elections and the Mainsprings of American Politics* (New York: W. W. Norton & Company, Inc., 1970).

[6] Louis Harris, *The Anguish of Change* (New York: W. W. Norton & Company, Inc., 1973), p. 257.

[7] For a discussion of these charges and a refutation of the "bandwagon effect," see Harold Mendelsohn and Irving Crespi, *Polls, Television, and the New Politics* (Scranton, Pa.: Chandler Publishing Company, 1970).

[8] John E. Mueller, *War, Presidents and Public Opinion* (New York: John Wiley & Sons, Inc., 1973), p. 9.

[9] Ibid., p. 44.

[10] Ibid., p. 9.

[11] Julian L. Woodward and Elmo Roper, "Political Activity of American Citizens," *American Political Science Review,* 44 (December 1950), 872–85.

[12] For a discussion of these techniques and the attendant problems and limitations, see A. N. Oppenheim, *Questionnaire Design and Attitude Measurement* (New York: Basic Books, Inc., 1966), ch. 6.

[13] This scale was developed by E. S. Bogardus. See E. S. Bogardus, "Measuring Social Distance," *Journal of Applied Sociology,* 9 (1950), 299–308; "A Social Distance Scale," *Sociological and Social Research,* 17 (1933), 265–71.

[14] See the discussion in John P. Robinson, Jerrold G. Rusk, and Kendra B. Head, *Measures of Political Attitudes* (Ann Arbor, Mich.: Survey Research Center, Institute for Social Research, 1968), pp. 12–14.

[15] The following discussion is heavily dependent upon Theodore M. Newcomb, Ralph H. Turner, and Philip E. Converse, *Social Psychology* (New York: Holt, Rinehart & Winston, Inc., 1965).

[16] Ibid., p. 40.

[17] Kurt Lang and Gladys E. Lang, "Ordeal by Debate: Viewer Reactions," *Public Opinion Quarterly* (Summer 1961), 277–88.

[18] Newcomb, Turner, and Converse, *Social Psychology,* p. 48.

[19] Ibid., p. 50.

[20] Ibid., p. 56.

[21] Richard M. Scammon and Ben J. Wattenberg, *The Real Majority* (New York: Coward, McCann & Geoghegan, Inc., 1970).

[22] Newcomb, Turner, and Converse, *Social Psychology,* p. 59.

[23] Ibid., pp. 58–63.

[24] See Harris, *The Anguish of Change,* pp. 250–51.

[25] Ole R. Holsti, "Cognitive Dynamics and Images of the Enemy," *Journal of International Affairs,* No. 1 (1967), 16–39.

[26] Ralph K. White, "Misperception of Aggression in Vietnam," *Journal of International Affairs,* No. 1 (1967), 123–40.

POLITICAL SOCIALIZATION: THE FORMATION OF ATTITUDES

3

In Chapter Two we were concerned with developing the concept of attitude and with the measurement and analysis of attitudes. From our discussion of the properties of attitudes and attitude systems, it should have been made clear that attitudes are *learned*. How attitudes are learned, though, is a most important topic that has been addressed by many psychologists interested in social learning. The political scientist asks himself how a culture transmits political attitudes to its citizens, and what kinds of attitudes are internalized by people being inducted into the political culture. These questions belong to the study of "political socialization."

This relatively new sub-field of political science is not, however, a new phenomenon; the study of political education, or civic training, is at least as old as Confucius and Plato. Formally, political socialization may be defined as "the acquisition of basic political orientations by new members of a political system," [1] or "the process by which people learn to adopt the norms, values, attitudes, and behaviors accepted and practiced by the ongoing system." [2] In studying the subject we can learn how attitudes are formed and influenced, how the citizen is assimilated into the political system, and how the normative valuations of that system operate. An examination of the political socialization process in the United States should reveal a great deal not only about what the political system expects from its citizens, but also about what the citizens expect from the system.

Political socialization
and the political system

THE POLITICAL COMMUNITY

The political system is, in the broadest sense, a political *community*. We are not referring here to villages, cities, or neighborhoods, but to persons who share a feeling of belonging to a particular culture or way of life. The sense of community means that there are individuals in the world who think of themselves as being "Americans," and these individuals distinguish themselves from Englishmen, Peruvians, and Algerians. Ordinarily, persons not only define themselves as being members of a political community, but place some attachment to that membership, and this attachment may be very emotional. We are referring here, of course, to nationalism, or "patriotism." Any political system is fundamentally weak if large numbers of people do not feel that they are members of the political community.

This feeling of belongingness, apparently a first step toward a complete induction into the political system, seems to begin with the recognition of and attachment to national symbols. This nascent nationalism has been evidenced among children of very young age. Lawson, for example, asked children to rate the flags of nineteen nations and that of the United Nations according to their attractiveness.[3] Children of all ages (from kindergarten through the twelfth grade) chose the United States flag as being attractive. Even kindergarten children showed a clear preference for the Stars and Stripes, and this attachment declined only slightly over the grades. High school students, while still liking the Stars and Stripes, also rated the U.N. flag highly. This flag evidently was not recognized by younger children (see Figure 3.1). What is especially interesting about this study is that the second most popular flag among children between kindergarten and Grade 5 was that of Liberia. The Liberian flag is a modified version of the Stars and Stripes, modeled after the American flag. Children at all ages rejected the Hammer and Sickle. As Lawson reports, "The Soviet flag is rejected immediately and has the lowest scores in the study. . . . It is chosen by 10 percent of the children in kindergarten, but declines to 1.25 percent in Grade 12." [4]

The perceptive student may ask whether children rate the flag of the United States as "better looking" because they in fact perceive it to be more aesthetically pleasing than other flags. Data reported by Lawson tend to repudiate this notion. Lawson administered a similar test to persons with professional art training, and the results bore no similarity to the preferences reported by the children. The artists, in fact, were inclined to view the

Figure 3.1
The Attractiveness of National Flags

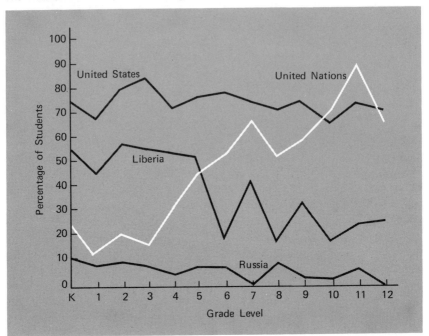

Source: Edwin D. Lawson, "Development of Patriotism in Children—a Second Look," *Journal of Psychology*, 55 (April, 1963), 283.

Hammer and Sickle as being quite attractive. The point is that the attachment to the political community emerges in very young children.

THE REGIME

Political scientists use the term *regime* to refer to the "rules of the game." Americans identify themselves as being distinct from other peoples of the world, and they also agree upon the terms of their political union, as they need to have some clear operating procedures for their governance. In the United States, some concepts that are operative at the regime level are constitutionalism, majority rule, the rule of law, minority rights, limited government, freedom, and equality.

An awareness of regime level ideas seems to emerge only after national symbols have been learned. The emergence of regime level ideas constitutes what Hess and Torney call a "second phase" in the acquisition of nationalistic feelings.[5] Instead of saying that he is proud to be an American because of "our beautiful parks and highways," or because of "our President," the child now uses such terms as "freedom" or the "right to vote." He is acquiring fundamental concepts that are quite sophisticated. The five-year-old who loves the flag or the Statue of Liberty has an attachment that may be very powerful but is essentially non-rational. The ten-year-old's "love of freedom" indicates that a certain level of rationality has been attained.

During the elementary school years children also learn what duties and responsibilities are assumed by the "good citizen." While younger children are likely to say that the good citizen keeps a clean house and is polite, older children understand that civic responsibilities include voting, keeping informed, etc. The citizen role is a regime level consideration, of course, since what is considered to be the proper citizen role is dependent upon the terms of the political union. Table 3.1 summarizes the changes that occur during the process of maturation in thinking about what constitutes good citizenship. The trends evident in this table are indicative of the regime level learning that takes place during these years. Children learn that participation, especially voting, is a good thing, and that citizens should not be politically passive.

THE GOVERNMENT

The term *government* is used to refer to the political authorities—the incumbents of authoritative decision making agencies and their political acts. The government is the most narrow and specific level of the political system. It is perhaps the least enduring and the least deep-seated. As we know, nations can continue to exist, and regime level attachments can be maintained while governments come and go.

Young children are introduced to the government level by exposure to political authorities that happen to be particularly visible. The President of the United States very often is the first contact that children have with politics. As we shall see, he is idealized by children, an experience that may predispose them toward a positive view of the political system in general. The policeman is another authority figure who is generally perceived positively by young children.

Through this exposure to individual authority figures the child acquires his first notion of government, in other words, the "structure of authority." This picture comes gradually into focus during the elementary school years as students learn about American history and the structure of the government. Children's changing perception of government is graphically illustrated in Figure 3.2. When asked to choose pictures that symbolize government, younger children are inclined to choose a picture of the incumbent

Table 3.1
Children's Perceptions of the Qualities of Good Citizenship, by Grade

GRADE	Works hard	Everybody likes him	Votes and gets others to vote	Helps others	Is interested in way country is run	Always obeys laws	Goes to church	Don't know "citizen"
				A CITIZEN IS SOMEONE WHO:				
4	13.5%	7.0%	26.4%	47.8%	28.2%	44.3%	23.6%	2.0%
5	11.3	8.5	29.8	42.1	41.8	42.0	20.6	.6
6	10.7	9.0	35.8	35.4	50.5	37.4	16.0	.6
7	11.1	8.3	35.9	34.2	57.7	32.7	14.6	.2
8	10.0	8.1	44.6	26.3	65.0	29.0	11.8	.7
Teachers	7.9	3.6	51.5	31.6	72.4	22.4	3.8	2.7

Source: Robert D. Hess and Judith V. Torney, *The Development of Political Attitudes in Children* (Chicago: Aldine–Atherton, Inc., 1967), p. 46.

Figure 3.2
Development of a Cognitive Image of Government:
The Four Dominant Symbolic Associations

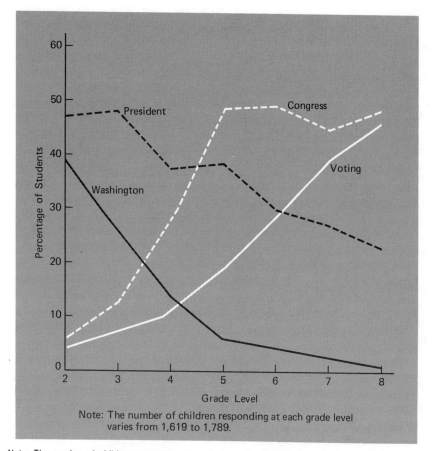

Note: The number of children responding at each grade level
varies from 1,619 to 1,789.

Note: *The number of children responding at each grade level varies from 1,619 to 1,789.*

Source: David Easton and Jack Dennis, *Children in the Political System* (New York: McGraw-Hill Book Company, 1969), p. 115.

President, or of George Washington. Later, government seems to be associated symbolically with Congress and with voting.

Obviously children become more sophisticated about government and politics as they grow older. They acquire an awareness of and knowledge about the other branches of government, they begin to understand the democratic processes of elections and campaigning, and they may even have some contact with political parties, pressure groups, etc. Even when they are able to distinguish the public from the private sectors, they still retain a rather sympathetic, if not enthusiastic, view of government. The typical American elementary school student reveals very little of the cynicism, alienation, or political negativism that may occur in later years. As Jennings and Niemi have shown, this is not even likely to be present among high school seniors.[6]

At the government level are the incumbents of authoritative decision making agencies, and a child's attitudes toward these persons and the policies they adopt are no doubt dependent in part upon party identification and ideology, both of which are likely to be acquired from parents. Interestingly, an incumbent whose office itself is held in disrepute is not likely to be viewed positively, regardless of his personal characteristics. That is why a child's orientation toward the offices and institutions themselves is so important.

What children learn about politics in the United States is important in shaping their later attitudes. It is, of course, in the interest of those who benefit from the prevailing system to see to it that children acquire this reservoir of support. As Easton and Dennis aptly remark: "Early orientations provide a solid supportive base for the regime as the members grow older. Even if later events should disillusion members about the structure of authority, the rate of decline in support might at least be restrained somewhat by the pull of latent childhood sentiments." [7]

It is not at all inevitable that children acquire such attitudes toward government. Laurence Wylie's description of political socialization in a small village in France shows us that the government can be an object of contempt, even when citizens are highly patriotic and share a deeply felt sense of political community. Wylie reports that French children:

constantly hear adults referring to Government as a source of evil and to the men who run it as instruments of evil. There is nothing personal in this belief. It does not concern one particular Government composed of one particular group of men. It concerns Government everywhere and at all times—French Governments, American Governments, Russian Governments, all Governments. Some are less bad than others, but all are essentially bad. . . .[8]

It should be clear that under such circumstances political stability is not assured, despite the high level of attachment that might prevail at the level of the political community.

The learning of basic political orientations

How is it that "basic political orientations" are acquired by members of political systems? And who does the teaching (socializing)? To answer these questions we must examine the social learning process itself and the "agents" involved in this process.

LEARNING ABOUT POLITICS:
FIVE MODELS OF POLITICAL SOCIALIZATION

Empirical evidence reported in the past two decades indicates that learning about politics begins very early in the life cycle, and that, as Easton and Hess have put it:

> . . . by the time the child has completed elementary school, many basic political attitudes and values have become firmly established. What is even more important, and dramatically contrary to expectations and implications of existing literature, it appears that by the time the child enters high school at the age of 14, his basic political orientations to regime and community have become quite firmly entrenched so that at least during the four years of high school little substantive change is visible. . . . for most young people, there is little evidence that fundamental attitudes and values with respect to the regime and political community are any different when they leave high school than they were upon entrance.
>
> The truly formative years of the maturing member of a political system would seem to be the years between the ages of three and thirteen. It is this period when rapid growth and development in political orientations take place, as in many areas of non-political socialization.[9]

Some more recent studies cast doubt on Easton and Hess' view that few changes occur during the high school years, but clearly the period between the ages of three and thirteen constitutes the major period of political socialization.

Just how are basic political orientations acquired? Learning psychologists do not agree on a methodology of learning, but some well-known theories of learning have been applied to political socialization in order to explain how attitude formation takes place in children. Each provides us with a different insight into how some basic political orientations are acquired. It must be stressed, though, that none of these theories has been in any way "proven," and none, when used alone, can account for the total body of empirical findings that have been reported. We shall now briefly discuss five "models" to show how each has been applied to substantive findings of political socialization research.

1. *The cognitive development model.* Technically speaking, this is not a learning theory, but rather a theory of child development. The famous child psychologist, Jean Piaget has shown how children's learning progresses through several stages.[10] According to Piaget, certain kinds of things cannot be learned by children until they have reached the proper maturational level. Piaget shows, for instance, that very young children (ages 5–6) are unable to understand that the city of Geneva is encompassed by Switzerland. When asked to draw the two, the young child draws Geneva and Switzerland as juxtaposed circles. Piaget concludes that this shows an "inability to understand how the part is included in the whole."

At the second stage, children are able to draw the correct spatial relationship but still do not understand how one logical category can be included in another—that is, they do not fully understand that one can be Genevese and Swiss at the same time. Finally, at age 11 or thereabouts, the child grasps the correct understanding of the relationship and of the concept of inclusiveness.

This kind of learning is called "cognitive" learning: it is strictly intellectual in that it involves the reception and storing of substantive information. But attitude formation also involves an evaluative component (in Chapter Two we said that attitudes are *valenced* cognitions). This evaluational kind of learning is called "affective" learning, and Piaget says that affective development closely parallels cognitive development.

During the first affective stage, children demonstrate no particular preference for Switzerland. This is due, says Piaget, to the fact that children at this stage are "egocentric"—that is, they think that the world revolves around them, and they have no appreciation of any relationship to other people. At the second stage, the child demonstrates a preference for Switzerland, but that preference is only due to the fact that he knows that he and his family are Swiss—that is, the expressed nationalism is actually derived from his egocentrism. At the third level, the child shows a preference for Switzerland that is rooted in his attachment to the society as a whole. At this point egocentrism is replaced by "sociocentrism." Sociocentrism involves a strong affective attachment to one's society that makes it difficult for one to empathize with a person from another culture. Sociocentrism is thus analogous to the more primitive egocentrism of young children. Piaget postulates a fourth stage, reciprocity, which must emerge if nationalism is to be any different from sociocentrism.

The Cognitive Development Model theorizes, then, that children are truly not able to learn certain things until they are mature enough to handle abstract concepts, to perform logical operations, and until they outgrow their childish egocentrism. For example, it would be pointless to try to explain what the United States Congress is to first-graders—such ideas as law making and representation are simply too complex.

2. *The accumulation model.* This model, so named by Hess and Torney, is the opposite of the Cognitive Development theory. The Accumulation Model suggests that even the very young child can understand complex matters if they are presented to him in a simplified way, compatible with his vocabulary and limited intellectual experience. Thus, the young child may be able to attain some understanding of the United States Congress if that institution is portrayed for him in the work of a single Senator. According to this theory, the child is a *tabula rasa* upon which the experiences of life are recorded in a more or less cumulative fashion, and physical matura-

tion is not necessarily correlated with set psychological stages which limit the kinds of things that can be learned. The Accumulation Model apparently underlies the thinking of those children's authors who attempt to convey abstract and difficult ideas to children within a simple framework.

With regard to political learning, even young children are often able to grasp the idea behind the United States Presidency, perhaps because they associate the President's role with authority in the family. They are also able to relate other political ideas, although often in a bizarre fashion. For example, consider this interview with a third-grader:

Q.: "Have you ever seen the President?"
A.: "I've seen him on television, and heard him on the radio, and seen him in the newspapers."
Q.: "What does the President do?"
A.: "He runs the country, he decides the decisions that we should try to get out of, and he goes to meetings and tries to make peace and things like that."
Q.: "When you say he runs the country, what do you mean?"
A.: "Well, he's just about the boss of everything . . ."
Q.: "And what kind of person do you think he is?"
A.: "Well, usually he's an honest one."
Q.: "Anything else?"
A.: "Well, loyal and usually is pretty smart."
Q.: "Usually, but not always?"
A.: "Well, they're all smart, but they aren't exactly perfect (pause) . . . most of them are."
Q.: "Who pays him?"
A.: "Well, gee, I don't know if anybody pays him, he probably doesn't get too much money for the job—I don't even know if he gets any money."
Q.: "Why would he take the job?"
A.: "Well, he loves his country and he wants this country to live in peace." [11]

As shown previously, children can recognize and express a preference for certain national symbols, and this may mean that children can, in a limited way, understand the concept of nation through these symbolic and simplistic devices. In any event, the Accumulation Model stands behind civics training in the public schools. Explicit efforts to socialize young children would not otherwise be attempted.

3. *The interpersonal transfer model.* One of the contributions Freud made to twentieth-century thought is the notion that very early childhood (or, even infancy or prenatal) experiences have an impact on later behavior. Experiences with parents, for example, can be reflected later in the kinds of attitudes one has toward other figures of authority, or authority in general.

It has been found that young children in the United States tend to idealize the President.[12] He is seen as omniscient, omnipotent, and benevolent—a kind of combination God, Superman, and Santa Claus. There are many interpretations of this phenomenon, but the Interpersonal Transfer

Model theorizes in the following way: the child knows his father, whom he tends to view as perfect—perhaps because of the child's ultimate physical vulnerability and dependence on the parent. The child then projects this image onto other figures of authority, such as the President, even though he may have very little cognitive knowledge of the office, the role, or the incumbent. This phenomenon will be discussed in more detail below.

4. *The identification model.*   Much learning seems to be best characterized as simple imitation, or what Bandura has called "modeling." [13] In this case a child imitates a role model, often one of his parents. Much learning seems to proceed in this fashion, including the acquisition of party identification.

Even very young children are often able to state a preference for one of the two major American political parties. Although the child may not have any conception of why one party is better than the other, if his parents are Republicans, he senses that Republicans are better, and he "becomes" one too. The learning of a party identification is probably not accounted for by Accumulation, since it is doubtful that parents sit down to teach the child why he should be a Republican or Democrat. Rather, the child overhears parental remarks and supports the same party as his parents simply because of his identification with them.

Greenstein's research, for example, shows that approximately 60 percent of fourth-graders can express a party preference. This is especially impressive when one considers that for 21–24-year-olds the rate of partisan identification is the same as for Greenstein's fourth-graders. [14] This, evidently, is a good example of a political orientation that is likely to be learned early in life through the process of identification.

5. *The "conditioning" model.*   This view of the political socialization process has a wide application to the study of political socialization. Based upon the "stimulus-response" idea, the classic example of this kind of learning is Pavlov's experiments with the salivation response in dogs. Pavlov introduced a stimulus (the sound of a bell) with a primary stimulus (food) when feeding the dog. After a while, the dog would salivate upon the introduction of the conditioned stimulus alone. Understanding this behavior does not require an examination of the dog's thought processes or his "cognitions," but instead an examination of the "conditions," that is, the procedures employed by the experimenter to elicit the response.

Because the Conditioning Model is basically non-cognitive, it is readily distinguished from the Accumulation Model, which can be best applied to conscious learning. For example, when teachers describe the structure and functions of the U.S. Congress, learning can be measured by evaluative instruments. The material is learned in much the same form that it is taught, and the content can be expressed verbally by the child. Attitudes (valenced cognitions) can of course be transmitted in precisely the same way.

The process of conditioning, though, illustrates how content can be taught and learned more or less unconsciously. A teacher may even be unaware of what he is transmitting and the learner, of what he is learning. Consider, for example, the fact that elementary school children have so well internalized the norm of compliance. The Accumulation Model would suggest that perhaps children have been lectured to by parents and teachers on "how good girls and boys always obey the rules." Although there are other possible explanations, it seems likely that compliance is learned simply by the child's experiencing certain reinforcement schedules that are stacked in favor of compliance. Parents and teachers have expectations—very often unarticulated—regarding the role of the child in the home and in the classroom, and behavior that conforms to their expectations is rewarded. These rewards may be blatant (expressions of love—or good grades) or subtle (approving nods, smiles, or simply, attention). Thus the child learns to comply with rules and authority figures generally.

Agents in the political socialization process

A great deal of research has been conducted with the aim of identifying the most important "agents" involved in the transmission of political orientations to young people. The political system may do a certain amount of explicit and implicit socializing itself, of course, but in the United States it is not thought to be wholly proper for the government to engage in wholesale political "indoctrination." Basic political orientations are, for the most part, transmitted by those social institutions that also contribute most to the nonpolitical socialization of children—for example, the family, the school, peer groups, and the mass media.

FAMILY

The family, as the basic social unit of most societies, is responsible for inculcating most cultural values and norms—although the family has in recent years relinquished some of its functions. The American family, for instance, no longer plays an important role in providing its children with jobs or job skills, nor does it assume full responsibility for health or sex education. Nevertheless, it is still thought to be crucial in implanting political ideas in young people. The Interpersonal Transfer, Accumulation, Identification, and Conditioning models all stress the role of the family.

Not all societies at all times have entrusted the family with the function of political socialization—in fact, some governments have thought themselves to be in competition with the family for the loyalty of the nation's youth. In the Soviet Union, for example, the new Bolshevik regime of the 1920s sought to minimize the influence of the family, since it considered the family an obsolete and subversive social unit, one that transmitted norms (e.g., religious values) not in the best interest of the state. In order to realize drastic cultural and political changes, the new Soviet government felt that it should socialize children in such a way as to make their values compatible with those of the new Communist government. The de-Nazification of West Germany required, to some extent also, that young Germans renounce their political heritage. The West German government could hardly afford to encourage youth to emulate their fathers.

With respect to Germany, it has been suggested that the structure of the German family and the authority relationships within it predisposed the German people to respond to the highly authoritarian appeals of the Nazis. According to this Interpersonal Transfer type of explanation, the "typical" German father—a strict, stern, demanding figure—contributed significantly to this phenomenon. This kind of socialization is for the most part inadvertent, but it may have ramifications of enormous importance. Observers of "national character" have often stressed the role of child-rearing methods.[15]

In a study of father-son relations in American families, Robert E. Lane contends that the American political culture is shaped by the nature of father-son relationships. Lane's conclusions appear below:

The history, political style, and future development of a political community reflect the quality of the relationship between fathers and sons. The permissive yet supportive character of model father-son relationships in the United States contributes to the following features of the American political style: (a) a relatively high consensualism combined with a capacity for direct and uninhibited criticism; (b) a relatively large amount of interest and political information combined with relatively low emotional commitment; and (c) a relatively strong idealism in foreign affairs (and in general social outlook).[16]

Modern American families are said to be child-oriented, and they tend to be responsive to the wants of their children out of a fear of inhibiting or restricting them. One indication of this is the degree to which Americans permit their children to be involved in family decision making. The American family structure tends to be democratic and egalitarian. This should presumably have political implications.

A well-known empirical study that tries to establish a causal link between family structure and political culture is the five-nation study of Almond and Verba.[17] One of the findings of this study was that persons who recall participation in the family decision making process during childhood are likely to be more politically efficacious as adults. This kind of experience was found to be much more prevalent in the United States and the United Kingdom than in Mexico, Italy, or Germany (see Table 3.2).

Most importantly, this study reveals that those people who recall participatory experiences within the family are more likely to have a positive view of themselves and of their own ability to cope successfully with their environment. Almond and Verba refer to this feeling as "subjective competence." Among those Americans in their sample who remembered having had influence over family decisions, 70 percent were high scorers on the "subjective competence scale." Among those who could recall no such influence, only 47 percent were high in subjective competence. From a political point of view, people who have had successful participatory experiences within the family are more likely to be politically efficacious and participatory individuals.

Attitudes can also be acquired within the family in the manner suggested by the Identification Model. The learning of sex roles is an obvious example of this type of learning, but a good deal of explicitly political learning occurs in this way also. The acquisition of party preferences by very young children may be explained by the process of identification. Statistical evidence that this identification is relatively permanent [18] is presented in Table 3.3. It can be seen from Table 3.3 that there is a fairly high correlation between the party identification of parents and children, and that this association tends to increase both with agreement between parents and with parental political activity.

In the United States party preferences seem to be transmitted by the parents more effectively than more subtle or abstract political orientations. Commenting on this, Hyman has said: "We have suggestive evidence that the socialization of the individual into a *party* is a much more direct process than the socialization of the logically congruent area of ideology." [19]

Much has been written in recent years on the subject of adolescent

Table 3.2
Remembered Influence in Family Decisions, by Nation

	UNITED STATES	GREAT BRITAIN	GERMANY	ITALY	MEXICO
Percentage who remember they had:					
some influence	73	69	54	48	57
no influence	22	26	37	37	40
don't know, don't remember, and other	5	5	9	15	3
Total percentage	100	100	100	100	100

Source: Gabriel A. Almond and Sidney Verba, *The Civic Culture* (Princeton: Princeton University Press, 1963), p. 331.

Table 3.3
Intergenerational Similarities in Party Identification, 1968

PARTY IDENTIFICATION OF OFFSPRING	BOTH PARENTS DEMOCRATS	BOTH PARENTS REPUBLICANS	ONE PARENT DEMOCRAT, ONE REPUBLICAN	BOTH PARENTS INDEPENDENT	BOTH PARENTS APOLITICAL
Strong Democrats	27.4%	8.3%	15.4%	11.9%	17.4%
Weak Democrats	40.1	10.8	16.3	2.4	21.7
Independent	23.4	20.4	36.5	78.6	39.1
Weak Republicans	5.2	34.1	15.4	2.4	8.7
Strong Republicans	2.8	25.8	16.3	4.8	4.3
Others (apolitical, etc.)	1.0	.6	0	0	8.7
Total	99.9%	100.0%	99.9%	100.1%	99.9%

Source: Frank J. Sorauf, *Party Politics in America*, 2nd ed. (Boston: Little, Brown and Company, 1972), p. 144. Original data source: Survey Research Center.

rebellion. The turbulence on college campuses during the 1960s, for example, was attributed to a rejection by college students of their families' values in favor of the very different values of the "counter-culture." While examples of this kind of rebellion seem to abound, there are good reasons for believing that the political protesters of the 1960s cannot properly be characterized as "rebels." Several studies, in fact, have indicated that the protesters were actually, as Kenneth Keniston put it, "acting out parental values." [20] Another study revealed that campus protesters tended to come from liberal families, and from homes where political issues were discussed frequently.[21] This would appear to be more like Identification, or Accumulation, than rebellion, and underscores the importance of the family as a socializing agent.

THE PUBLIC SCHOOL

If a government sees itself as competing with the family for the loyalty of the child, the public school becomes the agent of socialization that is relied upon to produce the kinds of citizens desired by the government. The early years of the Soviet Union are a case in point. Of course, if the family can be trusted by the state to train children in the "proper" ways, the state may wish to allocate some of these responsibilities to the family. That there is tension can be demonstrated by the following excerpt from Bronfenbrenner's description of the educational philosophy of a leading Soviet writer in this field:

Characteristic of Makarenko's thought is the view that the parent's authority over the child is delegated to him by the state and that duty to one's children is merely a particular instance of one's broader duty towards society. . . . In other words, when needs and values of the family conflict with those of society, there is no question about who gets priority. . . .[22]

Such a philosophy would dictate that the school have as complete control over the child as practicable, and would suggest boarding schools rather than day schools. In fact, Bronfenbrenner reports that the Soviet Union is promoting boarding schools. After describing the procedures of character education advocated by Makarenko, Bronfenbrenner notes that:

. . . they may be expected to receive even wider application in the years to come, for, in connection with these reforms, several new types of educational institutions are to be developed on a massive scale. The most important of these is the "internat," or boarding school, in which youngsters are to be entered as early as three months of age with parents visiting only on weekends. The internat is described in theses announcing the reforms as the kind of school which "creates the most favorable conditions for the education and communist upbringing of the rising generation." [23]

The boarding school can serve as a more effective socializing agent than the day school primarily because the role of the family is reduced, and if there is some incompatibility between the teachings of the school and those of the family, the former wins by default. Ordinarily we think of socialization or civic education as the conscious teaching of political orientations that will be internalized by the child in much the same form as they were transmitted. As we have seen, however, political socialization need not be so explicit. In fact, the public school can serve as an effective socializer by being a microcosm of society, or of an ideal society, so that the child learns by experience the kinds of roles that he will be expected to perform in later life. A good description of this kind of implicit and subtle socialization is contained in Wilkinson's description of the "public school" in Victorian England.[24] His thesis, in short, is that the public school trained an elite to fill important public roles by simulating the British government:

In Parliament and Public Schools alike, the political process depended on internalized, ethical restraints as much as on coercive law to curb the arbitrary exercise of power. A largely unwritten Constitution and a national executive whose control of the legislature was—as it is today—tempered by custom and usage found their counterparts in the organization of Public School government.[25]

Effective political socialization, then, can come in the form of providing occasions for the learning of particular roles as well as by way of explicit teaching. What we are saying here is that the public school socializes in two distinct ways: the first way can be understood most easily as the process of accumulation, and the second is a process by which children are encouraged to engage in certain kinds of behaviors and encouraged to eschew others through conditioning. The first tends always to be conscious and intentional, the second may even be inadvertent. In the United States, learning of both types occurs in the public school. The school makes a conscious attempt to transmit certain political attitudes, values, and knowledge to the student, and the methods employed and the milieu provided by the school prepare students for certain kinds of roles.

Although the evidence is not conclusive, it appears that the American school is highly successful, at least during the elementary years, in transmitting cognitive substance about politics to the mind of the child. It is especially effective in teaching the child about the structure of political authority, and in inculcating certain citizen roles. The school does not seem to have a major role in teaching loyalty to the political community, since that is probably established prior to the elementary grades. Neither does it attempt to influence certain attitudes (e.g., partisanship), deferring to the family in these realms.

When it comes to rote learning of certain structural and legalistic facts

Table 3.4
Changes in Children's Perception of the Source of Laws, by Grade

GRADE	N	CONGRESS MAKES LAWS	PRESIDENT MAKES LAWS	SUPREME COURT MAKES LAWS	DON'T KNOW
2	1,627	4.8%	75.6%	11.5%	8.2%
3	1,648	11.4	66.1	17.0	5.5
4	1,723	27.5	44.1	21.1	7.3
5	1,793	57.4	19.4	19.8	3.4
6	1,743	65.1	13.2	18.3	3.4
7	1,712	72.1	8.9	16.4	2.6
8	1,690	85.3	5.4	7.9	1.4
Teachers	384	96.4	.5	3.1	—[a]

[a]Option not provided.

about American government, though, the school plays a major role. Table 3.4, reproduced from the Hess and Torney study, shows the increase in knowledge about the government that occurs during seven elementary school years. While it is true that the high correlation between the responses of eighth-graders and teachers does not in itself prove that a causal relationship exists, it is safe to assume that the school has had a large role in producing these responses.

Again through explicit teaching, the school instructs the child about the duties and responsibilities of citizenship. The school also seems to be very concerned with teaching children that compliance with the laws is a central duty of citizens (and of students in school). Younger children feel that all rules are fair and that punishment is an inevitable consequence of violating the law. For obvious reasons, the school is not inclined to debunk completely this conception. And, in fact, the child's experiences in compliant roles in the home as well as in school tend to make him comfortable in this role. As the child becomes older two things happen: he no longer believes in the implicit fairness of the law and he becomes increasingly aware of alternative citizen roles. Another look at Table 3.1 will confirm this.

The school socializes young people in diverse ways. It provides a setting that unconsciously encourages children to learn appropriate norms about compliance and "good citizenship." That is to say, it "conditions" children. Much as the Victorian Public School prepared a stage on which boys would rehearse their future roles, so the American school facilitates a different kind of political learning. It teaches students not only that it is good to obey rules and regulations, but also publicly rewards students who behave "appropriately" and sanctions those who do not.

It is evident that the Victorian Public School used well-known methods of conditioning and had a very elaborate way of socializing boys. We may at first deny that American public schools employ the same techniques, but closer inspection confirms this fact. Almond and Verba, in their five-nation study, investigated how certain citizenship norms can be "taught." They asked respondents in the five countries whether or not they had been allowed to participate in classroom discussions and debates when they were in school. The responses, by country, are shown in Table 3.5.

Especially important about these data is the relationship between these participatory experiences in the public schools and later feelings of personal competence. Seventy-five percent of the participatory group were high scorers on the subjective competence scale, while only 54 percent of the non-participatory group scored high. Moreover, as expected, subjective competence increases with the absolute level of education, since increased exposure to the school's values and norms results in their assimilation.

Through explicit teaching, then, as well as through more subtle condi-

Table 3.5
Freedom to Participate in School Discussions and Debates, by Nation

	UNITED STATES	GREAT BRITAIN	GERMANY	ITALY	MEXICO
Percentage who remember they:					
could and did participate	40	16	12	11	15
could but did not participate	15	8	5	4	21
could not participate	34	68	68	56	54
Don't know (and other)	11	8	15	29	10
Total percentages	100	100	100	100	100

Source: Gabriel A. Almond and Sidney Verba, *The Civic Culture* (Princeton: Princeton University Press, 1963), p. 333. Excerpts from Gabriel A. Almond and Sidney Verba, *The Civic Culture: Political Attitudes and Democracy in Five Nations* (copyright ©1963 by Princeton University Press; Little Brown and Company, Inc. ©1965), pp. 304-474. Reprinted by permission of Princeton University Press.

tioning methods, the school is able to transmit political orientations to children. From the Almond and Verba study we can infer that the American political culture stresses citizen participation, and we can also observe that the school has methods of transmitting this effectively. These findings are consistent with those of Hess and Torney, who observed that the sense of political efficacy increases dramatically during the elementary school years (see Figure 3.3).

From this discussion the reader may have come to the conclusion that the school is potentially a very potent socializer, and that it plays a major role in the political socialization of American children. Hess and Torney went so far as to say that the school is the most important socializing agent in America. "It is our conclusion," report Hess and Torney, "that the school stands out as the central, salient, and dominant force in the political socialization of the young child." [26]

Figure 3.3
Comparison of Means of Grades 3 Through 8 in Sense of Political Efficacy

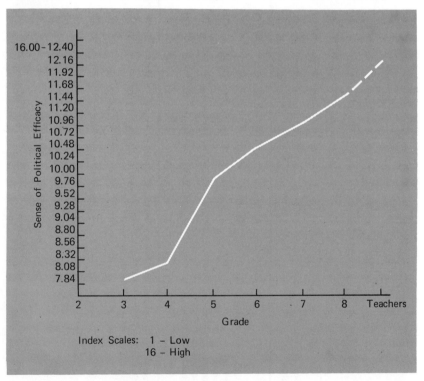

Index Scales: 1 – Low
                 16 – High

Source: Robert D. Hess and Judith V. Torney, *The Development of Political Attitudes in Children* (Chicago: Aldine-Atherton, Inc., 1967), p. 69.

Several caveats, though, must be entered with regard to this conclusion. It is customary in the United States for the teachings of the family and of the school to be compatible, if not mutually reinforcing. That is to say, we do not know for sure what happens when the teachings of the family are inconsistent or incompatible with those of the school. When a child is cross-pressured in this way, is he likely to adopt the values of the home or those of the school? And what are the control variables that determine which agent "wins" in such a situation? This question is not easy to answer, since extreme conflict does not often occur —the American family has, for the most part, been content to allow the school to adopt more and more of the socializing function.

It is also difficult to measure the impact of the school because of what Jennings and Langton have termed the "redundancy effect." [27] They found that high school civics courses have a measurable impact on the political orientations of black students but that white students were more likely already to have been exposed to the content of these courses, hence the term "redundancy effect." Blacks, for the most part, did not experience this effect. This agrees, too, with Hess and Torney's conclusion about class differences:

> The school is particularly important for children who come from working-class or low socioeconomic areas. Much of what working-class children learn at school is not reinforced by home and community. It may be for these reasons that the school seems to have somewhat less effect upon children from these areas of the city than it does on the children from more prosperous sections.[28]

Other studies of civics and political science courses at the secondary school or college level tend to agree that these courses do not produce dramatic changes in the political orientations of students.[29] For these reasons, then, it is difficult to evaluate the total impact of the school as a socializing agent.

PEER GROUPS

Since we all know from personal experience that groups influence the attitudes of their members, it is not surprising that children are socialized in part by their own peers. Socialization in peer groups tends, moreover, to be reciprocal, in the sense that children lead and are led by their peers.

The research conducted by social psychologist Theodore Newcomb at Bennington College during the 1930s was a pioneering study of how individuals are influenced by peers and by an academic institution.[30] The Bennington girls experienced great changes in political outlook (mainly from conservative to liberal) during four years at the school, and the extent to which they adopted Bennington's political values was in large part a function of their awareness of these values, and of the extent to which they used their peers as a "reference group." Some girls were either unaware of Bennington's politics, or indifferent to them, or both, and hence, unaffected by them. But most of the girls were aware of the liberalism that prevailed at the college, and since their peers were important to them, there was a tendency for them to become progressively liberal over the four-year period.

The Bennington study involved a discrepancy between peer group values and values that the girls had been exposed to in the home, since most were from rather well-to-do, conservative Republican homes. This is not always the case, however, since peer groups can also serve to reinforce the values held by the family, school, or other socializing agents.

This point is illustrated by the work of Urie Bronfenbrenner, who noted important differences between peer group socialization in the United States and in the Soviet Union.[31] Bronfenbrenner asked children in both countries what they would do in certain hypothetical situations involving moral behavior; for example, what they would do if they found an exam that their teacher had been planning to give to the class. Would they keep the test or would they return it to the teacher? Some children were told that their responses would be seen by their *parents*, and others were told that their *friends* would see their responses. In this way, Bronfenbrenner was able to observe whether pressure to conform to peers was greater in one of the two countries.

The main finding of this experiment was that American children were "cross-pressured"—they tended to reply that they would return the test if they thought their parents would see their response, but that they would keep it if their friends were to see their response. Soviet children, on the other hand, were pressured in the same direction under both conditions— to return the test. Bronfenbrenner's main finding was that "readiness to resist promptings to anti-social behavior, and responsiveness to adult influence, were greater among Russian than among American children." [32] Bronfenbrenner adds:

Where the peer group is to a large extent autonomous—as it often is in the United States—it can exert influence in opposition to values held by adult society. In other types of social systems, such as the U.S.S.R., the peer group—and its power to affect the attitudes and actions of its members—can be harnessed by the adult society for the furtherance of its own values and objectives. This fact carries with it significant educational and social implications.[33]

MASS MEDIA

The effect of the mass media in the political socialization process of children is uncertain. Of course the American child is exposed to politics through various media—television, radio, newspapers, and magazines—but the results of that exposure are not at all clear. In addition, media content that is not overtly political may or may not have political consequences.

One factor that probably mitigates the role of the mass media in shaping political attitudes is that people can choose, within limits, the media to which they wish to expose themselves. Liberals are not likely to subscribe to William Buckley's *National Review,* nor are conservatives likely to read *Rolling Stone.* Perhaps an even more important factor is selective perception, which we discussed in Chapter Two. People literally "see" things differently, depending on the attitudes and values that they bring to the media. Thus any "bias" contained in a message can often be distorted or ignored by the recipient of communication. In this way people can render themselves impervious to messages that are potentially painful or repugnant.

The sheer amount of media exposure does, however, seem to be related to the holding of certain attitudes. In their well-known study of racial attitudes in the South, for example, Matthews and Prothro discovered that for white southerners mass media exposure is negatively correlated with segregationist attitudes.[34] Likewise, the mass media probably are important in exposing members of subcultures to "mainstream" American attitudes. Hirsch's study of political socialization in Appalachia emphasized this effect of the mass media.[35]

It is not easy to state definitively how effective the media are in explicitly transmitting certain attitudes to the public, in the manner suggested by the Accumulation Model. But an even more controversial issue is the question of whether certain attitudes or behaviors are learned from the media through the process of "modeling," or identification. Do, for example, violent television programs "teach" viewers to engage in violent acts? This question should probably be answered with a qualified "yes," although it is not possible at this time to unravel all of the mysteries involved in this type of learning. Even if it were proven that television violence provokes real violence, the implications of this are not at all clear. Banning violent cartoon shows is one thing, but censoring news reports on wars or civil strife that involve violent acts is quite another. Political scientist Edward Banfield, for example, has urged that mass media coverage of urban riots such as those that occurred in many black communities during the late 1960s be banned.[36] His argument is simply that media coverage of these events caused them to spread from city to city. Obviously, this kind of censorship, even if essentially self-imposed by the television networks rather than mandated by the government, is a very controversial idea.

Discontinuities and differential
political socialization

We hope that we have not conveyed the impression that political socialization in the United States is merely a long, continuous, relatively painless process of receiving and internalizing political attitudes as they are transmitted by various socializing agents. This would not be at all accurate. For one thing, there are discontinuities in the process—that is, people may acquire political attitudes at one point in time that may become irrelevant, cumbersome, or positively dangerous at a later time. These persons may then undergo the difficult process of unlearning things that have been deeply internalized. Or, people sometimes undergo conflicting and incompatible socialization experiences. The political attitudes transmitted by the family, for example, may be so different from those to which a child is exposed in school that the socialization process might be exceedingly confusing and even painful.

Dramatic events can jar a person's attitude system, or they can almost single-handedly shape an individual's attitudes. Sputnik, the assassinations of the 1960s, and Watergate can be pointed to as dramatic events that seem to have profoundly affected America, and no doubt many Americans had their attitude systems shaken to their foundations by these events. Wars and depressions can have this effect. The Great Depression of the 1930s shaped the political attitudes of an entire generation of Americans, so much so that many voters today still regard the Republican party as the party of depression.

An important change in an individual's personal circumstances can involve discontinuous political socialization. A person who has risen or fallen on the social ladder may find that he must acquire new attitudes, or revise previously learned ones, in order to respond appropriately to his new circumstances. This is often very difficult, although most people are able eventually to cope with such changes. The phenomenon of "anticipatory socialization" (the adoption of new attitudes, values, or behaviors, in anticipation of new role expectations) helps.

An example of discontinuous political socialization involves gradual societal changes. For our grandparents, a high school diploma was a mark of honor and distinction, and a relatively small number of jobs required college or post-graduate training. Today, of course, employers tend to set very high educational requirements for job applicants, which has rendered a considerable number of older Americans "obsolete" in the job market. From a political point of view, it might also be noted that the gradual but substantial change in the racial attitudes of Americans has placed a heavy burden on white Americans whose attitudes stem from before the civil rights movement.

Even though we have made some broad generalizations about the political socialization process in the United States, one should also keep in mind the fact that ours is an extremely diverse, pluralistic country, and the heterogeneity of America can be easily seen in the political socialization process. For one thing, members of racial, ethnic, and subcultural minorities transmit very different attitudes to their children. We should not be surprised, for example, to discover that black children growing up in urban ghettoes have a very different view of the policeman as an object of political authority than white, suburban, middle-class children.

Class differences are also very important, and they are so extensive as to make a brief summary very difficult. Generally, it has been determined that basic attachment to the nation and to the norm of compliance both tend to be unrelated to social status. But class differences are observable with regard to the socialization of participatory norms and partisan orientation. Hess and Torney note that high-status children tend to be more participatory, more efficacious, and more involved politically than lower-class children.[37] This is no doubt to be explained in part by the fact that these norms are more likely to be transmitted to high-status children, as a study of three communities by Litt revealed. This study concluded that upper-class children tend to be encouraged to participate in politics, and they are led to believe that political involvement is rewarding. Children in the working class community are taught to view politics more passively, and to perceive political decision making as a kind of mechanical process that works well enough without citizen interference.[38] As Hess and Torney put it, low-status children are "retarded in their socialization into active involvement." [39] Moreover, some class differences seem to become more pronounced with age—that is, it seems that children are gradually socialized into social classes, and that class distinctions are more blurred among younger children.[40]

It is also reasonable to expect sex to be an important variable in the socialization process. Greenstein's 1965 New Haven study, while perhaps a bit dated, reports sex differences of considerable interest.

Even among the youngest respondents in Greenstein's sample, there are some sex differences in political responses. In short, boys are "more political" than girls:

. . . the amount of political information held by children of this age (nine) is infinitesimal. Even so, at the fourth grade level as well as for the total sample, boys were significantly better informed than girls. . . .[41]

And, interestingly, Greenstein found that both boys and girls are more likely to seek out their fathers rather than their mothers for advice about

Table 3.6
Sex Differences in Political Responses

QUESTIONNAIRE ITEMS	FOURTH GRADE SUBSAMPLE		TOTAL NEW HAVEN SAMPLE (GRADES 4 - 8)	
	Boys	Girls	Boys	Girls
SPECIFICALLY POLITICAL RESPONSES				
Political information score	3.30	2.77	4.69	4.31
Can name at least one party leader	41%	33%	56%	48%
Proposes "political" change in the world	13	5	41	34
Will vote when 21	76	77	80	81
Believes "elections are important"	69	72	72	73
POLITICALLY RELEVANT RESPONSES				
Names interesting news story	65	47	73	60
Story named is political	15	12	36	12
Names pleasant news story	39	28	54	41
Story named is political	9	2	26	17
Names unpleasant news story	37	35	53	43
Story named is political	18	9	33	20
Prefers Washington to New Haven news	52	35	38	26
Names someone from public life as "famous person you want to be like"	39	23	24	15
Names someone from public life as "famous person you *don't* want to be like"	22	14	32	13

Source: Fred I. Greenstein, *Children and Politics* (New Haven: Yale University Press, 1965), p. 117. Reprinted by permission of Yale University Press from *Children and Politics* by Fred I. Greenstein. Copyright © 1965 by Yale University.

voting—an apparent confirmation of the notion that even young girls think of politics as being properly the concern of males.[42]

Hess and Torney reported similar findings. Boys are not only "more political" than girls—a quantitative distinction— but there are qualitative differences in the ways that the sexes relate to politics. While boys seem to regard politics in impersonal and instrumental terms, girls are likely to view politics as personal and expressive. They also regard political life as being more benevolent and are made noticeably more uncomfortable by partisan division and conflict. Hess and Torney note that "the President was seen as more nurturant by girls, more likely to want to help them and more responsive if they wrote to him." [43] What is especially interesting is that this sex difference *increases* with age.

At all ages, boys are more likely to respond "yes" to the question: "Is it all right for the government to lie to protect America?" Hess and Torney conclude from this that "girls are more likely to apply personal morality to political actions, feeling that all lies are wrong, while boys judge governmental actions in terms of political expediency." [44] Once again, this difference *increases* with age.

Summary

There is no concise way to summarize the ways in which people come to hold political attitudes. What we can conclude from this chapter, however, is that political socialization is a process that tends to promote stability, at least in the United States. The attitudes that are internalized by new members of the political system are, generally speaking, supportive attitudes. There are numerous discontinuities, of course, and the various agents of political socialization may sometimes be in competition with one another. Still, the overall pattern is one that promotes the maintenance of the existing political system, and radical political change is rendered more difficult by the fact that Americans tend to acquire these supportive attitudes.

That political socialization processes tend to promote favorable perceptions of the community and regime does not, however, mean that similarly favorable attitudes will characterize responses to specific incumbents or specific policies. Beyond the shared attitudes relating to the Constitution or the flag, we might expect rather considerable disagreement among various groups relating to the more pedestrian aspects of the political process. And it is these types of group differences in public opinion that we will investigate in Chapter Four.

NOTES

1 David Easton and Robert D. Hess, "The Child's Political World," *American Journal of Political Science*, 6 (August 1962), 229–46. Reprinted from "The Child's Political World," *Midwest Journal of Political Science*, 6 (August 1962) by David Easton and Robert D. Hess by permission of the Wayne State University Press.

2 Roberta S. Sigel, ed., *Learning about Politics* (New York: Random House, Inc., 1970), p. xii.

3 Edwin D. Lawson, "Development of Patriotism in Children—A Second Look," *Journal of Psychology*, 55 (April 1963), 279–86.

4 Ibid., p. 284.

5 Robert D. Hess and Judith V. Torney, *The Development of Political Attitudes in Children* (Chicago: Aldine-Atherton, Inc., 1967), p. 30.

6 M. Kent Jennings and Richard G. Niemi, "The Transmission of Political Values from Parent to Child," *American Political Science Review*, 62 (March 1968), 169–84.

7 David Easton and Jack Dennis, *Children in the Political System* (New York: McGraw-Hill Book Company, 1969), p. 287.

8 Laurence Wylie, *Village in the Vaucluse* (New York: Harper & Row, Publishers, 1957), pp. 207–9.

9 Easton and Hess, "The Child's Political World," p. 236. Reprinted from "The Child's Political World," *Midwest Journal of Political Science*, 6 (August 1962) by David Easton and Robert D. Hess by permission of the Wayne State University Press.

10 See Jean Piaget, *The Moral Judgment of the Child* (New York: The Free Press, 1965).

11 Hess and Torney, *The Development of Political Attitudes in Children*, p. 36.

12 This literature is extensive, but see Fred I. Greenstein, "The Benevolent Leader: Children's Images of Political Authority," *American Political Science Review*, 54 (December 1960), 934–43, and Robert D. Hess and David Easton, "The Child's Changing Image of the President," *Public Opinion Quarterly*, 24 (Winter 1960), 632–44.

13 Albert Bandura and R. H. Walters, *Social Learning and Personality Development* (New York: Holt, Rinehart & Winston, Inc., 1963).

14 Fred I. Greenstein, *Children and Politics* (New Haven: Yale University Press, 1965), pp. 72–73.

15 See for example Lucian Pye, *Politics, Personality, and Nation Building* (New Haven: Yale University Press, 1962).

16 Robert E. Lane, "Fathers and Sons: Foundations of Political Belief," *American Sociological Review*, 24 (August 1959), 511.

17 Excerpts from Gabriel A. Almond and Sidney Verba, *The Civic Culture: Political Attitudes and Democracy in Five Nations* (copyright © 1963 by Princeton University Press; Little Brown and Company, Inc., © 1965), pp. 304–474. Reprinted by permission of Princeton University Press.

18 See Angus Campbell et al., *The American Voter* (New York: John Wiley & Sons, Inc., 1965).

19 Herbert Hyman, *Political Socialization* (New York: The Free Press, 1959), p. 56.

20 Kenneth Keniston, "The Sources of Student Dissent," *The Journal of Social Issues*, 23 (July 1967), 108–37.

21 J. Leiper Freeman, "Parents, It's Not *All* Your Fault, But. . . .," *Journal of Politics*, 31 (August 1969), 816–17.

[22] Urie Bronfenbrenner, "Soviet Methods of Character Education: Some Implications for Research," *Religious Education, Research Supplement,* 57 (July–August 1962), S–46.

[23] Ibid., p. S-50.

[24] Rupert Wilkinson, "Political Leadership and the Late Victorian Public School," *British Journal of Sociology,* 13 (December 1962), 320–30.

[25] Ibid., p. 322.

[26] Hess and Torney, *The Development of Political Attitudes in Children,* p. 219.

[27] Kenneth P. Langton and M. Kent Jennings, "Political Socialization and the High School Civics Curriculum in the United States," *American Political Science Review,* 62 (September 1968), 852–67.

[28] Hess and Torney, *The Development of Political Attitudes in Children,* p. 218.

[29] See, for example, Albert Somit, et al., "The Effect of the Introductory Political Science Course on Student Attitudes toward Personal Political Participation," *American Political Science Review,* 52 (December 1958), 1129–32.

[30] See Theodore M. Newcomb, "Attitude Development as a Function of Reference Groups: The Bennington Study," in *Readings in Social Psychology,* 3rd ed., eds. Eleanor E. Maccoby, Theodore M. Newcomb, and E. L. Hartley (New York: Holt, Rinehart & Winston, Inc., 1958), pp. 265–75.

[31] Urie Bronfenbrenner, "Response to Pressure from Peers Versus Adults among Soviets and American School Children," *International Journal of Psychology,* 2 (1967), 199–207.

[32] Ibid., p. 205.

[33] Ibid., p. 206.

[34] Donald R. Matthews and James W. Prothro, *Negroes and the New Southern Politics* (New York: Harcourt Brace Jovanovich, 1966), ch. 9.

[35] Herbert Hirsch, *Poverty and Politicization* (New York: The Free Press, 1971).

[36] Edward C. Banfield, *The Unheavenly City Revisited* (Boston: Little, Brown and Company, 1974), ch. 11.

[37] Hess and Torney, *The Development of Political Attitudes in Children,* ch. 7.

[38] Edgar Litt, "Civic Education, Community Norms, and Political Indoctrination," *The American Sociological Review,* 28 (February 1963), 74.

[39] Hess and Torney, *The Development of Political Attitudes in Children,* p. 171.

[40] Ibid., ch. 9.

[41] Greenstein, *Children and Politics,* p. 116.

[42] Ibid., p. 119.

[43] Hess and Torney, *The Development of Political Attitudes in Children,* p. 177.

[44] Ibid.

GROUP DIFFERENCES: PARTY IDENTIFICATION AND ISSUE OPINIONS

4

The political consequences of public opinion can be more easily and more meaningfully assessed by considering who has what kinds of opinions. And this generally involves our differentiating the mass public into groups or categories which have, or might be expected to have, political relevance. Traditionally, such an approach has resulted in a focus upon social class, race, religion, sex, region, and similar variables. In interpreting election results or public opinion surveys, political scientists and politicians are especially interested in which groups are on which side, why they are on that side, and which side they are likely to be on in the future. For the politician, these questions have a very practical application. They provide insights into the nature of his support (and opposition), and they also suggest the kinds of political issues to which he must devote his attention. For the political scientist, the focus upon group differences is helpful in analyzing patterns of stability and change within the electorate.

In recent years, certain traditional group divisions in the electorate have not provided the clear guides which they did in the past. The emergence of non-economic domestic issues along with demographic changes in the electorate has altered the economic and ethnic divisions which had dominated politics since Franklin Roosevelt established the New Deal "coalition" in the 1930s. But as the polarization of the electorate along economic lines has lessened, new cleavages based upon such factors as race, age, and education have emerged. The traditional stability of American party lines has also changed. The party electorates have become more heterogeneous, the proportion of Independent voters has risen, the amount of split-ticket voting has increased, and the effect of issues upon the voting decision has sometimes eclipsed that of party identification. These apparent instabilities, moreover, have prompted speculation about possible party realignments, third parties, and even the potential decomposition of the major parties.

In this chapter, then, we will examine the patterns of group divisions and differences in terms of partisan identification and issue opinions. And this should give us some insights into processes of stability and change within the electorate.

Party identification

One useful way to examine the differences in political behavior among social and economic groups is to focus upon party identification. Party identification is an individual's psychological allegiance toward a political party, and it usually represents the single most important influence upon his political behavior. The effects of party identification, moreover, are wide-ranging. It has a profound impact upon how people vote, of course, but it also affects their general political perceptions and political activities.[1]

Numerous studies have shown that patterns of party identification reflect important socioeconomic, racial, religious, and regional distinctions between the two major parties. But these distinctions often change over time and, in some instances, the extent of change has been rather dramatic. Over the last generation, for example, we have witnessed the disappearance of the "Solid South" in presidential politics. We have also seen a very substantial shift in the partisan identification of black voters, particularly in presidential politics. In addition to the changing identification of regions and groups, the degree of group polarization in partisan identification provides a convenient method for assessing the patterns of stability, change, and conflict within society, particularly as these patterns create demands which the political system must attempt to satisfy or to ameliorate.

GENERAL TRENDS

One of the most significant changes in public opinion over the past decade has been the increase in Independent identification. From the early 1940s (when survey research measurements of party identification distribution became available) through the early 1960s, Independent identification was consistently confined to about one-fifth of the electorate.[2] During the late 1960s, however, Independent identification started to rise rather steadily. In recent years, Independent identification has increased to include approximately one-third of the electorate, and more voters now identify as Independents than as Republicans (see Figure 4.1).

Figure 4.1
Party Identification Trend, 1965–1974

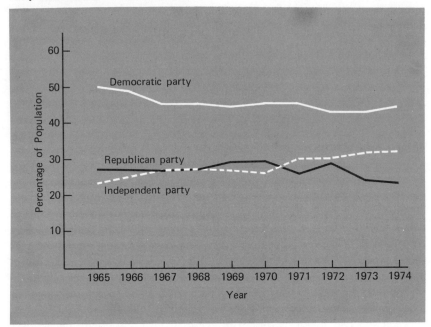

Source: *Gallup Opinion Index*, Report No. 112, (October 1974), p. 27.

The changes in Independent identification have been paralleled by other interesting trends. First, the proportion of strong party identifiers—those who consider themselves to be strong Democrats or strong Republicans—has declined to the point where their representation in the total electorate is approximately equal to that of Independents.[3] Second, the characteristics of Independent identification have apparently changed significantly. During the 1950s, survey research evidence indicated that Independents were less concerned about elections and were also less likely to be politically aware and politically active. In the 1956 presidential election, Independents were almost equally divided between those who were concerned about the outcome of the election and those who were unconcerned. In contrast, 82 percent of the strong party identifiers and 62 percent of the weak identifiers indicated that they were concerned about who won the election.[4]

By 1968, however, the Independent group had not only increased in size but had also changed rather markedly in its approach to politics.

Attention to campaigns, general interest in government and politics, and participation rates were quite similar between strong party identifiers and Independents.[5] It has been suggested that this change in the nature of Independent identification was largely attributable to the types of people who were added to the Independent category during the early 1960s. As shown in Table 4.1, shifts to the Independent category were concentrated in the higher socioeconomic (and younger) groups, and these groups tend to be more politically aware and interested than were the older Independents.[6]

These general trends in party identification over the past decade have no doubt reduced the stability of American parties and voting patterns. Independents, as might be expected, are unlikely to vote consistently for one party—periodic surveys have indicated, for example, that over 60 percent of the Independents have reported voting for presidential candidates of both parties.[7] In addition, Independents are more susceptible to third-party movements. In 1968, George Wallace received 25 percent of the Independent vote. This was appreciably higher than the proportion of support which he received from Democratic or, especially, from Republican identifiers. The fluidity of the electorate and the likelihood of its responding to short-term electoral forces and to issue candidacies have, therefore, been increased by the changes in party identification.[8]

Table 4.1
Shifts in Proportion of Independents, by Social Category,
June 1965 - September 1967

CATEGORY	INCREASE
Ages 30 - 49 years	11%
Highest income ($7,000 and over)	10
College education	10
Non-white	10
Ages 21 - 29 years	10
White-collar occupations	10
United States Total	8
Age 50 years and over	6
Women	6
Grade-school education	5
Middle income ($5,000 - $6,999)	5
Low income (under $3,000)	3
Farmers	2

Source: Walter Dean Burnham, *Critical Elections and the Mainsprings of American Politics* (New York: W. W. Norton & Company, Inc., 1970), p. 128. Original data source: AIPO (Gallup) data.

TABLE 4.2
Social Characteristics of Party Identifiers, 1968

	STRONG DEMOCRAT	WEAK DEMOCRAT	INDE-PENDENT	WEAK REPUBLICAN	STRONG REPUBLICAN	OTHERS
OCCUPATION						
Professional	11.6%	18.1%	37.1%	20.3%	12.9%	0%
Manager, official	17.1	22.0	33.6	16.6	9.3	1.5
Clerical, sales	15.3	23.5	32.3	17.6	11.2	0
Skilled, semiskilled	18.3	29.7	30.3	12.7	7.3	1.6
Unskilled, service	33.3	26.2	24.3	6.0	7.1	3.0
Farmer	25.7	27.0	10.9	23.0	12.2	1.4
Other (retired, etc.)	28.0	27.0	19.0	10.6	11.6	3.7
INCOME						
0 - $1,999	29.4	28.7	17.7	10.3	10.3	3.7
$2,000 - $3,999	28.2	25.8	24.0	10.8	8.9	2.3
$4,000 - $5,999	19.8	25.7	29.7	11.9	9.9	3.0
$6,000 - $9,999	18.6	25.3	30.8	13.9	10.1	1.3
$10,000 - $14,999	17.7	28.0	30.5	15.8	7.7	.3
$15,000 and over	9.4	16.5	39.5	24.1	10.0	.6
EDUCATION						
None - 8 grades	31.0	31.8	15.9	10.6	7.5	3.1
9 - 12 grades	19.2	27.3	28.9	14.6	8.3	1.7
Some college	10.8	18.8	42.5	15.7	11.7	.4
Baccalaureate degree	10.0	15.7	37.1	20.7	16.4	0
Advanced degree	21.0	12.9	40.3	12.9	12.9	0

Source: Adapted from Frank J. Sorauf, *Party Politics in America*, 2nd ed. (Boston: Little, Brown and Company, 1972), p. 149. Original data source: Survey Research Center.

SOCIAL CLASS DIFFERENCES

Since the New Deal of Franklin Roosevelt, the Democratic party has been generally characterized as the party of the "have-nots." Like the party systems of other Western democracies, the major parties in the United States have been associated with different class loyalties, but the American parties have not usually reflected the sharp status differences which characterize the party electorates in other industrial democracies.

As shown in Table 4.2, the relationships between party identification and such social class variables as occupation, income, and education are only moderately strong. The inter-party differences, moreover, are considerably muted by the large proportion of Independents in the middle and upper occupation, income, and education categories. We find, for example, that as income increases, there is a corresponding decrease in Democratic identification. Between the lowest and highest income groups, strong Democratic identification decreases by two-thirds and weak Democratic identification by about two-fifths. This decrease in Democratic identification, however, is not matched by a commensurate increase in Republican identification. Rather, while total Republican identification (weak and strong identifiers) increases to approximately 34 percent from the lowest to highest income classification, Independent identification increases to about 40 percent.

Similar patterns are evident in the occupation and education groupings. Very clear losses in Democratic identification occur as occupational status moves from the unskilled to the professional classification, or as education increases from grade school through college. But the Independent and Republican groups recoup the loss in Democratic identification, and in most instances, the Independents obtain the greater share.

In terms of social class distinctions, the major parties reflect an impressive degree of heterogeneity. While it is true that Democratic identification is disproportionately concentrated in the lower socioeconomic brackets, substantial numbers of individuals in these groups do identify as Independents or Republicans. And, conversely, a significant proportion of those in the upper socioeconomic categories identify with the Democratic party.

There is also evidence that the partisan implications of social class have been decreasing over time. Throughout the 1930s and 1940s, for example, there was a strong correlation between income and partisan support—the heavy support which low-income families gave to the Democratic party was accompanied by heavy support for the Republican party by high-income families.[9] As Table 4.3 illustrates, however, the relationship between income and partisan support declined rather markedly through

Table 4.3
Republican Proportion of the Two-Party Vote in Relation to Income and Education, 1948 - 1964

	1948	1952	1956	1960	1964
INCOME[a]					
Lower	36%	58%	54%	52%	26%
Lower middle	31	53	57	54	30
Upper middle	51	58	59	45	29
Upper	62	74	65	54	44
EDUCATION					
Some college (or completed college)	76	73	69	64	46
Some high school (or completed high school)	46	57	58	47	31
Some grade school (or completed grade school)	32	51	58	45	20

Source: Warren E. Miller, "The Political Behavior of the Electorate," in *Political Opinion and Behavior*, ed. E. Dreyer and W. Rosenbaum (Belmont, Calif.: Wadsworth Publishing Co., Inc., 1970), pp. 195, 198. Reprinted from *American Government Annual, 1960-1961*, ed. E. Latham et al. (New York: Holt, Rinehart and Winston, Inc., 1960).

[a]The income definitions used are as follows:

	1948	1952	1956	1960	1964
Lower	Under $2,000	Under $2,000	Under $3,000	Under $3,000	Under $3,000
Lower middle	$2,000 - 2,999	$2,000 - 3,999	$3,000 - 4,999	$3,000 - 4,999	$3,000 - 5,999
Upper middle	$3,000 - 3,999	$4,000 - 7,499	$5,000 - 7,499	$5,000 - 7,499	$6,000 - 9,999
Upper	Over $4,000	Over $7,500	Over $7,500	Over $7,500	Over $10,000

the 1950s and early 1960s. If we compare the lower and upper income categories, we see that there was a 26 percent differential in Republican support in 1948. This differential decreased to 16 percent in 1952, to 11 percent in 1956, to 2 percent in 1960, and then increased to 18 percent in 1964. The differential between the lower middle and upper middle categories (20 percent in 1948) declined steadily throughout the period and virtually disappeared by 1964.

Table 4.3 also provides an illustration of the relationship between education and partisan support. Here, again, there is a considerable decline in the distinctiveness characterizing the three groups. The 44 percent differential between the college and grade school classifications was reduced by approximately one-half in 1952, and in 1956, the difference was only 11 percent. In both 1960 and 1964, sharper differences emerged, but these were considerably lower than in 1948.

There are, then, differences in the social and economic composition of the party electorates. And it is apparent that these differences would be much more pronounced if Independent identification were less substantial. But the major parties provide at most a very moderate example of status polarization, and this polarization has been less evident in recent elections than it was during the Roosevelt and Truman administrations. There has not been complete depolarization, for social class is still linked to party identification, but the social class bases of party identification are quite modest.

AGE

Age is an interesting and important variable in analyzing partisan identification, particularly with the lowering of the minimum voting age to 18. It has been estimated, for example, that by 1976 this legal change coupled with demographic trends will result in an electorate in which 27 percent of the eligible voters will be under 30, an increase of approximately one-third since 1968.[10] Thus, to the extent that significant differences between age groups occur with respect to party identification (or other political phenomena), these differences will have a potentially greater impact in the future than they have had in the past.

Younger voters have traditionally been somewhat more prone than older voters to classify themselves as Independents rather than as Democrats or Republicans, and this tendency has become even more pronounced over the past decade. In 1965, the youngest and oldest age classes differed by about 12 percent in the proportion of Independents. By 1967–68, this had increased to 16 percent.[11] Independent identification was especially characteristic of the better educated young. Among college students in national samples, combined Democratic and Republican identification decreased from 61 percent in 1966 to a bare majority in 1974 (see Table 4.4).

According to Burnham, the increase in Independent identification among college students has been disproportionately high among those who describe themselves as "extremely liberal"—while only 23 percent of the "extreme conservatives" consider themselves Independents, 57 percent of the "extreme liberals" assume this classification.[12] Nevertheless, as Table 4.4 indicates, the Democratic party enjoys a very substantial lead over the Republican party in college student identification.

In addition to the differences in identification rates, there are also age-related differences in the evaluations of the parties. As Table 4.5 shows, a majority of the 50 and over age group evaluates either the Democratic or the Republican party in highly favorable terms. In the 18–24 age group, however, only 40 percent perceive the parties in similarly favorable terms, and the Democratic party has a considerably higher evaluation rate than does the Republican party.

The differences in party identification between younger and older voters are reflected in voting behavior. First, older citizens are decidedly more likely to vote than younger citizens, especially those who are newly enfranchised. In the 1968 presidential election, only 51 percent of the eligible population between the ages of 21 and 24 voted, while 72 percent of the 30–64-year-old age group voted, and 66 percent of those aged 65 and over voted.[13] And in 1974, the first midterm congressional election in which the 18–20-year-olds were eligible to vote, actual turnout in this group was only 21 percent (as opposed to 58 percent among those aged 55–64).[14] Given that education is strongly related to political participation, we might expect that younger voters would participate at a higher rate than older voters, since the younger age groups have more years of formal education. In attempting to explain this apparent contradiction, the authors of *The American Voter* emphasized the importance of perceptions and attitudes relating to political parties, since these are "the only elements that distinguish the motivational system of the older voter

Table 4.4
Trend in Party Affiliation among College Students, 1966 - 1974

YEAR	REPUBLICANS	DEMOCRATS	INDEPENDENTS
1966	26%	35%	39%
1967	22	30	48
1970	18	30	52
1972	21	38	41
1974	14	37	49

Source: *Gallup Opinion Index,* Report No. 109, July 1974, p. 15.

Table 4.5
Relationship between Age and Highly Favorable
Evaluations of the Parties, 1973

AGE	PERCENTAGE RATING REPUBLICANS HIGHLY FAVORABLE	PERCENTAGE RATING DEMOCRATS HIGHLY FAVORABLE
18-24 years	13	27
25-29 years	17	19
30-49 years	17	28
50 years and over	25	31

Source: *Gallup Opinion Index,* Report No. 100, October 1973, pp. 22-23.
Note: Data based on the Gallup definition of "highly favorable"—+ 5 and + 4 evaluations
on a scale ranging from + 5 to − 5.

from that of the younger. . . ."[15] Older voters are more likely to identify
with and to have strong commitments toward a political party, to evaluate
candidates and issues in party terms, and, hence, to vote more regularly
than are younger citizens. Participation by the young is likely to be not
only lower but also more variable, since it is more dependent upon short-
term electoral forces such as issues or personalities.

Second, lacking the anchor of party identification, younger voters
may be attracted to unconventional candidates and to third-party movements. In the 1968 election, George Wallace—whose campaign rhetoric
was especially notable for its rather negative depictions of college student
demonstrators—did exceptionally well among young voters. Outside the
South, Wallace received 13 percent of the votes of those under 30, but
only 3 percent of the votes of those over 70, and the degree of support
decreased regularly with age between these two extremes. Even among white
southerners, the correlation between age and the Wallace vote was slightly
negative. The higher degree of Wallace support among the young, moreover, was not matched by a disproportionately high affective rating for
Wallace—positive evaluations of Wallace were not correlated with age.
But older voters definitely tended to identify strongly with one of the
conventional parties, and the Wallace vote increased substantially as one
moved from the strong identifiers to the weak identifiers to the Independents.[16]

The Wallace experience suggests that one be exceptionally cautious
in assuming that the youth vote is in any sense monolithic. And it also
lends support to a prediction that the authors of *The American Voter*
voiced more than a decade ago: "It is probable that movements to reduce the voting age in effect imply a more fluid electorate. Whether such
fluidity is a matter for concern or a desirable source of 'flexibility' in the
political system depends upon our various normative persuasions."[17]

Table 4.6
Party Identification by Race, 1968

	BLACK	WHITE
Strong Democrat	55.7%	16.1%
Weak Democrat	28.9	24.8
Independent	10.1	31.0
Weak Republican	.7	16.1
Strong Republican	1.3	10.5
Others	3.4	1.4

Source: Frank J. Sorauf, *Party Politics in America,* 2nd ed.
(Boston: Little, Brown and Company, 1972), p. 149.

RACE

The partisan preference of blacks is now overwhelmingly Democratic. This represents a decided change from the pre-New Deal period, when a strong tie existed between the Republican party and the black voter. But the combination of New Deal economic liberalism and the civil rights record of the Democratic party since 1960 has served to draw most blacks into the Democratic party. As shown in Table 4.6, over 80 percent of the blacks identify as Democrats. Even more striking, approximately two-thirds of these classify themselves as strong Democrats. Republican identification, on the other hand, is almost nonexistent.

Black desertion of the Republican party is exemplified by the behavior of southern blacks during the early 1960s. In 1961, 10 percent of the southern blacks identified as Republicans, while 51 percent identified as Democrats. By 1964, however, strong Democratic identification had increased to 53 percent, total Democratic identification had increased to 75 percent, and total Republican identification had dropped to 2.5 percent.[18] Apparently, the Kennedy administration and the Goldwater campaign just about erased black Republicanism in the South.

The distinctiveness of the black vote, moreover, has become even sharper in recent elections. The six presidential elections shown in Table 4.7 indicate that black Democratic support has never fallen below 60 percent. But in the 1964 election, the black Democratic vote reached 94 percent, and in both 1968 and 1972, support was over 85 percent. Accordingly, black Democratic support was more than double white Democratic support in 1968 and almost three times higher in 1972. And the strength of black allegiance to the Democratic party is even more vividly shown by the fact that in 1968, black opposition to the war in Vietnam was even stronger than white opposition. According to the 1968 Survey Research Center Election Study, "Blacks stood out as the major demographic grouping most exercised about the entanglement in Vietnam." [19]

Nevertheless, black evaluations of Hubert Humphrey and Lyndon Johnson were considerably higher than white evaluations, and of course, black support for Humphrey was exceptionally distinctive.[20]

One of the most apparent social cleavages with respect to partisanship, then, is the black-white division. It is considerably deeper than class differentiations with respect to partisanship. Indeed, as class differentiations have become less sharp over the past 15 years, the black-white division has become even more pronounced.

RELIGION

The relationship between religion and party identification has been relatively consistent over time. Jewish voters have remained the most strongly Democratic religious grouping, and Catholics have also been predominantly Democratic. Protestants, on the other hand, have evidenced a stronger Republican identification than either Jews or Catholics, and with the exception of 1964, the Protestant vote has been decidedly Republican in recent presidential elections. Between 1960 and 1968, party identification within these three groupings showed some interesting changes (see Table 4.8). Among white Protestants, Republican and Democratic identification declined slightly, while Independent identification increased

Table 4.7
Vote in Presidential Elections, by Race, 1952 - 1972

	WHITE	NON-WHITE
1952		
Stevenson	43%	79%
Eisenhower	57	21
1956		
Stevenson	41	61
Eisenhower	59	39
1960		
Kennedy	49	68
Nixon	51	32
1964		
Johnson	59	94
Goldwater	41	6
1968		
Humphrey	38	85
Nixon	47	12
Wallace	15	3
1972		
McGovern	32	87
Nixon	68	13

Source: *Gallup Opinion Index,* Report No. 105, March 1974, p. 23.

Table 4.8

Changes in Party Identification, by Religious Group, 1960 - 1968

	1960					1968				
	Strong Democrat	Weak Democrat	Independent	Weak Republican	Strong Republican	Strong Democrat	Weak Democrat	Independent	Weak Republican	Strong Republican
White Protestant	18%	24%	22%	16%	21%	14%	24%	30%	19%	13%
White Catholic	29	33	21	10	6	22	30	32	10	6
Jewish	21	28	47	5	0	33	19	43	5	0

Source: Gerald M. Pomper, et al., *The Performance of American Government* (New York: The Free Press, 1972), pp. 68-69.

to 30 percent. Among Catholics, a similar increase in Independent identification occurred, but this was a result of a decrease in Democratic identification, since Republican identification remained stable. Jewish voters, however, showed a slight increase in Democratic identification, especially in the strong Democratic category. This increased from 21 percent in 1960 to 33 percent in 1968. And Independent identification dropped slightly during this period, from 47 percent to 43 percent. Republican identification among Jewish voters, however, remained minimal throughout the period and at considerably lower levels than Catholic identification or, especially, Protestant identification.

The direct salience of religion in any particular election is, of course, highly variable, but two recent presidential elections illustrate the manner in which religious identities can be increased by the candidates or issues in a given election. In 1960, John F. Kennedy's presidential candidacy was threatened by anti-Catholic attitudes. And while political and religious leaders attempted to minimize the issue of religion, this issue did have a very clear effect upon voting behavior. In particular, the Kennedy candidacy resulted in stronger Democratic support from Catholics than might normally have been expected, but it also reduced support among Protestants below the expected prediction of the Protestant vote.[21] Thus, Kennedy's Catholicism had a positive impact upon many Catholic Republicans but a negative impact upon many Protestant Democrats. And in 1972, the Nixon-McGovern race produced a diminution in Jewish Democratic support as a result of Jewish uncertainty about McGovern's position on military assistance to Israel. While McGovern did considerably better among Jewish voters than among most other groups (with the conspicuous exception of blacks), it appeared that Nixon was able to make much heavier inroads into the Jewish vote than would have been the case if this short-term influence had not affected the campaign.

REGION AND URBAN-RURAL DIFFERENCES

The regional distinctiveness of American politics has changed rather dramatically over the past generation. The Democratic "Solid South" has disappeared in recent presidential elections, and there is now a substantial contingent of Republican southerners in Congress. At the same time, however, the Democratic party has made substantial gains in both the East and the Midwest, and this has been particularly evident in congressional elections. If we examine the recent distribution of party identification by region, however, it is apparent that the South has retained some of its distinctiveness (see Table 4.9). But the other inter-regional differences are not especially striking. Democratic identification exceeds Republican identification in every region, but the differences in the East (16 percent), Midwest (15 percent), and West (23 percent) are relatively similar. In the South, the overall difference increases to 31 percent, with Democratic preference in the Deep South (41 percent) providing much of this distinctiveness. If we look at the southern states outside the Deep South, however, the Democratic-Republican distribution is closer to that in the rest of the nation.

In terms of urban-rural differences, Democratic strength is greatest in the larger urban areas (see Table 4.9). However, the level of Democratic identification is remarkably consistent, regardless of metropolitan size. Republican identification, on the other hand, is highest in the smaller towns and rural areas. It is also interesting to note that the lowest levels of Republican identification occur in those areas (500,000–999,999 and 50,000–499,999) where Independent identification is highest.

Regional and urban-rural differences have not disappeared from American politics, but the patterns of party identification indicate that many traditional differences have been considerably muted in the past two decades. And this change portends well for national politics, since it reduces the likelihood of intense regional conflicts such as those which plagued the nation during the early years of the civil rights movement. Moreover, this change indicates that politics has become, and is becoming, increasingly "nationalized."

Issues and ideology

In this section group differences will be examined from a second perspective—that of ideology and political opinions. Just as social and economic groups show differing patterns of party identification, they also provide an analytically useful means for examining patterns of ideological support as well as public policy issue positions. Political polarization and societal cleavages are often associated with differing social and economic segments of society. Proper understanding of the nature of mass public opinion requires knowledge of how the distribution of political opinions reflects the socioeconomic patterns of society.

There is little doubt that the socioeconomic conflicts within a society have an impact on the political order. If such cleavages are serious, violent eruptions may well occur. The religious (and economic) based hostilities in Northern Ireland, for example, have influenced the distribution of opinion within that nation. Catholics and Protestants generally support political views that are at variance. The wide breach separating these two religious groupings has manifested itself in open warfare. Cultural

Table 4.9
Party Identification by Region and City Size, 1974

	REPUBLICAN	DEMOCRAT	INDEPENDENT
REGION			
East	27%	43%	30%
Midwest	24	39	37
South	18	49	33
Deep South	12	53	35
Rest of South	20	48	32
West	24	47	29
CITY SIZE			
1,000,000 people and over	24	46	30
500,000 - 999,999 people	18	46	36
50,000 - 499,999 people	18	48	34
2,500 - 49,999 people	28	41	31
Under 2,500 people, rural	27	42	31

Source: *Gallup Opinion Index,* Report No. 112, October 1974, p. 28.

differences within a society have a similar impact on the distribution of political values. The history of conflict between Canadians of English and French backgrounds illustrates how such cultural patterns impose themselves on a nation's politics.

In the United States we have not been totally free of extreme hostilities based upon socioeconomic patterns within society. During the first century of our nation's history, regional differences were associated with political conflict to the extent that a civil war emerged as the only means by which the conflict could be resolved. As the nation entered the twentieth century political and economic differences between labor and management frequently led to violent outbursts; and in more contemporary periods racial and ethnic differences with their corresponding political ramifications prompted rioting in major urban centers such as Los Angeles and Detroit.

For the most part, however, socioeconomic differences within the United States have provoked political conflicts of a milder sort, resolvable by conventional methods. In the mid-1970s, for example, religious differences have manifested themselves on the issue of abortion reform. Many of the opponents of liberalized abortion policies have close ties to the Roman Catholic church. These groups have attempted to reverse the trend toward legalized abortion through organizing politically, supporting proposed constitutional amendments, lobbying legislators, and initiating court suits. The opposition of Catholic Americans to abortion reform is just one example of how demographic factors affect mass opinion. Additional examples readily come to mind—blacks' support of civil rights legislation, Jews' support of United States military aid to Israel, and fundamentalist Protestants' opposition to legalized gambling. So pervasive are the influences of social and economic factors on the distribution of citizen opinion that we should examine such relationships in greater depth.

POLITICAL PHILOSOPHY

American citizens are not known for espousing well-developed ideological positions. We tend to be much more a nation of pragmatists than of citizen-philosophers. Despite this fact, Americans do have general political beliefs that approximate philosophical positions on governmental affairs. Most citizens fall well within the center of the political spectrum, eschewing the more radical and reactionary poles. For this reason most commentators on public opinion generally use the terms "liberalism" and "conservatism" to distinguish the political views of the electorate. These terms, of course, lack precision. What is a liberal, or a conservative, position on a given issue may be subject to considerable debate. Similarly, an individual's attitudes on several different issues may range from conservative to liberal. How we would classify such a voter on a liberalism–conservatism scale is somewhat unclear. In spite of this imprecision, liberal–conservative distinctions give us an indication of the political philosophies of the citizenry.

Considerable public opinion polling has been devoted to analyzing trends in liberalism and conservatism among the American people. These polls have usually asked the respondents to classify themselves into liberal or conservative categories. This self-classification procedure has obvious disadvantages. Many people do not have an adequate comprehension of such terms, especially when used in a political context. Then, too, the respondents may give little thought to their answers. Yet even with these limitations, the self-ascribed political philosophies of the American public provide interesting information about the views of our citizens.

The results of this research reveal that over time there are few radical changes in the philosophical positions of the public on general political matters. There are, of course, shifts in public sentiment, but such alterations tend to occur gradually. While there may well be changes in the proportion of Americans who classify themselves as liberals or conservatives as the tenor of the times changes, the relative positions of various social and economic groupings are remarkably constant. For example, the proportion of Jews who classify themselves as liberals may fluctuate, but the Jewish population in this country is almost invariably more liberal than members of the Protestant faith. Given the persistence of several of these social and economic differences, it is profitable to discuss the pertinent research results.

Table 4.10 illustrates the 1972 distribution of self-ascribed liberalism-

Table 4.10
Demographic Characteristics and Self-Identified
Political Philosophy, 1972

	CONSERVATIVE	MIDDLE OF THE ROAD	LIBERAL	NO OPINION
AGE				
18 - 24 years	22%	30%	43%	5%
25 - 29 years	36	26	37	1
30 - 49 years	44	31	20	5
50 years and over	48	30	17	5
RACE				
White	43	31	22	4
Non-White	26	21	46	7
REGION				
East	37	30	28	5
Midwest	40	31	26	3
South	46	29	19	6
West	40	29	27	4

Source: *Gallup Opinion Index,* Report No. 86, August 1972, p. 9.

conservatism across three demographic characteristics—age, race, and region. In each case, clear opinion differences emerge.

The age variable results are clearly consistent with our general understanding of the impact of age on political attitudes. As a citizen grows older, he tends to become more conservative relative to the rest of the population. The reason for this tendency may well be twofold. First, experience may dull youthful reformist idealism, and the cloudiness of memories of the past may well portray the old ways as being better than they actually were. Second, even if an individual retains his original political philosophy over the years, his attitudes automatically become more conservative as the world "moves on." Whatever the reason, this relationship is a constantly recurring one. Consistently greater numbers of the young link themselves to liberal philosophies. This position moderates in the middle years and tends to become more conservative after the age of fifty.

Similarly clear-cut results are found on the race variable. It is not surprising to find that non-whites classify themselves as liberals much more frequently than do whites. This is due in large part to the economic and social deprivation experienced by non-white minorities in this country. Assuming that liberalism generally favors social and economic change and conservatism generally supports the status quo, it is understandable that the "haves" of society are substantially more conservative than the "have-nots."

The regional data also provide interesting and revealing information. As might have been anticipated, southerners are more likely to see themselves as conservative and easterners more likely to accept liberalism than citizens from other regions. The impact of region on political philosophies occurs in at least two ways. First, regionally oriented cultures have an impact on political thinking. A region such as the South with an agricultural and traditionalist history understandably has a conservatively oriented political culture. The West with its frontier culture, for example, places its political emphasis on different values than the East or Midwest. The second way region influences politics is through the types of groups which have settled in the various sections of the country. For example, the highly Jewish and Catholic populations of the East make that region more liberally oriented than the Protestant fundamentalist populations of the South.

Similar distributions are portrayed in Table 4.11 for socioeconomic characteristics. Three specific variables are analyzed—education, income, and occupation. The relationships, though interesting, are not as striking as those for the preceding factors.

Educational experiences are clearly related to the individual's choice of liberal or conservative political philosophy. As education increases, so too does the tendency to accept a more liberal political philosophy. As

Table 4.11
Socioeconomic Characteristics and Self-Identified Political Philosophy, 1972

	CONSERVATIVE	MIDDLE OF THE ROAD	LIBERAL	NO OPINION
EDUCATION				
College	37%	28%	34%	1%
High school	41	32	23	4
Grade school	47	27	16	10
INCOME				
$15,000 and over	38	32	29	1
$10,000-14,999	43	29	23	4
$7,000-9,999	46	31	19	4
$5,000-6,999	37	28	27	8
$3,000-4,999	45	30	20	5
Under $3,000	35	27	27	11
OCCUPATION				
Business/professional workers	37	32	30	1
White collar workers	34	26	36	4
Farm workers	41	35	18	6
Manual workers	41	30	18	7

Source: *Gallup Opinion Index,* Report No. 86, August 1972, p. 9.

Table 4.11 indicates, college educated individuals are almost evenly divided between self-described liberals and conservatives, while those with only grade school educations are almost three times as prone to accept conservatism over liberalism. Similar trends emerge on the occupational variable. The upper status occupations (business, the professions, and white collar workers) are much more evenly divided in their political beliefs than agricultural and manual workers who show a distinct propensity to adopt conservative views. Only on the income characteristics do clear patterns fail to manifest themselves.

In addition to the socioeconomic differences in political philosophy, Table 4.11 clearly reveals another important relationship. As socioeconomic status increases, in terms of education, income, and occupation, so too does the ability to classify one's own political philosophy. Those educated only to the grade school level, receiving incomes under $7,000, and having lower-class occupations are more often unable to label themselves as liberal or conservative. As we climb the socioeconomic ladder we find the percentage of the "politically naive" rapidly decreasing. Persons of higher socioeconomic status are usually better informed about and more active in politics than are lower status individuals. Thus they can better describe their own political views and philosophies.

PUBLIC POLICY ISSUES

We have seen how social and economic factors have predisposed individuals toward generally liberal or conservative political philosophies. We find similar distributions of differences on specific issues. In this section we shall discuss the way in which social, economic, and political characteristics affect mass public opinion.

In order to accomplish this objective we will examine opinion distributions on nine specific public policy issues. These specific issues were politically important as the nation entered the mid-1970s, and they encompass a rather wide variety of subjects.

1. Busing school children to achieve racial balance
2. The imposition of the death penalty for persons convicted of murder
3. Unconditional amnesty for Vietnam War draft evaders and deserters
4. The reduction of federal spending for military and defense purposes
5. The reduction in federal spending for Health, Education, and Welfare programs
6. Federal aid to parochial schools
7. Legalized abortion
8. Ratification of the Equal Rights Amendment
9. Registration of firearms

For each of these public policy questions we analyzed mass opinion over a number of social, economic, and political characteristics.

Table 4.12
Public Opinion by Sex, 1974

	MALE	FEMALE
Busing		
Favor	33%	36%
Oppose	67	64
Capital punishment		
Favor	69	59
Oppose	31	41
Vietnam amnesty		
Favor	38	44
Oppose	62	56
Defense spending reductions		
Favor	54	56
Oppose	46	44
HEW spending reductions		
Favor	37	32
Oppose	63	68
Aid to parochial schools		
Favor	52	54
Oppose	48	46
Legalized abortion		
Favor	54	48
Oppose	46	52
Equal rights amendment		
Favor	83	73
Oppose	17	27
Gun registration		
Favor	61	82
Oppose	39	18

Source: *Gallup Opinion Index,* Report No. 113, November 1974, pp. 4-17.

Sex differences. Table 4.12 presents public opinion data on each of the nine issues broken down by sex characteristics. The results provide an interesting illustration of differences between male and female citizens. Two specific findings are immediately apparent even from a casual examination of the data. First, the most radical male-female differences emerge on the three issues which are related to violence or bloodshed. And in each instance females assume a more humanitarian position. Women give far less support for capital punishment than men; they are more compassionate toward war resisters; and, above all else, they overwhelmingly support gun control legislation. These differences may well reflect early sexual socialization patterns that equate manhood with cowboys, war heroes, and firearms. The second interesting result occurs on the "women's issues" of legalized abortion and the Equal Rights Amendment. Justification for both of these reforms has been predicated on the personal rights of women.

Yet, interestingly, males support abortion and equal rights at a much higher rate than females.

Race differences.   In recent decades perhaps no other social or economic factor has received the same degree of attention as has race. On almost every controversial issue facing the nation, citizens and politicians alike have considered the possible reactions of racial groups. Table 4.13 shows the kinds of opinion differences that exist between whites and non-whites. On five of the nine issues—busing, capital punishment, Vietnam amnesty, aid to parochial schools, and abortion—there are fairly substantial differences by race. On busing, the differences are striking—while whites oppose busing by a 3-to-1 margin, non-whites support busing by almost the same ratio. On the issues of capital punishment and Vietnam amnesty, non-whites are somewhat more "liberal" than whites. These differences can perhaps be explained by (1) the disproportionate number of blacks

Table 4.13
Public Opinion by Race, 1974

	WHITE	NON-WHITE
Busing		
Favor	28%	75%
Oppose	72	25
Capital punishment		
Favor	66	50
Oppose	34	50
Vietnam amnesty		
Favor	39	54
Oppose	61	46
Defense spending reductions		
Favor	55	59
Oppose	45	41
HEW spending reductions		
Favor	35	30
Oppose	65	70
Aid to parochial schools		
Favor	51	68
Oppose	49	32
Legalized abortion		
Favor	53	40
Oppose	47	60
Equal rights amendment		
Favor	78	78
Oppose	22	22
Gun registration		
Favor	71	78
Oppose	29	22

Source: *Gallup Opinion Index,* Report No. 113, November 1974, pp. 4-17.

executed when the death penalty was in effect, and (2) the extremely high degree of non-white opposition to the war in Vietnam discussed earlier in this chapter. Non-whites are also more likely than whites to support aid to parochial schools, but they are also more opposed than whites to legalized abortion. This latter question has been especially controversial in the black community, with some black spokesmen arguing that issues of racial survival are at stake. While these differences are important, it is noteworthy that on several issues, distinctions based on race comparisons are relatively minor. White and non-white attitudes are remarkably similar on the defense and HEW spending issues, suggesting that there is considerable agreement on spending priorities.

Educational differences. Educational accomplishment has long been acknowledged as having a substantial impact on an individual's views about politics. Higher levels of educational attainment affect individuals in at

Table 4.14
Public Opinion by Education Level, 1974

	COLLEGE	HIGH SCHOOL	GRADE SCHOOL
Busing			
Favor	26%	34%	49%
Oppose	74	66	51
Capital punishment			
Favor	59	65	67
Oppose	41	35	33
Vietnam amnesty			
Favor	47	38	44
Oppose	53	62	56
Defense spending reductions			
Favor	58	53	57
Oppose	42	47	43
HEW spending reductions			
Favor	30	33	45
Oppose	70	67	55
Aid to parochial schools			
Favor	48	54	57
Oppose	52	46	43
Legalized abortion			
Favor	71	49	30
Oppose	29	51	70
Equal rights amendment			
Favor	83	79	66
Oppose	17	21	34
Gun registration			
Favor	71	72	73
Oppose	29	28	27

Source: *Gallup Opinion Index,* Report No. 113, November 1974, pp. 4-17.

Table 4.15
Public Opinion by Age, 1974

	18 - 29 YEARS	30 - 49 YEARS	50 YEARS AND OLDER
Busing			
Favor	45%	30%	30%
Oppose	55	70	70
Capital punishment			
Favor	52	66	71
Oppose	48	34	29
Vietnam amnesty			
Favor	54	38	34
Oppose	46	62	66
Defense spending reductions			
Favor	56	57	53
Oppose	44	43	47
HEW spending reductions			
Favor	22	35	43
Oppose	78	65	57
Aid to parochial schools			
Favor	55	54	51
Oppose	45	46	49
Legalized abortion			
Favor	64	48	43
Oppose	36	52	57
Equal rights amendment			
Favor	83	78	73
Oppose	17	22	27
Gun registration			
Favor	74	71	72
Oppose	26	29	28

Source: *Gallup Opinion Index,* Report No. 113, November 1974, pp. 4-17.

least two ways. First, education expands an individual's knowledge and experiences generally, and usually conveys some sense of the importance of politics. Second, educational level has a great impact on a person's occupational and income levels. Table 4.14 reveals fairly sizable differences among citizens with college, high school, or grade school educations with respect to stands on public issues. For the most part, the greatest difference pertains to the college educated group, who provide the greatest amount of support for amnesty, legalized abortion, and the Equal Rights Amendment—and the strongest opposition to busing, capital punishment, HEW spending reductions, and federal aid to church-related schools. Those with elementary school educations are conspicuous as being overwhelmingly opposed to legalized abortion.

Age differences. Age is perhaps one of the most interesting demographic variables because its influence is so clear. On six of the nine issues presented in Table 4.15 age differences are apparent. The younger the citizen the more likely he is to support busing, amnesty, abortion, and the Equal Rights Amendment; and oppose capital punishment and spending reductions for social programs. Only on the defense spending, gun control, and parochial school aid questions do substantial age differences fail to materialize. The generational differences among Americans are very real. The younger voters have assumed positions that are systematically different from those of the older generations. For the most part, these differences fall on the general liberalism–conservatism dimension, with youth taking more liberal stands on public policy questions.

Religious differences.   One of the major social forces in many societies is the church. The doctrines of the various religious faiths and how these doctrines are extended into the secular realm often have an impact on a nation's politics. The architects of our government provided for a separation of church and state, but such constitutional prohibitions do not block the possible influences of religious belief on the political opinions of the citizenry. The United States is primarily a Protestant nation with

Table 4.16
Public Opinion by Religious Affiliation, 1974

	PROTESTANT	CATHOLIC
Busing		
Favor	36%	30%
Oppose	64	70
Capital punishment		
Favor	65	67
Oppose	35	33
Vietnam amnesty		
Favor	35	44
Oppose	65	56
Defense spending reductions		
Favor	52	50
Oppose	48	50
HEW spending reductions		
Favor	38	32
Oppose	62	68
Aid to parochial schools		
Favor	46	73
Oppose	54	27
Legalized abortion		
Favor	52	41
Oppose	48	59
Equal rights amendment		
Favor	73	83
Oppose	27	17
Gun registration		
Favor	68	81
Oppose	32	19

Source: *Gallup Opinion Index,* Report No. 113, November 1974, pp. 4-17.

members of various denominations comprising approximately 70 percent of the electorate. But there is a sizeable Catholic minority accounting for about one-quarter of the population. Table 4.16 outlines the issue positions of Americans affiliated with these two major religious institutions. The differences between the two groups are not radical, but they do exist. Two of the nine issues have direct relevance to the American Catholic church, aid to parochial schools and legalized abortion. It is not surprising that Catholics support federal aid to church-related schools and oppose legalized abortion to a greater extent than do Protestants. What is rather remarkable is the substantial minority of Catholics (41 percent) who favor legalized abortion policies, seemingly in direct conflict with official church doctrine. On other issues which prompt substantial Catholic-Protestant differences (amnesty, the Equal Rights Amendment, and gun control) the Catholic population tends to assume the more "liberal" position.

Occupational differences. The way in which a person earns his living may have a substantial impact on how he views the world and the people around him. An occupation largely determines a person's income level, his associates, and the economic sector upon which he depends. Obviously these influences can potentially affect a person's political views. Table 4.17 indicates the distribution of public opinion broken down by occupational categories. Few clear patterns emerge from this information, but each of the four employment classifications has some distinguishing opinion characteristics. The business and professional class, for example, provides the greatest support for Vietnam amnesty and legalized abortion, but has disproportionately high opposition to parochial school aid and racial busing. The clerical and sales workers are perhaps the least distinguished by their political views. They vary from the other occupational categories only in their relatively high support of defense spending reductions, gun control, and the Equal Rights Amendment. Manual workers have often been stereotyped as having rather reactionary views. The data in Table 4.17 tend to reject this "hard hat" image. Manual workers, for example, support busing and aid to religious schools, and oppose HEW reductions more than any other occupational class. These could hardly be classified as reactionary positions. The responses of the non-labor force may be the most surprising among all occupational categories. Individuals in this class are those who are not employed and are not seeking employment (e.g., housewives and retired persons). This group opposes amnesty, abortion, and the Equal Rights Amendment more than any other occupational class. Furthermore, they are the only group of which a majority opposes defense reductions, and they accord the most support (42%) for HEW appropriations decreases.

Table 4.17
Public Opinion by Occupation, 1974

	BUSINESS / PROFESSIONAL WORKERS	CLERICAL / SALES WORKERS	MANUAL WORKERS	NON-LABOR FORCE
Busing				
Favor	25%	30%	41%	32%
Oppose	75	70	59	68
Capital punishment				
Favor	62	64	64	68
Oppose	38	36	36	32
Vietnam amnesty				
Favor	46	40	39	38
Oppose	54	60	61	62
Defense spending reductions				
Favor	56	62	55	46
Oppose	44	38	45	54
HEW spending reductions				
Favor	33	38	30	42
Oppose	67	62	70	58
Aid to parochial schools				
Favor	44	48	57	55
Oppose	56	52	43	45
Legalized abortion				
Favor	66	56	48	38
Oppose	34	44	52	62
Equal rights amendment				
Favor	80	87	77	73
Oppose	20	13	23	27
Gun registration				
Favor	73	77	70	73
Oppose	27	23	30	27

Source: *Gallup Opinion Index*, Report 113, November 1974, pp. 4-17.

Partisan differences.   If political parties have any force at all within the American society, we would expect partisan affiliations to have an impact on public opinion. Table 4.18 examines public opinion distributions broken down by party identification. The expected differences can be readily seen. With the exception of the legalized abortion issue, there are fairly substantial differences between Democrats and Republicans. And in each case, as might be anticipated, the self-identified Democrats take a more liberal stand than the Republicans. The Independent category presents even more interesting results. Two particular conclusions are especially relevant. First, Independent voters in almost every case fall somewhere between the Democrats and the Republicans. This, of course, enhances the position of Independents as holding the balance of power in American elections. Only on the abortion issue do Independents not take an intermediate position. Second, on most issues Independents fall closer to the views of Democrats than to those of Republicans.

Table 4.18
Public Opinion by Party Affiliation, 1974

	REPUBLICAN	DEMOCRAT	INDEPENDENT
Busing			
Favor	23%	42%	30%
Oppose	77	58	70
Capital punishment			
Favor	72	61	61
Oppose	28	39	39
Vietnam amnesty			
Favor	33	44	43
Oppose	67	56	57
Defense spending reductions			
Favor	50	58	55
Oppose	50	42	45
HEW spending reductions			
Favor	40	32	33
Oppose	60.	68	67
Aid to parochial schools			
Favor	43	59	51
Oppose	57	41	49
Legalized abortion			
Favor	50	49	53
Oppose	50	51	47
Equal rights amendment			
Favor	70	81	79
Oppose	30	19	21
Gun registration			
Favor	67	74	72
Oppose	33	26	28

Source: *Gallup Opinion Index,* Report No. 113, November 1974, pp. 4-17.

Summary

Demographic trends indicate that the makeup of the American electorate is changing. Certain groups which we have examined will be more heavily represented in future electorates—the college educated, younger persons, suburban residents, professionals, and those in upper-income categories. Conversely, the representation of poor and low-income voters, the less educated, union members, and small-town residents will continue to decrease. These changes may affect the patterns of party identification which have been discussed, and they no doubt will have a particular bearing upon the Independent proportion of the electorate.

As we have seen, certain of the traditional divisions between the party electorates have become less sharp in recent years. The degree of status polarization reflected in the Democratic and Republican electorates appears to have decreased, and the result has been increasing heterogeneity in the party followings. Moreover, Independent identification has increased disproportionately in the middle and upper socioeconomic categories, and this has further blurred the inter-party divisions.

Among younger voters, high levels of Independent identification have developed. Correspondingly, younger voters have tended to evaluate the major parties less favorably than have older voters. But the participation rates of the young have been relatively low and erratic, and their voting behavior has certainly not been monolithic. Indeed, the only group which appears to be nearly monolithic in its party identification and voting behavior is the black portion of the electorate.

When we move to the differences between groups in terms of issues, certain of these patterns are underscored. There appears to be a fairly substantial racial division on many issues, and the differences between age groups in terms of liberal–conservative philosophy and in terms of specific issues are substantial. Indeed, many of the most important differences are predicated upon race, age, and educational level. Other group differences, such as religion or sex, do exist but tend to be confined to specific issues which clearly impinge upon group interests.

The types of polarization which emerge from the analysis of issue differences between groups are not especially congruent with the patterns of partisan identification. This is particularly evident among younger voters and persons on a higher education level, where increased Independent identification rather than partisan differentiation has occurred. This suggests that the traditional parties have not yet provided the kinds of alternatives or leaders necessary to induce stable loyalties within a substantial portion of the electorate.

NOTES

[1] See Angus Campbell et al., *The American Voter* (New York: John Wiley & Sons, Inc., 1964), pp. 67–85.

[2] From 1940–1964, for example, Independent identification increased from 20 to 22 percent. There was, however, a significant change in the Democratic-Republican distribution. The Democratic edge in 1940 was only 4 percent (42 percent vs. 38 percent for the Republicans). Over the next two decades, Republican strength dropped rather steadily, and the Democratic advantage increased.

[3] Walter Dean Burnham, *Critical Elections and the Mainsprings of American Politics* (New York: W. W. Norton & Company, Inc., 1970), p. 121. During the 1950s and early 1960s, strong identifiers accounted for between 37–39 percent of the electorate. In 1966, this declined to 28 percent, slightly less than the Independent proportion of the electorate.

[4] Campbell et al., *The American Voter*, pp. 83–84.

[5] Frank J. Sorauf, *Party Politics in America*, 2nd ed. (Boston: Little, Brown and Company, 1972), pp. 173–75.

[6] Burnham, *Critical Elections*, pp. 122–29.

[7] William H. Flanigan, *Political Behavior of the American Electorate*, 2nd ed. (Boston: Allyn & Bacon, Inc., 1972), pp. 38–40.

[8] Interestingly, however, Independents do not support the idea of party realignment. When asked whether they would like to see two new parties—one liberal and one conservative—59 percent of the Indpendent identifiers, 57 percent of the Democrats, and 53 percent of the Republicans responded negatively. *Gallup Opinion Index*, Report No. 116, February 1975.

[9] Warren E. Miller, "The Political Behavior of the Electorate," in *Political Opinion and Behavior*, ed. E. Dreyer and W. Rosenbaum (Belmont, Calif.: Wadsworth Publishing Company, 1970), pp. 194–96.

[10] Louis Harris, *The Anguish of Change* (New York: W. W. Norton & Company, Inc., 1973), p. 273.

[11] Burnham, *Critical Elections*, p. 129.

[12] Ibid., p. 130.

[13] Richard M. Scammon and Ben J. Wattenberg, *The Real Majority* (New York: Coward, McCann & Geoghegan, Inc., 1971), p. 48.

[14] *Congressional Quarterly Weekly Report*, 33, No. 5 (February 1, 1975), p. 246.

[15] Campbell et al., *The American Voter*, p. 264.

[16] Philip E. Converse et al., "Continuity and Change in American Politics: Parties and Issues in the 1968 Election," *American Political Science Review*, 63 (December 1969), 1103–4.

[17] Campbell et al., *The American Voter*, pp. 264–65.

[18] Donald R. Matthews and James W. Prothro, *Negroes and the New Southern Politics* (New York: Harcourt Brace Jovanovich, Inc., 1966), p. 373.

[19] Converse et al., "Continuity and Change in American Politics," p. 1085.

[20] Ibid., p. 1088.

[21] See Philip E. Converse, "Religion and Politics: The 1960 Election," *Elections and the Political Order*, ed. A. Campbell et al. (New York: John Wiley & Sons, 1966), pp. 96–124.

THE AMERICAN
POLITICAL CULTURE:
ATTITUDES
ABOUT DEMOCRACY

5

In Chapter Two we were concerned with developing the concept of attitude and describing the dynamics of holding and changing attitudes. Chapter Three dealt with the formation of political attitudes. In Chapter Four we described public opinion in America, mainly from a demographic point of view. What we have not done as yet is to examine directly some of the issues that were raised in Chapter One.

In Chapter One we said that in order for a democracy to function properly there must be linkages between the mass public on the one hand and political elites on the other. We reviewed briefly the kinds of linkage mechanisms that can conceivably perform this function and suggested that this relationship between public opinion and government is a classic concern of democratic politics. In this chapter we will investigate this relationship from the viewpoint of the American people themselves. From the perspective of the mass public, we will focus on the expectations that Americans bring to bear on the issue of the mass-elite relationship. Are Americans indifferent to the ways in which public opinion and government are linked? Or does the public attach different values to the linkage models? Does the American political culture contain a natural affinity for one or another of the models of linkage?

We should, however, make clear what we will *not* be attempting to do in this chapter. First, although this chapter is concerned with "democratic theory," we do not mean to suggest that the common man in the United States is a political philosopher or a "theorist." It has often been said that Americans are a practical people and that they have little or no interest in "theoretical" (or better, hypothetical) matters. The average American may not think of himself as a theorist, but he does have very fundamental beliefs about democracy, and about what good citizenship in a democracy entails. These beliefs are difficult to study, especially since most of us are hard put to articulate them, but they are important because in the aggregate these beliefs constitute an important element of the American belief system and political culture.

Second, it is not our intention to compare American attitudes about democracy with the way in which our government actually functions. In this chapter we are not asking "Is the American political system really democratic?" Rather, we are asking whether the American public *believes* that our political system is democratic, and we are asking what criteria the American people employ for making such a judgment.

In sum, we are not claiming that Americans are democratic theorists, nor do we intend to describe the actual performance of American democracy. We wish to address two basic questions. What do Americans believe about democracy? What are the implications of these beliefs for linkage politics?

Direct democracy

Direct democracy can be best understood by thinking of the New England town meeting, which remains the formal governing body in many parts of New Enlgand. The town meeting conjures up an image of widespread citizen participation in political decision making. There is no discrepancy between the rulers and the ruled, since if every citizen attends the town meeting, all of the rulers are also all of the ruled.

Since access to the government is easy (all one has to do is to show up at the town hall), every citizen can participate in this political system. There are no structural barriers to "making inputs." Moreover, since there is no rank among the citizens, and since all votes are weighted the same (one-person, one-vote), equality is assured. And not only is there considerable freedom to participate, but freedom from oppression is virtually guaranteed, unless of course the citizens decide to oppress themselves. The town meeting is, therefore, a case of direct democracy—"government by the people" in the most literal sense—and the problem of linking the mass public with political elites is resolved by abolishing the distinction at the outset.

Direct democracy has had some persuasive advocates. Rousseau described it in the following terms:

If I had to choose my birthplace, ...I would have wished to be born in a country where the sovereign and the people could have only one and the same interest, so that all movements of the machine always tended only to the common happiness. Since that would not be possible unless the people and the sovereign were the same person, it follows that I would have wished to be born under a democratic government, wisely tempered.[1]

Jefferson, of course, thought that he saw possibilities in America for such governments as Rousseau described. Recognizing with Rousseau that a "general will" is not likely to be achieved unless the community remains small and relatively homogeneous, Jefferson thought that rural townships might become "republics-in-miniature" where citizens (the majority of whom would be yeoman farmers) would govern themselves. "I think our governments will remain virtuous for many centuries," he wrote, "as long as they are chiefly agricultural; and this will be as long as there shall be vacant lands in any part of America." [2]

The fact is that perfect unanimity, even in Orwell's *1984*,[3] is rare and unlikely to prevail on most public issues. Consequently, there are likely to be minorities even in New England town meetings. Of course the town meeting is not incapacitated by the lone dissenter, or even by large and vocal minorities, because even in the pure cases of democracy, policies are made by a majority of the people. The principle of majority rule is a convenient and obvious way of producing policies in the absence of unanimity.

One problem caused by the principle of majority rule is familiar to all of us. There are times when the operation of this principle appears to be incompatible with another principle that is of paramount importance in democratic theory—minority rights. The New England town which outlaws all religions except Congregationalism over the vigorous objections of a few "heretics" is obvious sacrificing minority rights to the majoritarian principle. The reconciliation of majority rule with minority rights is always difficult, and striking a prudent balance between the two is one of the classic problems of democracy.

Theoretically prudence cannot really contribute to the resolution of the minority rights problem. To put the matter simply, the principle of majority rule just does not square well with the notion of "government by the people." There is nothing particularly sacred about the majoritarian principle; it is simply a useful way of dealing with the inevitable lack of consensus. Since majority rule is merely a practical, and not a theoretical (or ethical) solution, it circumvents the idea of self-government. The distinction between the rulers and the ruled, which direct democracy seeks to obliterate, prevails so long as unanimity is absent. And as long as there is a distinction between the rulers and the ruled, there will be a linkage problem.

Minorities simply have a different relationship to the government, even in direct democracy, than those citizens who are in the majority. Whatever else can be said about the town meeting, there is no hiding the fact that when conflict is present the town meeting is not government by all the people. It is, with majority rule, government by *most* of the people, even if that means only 51 percent. So long as the principle of majority rule is operative, there will always be a discrepancy in the notion of "government by the people," even if minority rights are guaranteed (in a document, perhaps, such as the Bill of Rights), and even if they are in fact scrupulously respected.

Saying that "government by the people" is not possible without consensus should not be taken as an indictment of American democracy. We are simply making the point that "participation by the people" and "government by the people" are not synonymous. In any event, the framers of our Constitution never intended for the United States to be governed by direct democracy. Rather, they had in mind a representative democracy.

Representative democracy

American democracy has never been of the pure, direct form. Although we traditionally refer to our system of government as a democracy, the citizens of the United States do not, and never did, "govern themselves" directly. The distinction between "democratic" and "republican" forms of government (which are synonymous with "direct democracy" and "representative democracy," respectively) was thus characterized by Madison in the 14th *Federalist:*

The true distinction between these forms . . . is that in a democracy the people meet and exercise the government in person; in a republic they assemble and administer it by their representatives and agents.[4]

In fact, the framers of our Constitution established a national government that was in certain respects designed to *prevent* the people from governing themselves. A republican form of government was thought to be necessary for the preservation of liberty.

In a representative form of government, the people delegate political authority to public servants who perform the actual tasks of governing. Despite the fact that this creates a distinction between the political leadership and the public, this form of government is considered democratic because the people continue to be sovereign. The governors can claim no "divine right" to rule, they can only claim an authority to govern that is derived from the people—and which the people may revoke. Robert Dahl's description of the delegation of authority in democracies appears below:

In a democratic association, whether governed by committee, town meeting, referendum, or representative body, the authority of the delegate, agent, or subordinate is legitimate simply because (and only to the extent that) he carries out the policies of his superior, that is, the democratic body.[5]

Most of us would probably be willing to concede that governments can be republican and still be democratic, so long as the people remain sovereign. Republican institutions can be considered compatible with democracy by substituting, as a definition of democracy, "government by the consent of the governed" for "government by the people." If this is to be done, then direct democracies and representative democracies should be judged by different standards. Nevertheless, most of us still tend to think of direct democracy as being "pure," and of representative democracy as being somewhat less pure. The question needs to be asked, then, why we have representative government instead of direct democracy.

THE MADISONIAN JUSTIFICATION

The *Federalist* papers provide us with a defense of republicanism that reveals the views of the "father of the Constitution," James Madison. Madison considered representative democracy to be superior to direct democracy. The following is from the 10th *Federalist:*

. . . It may be concluded that a pure democracy, by which I mean a society consisting of a small number of citizens, who assemble and administer the government in person, can admit of no cure for the mischiefs of faction. A common passion or interest will, in almost every case, be felt by the majority of the whole; a communication and concert results from the form of government itself; and there is nothing to check the inducements to sacrifice the weaker party or an obnoxious individual.[6]

Madison's view was that the absence of unanimity creates a factious spirit and results in the "tyranny of the majority." Minorities are forced to submit to the will of the many. This problem, according to Madison, "admits of no cure" in a direct democracy.

It is clear that Madison viewed direct democracy as being potentially tyrannical, and it is also clear that he assumed that pure democracy could exist only at the local level. "A democracy," according to Madison, "must be confined to a small spot. A republic may be extended over a large region." Not only did Madison think that republics are more appropriate for large nations, he also argued that *large* republics are in principle superior to *small* ones.

Madison defined a republic as "a government in which the scheme of representation takes place." His argument, that representation works much better in large than in small republics, runs something like this. In a small republic, the representatives have too few constituents—consequently they are bound too closely by the "passions" and interests of the people whom they represent. In other words, the representative is so closely identified with and attached to the interests of his constituents that he finds it impossible to perceive the larger, national interest.

In a large republic, on the other hand, the representative is able to consider the national interest, since the existence of "factions" within his own constituency forces him to take the wider view.

Representative institutions in a large nation, then, are defended by Madison on the ground that they will dilute the effects of faction. No single faction will be able to attain control of the government so as to tyrannize the rest. In this kind of national government, the potentially tyrannical factions in effect cancel each other out. Thus even though factious interests may be able to dominate at the state or local level, liberty will be preserved at the national level:

The influence of factious leaders may kindle a flame within their particular States but will be unable to spread a general conflagration through the other States. A religious sect may degenerate into a political faction in a part of the Confederacy; but the variety of sects dispersed over the entire face of it must secure the national councils against any danger from that source. A rage for paper money, for an abolition of debts, for an equal division of property, or for any other improper or wicked project, will be less apt to pervade the whole body of the Union than a particular member of it, in the same proportion as such a malady is more likely to taint a particular county or district than an entire State.[7]

The traditional justification for representative government, then, reduces to this. Direct democracy is to be feared because it is vulnerable to majority tyranny, and republican governments are to be preferred, especially in large nations, because they preserve liberty by mitigating the "mischiefs of faction." Madison was essentially pessimistic about human nature, and he considered conflict to be endemic to politics. His constitutional scheme had, from his point of view, the twin virtues of controlling conflict and preserving liberty. It should be clear that Madison was no lover of direct democracy, and it was not his aim to promote government by the people to its logical conclusion.

Madison was even willing to go so far as to say that the common good is more likely to be known to representatives than to the people themselves. "It may well happen," Madison asserted, "that the public voice, pronounced by the representatives of the people, will be more consonant to the public good than if pronounced by the people themselves, convened for the purpose." [8]

THE MAJORITARIAN JUSTIFICATION

One does not often hear the Madisonian justification for representative government, nor is Madison's distinction between democracies and republics generally understood, since most people consider republicanism to be just one form of democratic government. Because sovereignty is vested in the people, and because there exist numerous opportunities for popular political participation, the American political system is usually regarded as democratic despite its republican institutions.

The majoritarian justification of our representative system is essentially rooted in Jefferson's philosophy, which does not regard democracy as necessarily turbulent, violent, or inimical to liberty. The Jeffersonian notion of small, agrarian democracies that would comprise the moral backbone of the nation is, in fact, derived from a rather optimistic view of human nature.

The majoritarian view enshrines pure democracy as the ideal form of government, and since direct democracy is feasible only at the local level this view has a special sympathy for smallness. The American idiom "grass roots democracy" is particularly apt. Even though the age of Jefferson's beloved yeoman farmer has long since passed, Americans retain a special affection for grass roots democracy.

The majoritarian justification of our representative system fundamentally rejects the Madisonian fear of the mischiefs of faction and majority tyranny. Proponents of majority rule argue that in a nation as large and heterogeneous as the United States any majority will of necessity be composed of many minorities. Thus majority tyranny cannot constitute a threat because any party, policy, or program that appeals to enough minorities so as to constitute a majority would of necessity have to be moderate. Majority rule, then, is tempered, or restrained, from within. Many spokesmen for majority rule contend that the American constitution contains too many unnecessary restraints against majority action—federalism, separation of powers, judicial review, etc. Such institutions, it is contended, result in a system in which minorities exercise a negative kind of power—the power to frustrate majority rule. This system, often called "democratic pluralism," is rather unwillingly tolerated by believers in direct democracy, who are forced to recognize that pure democracy is not feasible except at the grass roots level.

The majoritarian justification of representative government in America then stresses the importance of size and diversity. This view basically regards representative government as an evil made necessary by the sheer physical size of the United States and its more than 210 million citizens. E. E. Schaatschneider has made this very simple point in the following way:

No one has ever seen the American people because the human eye is not able to take in the view of the four million square miles over which they are scattered. What would they look like if (ignoring all logistical difficulties) they could be brought together in one place? Standing shoulder to shoulder in military formation, they would occupy an area of about sixty-six square miles. . . .
Merely to shake hands with that many people would take a century. . . . A single round of five-minute speeches would require five thousand years. If only 1

percent of those present spoke, the assembly would be forced to listen to two million speeches. . . .

In other words, an all-American town meeting in Rousseau's style would be the largest, longest, and most boring and frustrating meeting imaginable. What could such a meeting produce? Total paralysis. What could it do? Nothing.[9]

The point, obviously, is that there are too many people for direct democracy to work in the United States. Madison took this as incontrovertible when he said that "the natural limit of a democracy is that distance from the central point which will just permit the most remote citizens to assemble as often as their public functions demand, and will include no greater number than can join in those functions." [10] Robert Dahl estimates the maximum number to be about 600:

It is hard to say what the practical limits of primary democracy are. . . . My own experience leads me to believe that an assembly of one thousand people is probably too large, not only because of the difficulty of assuring that everyone can speak but also because increasing quantity means decreasing quality as the arts of rhetoric and crowd manipulation take over. It is significant that in the modern world, six hundred seems to be about the limit for legislative bodies.[11]

So, if we were to break down the American republic so that direct democracies of 600 citizens apiece would result, we would find ourselves living in more than 350,000 autonomous pure democracies.

To summarize, the majoritarian justification for representative government is that America is simply too large and diverse for direct democracy. Representatives institutions, then, merely facilitate a realistic division of labor.

THE PROBLEM OF REPRESENTATION

As we have seen, Madison had no trouble justifying representation—in fact, he preferred representative government to direct democracy. He envisioned the national legislature, especially the Senate, as being a kind of council of elders that would govern more wisely than the people could "if convened for the purpose." For Madison, representation was not a "problem," it was a positive good. But for anyone who holds direct democracy to be in principle the most "virtuous" form of government, representation is always a "problem" to one extent or another.

Representation is considered to be a constraint upon democracy, because it necessitates the construction of mechanisms to link the people with their spokesmen. But there are certain ways in which this linkage can occur and in which representation can be made more compatible with "government by the people." Specifically, there are several features of representative government that, when present, make representation compatible with democratic theory.

First, representatives should be elected, not appointed or selected in any other way. Democratic theory dictates that popular election is really the only legitimate way to select representatives in accordance with the principle of popular sovereignty.

Second, the apportionment of representatives should be equitable, that is, on a "one-person, one-vote" basis. An inequitable apportionment scheme is undemocratic in the sense that some persons' votes are diluted, and others have power disproportionate to their numbers. The public's voice is distorted when votes are translated in this fashion.

Third, because the representative institution should resemble a town meeting of the whole population writ small, the representative should keep his "ear to the ground" so that he may hear public opinion and transmit the voice of his constituency to the legislative chamber.

To summarize, the American concept of representative democracy is that it is a device by which the town meeting is made workable in a large, expansive nation. Since representative democracy is measured against the standard of direct democracy, universal suffrage and "one-person, one-vote" are prerequisites. Ideally, representatives should either "personify" their constituencies or be able to synthesize all of their constituents' voices. In other words, legislative bodies must not consist, in the aggregate, of councils of elders convened for the purpose of restraining popular rule—Madison notwithstanding.

The problem of representation, then, is that it is not self-evident that a single man or woman can in reality personify a large number of persons living in a geographical area, and that it is not easy to understand how such an individual can follow instructions that may be, in many cases, ambiguous or contradictory. Basically, representation is a problem because it falls short of the pure democratic standard against which it is judged.

Citizen roles

Direct democracy is considered feasible where government is small, and where the citizens are not too numerous. Since American circumstances are not compatible with direct democracy, majority rule democrats must be content with an approximation of the ideal. The important point to be made here, though, is that in the American public *direct democracy is held as the ideal*. This has numerous implications, not the least of which is that it affects what Americans think about their own roles in the linkage of public opinion and government.

In this section we will examine attitudes about citizenship and the roles that citizens might play vis-à-vis the government. We are looking at this from the perspective of the mass public, that is, what concept of citizenship does the public in our particular version of democracy hold? The thesis that will be developed is that even though ours is a republican form of government, the American political culture favors citizen roles that correspond with the theory of direct democracy.

What is the proper relationship between the individual citizen and the government? What role should the citizen play in the political process? What are his duties, responsibilities, and rights vis-à-vis the state? These questions have preoccupied political scientists since men began to study politics. It might make sense to think of the alternatives as being essentially threefold.[12]

The parochial. In a parochial political culture, the individual citizen is related to the political system in an indirect and nebulous way. He is not really aware of the political system and does not play any explicitly political role. The citizen may assume religious, social, or economic roles, but he does not think of himself as being a political actor. In fact, he probably does not usually regard himself as being subject to a political authority.

Parochial political cultures tend to be found only in very simple, traditional, pre-modern societies. In these societies religious, social, political, and economic roles tend to be blended together and are not consciously distinguished by the citizen. He has no expectations regarding the political system, and he is oblivious to any political duties that might devolve upon him.

Even in modern political systems, some citizens may adopt the parochial role. Such persons have almost certainly been inadequately socialized, however, and remain isolated from the dominant culture. It should be clear that the parochial role is anathema to modern Western democracies.

The subject. As subject, the citizen has an explicit relationship to the political system. However, the subject role is without initiative and largely passive. The subject understands that the political system makes some claims upon him and that he is affected by politics—in this sense his orientation is a conscious political role. But he sees himself as being on the "output" side of the political process. He may or may not view the political system as being legitimate. He may have a strong attachment to the system, or he may be completely hostile toward it. Regardless of his attitudes, though, his relationship to the system remains exclusively passive. The subject, then, does not think of his citizenship as having an active dimension. He does not think of himself as having an "input" role, either positive or negative. The subject type of citizen is common in Western democracies. He may be a contented, acquiescent individual, or he may be alienated from the political system to such an extent that he has retreated from any active involvement with it.

The participant. This type of citizen is found most often in modern political systems which have democratic institutions. Like the subject, the
participant is a conscious political actor, and his affective orientation toward
government may be either positive or negative. The participant, though,
plays an active role in the system and understands his relationship to the
system to be as much on the input side as on the output side. The participant
is ordinarily encouraged by the political culture to participate, and he may
even feel that he has a duty to participate.

Obviously, this is the citizen role that is most compatible with direct
democracy. Proponents of direct democracy advocate the participant role.
The "general will" cannot be known if the citizens are mute.

The American participant

It has been suggested that Americans regard direct democracy as a preferable form of government, and that they evidently do not recognize the
important theoretical differences between pure democracy and the representative form. Schaatschneider makes this point, characterizing the American conception of democracy as a precarious juxtaposition of Aristotle and
the New England town meeting:

With some juggling, the New England town meeting could be fitted into what people supposed that Aristotle had in mind 2500 years ago. Thus Americans acquired
the notion that the town meeting was the perfect form of democratic government.
That is how the town meeting became the standard by which all democratic governments were judged; governments were democratic in the exact proportion in
which they conformed to the model and were undemocratic to the extent that they
departed from it.[13]

If Americans believe that direct democracy is the ideal form of government, we should not be surprised to learn that in the United States the
parochial and subject roles are strongly discouraged, and that the American
political culture demonstrates a firm commitment to the participant role.
The conclusion of Almond and Verba's well-known study confirms this:

Civics texts would have us believe that the problem facing the citizen in a democracy is, to quote the title of a recent book in the field, *How to Be an Active Citizen.*
According to this . . . view, a successful democracy requires that citizens be involved and active in politics, informed about politics, and influential. Furthermore,
when they make decisions, particularly the important decision of how to cast their
vote, they must make them on the basis of careful evaluation of evidence and
careful weighing of alternatives. The passive citizen, the nonvoter, the poorly informed or apathetic citizen—all indicate a weak democracy. This view of democratic citizenship stresses activity, involvement, rationality. To use the terminology
we have developed, it stresses the role of the participant and says little about the
role of the subject or parochial.[14]

The political socialization studies conducted in recent years have tended to show much the same thing. Children are taught that the good citizen is a participant, and that participation is essential to our form of government. Consider, for example, Table 5.1, which shows the changes in children's conceptions of democracy during the elementary school years. Popular government, the act of voting, and the principle of equality come to be the dominant conceptions of democracy by grade eight. Democracy as a political system where "the people rule" is especially interesting, because Hess and Torney's sample of teachers was nearly unanimous in choosing this as a definition of democracy. It should be rather clear that the participant role is transmitted by the agents of political socialization in the United States.

The Easton and Dennis political socialization study shows a similar pattern. When asked to choose a symbol of American government from a series of pictures, young children were likely to choose portraits of George Washington or John F. Kennedy. Later, they were much more likely to select the picture of a hand placing a ballot into a voting box. Only four percent of the second graders, for example, chose this "voting" picture, compared to 47 percent of the eighth graders. Fully 72 percent of the teachers surveyed chose this as the best way to characterize American government.[15]

Further evidence that children learn the participant role during the political socialization process is that children have surprisingly high rates of political participation even in the elementary school years. Hess and Torney report, for example, that the seventh graders they surveyed had higher scores on their "activity index" than did their own teachers![16] Some of these intriguing data can be seen in Table 5.2.

Evidently the schools encourage children to think that they are very effective political actors so as to promote the norm of participation. The

Table 5.1
Changes in Concept of Democracy, by Grade

GRADE	THE PEOPLE RULE	ALL GROWN-UPS CAN VOTE	ALL HAVE EQUAL CHANCE
4	26.0%	39.4%	35.8%
5	35.9	52.4	50.2
6	51.9	69.0	66.4
7	64.3	75.4	76.8
8	76.4	75.3	82.8
Teachers	98.4	76.5	88.3

Source: Robert D. Hess and Judith V. Torney, *The Development of Political Attitudes in Children* (Chicago: Aldine-Atherton, Inc., 1967), p. 66.

Table 5.2
Changes in Participation in Political Activities, by Grade

GRADE	READ ABOUT CANDIDATES	WORE A CAMPAIGN BUTTON	HANDED OUT BUTTONS AND HANDBILLS
3	59.7%	43.5%	21.6%
4	75.0	45.9	20.9
5	87.5	56.8	22.4
6	91.9	62.2	26.1
7	95.1	65.4	28.6
8	95.0	63.4	26.9
Teachers	100.0	49.3	34.7

Source: Robert D. Hess and Judith V. Torney, *The Development of Political Attitudes in Children* (Chicago: Aldine-Atherton, Inc., 1967), p. 88.

socialization studies show that children acquire a very lofty sense of their own political competence and abilities as they progress through elementary school. The sense of political efficacy rises rather sharply between the lower elementary and the fourth or fifth grades. Even more important is that children associate the most efficacious *mode* of political action with individual action. The vote is stressed, but generally it is the single citizen acting individually, not through groups or parties, that comes to be viewed as the best possible kind of participant. So while it is fair to say that the school transmits the participant role and encourages a sense of political efficacy, it is even more accurate to say that the school stresses the value and efficacy of the individual participant. Hess and Torney refer to this belief in the power of the citizen to exercise control over government through his individual action as the "personal clout illusion." [17]

But personal clout should not be employed merely to serve one's own private interest. Americans are groomed to be participants also in the wider sense of acting in a "public-regarding" and nonpartisan way.

PUBLIC-REGARDINGNESS

Early in this chapter we discussed the problem of conflict and said that conflict is especially troublesome in the town meeting because the absence of unanimity reduces "government by the people" to "government by the many," and therefore establishes a mass-elite distinction, creating the classic linkage problem. We said also that American democrats who start with less gloomy premises about human nature than James Madison are reluctant to concur with the Madisonian contention that conflict is endemic to politics.

One possible solution to the existence of conflict lies in man's reasoning capacity. If each individual were to apply disinterested logic to political questions, it would be possible to come to a consensus on the common good. The good citizen in a democracy must therefore allow his political action to be guided by rationality and a sense of "public-regardingness."

Banfield and Wilson have characterized this ethos as being mainly a Yankee Protestant, middle-class point of view which stresses "the obligation of the individual to participate in public affairs and to seek the good of the community 'as a whole.' " [18] This ethos, according to Banfield and Wilson, is becoming more necessary all the time; it explains why some citizens are able to sacrifice their own interest in deference to the common good, why an affluent suburban voter, for example, might vote for tax increases to improve public services to the inner-city poor.

NONPARTISANSHIP

We have already seen that during the political socialization process children are encouraged to be individual participants and to exercise their political influence in an independent fashion. Nonpartisanship is also taught quite explicitly. Hess and Torney asked their young respondents whether it was better to "join a party and always vote for its candidate," or to not join a party and "vote for the best man." The results indicate that the norm of nonpartisanship is acquired slowly but surely as the child matures (see Table 5.3). In the words of Hess and Torney, the child is "socialized toward independence." [19]

It is also interesting that children seem to be sheltered from knowledge about political parties and political conflict. Easton and Hess have likened this phenomenon to the prudery of the Victorian era which sheltered the innocent child from knowledge about "the sordid facts of sex":

He is too young, he will not understand, it will disillusion him too soon, awareness of conflict among adults will be disturbing, are some of the arguments raised against telling the whole truth.[20]

This denial that conflict is an inevitable fact of political life might also explain why Americans have such a curiously paradoxical view of their political system. Monsma, for example, has noted that six of the ten most highly respected occupations in the country are public offices—Supreme Court Justice, cabinet member, diplomat, mayor, governor, and Congressman. And yet, 54 percent of the respondents to a Gallup poll oppose the idea of their sons' entering a political career! [21] It seems even the very word "politics" has a bad connotation. In one study, for example, 89.6 percent of the respondents said that they "usually have confidence that the government will do what is right," but only 58.9 percent agreed that "most poli-

Table 5.3
Changes in Basis of the Good Citizen's Candidate Preference, by Grade

GRADE	JOINS PARTY; ALWAYS VOTES FOR ITS CANDIDATE	DOES NOT JOIN PARTY; VOTES FOR MEN HE THINKS ARE BEST
4	48.8%	51.2%
5	40.6	59.3
6	35.3	64.7
7	34.1	65.9
8	26.4	73.6
Teachers	12.6	87.4

Source: Robert D. Hess and Judith V. Torney, *The Development of Political Attitudes in Children* (Chicago: Aldine-Atherton, Inc., 1967), p. 84.

ticians can be trusted to do what they think is best for the country." [22] "Politics" and "politicians" seem to suggest all of those squalid and seamy things, like conflict, which prevent government by all the people from being a reality.

Partisanship appears to be declining in the United States. As we have seen, Americans in increasing numbers consider themselves Independents and this is especially true of younger people.[23] American voters are also less inclined than before to vote a straight party ticket.[24] Increasingly, they prefer to vote "for the man, not the party."

Public-regardingness and nonpartisanship have the same aim: to transcend divisiveness and to thereby create the consensus in which pure democracy thrives. To be a participant in a democracy is not enough. One must participate as an individual, without blind partisan and factional loyalties, and one must be willing to sacrifice private gain to the common good.

Summary

What conclusions can we draw about linkage politics as the system is perceived by the mass public? First, the American public generally accepts the distinction between the rulers and the ruled in the United States, and the fact that the American people do not directly, literally, "govern themselves." The classic concern of democratic politics, and the primary concern of this book, however—the relationship between public opinion and government— also occupies the political thinking of the American public. Some rather definite opinions on the subject emerge.

Americans at the mass level tend to view direct citizen action as the most desirable type of political linkage. In fact, all other linkage models are to some degree suspect. In other words, direct public participation is considered the most legitimate mode of linking the mass public with the political leadership. This is so because a basic premise in America is that the distinction between rulers and ruled is *in itself* a deviation from the ideal type of democracy. Americans therefore prefer direct influence because it is the least compromising way to bring about change. Perhaps it is even fair to say that for Americans, direct influence symbolizes the suspension of the mass-elite dichotomy. All other linkage models are compromising ·in the sense that they accept this dichotomy as legitimate, or at least as inevitable.

The preference that Americans have for individual citizen action as a participatory mode has several implications. First, as we have seen, it causes Americans to view the other linkage models unfavorably. Second, it means that the institutions which might act as intermediaries between the mass public and the government are seen to be ineffective and even potentially disruptive. Third, even if public opinion were to be regularly and efficiently translated into public opinion policy *indirectly*—through one of the other models—the reaction would still be negative.

As we conclude this section and prepare to move to an examination of American political elites, we should simply note that the concept of elites is controversial in a country which is enamored with the idea of direct democracy. And so long as these elites and the institutions over which they maintain control continue to exist, they can expect to come under continued attack from democratic reformers. Popular dissatisfaction with the American political system will not soon dissipate, because the anti-political biases of the American people are substantial and we should not make the mistake of hoping that political cynicism is merely a temporary phenomenon.

NOTES

[1] Jean-Jacques Rousseau, *Second Discourse,* ed. Roger D. Masters (New York: St. Martin's Press, Inc., 1964), pp. 78–79.

[2] Quoted in Roscoe C. Martin, *Grass Roots: Rural Democracy in America* (New York: Harper & Row, Publishers, 1957), pp. 5–6.

[3] George Orwell, *1984* (New York: Harcourt Brace Jovanovich, Inc., 1949).

[4] *The Federalist, Number* 14 (New York: The New American Library, 1961), p. 100.

[5] Robert A. Dahl, *After the Revolution?* (New Haven: Yale University Press, 1970), p. 77.

[6] *The Federalist,* Number 10, p. 81.

[7] Ibid., p. 84.

[8] Ibid., p. 82.

[9] E. E. Schaatschneider, *Two Hundred Million Americans in Search of a Government* (New York: Holt, Rinehart & Winston, Inc., 1969), pp. 60–61.

[10] *The Federalist,* Number 14, p. 101.

[11] Dahl, After the Revolution? pp. 69–70.

[12] The discussion which follows is drawn from Gabriel A. Almond and Sidney Verba, *The Civic Culture: Political Attitudes and Democracy in Five Nations* (copyright © 1963 by Princeton University Press; Little, Brown and Company, Inc. © 1965), pp. 304–474. Reprinted by permission of Princeton University Press.

[13] Schaatschneider, *Two Hundred Million Americans*, p. 59.

[14] Almond and Verba, *The Civic Culture*, pp. 473–74.

[15] David Easton and Jack Dennis, *Children in the Political System* (New York: McGraw-Hill Book Company, 1969).

[16] Robert D. Hess and Judith V. Torney, *The Development of Political Attitudes in Children* (Chicago: Aldine-Atherton, Inc., 1967), p. 66.

[17] Ibid., p. 199.

[18] Edward C. Banfield and James Q. Wilson, *City Politics* (New York: Vintage Books, 1963), p. 41.

[19] Hess and Torney, ch. 9.

[20] David Easton and Robert D. Hess, "The Child's Political World," *Midwest Journal of Political Science*, 6 (August 1962), 244.

[21] Stephen V. Monsma, *American Politics: A Systems Approach* (New York: Holt, Rinehart & Winston, Inc., 1969), pp. 26–27.

[22] Herbert McClosky, "Consensus and Ideology in American Politics," *American Political Science Review*, 58 (June 1964), 361–79.

[23] See, for example, *Gallup Opinion Index*, Report No. 109, July 1974, p. 15.

[24] Walter Dean Burnham, *Critical Elections and the Mainsprings of American Politics* (New York: W. W. Norton & Company, 1970), p. 120.

Part two
Elite opinion

POLITICAL ELITES, LEADERSHIP, AND AMERICAN DEMOCRACY

6

Under all existing forms of government the distinction between leaders and followers, elites and masses, inevitably occurs. In some societies this division is based upon wealth, in others genealogy, and in still others divine ordination. Under democratic systems the distinction is usually made on the basis of electoral victory. Regardless of the determining factor, however, the results are similar. The elites possess power, status, and direct influence over the directions of governmental policy.

There is considerable variation, however, in the relative value placed upon mass opinion and the opinions of elites. Under a military junta or an absolute monarchy, for example, the only opinions of consequence are those held by the ruling elite. Mass opinion remains passive and inconsequential until such time as popular dissatisfaction manifests itself in overt rebellion. Under those systems of government which are at least theoretically democratic, public opinion is given much greater status. The selection of governmental elites is predicated on the expression of popular opinion through ballot box procedures. Elected officials are generally held accountable to the public by means of periodic reelection requirements. There are legitimate means, such as political party or interest group membership, for the citizenry to express its preferences to elected and appointed leaders. The leaders, of course, are expected to heed these expressions. The result is a mixture of elite and public views each time the cauldron of public policy formation is stirred. The proportion of each, however, varies considerably from issue to issue and decision to decision.

The study of political elites is necessary to any comprehensive understanding of public opinion. In a democracy the masses select political elites to rule in their behalf. Theoretically the people retain control over their leaders through rewards and sanctions. The success of mass-elite interaction depends largely upon the nature of the country's political leadership. In this chapter we attempt to define the role of political elites in the American governmental process. In order to do so, we must consider each of the following: (1) the meaning of a democratic political elite; (2) our expectations that the political elite will respond to the public's needs; (3) the process by which citizens are recruited into political elite capacities.

Political elites
and democratic government

THE CONCEPT OF POLITICAL ELITE

The term "elite" originally came into popular usage in seventeenth-century Europe to describe commodities of particularly high quality. Later it evolved as a theological term to depict the "elect of God," the chosen people. From this point the meaning of the word expanded to envelop excellence in various forms of human activity. But not until the late nineteenth century was it used to characterize the politically powerful.

The concept "elite" denotes two defining characteristics. First, the elite, as distinguished from the masses, are a highly placed minority. And second, because of their position, resources, or ability, elites are influential. They compose the upper echelon of their respective spheres of human activity. Vilfredo Pareto, an early twentieth-century elite theorist, provided a general description of elites in the following passage:

> Let us assume that in every branch of human activity each individual is given an index which stands as a sign of his capacity, very much the way grades are given in various subjects in examinations in school. The highest type of lawyer, for instance, will be given 10. The man who does not get a client will be given 1—reserving zero for the out-and-out idiot. To the man who has made millions—honestly or dishonestly as the case may be—we will give 10. To the man who has earned his thousands we will give 6; to such as just manage to keep out of the poor-house 1, keeping zero for those who get in. . . . And so on for all the branches of human activity. . . So let us make a class of people who have the highest indices in their branch of activity, and to that class give the name of *elite*.[1]

The elite, then, are those individuals who occupy the highest strata or pivotal positions in society. In religious orders the elite are those elevated to the priesthood. In the world of corporations the elite occupy positions on the boards of directors. In politics the elite hold governmental office.

The distinction between elites and masses has often been represented by the shape of a pyramid (see Figure 6.1). The pyramid, of course, is a

Figure 6.1
The Pyramid Model of Elites and Masses

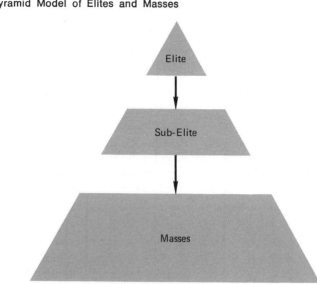

graphic way of illustrating many forms of human organization—the military, for example, from its generals and several ranks of officers down to its foot soldiers. The highest point on our political pyramid represents the top elite, the smallest number of individuals with the most power and influence. The base of the pyramid symbolizes the masses, the largest numbers of individuals with the least power. The area of the pyramid falling between the pinnacle and the base represents various strata of sub-elites, whose numbers are always in inverse proportion to the amount of power exercised. The primary avenues for the flow of influence in this model are always downward.

The term political elite refers to those directly involved with governmental affairs. These individuals constitute the top power class which rules a society or a segment of society. For our purposes, we will use the term political elite to describe those individuals who hold political office or who are leaders in legitimate forms of political activity related to the functions of government. Under a democratic system, a large number of individuals fall under this definition. Federalism as practiced in the United States multiplies this number by providing for political officeholders at the national, state, and local levels. In addition influential persons active in political parties and interest groups must be considered as members of the political elite. The net result is a myriad of politically active persons, each in his own area of governmental concern: the President, governors, legislators, mayors, administrators, judges, councilmen, law enforcement officials, and leaders of citizen organizations, political parties, and lobby groups. We are most concerned in the following pages with those who hold governmental positions, since it is the responsiveness of these public officials to mass opinion that we wish to evaluate.

It is important to understand that political elites are not the only individuals who wield political power. Nongovernmental elites often have a substantial impact on public policy outcomes. Two obvious examples of nongovernmental elites entering the political process occurred during the 1972 presidential campaign. One of these incidents was AFL-CIO President George Meany's refusal to support either George McGovern or Richard Nixon. The effect of this action by the head of the nation's largest trade union organization was to deny a large amount of traditionally Democratic campaign funds, along with organizational support and votes, from McGovern's presidential bid. The second incident involved corporate funds in the drive to reelect President Nixon. In early 1972, it was discovered that a large campaign pledge had allegedly been made by the ITT corporation in exchange for favorable action by the Nixon administration on antitrust charges filed against the company. Estimates of the size of the pledge ranged as high as $400,000. The antitrust action which ITT sought to have dropped centered on the acquisition of the giant Hartford Insurance Company.

Political elites are acutely aware of the influence nongovernmental elites may have and often attempt to use such support to their political advantages. Usually the means of translating the support of nongovernmental elites into political backing are kept within ethical bounds. An example of this is the growing tendency of politicians to enlist the support of leaders in the educational, scientific, business, professional, and even entertainment fields. If the political elite are unable to enlist the support of these influential persons, they at least attempt to ensure neutrality. This, of course, stems from fear of the vast amount of potential power held by these nongovernmental elites. As Edward Banfield noted in his study of Chicago politics, "If the twenty or thirty wealthiest men in Chicago acted as one and put all their wealth into the fight, they could easily destroy or capture the machine." [2]

The essential difference between political and nonpolitical elites is one of accountability. The nongovernmental elite are accountable only to themselves (or to a relatively small number of individuals). The wealthy industrialist who wishes to influence public policy outcomes by making large campaign contributions to the candidate or party of his preference need account to no one. He may spend his fortune as recklessly as he desires. Similarly, a corporation president who attempts to enter the political arena with company resources may ultimately be sanctioned only by the corporation's shareholders—or perhaps by the courts if campaign contributions are taken illegally from corporate coffers.

The democratic method is an institutional arrangement for arriving at political decisions in which individuals (candidates) acquire decision making power by means of a competitive struggle for the people's vote.[3] The fundamental basis of authority held by political elites is popular accountability. Government officials, with some exceptions such as life-tenured federal judges, must periodically return to their constituencies for approval and must account for their actions while in office. It is this obligation to undergo frequent popular reappraisals of their behavior that distinguishes political from nonpolitical elites.

POLITICAL ELITES
AND DEMOCRATIC THEORY

A basic assumption of traditional democratic thought is that popular participation is good. Public policy most beneficial for the common good results when reasonable and informed citizens engage in widespread debate. From this open discussion the citizenry will perceive the most prudent course of political action and direct the government to take that course. The values of this system are threefold: (1) it provides equal opportunity for all persons of all beliefs to participate directly in the decision making process; (2) it insures against tyrannical governmental actions taken by a few political officials; and (3) it educates and improves those citizens who accept their responsibility to participate in the polity. It is generally agreed that the closest approximation to classical democracy existing in this country was the New England town meeting, a practice in which all the citizens of a small locality met, debated issues, and collectively arrived at decisions governing the town. Since the town meeting is not feasible for mass societies, popular election of political representatives has evolved as an alternative.

Despite its emphasis on public participation in politics, democracy is not inconsistent with the existence of political elites. In recent years there has been substantial discussion of an "elitist theory of democracy." [4] This theory holds that American society is best analyzed as a fundamentally democratic system in which elites play a crucial role. The position of elites in the American political system must be thoroughly understood in order to appreciate the way in which democracy functions. The reason that a political elite is not inconsistent with democracy in America is because it operates under *democratic* rules.[5] First, our political leadership forms a non-monolithic class that is generally open to new membership through the electoral process. Second, the political elite in this country must compete among themselves for the favor of the voters. Third, public opinion sets bounds within which the behavior of elites must stay. Fourth, if for no other reason than political survival, the governmental leaders of the United States believe that they should respond to public opinion. After all, the political graveyards are filled with the broken careers of politicians who failed to recognize and respond to the will of the people. Generally speaking, American democracy is a system in which political power is shared by the electorate and their duly selected leaders, and governmental policy is determined largely by the interactions of masses and elites.

POLITICAL LEADERSHIP AND POLITICAL POWER

Political elites in the United States are placed in a leadership capacity. The citizens expect that governmental officials will not only respond to the dictates of reasonable public opinion, but will also educate and lead the populace in the formation of public opinion. The elevation of an individual to public office carries with it access to leadership resources. The President of the United States, for example, is given command over the resources for the conduct of foreign policy. His position as director of the nation's diplomatic and military machinery provides him a near monopoly over the foreign policy making process. Cognizant of this, the electorate expects the President to assume leadership over the nation's foreign affairs and allows him considerable latitude of action. During the Vietnam conflict President Johnson received initial support for his policies. Early criticism of the war effort was unfavorably received by the public. Only when the Johnson administration's promises that the end of the war was "just around the corner" never materialized did a broadly based anti-war sentiment finally emerge. But until reasonable doubt had been exhausted the President was able to muster more than adequate support.

Often the politician is faced with the choice of either following existing public opinion or attempting to modify public beliefs. The choice is always difficult and the stakes are often quite high—especially when the issue evokes intensely held feelings. If the politician elects to conform to existing public views, he can usually count on political survival—at least in the short run. However, if he elects to wage an effort to convince the public to change its views, the consequences can be uncertain. A successful attempt often transforms the official into a public hero. He becomes known as a man of unusual foresight and courage. But if he fails, political suicide is quite often the result. An excellent example is President Wilson's campaign to convince the country to join the League of Nations following the First World War. Wilson was unsuccessful. The Senate refused to ratify the treaty which would have permitted the United States to enter the

League. The personal results to Wilson were disastrous. The campaign itself had a pronounced effect on his already serious health problems and his lack of success cost him a substantial loss of personal prestige and political power. Wilson's only consolation has been that history has vindicated him.

A more recent example of contrasting strategies occurred during the 1972 Florida presidential primary election. In that state the issue of forced busing of children to create a racial balance in the public schools was paramount. Opponents of forced busing placed on the ballot a public referendum calling for the prohibition of this desegregation tool. The vote on this referendum had national importance because it was the first statewide expression of voter sentiment on what loomed as a major campaign issue. Florida Governor Reubin Askew, a supporter of action to end segregation in schools, opposed this referendum. In addition, his supporters placed a second referendum on the ballot calling for the people of the state to affirm their belief in equal educational opportunities for all children and to renounce the notion of returning to a dual school system. Askew waged an active campaign against the busing amendment and in support of equal educational opportunity. Voter opinion was decidedly against forced busing, and Askew's campaign was designed to reverse this trend. At the same time, President Nixon was being urged by the forced busing foes to take a firm stand on the issue. Selecting a cautious course, however, the President declared that he would refrain from announcing a position until the voters had expressed their opinions. The results of the election were dramatically clear. Of the eleven Democratic presidential aspirants on the ballot the most vocal opponent of forced busing, Alabama's Governor George Wallace, captured the election by a huge margin. The antibusing referendum gained the support of 74 percent of the voters. The equal educational opportunity measure also passed, but this had little impact on the victory of the forced busing foes. Only days after the Florida primary, President Nixon announced a strong antibusing program; and while political pundits began projecting the political demise of Reubin Askew, the governor survived the setback and was easily re-elected two years later.

The effectiveness of representative democracy is largely dependent on the quality of political leadership. Within the bounds set by public opinion and the American political culture, the political elite in the United States are given the responsibility of charting the course of governmental policy making. The citizenry expects this type of leadership and will usually reject candidates who fail to inspire confidence in their leadership qualities. One of the major problems facing the McGovern presidential campaign in 1972 was the image held by a large segment of the electorate that the Democratic standard bearer was indecisive and switched his political stands much too frequently. Of course, candidates may suffer a similar fate if their image appears too inflexible and extreme. This situation faced supporters of Senator Barry Goldwater's presidential bid in 1964. To the American public Goldwater appeared far too radical in his conservative domestic and foreign policy pronouncements. And perhaps more importantly, Goldwater refused to modify his views in response to political realities. His campaign slogan that he would "rather be right than President" adequately reflected his severely rigid political perspective; and the American public rejected this brand of leadership.

Inexorably tied to political leadership is the concept of political power.[6] In fact, political power has often been called the most central concern of political science. This centrality is evident from the fact that every important political philosopher has devoted considerable effort to the explication of this concept. Political elites strive for power and exercise it in the name of the people. So important is the notion of political power to governmental leadership that we need to stop at this point and discuss the basic facets of this concept.

The concept of power connotes a relationship. The most simple of power relationships are those based upon physical force. When a person lifts a heavy weight we say that he exercises power over the object. While power associations may be man over object, we are more concerned with person-over-person relationships. This too may be based upon physical dominance, but may also hinge on several other factors. For example, the third-grade bully holds power over his classmates not only because of his physical superiority, but also because of the fear he instills in them. Power relations among people may be based upon prestige, force, status, position, money, the ability to mobilze others, or a host of additional factors. But the result is the same: one person having a certain degree of dominance or authority over another.

The power exerted by political elites is variable, not only in amount but also with respect to the bases of that power. Some leaders are forced to rely on informal personal power because their positions are not accorded great amounts of formal authority. The most important example of this is the United States' Presidency, a position with few constitutional powers attached to it. Yet the individual who serves as President is often the most influential member of the governmental elite. This influence is largely due to his own ability to convert the office into a vehicle for persuading others to act according to his preferences.[7] Other governmental elites must rely on professional expertise. Congressmen, for example, fall into this category. The most effective legislators are usually those who develop superior knowledge in a given area of specialization and devote large segments of time to maintaining that expertise. Other elites owe their power to informal norms. A committee chairman in the United

States Senate wields considerable influence over policy making largely because the seniority system has rewarded long tenure with an immensely powerful position. Still others must rest their power on cultivating feelings of legitimacy. Judges, for example, lack enforcement powers for their decisions, but usually court rulings are implemented because the populace as well as other political elites believe that judicial decrees should be followed.

Political leadership, therefore, is completely intertwined with the phenomenon of political power. The impact a leader can effect depends upon the amount of authority he is able to wield. How an official exercises his power usually determines the degree of success he will enjoy, and his success at fulfilling his duties often decides his political future. Because of the importance of power and leadership to the understanding of elite opinion and behavior, we will frequently refer to these two concepts in subsequent pages.

Political leadership:
Responsiveness, responsibility, and accountability

We have already made several references in this chapter to three concepts associated with a well-functioning democracy: responsiveness, responsibility, and accountability. Because of the importance of these concepts to the major theme of this book, we should discuss them in greater detail and demonstrate their relevance to public opinion, political leadership, and governmental action.

RESPONSIVENESS

The term "responsive government" is often used when individuals discuss the impact of public opinion. If government is not responsive to the will of the people, then public opinion might just as well be ignored by students of politics. If political leaders do not respond to citizen attitudes and if, therefore, the feelings of the populace have no influence on governmental policy, then public opinion would be a topic of only tangential interest to political scientists. But if political elites do respond to public opinion, then citizen attitudes become matters of crucial importance to the understanding of politics. Throughout the remainder of this book we will discuss why, how, and under what conditions political leaders respond to expressions of mass opinion.

There is no question that political leaders respond. The question is, to what or to whom are they responsive. There are innumerable forces to which an elected official might respond; he might, for example, respond in accordance with his own political or moral values or social background experiences. External demands might include those from political party organizations, interest groups, friends, or big campaign contributors. Hopefully, political leaders respond in at least some measure to public opinion. But even this rather simple hope is a complicated matter because defining, isolating, and understanding the will of the people are difficult processes. To what is a congressman to respond if he wishes to have his behavior guided by citizen attitudes—constituent mail? National public opinion polls? Opinion as expressed in the local press? The feeling he gets from public gatherings when he returns to his district? Should he respond to the perceived will of all the people or just those groups who contributed most to his election? Responsiveness, then, is a much clearer concept theoretically than it is in practice.

What we might hope is that more legitimate forms of responsiveness can be enhanced by the systematic elimination of less preferable forms. For example, in the 1974 House Judiciary Committee hearings on the question of impeaching Richard Nixon, a major charge against the President concerned his acceptance of large campaign contributions donated by segments of the dairy industry. The 1972 Nixon reelection campaign was alleged to have received $727,500 over a three-year period and to have been promised a total of two million dollars by the donor dairy cooperatives. Immediately following the receipt of these contributions and promises, the Nixon administration initiated milk price support actions favorable to the industry. The clear implication from this is that President Nixon acted in a responsive fashion—responsive to the monetary contributions of a special interest group. Whether the administration's actions in behalf of the milk industry constituted a thinly disguised response to what might well be characterized as a bribe or whether the contributions and governmental actions were unrelated is a question which may never be finally determined. But the possibility of the government's responding to large contributors contrary to the public interest is indeed a very real danger to democratic responsiveness.

What makes this example even more significant is that, in June of 1974, the news was released that sixteen members of the House Judiciary Committee had also accepted campaign contributions from large dairy cooperatives. Thus, that very body entrusted with the impeachment decision was itself staffed by congressmen who had accepted money from the same special interest. The contributions were not distributed according to partisan affiliation (nine Democrats and seven Republicans received such funds) nor by any type of district. Committee Chairman Peter Rodino was one of the recipients; and, needless to say, Rodino's Newark, New Jersey constituency contained no dairy farmers. The majority of those congressmen who had received these campaign funds had supported dairy industry price support legislation.

What then do we mean when we refer to governmental responsiveness? By this term we mean nothing more than a governmental official's taking seriously into account the will of the people before he acts. The political leader is responsive when he acts as if he cares about the legitimate demands and expectations of the voters.[8] In a society such as ours this is certainly not too much to ask of our political elite.

Responsiveness is a governmental quality with which the American people have become increasingly concerned in recent years. Too often it has appeared that the political leaders of this country have turned a deaf ear to the needs of the public and the demands of the electorate. Disenchantment with our government has become a serious problem because of this lack of confidence in our political leaders. For democracy to work effectively the people must be able to see and appreciate the fact that political leaders have the public good at heart and do in fact respond to the reasonable demands of the citizenry.

RESPONSIBILITY

If government is to work effectively responsiveness must be tempered with responsibility. Political leaders exercise responsibility when they make an intelligent judgment concerning public demands.[9] Obviously, not all citizen demands, even those supported by the majority, are wise, prudent, or thoughtful. Responsible public officials listen to demands from the people, carefully consider these demands, and are able to reject those public sentiments which are disadvantageous to the common welfare.

Several factors demand the exercise of responsibility. First, as noted in Part One of this volume, despite the relatively high educational and socio-economic levels of the American citizenry, its political knowledgeability is rather limited. A good deal of public opinion is uninformed opinion. Second, public opinion is subject to a great deal of fluctuation. For example, prior to the 1973 resignation of Vice-President Spiro Agnew, the name of Gerald Ford was recognized by only a small percentage of the electorate. Yet within weeks of Ford's elevation to the Vice-Presidency public opinion polls showed him to be one of the front runners for the 1976 presidential election. Obviously the government cannot abruptly change its course each time the electorate undergoes temporary mood changes. Third, the public official in many instances has superior knowledge of the governmental process. He may realize that a popular course of action can have deleterious long-range effects. He also understands the technical side of governing, which may at times provide barriers to the implementation of policies widely supported by the electorate.

Responsibility not only implies distinguishing legitimate from dysfunctional public demands, but it also includes the obligation to act affirmatively for the good of the polity in the absence of supporting public opinion. Woodrow Wilson's long, losing battle to convince the American people to support U.S. entry into the League of Nations following the First World War is a classic example of responsible behavior by a political leader.

Responsiveness and responsibility, then, are both necessary for effective democratic government. Since these values may be contradictory in certain situations, we raise the question as to which should be emphasized, responsiveness or responsibility? To a great extent this question is answered by the nature and structure of the governmental body being discussed. For example, the structure of the United States House of Representatives stresses responsiveness. This is largely due to the fact that every two years the members of the House must return to their districts for reelection. Unpopular behavior is relatively easily remembered for this short period of time and the congressman can be kept in close check by his district (or at least the representative may perceive this to be the case). The United States Senate, on the other hand, with its six-year terms, allows a much greater opportunity to exercise responsibility. The senator is not constantly returning to his home district to ask for reapproval and, therefore, is not on as short a leash as is the representative. The Presidency was originally designed to be a position of responsibility rather than responsiveness. The very existence of an Electoral College to select the chief executive buffered him from the winds of public opinion. Yet with the erosion of the Electoral College the President has been forced to pay increasing attention to the responsiveness function. During his first term of office the President must be concerned with responding to the will of the people. But since 1951 with the ratification of the 22nd Amendment (which prohibits more than two full terms of office), the President can substantially decrease the emphasis placed on responsivness. The only real danger he faces during his second term is the once improbable sanction of impeachment. Finally, there is the judiciary. Here we expect overwhelming emphasis to be placed on responsibility. The very Canons of Judicial Ethics directs that public opinion shall not enter into the decision making of the judge.[10] This is particularly true at the federal level where elevation to the bench is by appointment and tenure is for life.

ACCOUNTABILITY

Responsiveness and responsibility are twin virtues of a well-run democratic society. But what recourse do the people have when a government is found lacking in these qualities? What restraints are placed upon a democratic system to keep it both responsive and responsible? These questions lead us to our third major concept, accountability.

By accountability we mean the existence of checks on public officials to insure that they will function in a responsive and responsible manner and the potential levying of negative sanctions on a political leader who strays from these standards. We can examine the subject of accountability by analyzing its three basic forms: institutional accountability, electoral accountability, and internal accountability.[11]

Institutionally based accountability finds its roots primarily in the notions of political power and authority incorporated into our system of government by the framers of the Constitution.[12] It is essentially a consti- tutionally based form of accountability proposed for the most part by individuals such as James Madison. Madison's chief premise was the hypothesis that if unrestrained by external checks political leaders will tend to tyrannize others.[13] Madison scoffed at the idea that frequent popular elections would provide sufficient accountability to insure that political elites would exercise their authority in an acceptable fashion. He believed that the only sure way to control political power was to create equal and offsetting power. For this reason Madison's ideal government was one of checks and balances and separation of powers. If each political office- holder is checked by other officeholders, he will not stray too far afield from legitimate standards of behavior. Hence, through a system of counter- vailing institutional forces political power remains in check. For these reasons Madison supported ratification of the federal Constitution, for that document contained a bicameral legislature; separate constituencies for selecting the President, House, and Senate; presidential veto; senatorial confirmation of executive appointments; and a separation of state and federal spheres of authority. In addition, the development of judicial re- view further contributed to institutional checks on the exercise of political power. Institutional accountability in the Madisonian tradition is based upon offsetting powers, so that if one leader or political branch acts in an irresponsible manner, that action may be checked by another leader or branch. This form of accountability ignores the role of the public as a possible agency for accountability. Instead, it places its faith in political elites checking other political elites.

Electoral accountability is in direct contradiction with much of what institutional accountability is based upon. Electoral accountability places its primary value on the ultimate wisdom of the people. The election is the critical technique for insuring that governmental leaders will be rela- tively responsive to non-leaders.[14] Electoral accountability holds that the very fact that political leaders must periodically return to their constit- uencies for approval guarantees that governmental officials will not become too unresponsive or irresponsible. Electoral accountability, of course, is based upon two rather fundamental assumptions. First, it assumes that political officeholders want to be reelected. And second, it assumes that the people are sufficiently informed to reject an unresponsive or irresponsible leader. The first assumption is undoubtedly valid in most cases. The validity of the second assumption, based upon what we have learned from earlier sections of this volume, may be seriously questioned. But even if the public is not well informed, as long as the political leader perceives the voter as intelligent or fears electoral reprisals, the existence of electoral accountability is a real possibility.

Internal accountability is a much more elusive subject than either institutionally or electorally based accountability. Internal accountability argues that political elites will behave in a responsive and responsible fashion because they have internalized these values. Ideally, *political elites hold themselves accountable* and do not require external checks. One student of political leadership has succinctly stated this internal accountability position by noting, "The elected leaders are solicitous of the views of the masses not because the elected fear voter sanctions; rather, the governors remain sensitive to shifts in public sentiment because that is what men holding office *are supposed to do.*" [15] The existence of self-imposed responsiveness and responsibility is indeed difficult to substantiate, but it is obviously not a far-fetched theory—in spite of events during the past few years which have prompted many to doubt that politicians have any decent motives whatsoever. One proponent of this theory, V.O. Key, finds the seeds of self-imposed accountability in the political socialization of the leadership echelon.[16] Americans are taught that leaders should respond to the will of the people and that holding office is accepting a public trust. These lessons, ingrained at an early age, are reinforced as a citizen assumes and serves in a leadership capacity. He wants to do a good job. He desires to fulfill the obligations of his office. To satisfy the normative role of an officeholder a leader's values, attitudes, and conscience hold his behavior accountable to the standards of responsiveness and responsibility.

These three forms of accountability are not mutually exclusive. They are not competing theories of reality. Accepting one does not necessitate rejecting the other two. In fact, all three undoubtedly exist simultaneously. Institutional checks do provide a means by which one political agency can thwart the irresponsible acts of another. Electoral accountability encourages responsiveness and responsible behavior both because it poses a constant and perceived threat to inappropriate leadership behavior and because it provides an actual means of removing errant officeholders. Internal accountability is the most subtle and least apparent of the three, but it may well be the most pervasive. Each action which an officeholder takes is weighed in his own mind for acceptability. Assuming that a leader's values include responsiveness and responsibility, this means that each of his actions is evaluated according to these standards—even those actions which are sufficiently insignificant to escape the view of other elites and the eyes of the public.

The three concepts of responsiveness, responsibility, and account-ability are critical to our evaluation of the way in which public opinion has an impact on political leaders and public policy formation. By ex-amining these concepts we can see the role of democratic political elites much more clearly. Governmental officials in a democracy must be both followers and leaders. Political elites must follow public opinion in carry-ing out the process of governmental responsiveness, listening to and executing the general directives of the citizenry. Elites behave as leaders in implementing the responsibility function. The political leadership must discriminate among the demands articulated by various segments of society as well as guide public opinion to support wise and prudent governmental policies. Finally, political elites are kept in check through accountability processes. Should the leadership stray too far from public expectations of responsive and responsible behavior new leadership may be ushered into office.

Recruiting political elites

Thus far in this chapter we have discussed the role of political elites in the American democracy. For the most part we have remained at a theoretical level, examining the way in which political elites should behave in a democratic system if that system is to approximate its ideals. The final point which is necessary to consider in this chapter is less theoretical and much more practical. This is the question of how citizens become mem-bers of the American political leadership.

If political elites were selected through some random procedure from the citizenry at large, the task of understanding how mass opinion trans-lates into public policy would be a relatively easy one. We could simply extrapolate from the numerous studies of mass political behavior to the political behavior of elites. But this is not the case. In a governmental system such as ours, holding public office is dependent upon a commit-ment to seek and maintain an elite position. The requirements for success-fully obtaining political office screen out the vast majority of Americans. Those remaining are eligible to compete for voter approval. This, of course, means that the political elite are a rather select group of individuals whose characteristics may not be reflective of the general population.

The leap from a casual interest in politics to a declaration for public office is an enormous one. The qualitative differences between supporting or working for a candidate and being one are vast. It is possible to support another for public office with little personal cost involved. Such political activists may donate spare time, excess cash, and otherwise unexpended energy to a political campaign. If the candidate is victorious, the campaign worker may experience a feeling of euphoria, vicarious pleasure, and even a great sense of accomplishment. On the other hand, if the candidate is defeated, his supporters can curse those real or imagined causes of the defeat and then return to their normal occupational and family duties with no substantial personal loss.

However, when an individual crosses the Rubicon dividing political interest and political candidacy, the required ante immediately soars. It is no longer the name of someone else on the campaign posters, attacked in the press, slandered from the stump, and possibly smothered under an electoral avalanche. The campaign becomes a personal one with the stakes often including personal pride, status, financial security, family solidarity, health, and a host of other values. If the candidate loses, he cannot normally return to his previous lifestyle as if nothing had happened, but must mentally relive the campaign a countless number of times. In the end he may conclude that the experience was nothing more than offering himself for public abuse. But if the campaign has not been too ego shattering and has not left too many personal scars, there is a high probability that the candidate will once again at later date declare for public office. The question which naturally arises is, Why? What makes an otherwise normal and well-adjusted individual risk so much to run for office? The answer to this question can be found by analyzing four requirements of political recruitment: interest, motivation, resources, and opportunity.

POLITICAL INTEREST AND ELITE SOCIALIZATION

In Chapter Three we discussed the phenomenon of political socialization of the American citizenry. Both the process and content of political socialization are also important to our understanding of political elites and their recruitment. While the socialization process continues throughout one's life, the greater proportion of political learning is achieved by the time most individuals reach adulthood. By this time the average American's interest in politics is insufficient to prompt a challenge for public office. Therefore, we might expect that those Americans who do decide to run for office undergo political socialization in a different manner than does the typical citizen. Empirical research has demonstrated that this expectation is at least partially valid.

One of the more documented findings is that those in political office have been socialized at a much earlier age than the average citizen. Furthermore, the elite socialization process instills sufficient interest in political matters to prompt these individuals to enter the political arena. In the now classic study of four state legislatures conducted by John Wahlke and his associates, the conclusion was reached that state legislators are exposed to political stimuli at a much earlier stage of development than are average citizens.[17] Studies of American political party officials have discovered similar patterns of early socialization experiences.[18]

The political socialization processes experienced by masses and elites are, however, similar in several respects. The same socializing agents occur in the backgrounds of both groups, with the family being the most important. What does differ is the nature and intensity of the socializing message to which the child is subjected. Those in political office have often been exposed at an early age to the possibility of running for a governmental position. This, perhaps, makes politics more exciting and real to the child in his developmental years.

Political elites tend to beget political elites. There is a greater tendency for those in political office to have been raised in families in which politics was discussed—if not practiced. One study of elementary-school children from socioeconomic elite families indicated that ninety percent of the children's parents *always* voted and that all of the surveyed children had at one time or another discussed a political candidate with their parents.[19] These figures are substantially higher than would be expected from children raised in non-elite families. One study of state legislative officials revealed that one-half of the interviewed solons had one or more relatives who were politicians of one variety or another.[20] For some positions within the political elite there seems to be an even greater dependence upon specialized socialization within the home. One comprehensive survey of the social backgrounds of Supreme Court justices, for example, discovered that one-third of the individuals who have occupied seats on the nation's highest court were related to jurists and intimately connected with families possessing a tradition of judicial service.[21] It is apparent, then, that when a child's family is active or interested in politics the child's lifelong awareness and knowledge of public issues is heightened.

Those who run for public office and successfully attain leadership positions are those who have intense interest in politics. For the most part the roots of this interest can be found in the early political socialization experiences. Political elites have undergone socialization experiences of a nature different from that of the general citizenry. They tend to be exposed to politics at an early age, to grow up in politically oriented families, and to be exposed to political matters much more intensely. This partially explains the recruitment process. Early and intense political socialization tends to produce high levels of political interest; and as political interest increases so too do the probabilities that a person will seek public office.

POLITICAL MOTIVATION AND AMBITION

The question of motivation may be uppermost in the minds of many potential office seekers. There are few candidates who can honestly say that the office seeks the man. This notion is a fairly obvious myth which for some unknown reason fails to die.[22] Perhaps this is because the exceptions, such as Presidents Washington and Eisenhower, are so notable. For the vast majority of political candidates there is little doubt that the person seeks the office and not vice versa. Usually motivation boils down to a question of ambition.[23] If a potential candidate is sufficiently ambitious either for personal or policy reasons, he will be heavily predisposed to running for public office.

According to one well-known study, political ambitions can assume three basic forms: discrete, static, and progressive.[24] An individual with discrete political ambitions desires a particular office for a specific period of time. We usually find these individuals in those governmental positions with high rates of turnover, such as in state legislatures and state or federal cabinet positions. A person with static motivations has his sights set on a specific office but desires to serve in that capacity for an extended period of time. Congressmen are obvious examples, as are members of the judiciary, who may consider sitting on the bench as the capstone of a legal career. Progressive ambition is characteristic of those politicians who see holding a particular office as a stepping stone for higher governmental service. The political career of Senator Mark Hatfield of Oregon is exemplary of this stepping stone approach.[25] Hatfield progressively moved from his private career as a professor to the State House of Representatives, to State Senate, to Oregon's Secretary of State, to Governor and finally to United States Senator.

The immediate source of political motivation may be self-initiated or initiated by others. The self-starter is the candidate who on his own decides to run for public office. The candidate whose desire is spurred by others often had never seriously considered mounting a political campaign before being approached by influential persons or groups. These outside forces whet the latent political appetite of the potential candidate and in that manner may kindle political motivation. The recruiting forces usually are in the form of political leaders, interest groups, or local community influentials.[26] There is a tendency for self-starters to have been politically socialized at a very early age.[27] Those initiated by others, however, have usually developed high levels of political interest at a later point in their personal development. For many "drafted" candidates the decision to run for public office is in response to pleas from party leaders looking for a candidate. Often this process reduces to the simple need for party leaders to field a candidate—any respectable candidate—to oppose a popular and rarely vulnerable incumbent. This fact was demonstrated in one study of congressional candidates which revealed that two-thirds of the losing candidates cited party leaders as key agents in their decisions to run for Congress.[28]

RESOURCES

A realistic appraisal of a potential candidacy must include an evaluation of available resources. These resources are pertinent to two different aspects of the elite recruitment process. First, the potential candidate must answer the question of whether or not he has the personal resources to serve competently in the office for which he is considering running. These resources, of course, include such attributes as talent, intelligence, educational level, aptitude, and experience. If the individual does not have the ability to serve well and realizes this deficiency, the probability of his entering the campaign is reduced. A person trained in library administration, for example, would probably never consent to run for county sheriff simply because of the lack of confidence in his own abilities in the area of law enforcement. On the other hand, an individual with well developed skills corresponding to the responsibilities of a particular office might decide to launch a campaign because he may be convinced that he can do a credible job. A Certified Public Accountant, for example, may be tempted to declare for State Auditor because of both professional interest and confidence in his own abilities to master the tasks facing that office.

The second resource consideration is whether the potential candidate can muster the wherewithal to win an election. Even if an individual possesses the motivation and confidence necessary to enter the political arena, he may refrain from doing so because he cannot mount an effective campaign. Determinants of successful campaigning often reduce to two major resources: money and organization.

The high cost of running for political office restricts electoral opportunities to those who are independently wealthy or have access to financial support from others. The problem of financing elections has become increasingly serious in recent years. The costs tied to today's mass media campaigns have made financial requirements soar. This, of course, has made it necessary for candidates to accept large campaign contributions from wealthy individuals and interest groups. The financial obligations inherent in contemporary campaigning have prompted several proposals for reform, and some of these have been adopted, but fundamental change has yet to occur.

The other major campaign resource is organizational support. If the voters are to be mobilized, massive organizational efforts are often required. While many types of organizational support are common, the most frequently encountered are political party, interest group, and voluntary action organizations. The most prevalent form is based upon party membership. Parties in most sections of the country have long-standing organizational structures that are capable of being mobilized during a campaign. Gaining the full support of the party machinery is often essential to any hopes of winning elective office. If party support is not total or if the party organization is not sufficient to guarantee victory, candidates may turn to interest group support. In terms of organizational strength the mass membership interest groups are most crucial. The labor movement, for example, has historically lent organizational support to favored candidates. Another common form of political organization is based upon voluntary action groups, which often form for the sole purpose of advancing the cause of a single candidate. The thousands of young Americans who flocked to the support of Eugene McCarthy in 1968 and George McGovern in 1972 are representative of the types of voluntary organizational support a candidate may be able to attract. Regardless of type, however, some organizational support is necessary if the potential candidate hopes to have any realistic chance of winning a contested election.

OPPORTUNITY

The final consideration in the recruitment process is an evaluation of political opportunity. The potential candidate, regardless of his interest, motivation, and resources, must weigh the probabilities of breaking into the elite strata at a given point in time. The calculation of political opportunity must take into account a long list of personal and system characteristics.

Despite the old adage that any child can grow up to be President, social status can have considerable impact on a contender's chances. High social status usually is associated with commensurate political status.[29] High social status not only automatically confers political status, but is also associated with access to quality education and financial resources. People from lower social status levels are often confronted with considerably greater obstacles blocking the entrance to political candidacy. Individuals from lower socioeconomic levels are less often socialized to value political action, are more likely to have occupational positions which do not allow sufficient free time to run for public office, are less likely to possess the economic resources to engage in an effective campaign, and are more prone to have suffered educational disadvantages. This naturally biases the recruitment process toward the higher social classes.

Opportunity may also be related to family background. The family in which one is raised places the individual in a geographical area, an ethnic or racial group, a religious tradition, and a socioeconomic level. Each of these factors may have a bearing on the opportunities available to politically interested individuals. Areas densely populated with a certain ethnic or racial group are prone to choose members of that group for political office. Districts with agriculturally based economies are not likely to elect industrialists to office. Predominantly Catholic areas will give electoral preference to those candidates of similar religious persuasion.

Educational attainment provides a means of enhancing political opportunity. Through educational accomplishments an individual can often break the barriers imposed by family and social status factors. Through education a person may gain professional, economic, and social status. Furthermore, education is likely to increase an individual's political awareness and make him more attractive to the electorate. Certain types of education are more likely to expand political opportunities than others. Obtaining a legal education, for example, almost immediately makes a person eligible for any governmental position, including the judiciary which is for all practical purposes open only to members of the Bar. Specialized educational backgrounds are often important in gaining bureaucratic positions. Tax accountants and foreign affairs specialists, for example, are prime candidates for appointment to Treasury and State Department posts.

Electoral opportunity is also greatly determined by political party activity. If a party has done an effective job of organizing and educating the citizenry, recruiting and grooming potential candidates, and accumulating campaign funds, then candidates nominated by the party have excellent opportunities to obtain public office. If the party has not done its job, then opportunities are severely reduced. A Republican candidate for local office in Mississippi, for example, has little to bolster his optimism because the Republican party in that state is of fledgling strength.

A final, but absolutely essential, opportunity factor is the availability of a political office. Availability depends upon a number of factors including the office's length of term, turnover rates, and the number of potential openings. For example, a person interested in campaigning for the U.S. Senate knows that a particular Senate seat is up for election only once every six years, that turnover for that position is very low, and that for each state two such Senate seats exist. In addition to these structural factors, an individual contemplating an election campaign must consider the strength of the incumbent and the incumbent's desire to retain office. A popular, well entrenched incumbent may be practically unbeatable and this, of course, means that political opportunity is substantially decreased.

If a potential candidate concludes on the basis of considering the motivation, resource, and opportunity factors that an attempt at political office will be his course of action, he assumes a large degree of political risk. He commits time, money, effort, and a physical and psychological strain on himself and his family to a venture which may well prove disastrous. A winner in American political life gains everything. The loser has little tangible to show for his efforts aside from possible campaign debts. While he may lay the groundwork for future political campaigns, the defeated candidate may more likely feel bitterness and resentment; and if he has lost too badly, his political ambitions may have been permanently extinguished. If, however, he has calculated his chances accurately and has executed an effective and successful campaign, the candidate wins office and becomes a member of our political elite. Along with other elected and appointed officials, the successful candidate accepts the trust of the public to carry out governmental duties and exercise official powers granted to the government by the people.

Summary

The purpose of this chapter has been to introduce the role of political elites in the American democracy. Political elites are those individuals who are selected directly or indirectly by regularized election procedures to lead the country and exercise political power. They constitute the top strata in society, ruling in the name of the people and upon authority granted by the people. Elites are essential to a well-functioning democracy. For reasons of practicality there must be some officially specified group of individuals chosen to carry out the will of the people. Those citizens chosen for leadership positions are given the resources and the popular consent necessary to execute their duties. The elite wield the official power of the government through authority granted by the people.

In democratic societies there are certain expectations about how elites are to behave. By accepting leadership positions the political elite incur certain obligations. The people expect the elite to be responsive, to act as if serious consideration is being given to the needs and desires of the people. Similarly, the people expect democratic elites to act responsibly. This entails not only responding to the will of the people, but providing positive leadership which educates the populace and creates prudent public opinion. Should political leaders fail to carry out the public trust granted them, they may be removed or checked through accountability procedures. Elites are held accountable by other elites, by the voters, and by their own internalized values. In democratic societies, the public retains authority over its political leaders and should the elite fail to meet popular expectations they can be replaced.

Under other forms of government, citizens are chosen to occupy elite positions by the military, the church, a political party, or by heredity. In democratic systems, citizens become members of the political elite through open competition for the votes of the electorate. Not all citizens can be reasonably expected to vie for political office. Politics is a demanding activity. Unless a citizen possesses intense political interest, a great deal of motivation, access to sufficient resources, and excellent political opportunities, there is very little likelihood that he or she will ever enter the ranks of our political leadership.

In subsequent chapters we will analyze those citizens who survive the political recruitment process. What characteristics they possess, what personalities they have acquired, and what attitudes they hold have a great deal of impact on the way in which our democracy functions. It is to these subjects that we now need to turn our attention.

NOTES

[1] Vilfredo Pareto, *The Mind and Society,* Vol. 3 (London: Jonathan Cape, 1935), pp. 1422–23.

[2] Edward Banfield, *Political Influence* (New York: Free Press, 1961), p. 290.

[3] Joseph A. Schumpeter, *Capitalism, Socialism, and Democracy,* 3rd ed. (New York: Harper & Row, 1950), p. 269.

[4] For a discussion and debate on the "elitist theory of democracy" see Peter Y. Medding, " 'Elitist' Democracy: An Unsuccessful Critique of a Misunderstood Theory," *Journal of Politics,* 31 (August 1969), 641–54; Jack L. Walker, "A Critique of the Elitist Theory of Democracy," *American Political Science Review,* 60 (June 1966), 285–95; and Robert Dahl, "Further Reflection on 'The Elitist Theory of Democracy'," *American Political Science Review,* 60 (June 1966), 296–305.

[5] Steven V. Monsma, "Potential Leaders and Democratic Values," *Public Opinion Quarterly,* 35 (Fall 1971), 351.

[6] Kenneth F. Janda, "Toward the Explication of the Concept of Leadership in Terms of the Concept of Power," *Human Relations,* 13, No. 4 (1960), 345–63.

[7] Richard E. Neustadt, *Presidential Power: The Politics of Leadership* (New York: John Wiley & Sons, 1960).

[8] William C. Mitchell, *Public Choice in America* (Chicago: Markham Publishing Company, 1971), p. 373.

[9] Ibid.

[10] Canon 34, *Canons of Judicial Ethics.*

[11] Kenneth Prewitt, *The Recruitment of Political Leaders* (Indianapolis: Bobbs-Merrill, 1970), esp. ch. 9.

[12] See Alpheus Thomas Mason and Richard H. Leach, *In Quest of Freedom* (Englewood Cliffs, N.J.: Prentice-Hall, 1959), esp. pp. 148–52.

[13] Robert A. Dahl, *A Preface to Democratic Theory* (Chicago: University of Chicago Press, 1956), p. 6.

[14] Ibid., p. 125.

[15] Prewitt, *The Recruitment of Political Leaders,* p. 123.

[16] V. O. Key, *Public Opinion and American Democracy* (New York: Knopf, 1964).

[17] John C. Wahlke, Heinz Eulau, William Buchanan, and LeRoy Ferguson, *The Legislative System* (New York: John Wiley & Sons, 1962), pp. 80–81. See also Herbert Hirsch, "The Political Socialization of State Legislators: A Re-examination," in *Comparative Legislative Systems,* eds. Herbert Hirsch and M. Donald Hancock (New York: Free Press, 1971), pp. 98–106.

[18] Allan Kornberg, Joel Smith and David Bromley, "Some Differences in the Political Socialization Patterns of Canadian and American Party Officials: A Preliminary Report," *Canadian Journal of Political Science,* 2 (March 1969), 151–62.

[19] Joan E. Laurence and Harry M. Scoble, "Ideology and Consensus among Children of the Metropolitan Socio-economic Elite," *Western Political Quarterly,* 22 (March 1969), 151–62.

[20] Wahlke, et al., *The Legislative System,* p. 82.

[21] John R. Schmidhauser, "The Justices of the Supreme Court: A Collective Portrait," *Midwest Journal of Political Science,* 3 (February 1959), 14.

[22] Conrad Joyner, *The American Politician* (Tucson: University of Arizona Press, 1971), esp. ch. 12.

[23] For discussions of political ambition see Michael L. Mezey, "Ambition Theory and the Office of Congressman," *Journal of Politics,* 32 (August 1970), 563–79; Joseph A. Schlesinger, *Ambition and Politics* (Chicago: Rand McNally, 1966); Gordon S. Black, "A Theory of Political Ambition: Career Choices and the Role of Structural Incentives," *American Political Science Review,* 66 (March 1972), 144–59; Paul L. Hain, "Age, Ambitions and Political Careers: The Middle-Age Crisis," *Western Political Quarterly,* 27 (June 1974), 265–74.

[24] Schlesinger, *Ambition and Politics.*

[25] Joyner, *The American Politician,* p. 144.

[26] Samuel Patterson and G. R. Boynton, "Legislative Recruitment in a Civic Culture," *Social Science Quarterly,* 50 (September 1969), 243–63.

[27] Harmon Zeigler and Michael A. Baer, "The Recruitment of Lobbyists and Legislators," *Midwest Journal of Political Science,* 12 (November 1968), 493–513.

[28] Robert J. Huckshorn and Robert C. Spencer, *The Politics of Defeat* (Amherst: University of Massachusetts Press, 1971).

[29] Lester G. Seligman, *Recruiting Political Elites* (New York: General Learning Press, 1971), p. 5.

ELITE OPINION
AND POLITICAL
DECISION MAKING:
INDIVIDUAL FACTORS

7

In Chapter Six we introduced the role of political elites in the democratic process. For the most part we remained at an abstract level. We examined the relationship between elites and masses as postulated in democratic theory, particularly with respect to our expectations of how the political leadership should behave relative to public opinion. To achieve a more adequate appraisal of political leadership, we need to move from this relatively theoretical discussion of elites to a much more concrete analysis of our political decision makers. We should not lose sight of the fact that political elites are human beings. They are not abstract agencies or organizations drawn on the blueprint of democratic theory. As human beings, governmental leaders are subject to the same personal, social, and political forces as citizens are. To understand elite opinion and decision making, then, we need to inquire as to the types of individuals who staff our political offices.

The purpose of this chapter is to draw a profile of the characteristics possessed by our political leaders. From our discussion of political recruitment in Chapter Six, we might well suspect that our governmental decision makers are not representative of the general population. The recruiting process screens out all but a select group of Americans. In this chapter we will devote our attention to the personal characteristics of public officials— the social backgrounds they possess, the personalities they manifest, and the attitudes they hold. In our examination of these three categories of elite characteristics, we will be concerned with answering two basic questions: how do political elites differ from the general population and how do elite characteristics affect governmental decision making?

Social background factors

BACKGROUND CHARACTERISTICS
OF POLITICAL ELITES

The writings of sociologist C. Wright Mills during the 1940s and 1950s encompassed some of the first attempts to examine the backgrounds of elites in the United States.[1] The result was a graphic portrayal of what most Americans already suspected: that those in power were of the higher socioeconomic classes and that notables such as the log cabin born Abraham Lincoln were exceptions to the general rule. While there is the possibility that every little boy or girl may grow up to be President, some have distinctly higher probabilities of attaining that goal because of advantages granted at birth. Such a conclusion should not be surprising given what we have noted earlier with respect to the political socialization and recruitment processes. The deck from which political elites are drawn is obviously stacked in favor of the higher socioeconomic classes. In order to discover just how stacked the deck is, we need to examine the backgrounds of those individuals who have held political office in the United States.[2]

Age, sex, and race. On the basis of age, sex, and racial characteristics political elites in the United States tend to be middle-aged, white males. This pattern has held throughout the nation's history and only in recent years has there been any evidence of modification in that standard. In terms of age, individuals serving at the higher levels of governmental power tend to be older than those serving at the lower levels. Then, too, federal officeholders are generally older than state and local officeholders. The United States Supreme Court with its provisions for life tenure has the greatest propensity for having elderly officeholders. It is not uncommon for the Court to have more than one of its nine members over the age of 80. There is an even sharper bias in the sexual characteristics of political elites in this country. More than 95 percent of the individuals currently holding major offices in the United States are men. The Supreme Court and the Presidency have been in the exclusive control of men. While there has been considerable evidence that the first woman may soon be appointed to the Court, the probabilities of a woman being elected to the Presidency in the near future are still exceptionally low. Members of the Caucasian race similarly have dominated positions of political power. While blacks have made some progress in legislative positions and have gained municipal offices in many cities, electoral success by black candidates has normally occurred only in those areas densely populated by blacks. It was not until 1967 when Lyndon Johnson appointed Thurgood Marshall that a black first wore the robes of a Supreme Court Justice.

Religious affiliation. Generally political elites in the United States are overwhelmingly Protestant in religious affiliation. As with racial minorities, religious minorities in this country have thus far achieved their greatest electoral successes in legislative positions where their constituencies share their religious beliefs. Members of religious minorities have achieved far greater success under the Democratic than under the Republican banner. This fact is largely due to the efforts made by the Democrats to cultivate support from ethnic groups. Until the 1960 election of John Kennedy, a Roman Catholic, no person of any religious membership other than Protestant had ever attained the Presidency. But perhaps the most curious example of religious representation has occurred on the Supreme Court. Over the last three-quarters of a century the tradition of appointing one Catholic and one Jew to the high court has developed. The "Catholic seat" has been filled from 1894 when Grover Cleveland appointed Edward White to the Court until the present, with sole exception of the years 1950–1956. A "Jewish seat" was first established with Woodrow Wilson's appointment of Louis Brandeis in 1916. Brandeis was followed by Benjamin Cardozo, Felix Frankfurter, Arthur Goldberg, and Abe Fortas. With the Fortas resignation from the Court in 1969, however, the "Jewish seat" was not maintained. President Nixon expressly declared that he did not believe in religious considerations when making appointments to high office.

Education. In terms of educational attainment, American political elites form one of the most highly educated groups in the world. An overwhelming proportion of officeholders at all levels of government has received some form of college education with most possessing college degrees— often from prestigious institutions. Large numbers of elites in this country also hold advanced degrees, the most common of which is the law degree. The facts indicate the great boost to one's political chances that an education can provide. The association between education and a political career should be fairly obvious. A college or advanced degree is likely to be held by an individual who is ambitious, upwardly mobile, and intelligent. Furthermore, such persons are likely to have gained some interest in politics or at least to have learned the importance of government as a regulator of society. And perhaps most importantly, a well-educated person is more apt to choose an occupation in which the combination of free time and financial reward allows the individual to engage in some form of political activity if he so desires.

Occupational background. Consistent with their levels of educational attainment, American political elites have been primarily of white collar occupational backgrounds. The most prevalent occupation of political elites has been that of practicing attorney. From the very beginning of this nation, lawyers have held a special position in politics. Almost one-half of the signatures on the Declaration of Independence were those of attorneys and three-fifths of the delegates to the Continental Congress were lawyers.[3] The frequent appearance of attorneys among the ranks of the political elite continues today. In legislative bodies, for example, it is not unusual to find that well over half the members have occupational roots in the legal profession. Seventy percent of the Presidents have been attorneys and every Justice of the Supreme Court has been a member of the Bar. A number of explanations have been offered for the predominance of the legal profession in American politics.[4] Lawyers tend to be highly educated, to have high incomes, and to be socialized and enter political life at a much younger age than non-attorneys. Furthermore, there appears to be a convergence of professional roles between legal and political life. Both are affected with a sense of public service and professional independence. Politics and the law are highly compatible, with many governmental positions revolving around the development, interpretation, and enforcement of the law.

The second group which tends to be over-represented among the political elite is the business and finance occupational sector. While businessmen receive more than their share of elite positions under both major parties, the Republican party in particular has advanced members of the business community to high rungs on the political ladder. The reasons for the high participation of business and financial interests in politics should be apparent. Members of this occupational classification are generally from the higher economic strata and are able to call upon the backing of powerful and wealthy economic concerns. It is perhaps the business community above all others which has realized the importance of governmental policy making as a determining factor in the success or failure of economic ventures. For that reason business has attempted to influence the policy making process by encouraging members of its community to achieve political success.

Political elites in the United States, then, can be characterized as middle-aged, male, white, Anglo-Saxon, Protestant, highly educated professionals. As unrepresentative as such an elite may seem we have not yet proven it to be unresponsive. It is possible that an enlightened elite could rule with the best interests of all and the common good at heart. But before we are able to arrive at any conclusions in this regard, we need to tackle the fundamental question of whether social background factors significantly affect the opinions and behavior of political elites.

SOCIAL BACKGROUND THEORY
AND POLITICAL DECISION MAKING

Social scientists commonly have approached the study of political decision making by examining the social backgrounds of political elites. This is done under the assumption that a decision maker's past will influence his decision making process. Social background theorists rarely take the extreme position that a person's background absolutely determines his behavior. What social background theory argues is that an individual's past experiences form a screen upon which current issues, questions, and actions are projected. This screen can at least partially form or even distort perceptions. For example, two persons residing in an urban ghetto area, one a white merchant and the other a seventeen-year-old black youth, may evaluate the police in entirely different ways. Similarly, a Congressman whose family once received social assistance may react differently to proposed welfare legislation than another who grew up in luxury.

A complete test of social background theory is extremely difficult. This is because it is virtually impossible to determine all of the relevant factors in a particular decision maker's background which may affect his behavior while in office. If Freud was correct, these background experiences may be subtle and unknown even to the decision maker himself, much less to a political scientist attempting to explore the effect of background variables on political behavior. Furthermore, these experiences may have occurred as early as infancy. Because of these problems, social scientists have attempted to isolate those factors which theoretically should affect political decision making. Relevant factors have included such variables as political party affiliation, religious membership, race, occupational background, and educational level. Studies which have attempted to relate background variables with decision making behavior have yielded mixed results. Social background factors appear to have some impact on elite opinions and behavior, but certainly are not the sole determinants of elite decision making.

What social background factors provide is a sign or tip-off that under certain conditions a particular decision maker may act in a predictable fashion. As an example we can use the decision reached by the U.S. Supreme Court in the case of *Buck* v. *Bell* in 1927.[5] The principal in this case was Carrie Buck, a feebleminded eighteen-year-old woman who had been committed to the Virginia State Colony for Epileptics and Feebleminded. Miss Buck was the daughter of a feebleminded mother and had given birth to an illegitimate feebleminded child. Virginia law, with certain safeguards, allowed for the compulsory sterilization of mental defectives. Following a hearing on this matter, the state ordered the sexual sterilization of Carrie Buck. Miss Buck appealed on the grounds that compulsory steriliza- tion violated the 14th Amendment's due process and equal protection clauses. The Supreme Court rejected Buck's argument and upheld the validity of the Virginia statute. The majority opinion was written by Justice Oliver Wendell Holmes in which he made his famous statement that "three generations of imbeciles are quite enough." The vote on the decision was 8 to 1. The lone Justice dissenting was Pierce Butler. Butler was also the only Roman Catholic on the Court at that time. While Justice Butler did not write a dissenting opinion explaining the reason for his vote, the case can be made that his strong ties with the Catholic church and its corresponding teachings against sterilization, artificial birth control, and abortion may have been the reason for his action. While this is an isolated example, it does illustrate the possibility that under certain circumstances background characteristics may activate certain decisional propensities.

One of the first major works applying social background theory to political phenomena was the classic 1913 study by Charles Beard, *An Economic Interpretation of the Constitution.*[6] In this work Beard argues that the Constitution of the United States was the product of delegates who had economic stakes in the outcome of deliberations. At least five-sixths of the representatives, according to Beard, stood to gain economically from the ratification of the Constitution. The delegates were generally from the upper economic, social, and educational classes. Most were engaged in professional, business, and agricultural occupations, success in which was dependent upon a stable government and economy. While Beard did not argue that the delegates were motivated by personal selfishness, he did demonstrate convincingly that the decisions reached at the Convention corresponded with the best interests of the assembled individuals.

More contemporary efforts to evaluate empirically the validity of social background theory have concentrated largely on legislative and judi- cial behavior. Applying the propositions of social background theory to legislatures and collegial courts has the distinct advantage of examining the behavior of multiple elites with differing background experiences responding to similar if not identical public policy questions.

In legislative voting behavior studies, the background factor most frequently cited is political party affiliation.[7] This variable is most useful in predicting the way a legislator will cast his vote—at least in those legisla- tures which have two competitive parties. Legislatures generally organize, select leaders, and distribute legislative rewards and punishments according to political party membership. Furthermore, legislators run for office with a political party label, on a political party platform, and receive political party support and organization. Because of these factors, it is likely that legisla- tors will vote as often as possible according to the "party line." But political party affiliation means much more. It usually indicates a long-standing commitment to the party often extending as far back as early childhood. It also indicates acceptance of a general and perhaps loosely defined ideological position.

What might be more surprising to most students is that similar political party differences have been discovered in the behavior of judges. This phenomenon is particularly interesting because judges are popularly regarded as being non-partisan. Judges after all are supposed to be objective and free from political party influence. Yet subtle partisan influences have been discovered in several studies of judicial decision making.[8] The differences between the decisions of Democratic and Republican judges are in the directions we might have anticipated. Democrats tend to support criminal defendants, government regulation of the economy, and the underprivileged (employees, tenants, consumers, and the injured) to a significantly higher degree than Republicans. The stereotyped view of Democrats supporting the average citizen and Republicans favoring the interests of big business fits in with these findings. While other studies have provided mixed results on the effect of party affiliation on judicial decision making,[9] the general conclusion has been that partisan memberships do influence court rulings on various types of cases. However, the extent of this influence has not yet been adequately measured.

Additional research has examined the impact of social background factors such as age, occupation, and religious affiliation on the opinions and behavior of political elites. As we might expect, political leaders of advanced age, those from agricultural backgrounds, and those with fundamentalist Protestant religious views tend to be more conservative.[10] These social background characteristics appear to operate similarly on elites and on the general citizenry.

Finally, because of the predominance of the legal profession in American politics, we need to discuss the possible impact of the attorney as a political decision maker. If we believed the common folklore about lawyers in politics, we would picture them as an ultra-conservative, highly cohesive group of professionals whose primary political aim is the passage of excessively complicated laws which baffle the layman and necessitate his retaining the aid of an exorbitantly expensive attorney.

Generally, however, this rather cynical view of the lawyer-politician has been discredited. Studies comparing lawyer and non-lawyer legislators have found relatively few differences. Political conservatism, for example, has not been demonstrated to be an identifying characteristic of the attorney. Rather, state legislative research has indicated that the ideological stance of attorneys is actually slightly more liberal than non-attorney lawmakers.[11] Nor, contrary to popular myth, do lawyer-legislators vote together as a bloc,[12] even when the issues involved deal with matters relevant to the judiciary.[13] However, on at least one dimension, legislative activity, the lawyer-legislator distinguishes himself from his non-lawyer colleagues: representatives with legal backgrounds have much higher rates of authoring and introducing legislation.[14]

From evidence assembled by numerous scholars, we can conclude that social background factors have at least some impact on the opinions and behavior of elites. The general backdrop that these experiences provide for political stimuli should not be underestimated, but unless we examine other factors our knowledge of elite opinion and behavior will be noticeably incomplete.

Personality factors

PERSONALITY AND POLITICS

Since the publication of Sigmund Freud's pioneering work in the late nineteenth century, scholars have been aware of the relationship between personality and social behavior. The systematic study of the impact of personality factors on political behavior, however, did not receive its deserved attention until the efforts of Harold Lasswell became widely circulated in the mid-twentieth century.[15] Personality theories share with the social background approach an emphasis upon previous life experiences. The personality approach, however, focuses on those experiences which contribute to the development of the subconscious, while social background theorists concentrate on demographic factors. Personality theorists often examine childhood experiences, parental relationships, attitudes toward sexual matters, and conceptualizations of self. The personality approach, then, attempts to go beyond the "simplistic" demographic approach by examining the inner man.[16]

When we apply personality theories to elite behavior and decision making, we implicitly assume that political elites possess systematically different personalities than average citizens. This distinction between *homo civicus* and *homo politicus*—civic man and political man—was examined by Robert Dahl.[17]

Civic man, according to Dahl, is simply man as a social being. This creature learns at an early age that he possesses certain biological and psychological needs and wants, including food, work, play, rest, sex, friendships, and a desire for love. But he knows that the fulfillment of these needs involves social behavior and that gratification is constrained by society. Society, however, not only places limitations on certain forms of behavior, but also provides opportunities by means of which the individual receives aid in attaining his primary goals. Because of this he has developed certain strategies to enhance these relationships with others. One of the most important social institutions which limits as well as expands opportunities is government. Other forms of activity, such as earning a living, joining a club, or planning for financial security, are usually placed above the political. Political activity may only become paramount if government threatens to limit an individual's interests. The sportsman, for example, may never become active in politics until government considers gun control legislation.

Homo politicus is of a different variety. He regards political action as a means of gratifying his needs and, therefore, allocates sizable resources to politics. Political man attempts to gain control over civic man. He may pursue this end by running for public office. However, as in all forms of social behavior, political action is constrained by societal norms. When *homo civicus* perceives political man as a threat to his preferred activities, civic man will take political action to thwart *homo politicus*. Political man's preoccupation with dominance over civic man may include gratification of such needs as power, wealth, popularity, social standing, and respect. Political man will use any approved resources at his disposal to gain influence, and then he will use that influence to gain more resources. Therefore, while all men place value on certain types of social behavior, political man places primary importance on political activity.

When we speak of political elites, then, we are discussing *homo politicus*. He may be a distinct personality type whose psychic needs are much different from those of the average citizen. The personality traits of elites are almost by definition dissimilar to the traits possessed by the masses. After all, it takes a particular type of person to assume political risks, to visualize himself as a ruler of society, to seek office, and to desire political power. Many politicians think of themselves as a breed apart. Just how different the personality of political man is has yet to be adequately determined. The notion that the ruling elite may possess special types of psychic needs is an interesting one; for if political man is psychologically aberrant, then perhaps psychological studies of members of the public cannot be generalized to political officeholders.

According to Harold Lasswell's seminal works, political man can be easily distinguished from the average citizen. The primary distinguishing characteristic is the personality need to exercise power. As Lasswell has noted:

If there is a political type . . . , the basic characteristic will be the *accentuation of power in relation to other values within the personality when compared with other persons.*[18]

However, the mere personality need is insufficient to thrust an individual into a position of political power. The potential elite must garner the appropriate political skills to satisfy the power needs of his personality. For

Lasswell, the power need, i.e., the need to obtain deference from others, stems from a desire to overcome low estimates of the self. Attaining high political office with its corresponding status and power may be one of the ultimate accomplishments in the drive to achieve deference. Based upon this theoretical premise, Lasswell lays down five postulates describing the behavior of an individual who possesses the political personality:

1. He demands power and seeks other values only as a basis for power.
2. He is insatiable in his demand for power.
3. He demands power for himself only, conceived as an ego separate from others.
4. His expectations are focused upon the past history and future possibilities affecting power.
5. He is sufficiently capable to acquire and supply the skills appropriate to his demands.[19]

Lasswell's theories of the political personality, while receiving well-deserved acclaim for their contributions to our knowledge of political leadership, have also been subject to considerable criticism and modification on the grounds that they are far too simplistic. In reality, critics argue, the political personality cannot be reduced to a single power-seeking dimension. Instead, political leaders are more likely to possess multi-valued political personalities. Then, too, political power may be an instrumental value rather than an end value of the political personality, desired in order to satisfy deeper personal needs, such as a need for achievement, for respect, or for security.[20]

At least one study has empirically tested the Lasswell thesis of the power motive of political elites.[21] Researchers were able to administer personality questionnaires to groups of local politicians and businessmen. The results indicated that political leaders did not have abnormally intense power motivations—at least in comparison with businessmen. This evidence, of course, does not totally discredit Lasswell's theories. It may well be that relatively high power needs are common to persons who choose achievement-oriented careers. Similarly, the intensity of power motivation among political elites increases as one climbs to higher rungs on the political ladder.

Later studies examining the question of personality differences between political elites and the masses have generally followed the power theories advanced by Lasswell. However, power oriented research has not been the only personality related study that has been conducted. In a 1950 study comparing the personality traits of legislators and citizens,[22] John McConaughy examined several personality dimensions. His research was inspired by Lasswell's insight that politics might be best understood by an analysis of the motivations and personalities of political elites. Accordingly,

McConaughy compared the personality traits of members of the South Carolina state legislature with the personality factors of a group of male citizens of that state. While the results of this study are somewhat tenuous because of the exploratory nature of the research, the findings tend to make intuitive sense.

In comparison with the state population, McConaughy found the legislators to be much less neurotic, decidedly more self-sufficient and extroverted, and slightly more dominant. Furthermore, the representatives were found to be more active and self-confident. Conversely, these political elites were less tense and irritable and possessed fewer feelings of inferiority. On more politically related dimensions, the South Carolina representatives were less fascist and only slightly more conservative than members of the general population who were used as a control group. A legislator's tendency to accept fascist ideas and espouse a conservative philosophy decreased with the prosperity, commercial development, education, and urbanity of the district represented.

Studies comparing personality characteristics of political elites and the general citizenry have not been numerous. This is largely due to the methodological problems confronting such research. It is extremely difficult to find political leaders who are willing to subject themselves to an inventory of personality tests. The task becomes more arduous as we attempt to obtain access to higher level leaders. Political researchers generally have to content themselves with interviewing local elites. More powerful, national political leaders must be studied from afar, inferring personality characteristics from their behavior, writings, and speeches.

Despite the paucity of research, our findings about the personalities of political leaders have been consistent with our theoretical expectations. We would expect political leaders to differ from the general population, to be more extroverted than the masses, as well as more dominant and active. These characteristics are prerequisites to declaring for public office and waging a campaign. Similarly, we should not be shocked to discover that successful candidates have high achievement needs and enjoy political power. The competitive nature of politics and the power associated with public office would appear to screen out persons without such traits.

PERSONALITIES AND ELITE OPINION

Research exploring the relationship between personality traits and political behavior has demonstrated that a linkage between the two clearly exists.[23] Personality factors affect most aspects of an individual's private as well as social behavior, and there is no reason to suspect that the political sphere of one's activity should be exempt from this influence. However, while our awareness of the personality-politics relationship has deepened significantly over the past two decades, our understanding of the intricacies of this relationship remains peripheral.

Personality and political beliefs. Several scholars have sought to compare personality characteristics with political beliefs and ideologies. Herbert McClosky's pioneering studies in the 1950s explored the relationship between personality and political liberalism/conservatism.[24] McClosky surveyed more than one thousand Americans in order to examine their personality traits and political attitudes.

McClosky's results challenge the validity of the traditional belief that conservatives comprise the intelligent, elite, upper-class aristocrats of society. Instead, he concludes that conservatives (in comparison to liberals) tend to be social isolates, who are timid, frustrated, and do not think highly of themselves. Conservatives are often people who lack a clear sense of direction and purpose and look at society as too complex to understand. Conversely, liberals included in the McClosky analysis were less hostile, suspicious, compulsive, and intolerant than their more conservative counterparts.

McClosky's findings are certainly not flattering to more conservative individuals and have been criticized as being based upon methodologically flawed procedures.[25] Yet his research suggests that individuals of similar political persuasions have certain personality attributes in common. There appear to be real differences between groups of citizens who subscribe to a liberal or a conservative credo.

Several studies following McClosky's early efforts have uncovered little evidence linking personality traits with moderate, conventional political beliefs. However, research has established an association between the more extremist political ideologies and the personality attributes of authoritarianism, dogmatism, and alienation. Significantly, each of these personality characteristics has been shown to be related to the acceptance of extremist political views, and particularly to extremism of the political right.[26]

Although this hypothesis has yet to receive rigorous testing, historical examples suggest that those political leaders who exhibit extreme authoritarianism or dogmatism have been associated with extreme right wing political movements. Adolf Hitler perhaps provides the most outstanding historical case. In our own country, Senator Joseph McCarthy's anti-communist crusade of the 1950s serves as a possible, albeit less extreme, illustration.

Given the structure and traditions of American politics, individuals who espouse extreme views have rarely achieved elite positions. Extreme or defective personalities can only gravitate to extremist political movements *if such ideological groups exist.* In the United States, a tradition of diversified ideological choices has not emerged in any viable form. And where extremist groups have survived more than a short period of time, they have never attained electoral acceptance. Therefore, those with uncommon personality traits who have been attracted to extremist ideological philosophies have never achieved serious positions of political power. Instead, they have remained largely on the fringes of American politics rather than becoming an integral part of our political leadership.

Personality and elite behavior.   The question of the impact of personality factors on elite opinion and behavior is a central one. If personalities influence the way in which political elites perceive their obligations of office, act in response to public opinion, and generally conduct their duties, then it is important that we understand this influence.

Personality studies of American political elites have generally been of two varieties. The first has been the case study, in which the personality attributes of individual political leaders and the impact of those attributes have been analyzed in considerable depth.[27] The second approach has used typological analysis, pursuing the personality-politics linkage by evaluating classifications of political actors in psychological terms.[28] For the most part, these studies of American political leaders have focused on Presidents and legislators.

Studies of the personalities of political chief executives are the most numerous of those dealing with the psychological traits of governmental elites. Very few American Presidents have escaped having their personality attributes and needs analyzed by scholars. For the most part, these studies have lacked rigor and analytical depth because they have been conducted by historians and biographers untrained in psychological analysis. Political scientists have only recently adopted more rigorous methods. Psychological studies of the Presidency have usually fallen into the category of individual case studies rather than systematic comparative analyses across several presidential administrations.

Studies of presidential personalities have in many ways contributed more to our knowledge of the political process than have psychological studies of other types of elites. The reason for this discrepancy is not so much the quality of the presidential studies, but the institutional setting in which the President operates. In a very real sense the Presidency is a shapeless, undefined office. There are very few constitutional requirements or specific obligations. The President, through his policies, appointments, and actions, molds the executive branch into what he desires it to be. The President's power is unstructured and informal [29]—only the traditions set by previous officeholders guide him. The Presidency, then, becomes largely an extension of the personality of the individual chosen for that office. The psychological needs, self-concept, and perception of roles of the incumbent determine the tenor of the Executive Branch. Thus, the impact of the chief executive's personality is much greater than that of elites in other governmental spheres. The functioning Congress is not radically altered by a particular senator's personality, nor is the complexion of the judiciary changed markedly by a newly appointed judge's psychological attributes. But like a chameleon, the Executive Branch changes color with the inauguration of each new President.

Erwin C. Hargrove has provided one of the few analyses of presidential personalities in comparative perspective.[30] He examines the political personalities of six chief executives and classifies them into two types: Presidents of Action and Presidents of Restraint. Into the action category, Hargrove places Theodore Roosevelt ("The Dramatizing Leader"), Woodrow Wilson ("The Moralizing Leader"), and Franklin Roosevelt ("The Manipulative Leader"). Hargrove's restraint classification includes William Howard Taft ("The Judge"), Herbert Hoover ("The Engineer"), and Dwight Eisenhower ("The General").

Hargrove's two presidential types are distinguished through an examination of four personality attributes: needs, mental traits, values, and the ego. Presidents of Action are driven to seek their positions, according to Hargrove, by a need for personal power. This need is evident in their early lives when leadership skills were gained not as a response to policy situations but because of a psychological need to exercise control over others. The mental traits and abilities of Presidents of Action are important only inasmuch as there exists a congruence between the qualities of the mind and of the temperament. For an individual to become a President of Action, his mental traits must provide the wherewithal to satisfy his needs. These mental traits may include such attributes as the ability to interact well with others, flexibility, practicality, and sensitivity to power situations. Values give direction to the political lives of the Action Presidents. They provide an avenue within which to aim the drive for political power. Normally for Presidents of Action this direction has taken the shape of some variety of reformism. The ego, of course, is the force unifying each of the previous attributes into a single personality type. The consequence of this unification is a chief executive with an activist conception of his role as President.

Taft, Hoover, and Eisenhower, the Presidents of Restraint, possessed radically different personality traits from the Presidents of Action. According to the analysis provided by Hargrove, none of the Restraint Presidents were the subjects of intense needs for personal power. Instead, each valued order, harmony, and self-restraint. The needs of these Presidents led them to develop nonpolitical skills in their respective occupational areas of the law, engineering, and the military. Technical skills were paramount in the developing character of these more passive politicians. Each exhibited mental abilities emphasizing order, logic, and regularity. They tended to prefer very structured situations and performed well under such conditions. But in the fast-paced political world each displayed an inability to cope with unstructured conditions. Each also possessed values which reinforced political passivity. They were all essentially conservative and doubted the need for governmental action unless the private sector was proven to be totally incapable of handling situational needs. The integration of these elements into a single personality dictated that these individuals would never become active leaders, nor would they ever be known in their political lives as contributors to the improvement of society or the growth of the Presidency.

Hargrove's analysis, while certainly subject to criticism for its intuitive basis and corresponding simplicity, is nontheless significant for its contribution to the comparative examination of executive personalities. In 1972, twelve years after the publication of the Hargrove study, a more refined attempt at comparative evaluation of presidential personalities was produced by James David Barber in a work entitled *The Presidential Character*.[31]

Barber's analysis moves from Hargrove's one-dimensional (action/restraint) examination of the presidential personality to a two-dimensional evaluation. According to Barber, we can predict with a certain degree of confidence a President's performance if we look at two basic questions: (1) How active is he? and (2) To what extent does he appear to enjoy his political life? By answering these two questions, Barber is able to classify Presidents into four basic personality types.

1. *The active-positive presidents.*   Chief Executives falling into this category exhibit a high degree of political activity and a high sense of enjoyment of political experiences. Barber includes three recent Democratic Presidents in this category: Franklin Roosevelt, Harry Truman, and John Kennedy. Each exemplified an orientation toward productivity and progress, mixing idealism and reformism with practicality. Active-positive Presidents emphasize rationality and reject the overemotional and irrational aspects of politics. Presidents of this personality type enjoy political life to the fullest and quite probably their political histories extend back to early childhood. This personality variety is a congruent one, coupling high activity with the enjoyment of that activity.

2. *The active-negative presidents.*   The Presidents with personalities of this classification are plagued with inconsistency and lack of congruence. Their high activity levels and low levels of enjoyment are indicative of intense effort and low emotional reward for that effort. Their work is spurred on simply by compulsion. These Presidents appear ambitious and

power seeking. They are aggressive and are tormented by a perfectionist conscience. They do not enjoy their tasks but respond with a high activity level to some inner need. Barber classifies Woodrow Wilson, Herbert Hoover, and Lyndon Johnson in this category. While at first glance these men appear to have little in common, close analysis reveals that they shared many of the same attributes. In spite of varying policy objectives, each pursued his duties with high levels of effort. Each was a driven man. Each refused to change when faced with impossible situations, thus demonstrating an inability to be flexible, practical, or compromising. And, of course, each ended his political career in a losing effort to impose his policy preferences on an unwilling nation. Wilson failed in his fight for United States admission to the League of Nations; Hoover failed to respond to economic chaos by modifying his laissez faire economic beliefs; and Johnson failed by escalating an unpopular and unsuccessful war.

3. *The passive-positive presidents.* Passive-positive executives are low on political activity, but receive a high degree of satisfaction from holding a political position. They have intense needs to be received well by others, become objects of affection, and have doubt dispelled by others. Hence, the passive-positive President is receptive, compliant, and other-directed. He rarely asserts himself, preferring to be agreeable and cooperative. He is a nonaggressive and quite fragile personality type. Passive-positive Presidents, like William Howard Taft, often have difficulty using advisers effectively, since their desire for loyalty and affection precludes any toleration of brutal frankness. Warren Harding was perhaps the passive-positive President in its ideal type. A totally compliant man, Harding was a friend to all, but close to few. He became a puppet of his advisers and longed for interpersonal affection. On the occasion of his death Charles Evans Hughes delivered a funeral oration to the House of Representatives in which he said, "President Harding had no ossification of the heart. He literally wore himself out in the endeavor to be friendly." [32] The passive-positive Presidents almost always fit the description of "a nice guy," but too often in presidential politics nice guys finish last.

4. *The passive-negative presidents.* The passive-negative President is low on both the activity and enjoyment dimensions. A President of this variety does little and what he does do provides him with almost no satisfaction. Individuals of this personality variety are usually withdrawn and have a pronounced tendency to avoid conflict. The key to the passive-negative personality is devotion to duty, a sense of obligation. While in office these men emphasize enforcing procedural niceties rather than substantive policy making. Barber classifies Calvin Coolidge as exemplary of the passive-negative President. Coolidge was never satisfied with the major obligations

of his work. He constantly felt busy and rushed, a feeling for which he compensated by rarely engaging in physical activity and permitting himself eleven hours of nightly sleep plus an afternoon nap. He stressed patience and refused to let himself become excited. Coolidge rarely wanted to be bothered by problems or conflict and therefore avoided these two un-pleasantries at all costs.

The research by Hargrove and Barber, along with the earlier bio-graphical case studies of individual Presidents, provides interesting insights into the presidential personality. But all suffer from a common method-ological weakness which is perhaps unavoidable. This weakness is the ex-clusive reliance on public records, previous biographical studies, speeches, and private papers. Such research is at the mercy of available materials. While some advances have been made in interpreting research materials of this variety,[33] no scholar has ever become sufficiently close to a President to attain a real measure of his personality. No President has undergone psychoanalytic testing for scholarly purposes, and it is quite doubtful that any President ever will. Therefore, students should be cautious when inter-preting psychological studies done from afar. There is too much room for the possibility of misinformation and misinterpretation by the scholar en-gaged in such research, no matter how objectively he pursues his analysis. This factor, of course, does not eliminate the total worth of such studies, but it is a limitation that should be noted.

Personality research focusing on the legislative branch has been less frequent than studies of the executive personality. Examinations of the legislative personality have also differed from those done on the Presidents by employing moderate-size groups of legislators rated on several person-ality dimensions. Unfortunately, the data base for such analyses has been generally confined to a single state legislative chamber.

Once again, James David Barber has been one of the leaders in apply-ing personality research to behavior and opinions of political elites.[34] Barber's analysis focused on newly elected members of the Connecticut state legislature. Through a lengthy interviewing process, Barber accumu-lated sufficient amounts of personality and career-related data about the freshmen legislators to enable him to classify his legislators into four basic types. Each legislative type is defined by its position on two major scales: activity level and willingness to return to the legislature for subsequent sessions. These four types of legislators—Spectators, Reluctants, Adver-tisers and Lawmakers—fell into different personality types and displayed corresponding variations in behavior during the legislative session.

1. *The spectator.* Barber defines the spectator as a legislator who has a low activity level but a high willingness to return. In terms of personality considerations, the spectator is other-directed with little sense of individual-

ity. He is plagued with a pervasive sense of personal inadequacy and unattractiveness. In order to accommodate his personality needs, the spectator engages in superficial socializing and vicarious participation. He enjoys watching the legislative rituals and being entertained by them and is psychically rewarded by membership in a prestigious group. The spectator contributes little to the substantive work of the legislature but adds to the ceremony, color, and traditions of that branch. Spectators tend to be middle aged, often female, with limited ambitions.

2. *The reluctant.*   Barber's reluctant is characterized by a low level of legislative activity and a disinclination to return. The reluctant's personality incorporates a strong moral sense of social responsibility. He feels duty bound to carry out the legislative tasks he had been assigned, but does not enjoy his work because of feelings of inadequacy and uselessness. He tends to withdraw from legislative conflict and to perform functions that increase harmony. He is bewildered by the complexities of the legislative process and the varied types of people with whom he must work. The reluctant, whose roots are generally in traditional, rural towns, embodies the values of his constituency. He is generally an elderly, retired person of moderate accomplishments who is carrying out what he perceives as an unpleasant civic duty.

3. *The advertiser.*   The advertiser is defined in Barber's analysis as the legislator who performs at a very high activity level, but has no intentions of remaining in public office for any significant period of time. The personality of the advertiser combines intense ambition, anxiety, suffering, and a sense of impotence. His goal in the legislature is occupational advancement. He displays a flurry of activity, making as many contacts as possible and attempting to capture the attention of the news media. The contacts and publicity are part of an overall strategy to enhance his occupational goals, which most frequently fall into categories such as law, insurance, and real estate. His whirlwind pace does not conform to legislative conceptions of the role of the freshman representative. His emphasis on activity for personal advancement rather than for legislative goals often causes a decrease in morale within the legislative chamber. The typical advertiser is a young, upward-mobile attorney who has experienced difficulties in his occupational activity. He tends to rise out of politically uncertain districts in which his constant level of activity impresses undecided voters.

4. *The lawmaker.*   The lawmaker is Barber's ideal legislator. He is defined as a representative with high levels of legislative activity and an exceptionally high interest in continuing in public office. His personality is well-

adjusted with a strong sense of self-identity. He prides himself on his rationality and self-control. The lawmaker's activity is directed at substantive goals rather than personal advancement. He has a conscious knowledge of important legislative concerns and does not become entranced with trivial or procedural details. He concentrates on bills and issues rather than on ceremony and ritual. The lawmaker, like the advertiser, is usually young and upwardly mobile. He tends to be spawned in an educated, moderately competitive district. He offers his constituents concern and competence over issues of interest to the district. The lawmaker is committed to political office and will continue to seek reelection until his ambitions move him to run for higher political office.

Barber's analysis provides an interesting approach to the subject of the legislative personality. It allows us to see how personality factors may affect political motivations, styles, and activity. The psychological needs of each type of representative prompt certain varieties of legislative behavior that are intended to satisfy those needs. Of course, Barber's study is far from a definitive work on the legislative personality. Its twofold classification system into four types of personalities is no doubt an over-simplification and the methodological techniques used do not allow for anything but the most shallow appraisal of a legislator's personality attributes. Nonetheless, Barber forcefully demonstrates the value of personality study in the process of understanding behavior in the legislative branch.

Attitudinal factors

ELITE-MASS
ATTITUDE DIFFERENCES

In previous sections of this chapter we have examined elite-mass differences in two areas of individual characteristics: social background experiences and personality factors. In both of these areas we have discovered distinguishing characteristics between leaders and followers. Meaningful differences between elites and masses also appear in the nature and intensity of the attitudinal positions held by each. It is to these differences that we now turn our attention.

The student will remember from earlier discussions on mass beliefs and opinions that we have defined the concept "attitude" as a cognition with valence and intensity. An attitude connotes a mental predisposition or action tendency. Individuals exhibit immediate mental reactions to such concepts as labor unions, the military, and communism. They react positively or negatively depending upon the valence attached to that particular concept. How strongly the individual reacts depends upon the intensity or strength of the attitude. A strong segregationist, for example, may react violently to the mere mention of the civil rights movement, whereas a racial moderate may evince only a mild response. Political elites and their attitudes may be described in this same fashion. What differences may exist between the attitudes and opinions of elites versus masses lies not in definitional considerations but along three basic dimensions: (1) the substantive content of the attitudes held; (2) the interconnection of various independent attitudes into what has become known as "belief systems"; and (3) the resistance of attitudes to change.

There have been relatively few studies of elite-mass differences in terms of attitude content, but the research conducted to date has indicated substantial variations between opinions held by leaders and followers.[35] At least three basic conclusions can be drawn from this research. First, elite opinion tends to differ from mass opinion both on basic attitudes toward democracy and on public policy issues. For example, on matters involving civil rights and liberties, political elites have been shown to be substantially more liberal than the general electorate. These differences extend to questions of procedural safeguards, freedom of expression, and democratic "rules of the game." Such differences may well be attributable to the fact that political elites are more completely immersed in governmental affairs and engage in much more thought about political matters than the masses. This increased involvement may well lead to a well thought out understanding of democratic principles, both in theory and in application.

Second, there are greater attitudinal differences between elites from competing political parties than among rank-and-file party members. A survey of elite and mass opinions on various policy areas revealed definite differences, but the degree of these differences depended greatly on political party identification. Differences between Democratic leaders and followers were relatively slight. On most of the issues where differences appeared, the Democratic elites tended to possess more progressive attitudes. An examination of Republican leaders and followers yielded entirely different results. Here the attitudinal gap between elites and masses was substantial. The Republican leadership was consistently more conservative than Republican voters. In fact, Republican voters' attitudes were often judged closer to the Democratic leadership than to the Republican. This finding supports the argument that where Republican party leaders cling to the economic policies of the business community and conservative intellectual philosophies of leaders such as the late Robert Taft, the party will continue to suffer loss of membership.

The third basic conclusion derived from these studies comparing elite and mass attitudes is that the opinions of political leaders are relatively more ordered and coherent than the attitudes held by the masses. Political leaders possess reasonably consistent attitude systems in which various beliefs and opinions form interconnected relationships. Members of the citizenry are much less likely to exhibit such well organized and consistent attitudinal systems.

This final conclusion has spurred recent interest in the subject of political belief systems.[36] Political scientists have defined a belief system as a configuration of ideas and attitudes in which the elements are bound together by some form of constraint or functional interdependence.[37] This interdependence or constraint means, for example, that if an individual holds attitudes strongly supportive of freedom of speech, he is likely to have similarly supportive attitudes toward other civil libertarian issues, such as constitutional rights for racial minorities. Constraint also dictates that when one element of the belief system is altered other elements must undergo a certain degree of change so that the system will be maintained. If, for example, our civil libertarian modifies his position on freedom of speech for some reason (say, for national security considerations) it is likely that his support for other provisions of the Bill of Rights will also diminish.

Each attitude or idea element within the belief system is accorded a certain degree of centrality which determines the importance of the element to the system as a whole. The crucial elements in a belief system lie at its very core. Alteration of these elements often causes radical modifications in the entire system. By contrast, attitude elements that exist on the periphery are not highly interrelated with other attitudes, and, therefore, major changes in them may require only minor modifications in the system.

There are at least three basic reasons for the existence of a highly constrained system of attitude elements.[38] The first cause of constraint is logical interdependence. An individual, for example, may have highly related attitudes toward government taxation and government expenditures simply because the two are logically related. Constraint based on logic presupposes, of course, that a person has devoted a good deal of thought to the potential interrelationships among various concepts and ideas. For this reason theorists have suggested that highly educated, intelligent, and active individuals are likely to possess highly constrained attitudes and opinions. Since political elites often fall into this class, it follows that they are more likely to possess highly constrained belief systems than are the masses. A Congressman who favors large tax cuts might logically be expected to opt for a reduction in government spending. The average citizen, on the other hand, may argue for both tax cuts and increased governmental services without realizing the logically interdependent character of these two policies.

Belief systems may also be held together by psychologically based constraint. Often groups of ideas or attitude elements not strictly linked appear to be rationally related because of certain psychological attachments. The liberal Jewish university student of the early 1970s who militantly protested U.S. bombing in the Indochina war and yet supported Israeli air strikes against the Arabs is an example of such psychologically based constraint. Although these two positions may seem logically incompatible, psychological constraint enables him to see both positions as consistent with certain principles of justice and humanity.

The third form of constraint has a social base. Certain idea elements are often highly correlated with an individual's social status. The American worker who has strong ties to the organized labor movement for example, will predictably possess the related attitude elements of support for minimum wage laws, the right to strike, collective bargaining, Social Security, and a host of similar positions. These elements may or may not be logically related. For example, many American workers, while espousing these forms of domestic liberalism, have strong feelings against communism and support aggressive United States military action. Many union members supported George Wallace in 1968 and 1972. While all of these attitude elements elude logical unity, they may make sense in terms of social constraint.

It has been generally assumed that elites are more likely to hold highly constrained, predictable belief systems than will the masses. Be the source of the constraint logic, psychological predispositions, or social ties, the elite may be better equipped to realize the interrelation of certain attitudes or ideas. Better education and broader experience make the elite more aware of the need for rationality and consistency in their attitudes and for modifying idea elements to achieve consistency. The initial studies designed to test the hypothesis that elites, because of education and political involvement, have more highly constrained political belief systems generally confirmed this proposition.[39] However, subsequent research efforts, particularly those dealing with local political leaders, did not find the expected elite-mass differences.[40]

Political attitudes among elites and masses also differ with respect to the phenomenon of attitude change. Political elites generally display stable, well thought out attitudes that tend to resist change. Elites are obviously more committed to their opinions and attitudes and cling to them more tenaciously than do the masses.[41] In addition to the relatively high levels of educational attainment, the reasons for the soundly entrenched character of elite attitudes is that they have been tested by experience, and found to be valid and valuable. As such they are not readily discarded. This means, practically, that political leaders will modify their attitudes only in response to change in environmental conditions or new information of a sufficiently compelling nature. Hence, attitude change among the elite is more rational and deliberate than among the citizenry who do not attach great importance to political matters and whose opinions are therefore subject to change in the face of low intensity stimuli. Attitude change among political elites may be characterized, then, as relatively deliberate, informed, and predictable, and likely to occur in a gradual and incremental fashion.[42]

To review, attitudinal differences between political elites and the masses can be found along three basic dimensions. First, pronounced differences in attitude content are apparent. Study after study has detected variation between leaders and followers in both the substantive nature of the attitudes held as well as the cognitive structuring of these attitudes. Second, there is substantial evidence to indicate elite-mass differences in belief system constraint. While support for this proposition is not as compelling as for the first, the preponderance of evidence suggests that the belief systems of political elites are more highly constrained than those of the masses. Third, elite attitudes are more resistant to change than mass attitudes. For the leader a political attitude is an important, relevant predisposition which guides his official behavior. Such guiding opinions are not easily swayed. For the masses political attitudes are peripheral in importance, and, therefore, readily subject to modification.

POLITICAL ATTITUDES AND ELITE BEHAVIOR

The study of elite attitudes would be a meaningless exercise if attitudes had no impact on political decision making. However, common knowledge alone tells us that attitudes affect behavior. In everyday life we make behavioral assumptions and predictions from known attitudes. For example, if a high school student knows that his English teacher has extremely negative attitudes toward athletics he is not likely to use the demands of football practice as an excuse for failing to complete an assigned essay. In a similar vein, a worker who realizes that his employer places a high value on promptness will take pains to arrive at work on time. These two commonplace examples demonstrate how people assume the connection between attitudes and behavior and alter their own actions based upon predicted attitudinal-behavioral responses.

When a citizen accepts public employment he does not leave behind his attitudes, opinions, or prejudices. Public servants respond in general conformance with their personal attitudes in the same ways citizens do. A police officer, for example, who has "progressive" attitudes toward moral offenses may well refrain from conducting an investigation of certain activities that have all the outward signs of prostitution. On the other hand, if police harbor negative feelings toward certain racial or ethnic groups they may enforce the law in a much more severe fashion in their relationships with these persons than with members of the dominant white majority.

The behavior of political elites is most definitely influenced by their attitudes. We might expect, then, that a state legislator with generally liberal attitudes toward social issues will support increased appropriations for aid-to-dependent children, education, and vocational rehabilitation. A mayor of conservative political leaning will predictably respond to rising crime rates by strengthening police rather than attacking the social ills that may be giving birth to the increasing criminality.

The degree to which attitudes affect the behavior of elites is an important empirical question which political scientists have long studied. For the most part, attitude studies have focused on the behavior of legislators and collegial court judges. The reason for this is basically a methodological one. A study of the relationship between attitudes and behavior can best be conducted when several of the elite are forced to respond to the same stimuli at the same point in time. In the United States Senate, for example, as many as 100 legislators vote on every proposed law that reaches the floor. On the Supreme Court nine judges reach decisions on each case docketed. These collective decision making situations allow for meaningful comparisons. If we knew certain political attitudes of members of the Senate we could compare the votes of, say, fiscal liberals and fiscal conservatives on issues such as a particular defense spending measure. We do not have such an advantage when analyzing unique decision making actions such as those of the President.

Studies of legislative behavior have consistently indicated that attitudes influence the way in which lawmakers conduct their business.[43] This influence has been difficult to observe directly, however, because of the close correspondence between attitudes and political party affiliation. Research has demonstrated, for example, that almost without exception Democratic candidates for Congress have more liberal attitudes on public policy issues than their intra-district Republican opposition.[44] It is not surprising therefore that, once elected, Democratic legislators have more liberal voting records than their Republican counterparts. Attitudes affect a legislator's behavior on a wide range of political issues, but these attitudes often coincide with the positions of his political party. We come full circle when we say that the political leader's choice of party is at least partially determined by his own attitudes—that he will gravitate to a party organization in which he can be ideologically comfortable. The political party as a membership and reference group for the politician molds and reinforces his opinions. Both party and attitude factors influence the legislator to the point where he exhibits highly predictable behavioral patterns.

In sum, research on legislative attitudes has demonstrated that political elites behave in a manner consistent with their predispositions. Along with political party and constituency demands, attitudes play a determining role in legislative behavior. Of course, certain issues are associated with more intense attitudes than others. Fiscal policy, social welfare, civil rights, governmental power, foreign policy, administration proposals, and morality issues are some of those on which legislators have strong predispositions to guide them in performing their lawmaking functions.

The judiciary provides a much different setting within which to study the attitude-behavior relationship. On the one hand, we might expect attitudes to play a minor role in judicial decision making. After all, a judge is supposed to be above prejudice and to hand down his decisions objectively. Judges are often thought to be bound by the restraints of law, tradition, and precedent. On the other hand, for most judges, political party affiliation no longer looms as important as perhaps it was prior to ascendance to the bench. Similarly, a judge may have no official constituency or district to serve. A federal judge, of course, need not worry about reelection and, therefore, will not feel obligated to comply with current public opinion. This line of reasoning might lead us to expect attitudes to be the primary guiding force behind judicial decisions. Somewhere between the objective impartial judge and the attitudinally biased judge lies the vast majority of American jurists. Just where between these two extremes *most* judges fall is a question to which judicial behavioralists have been addressing their efforts.[45]

There is little doubt that judges have attitudes and that these attitudes have some impact on their rulings. In almost every jurisdiction there are some judges who are known as "hanging judges," those who mete out criminal sentences with extreme severity. They do so because their personal attitudes prompt them to be harsh with criminal offenders. Federal Judge John Sirica who heard the 1972–1974 Watergate political espionage cases has earned the informal title of "Maximum John," referring to his well-deserved reputation for handing out maximum sentences to criminal offenders. Conversely, many other judges are known as "soft" because they are lenient with the criminally accused.

There is, of course, always a certain degree of attitudinal variation among judges sitting together on collegial courts. For example, as the United States Supreme Court entered the 1970s the ideologies espoused by the Justices included almost every philosophical position. There existed a solid liberal block made up of Justices William Douglas, William Brennan, and Thurgood Marshall. Of these three, Douglas holds the most ideologically extreme position. He has often expressed views from the bench and in his writings which make his liberal learnings patently clear. In 1970, for example, Douglas in reference to contemporary America wrote:

Violence has no constitutional sanction; and every government from the beginning has moved against it.

But where grievances pile high and most of the elected spokesmen represent the Establishment, violence may be the only effective response.[46]

An opposing group of Nixon-appointed conservatives has offset the liberal contingent from the Warren Court years. The most extreme conservatives have been Chief Justice Warren Burger and Justice William Rehnquist. Rehnquist has long been engaged in conservative causes. Not only was he active in the Goldwater presidential campaign of 1964, but as a law clerk for Justice Jackson in 1952–53 he has been said to have urged the Justice to vote to maintain the "separate, but equal" doctrine which was later struck down by a unanimous Court in the 1954 *Brown v. Board of Education* decision.

If personal attitudes make a difference in judicial decision making, we would expect judges to vote in accordance with their personal values and to be joined by other justices who have similar attitudes. The recent history of the Supreme Court clearly demonstrates this to be the case. The conservative and liberal blocs on the Court often divide along ideological lines. Douglas and Rehnquist vote together only when the case before the Court is so clear that a unanimous or nearly unanimous verdict results.

Political scientists who have examined decision making processes in federal courts from an attitude theory perspective have argued that most judicial decisions can be explained on the basis of two general attitudes.[47] The first of these is the judge's position on issues involving a conflict between personal rights and governmental authority. This includes such questions as political freedom, equality, religious liberty, privacy, and criminal due process. A judge's civil liberties attitudes indicate how much personal freedom he will allow before he thinks governmental interference is justifiable. For example, on censorship matters Judge X may define obscenity only in terms of the most hardcore pornography imaginable and consequently rule to protect freedom of expression from governmental restraint in almost every instance. Judge Y, on the other hand, may feel that any form of nudity is obscene and therefore would uphold governmental restrictions on any suggestive books, movies, or magazines. The differences between the two judges reduce simply to dissimilar attitudes toward personal freedom. The second general attitude dimension represents the judge's attitudes toward economic matters. A liberal economic attitude means that the judge normally favors the interests of the economically underprivileged and is opposed to disproportionate accumulation of wealth and economic power. A judge possessing such liberal attitudes would tend to favor the legal interests of labor unions and consumers, as well as be sympathetic to government regulation of big business. By knowing a judge's attitudinal positions on personal liberty and economic questions, we are able to understand and to predict decisions more accurately.

There is little doubt that attitudes affect judicial behavior in much the same manner as they affect the behaviors of other governmental elites, or of the masses for that matter. That political elites respond to their personal attitudes in conducting their official duties is not necessarily an improper or disturbing thing. Many attitudes are based upon experience, education, and knowledge. Attitudes need not be associated with invidious bias or prejudice. Rather they should be seen as guiding principles or predispositions. Successful political elites tend to have stable attitudes that lend consistency to their official behavior. This in turn makes their behavior more predictable; and consistent behavior (i.e., predictability) enables an informed electorate to rely on the product it is directly or indirectly purchasing with its votes.

Summary

In this chapter we have examined three formative influences upon the opinions and behavior of political elites: social backgrounds, personalities, and attitudes. These internalized forces constantly influence the way in which political elites carry out their duties. They are forces which the political leader cannot totally shed. He may take actions to reduce the impact which these personal characteristics have on him. He may even take action to change certain aspects of these characteristics. But at any given point in time background experiences, personality traits, and attitudinal predispositions weigh heavily in his decision making processes.

Two major points are made in this chapter. The first is that with respect to each of these three personal characteristics there exist substantial differences between elites and masses. Perhaps the greatest discrepancies can be found along the social background dimension. Elites tend to be more highly educated, from higher status social and occupational backgrounds, and more knowledgeable and interested in politics. They are older and a disproportionate number of them are male, Caucasian, and Protestant.

In terms of personality characteristics, elites have been said to possess a greater need to hold and exercise power. The political elite, more than the average citizen, must have a high tolerance for political risks. He must have sufficient ego strength to believe that he is more qualified than his opponents and to repel personally directed attacks. He must be sufficiently extroverted to place himself constantly in the public view. He is normally highly motivated and ambitious.

There is also substantial variation between elites and masses on the attitude dimension. Elites tend to give greater support to democratic principles and procedural safeguards. They appear to be more libertarian and tolerant. Furthermore, their attitudes are characteristically more stable and consistent, reflecting highly constrained belief systems. This factor prevents their being swayed by arbitrary influences or momentary environmental changes.

The second major point made in this chapter is that the personal attributes of elites affect opinions and decision making. Where there exists substantial variation among elites along the lines of individual characteristics, there will also be variations in behavior.

Social background experiences often have an impact upon political decision making and the behavior of elites. Whatever stimuli a leader perceives are evaluated according to his background experiences. We know that social class, political party affiliation, occupational background, age, and religious preference all have an impact on elite behavior. This is because these general background experiences provide criteria against which to judge political questions and weigh political events.

Personality factors likewise affect the opinions and behavior of elites. Personality needs, temperament, ego strength, and rigidity all have an impact on how a particular leader will carry out his responsibilities. Furthermore, personality will guide him in constructing role preferences which are appropriate to his perception of his office.

The most direct link between the personal characteristics of elites and their behavior is probably found in the attitude-behavior relationship. If a legislator evaluates the civil rights movement favorably, places a high value on education, and abhors war, his voting record will undoubtedly reflect these attitudinal positions at least to a certain degree. Political officials have strong feelings on issues such as fiscal policy, foreign affairs, social welfare needs, and civil liberties. Usually the behavior of political leaders is consistent with these predispositions.

Knowledge of the influences of individual characteristics on elite behavior is crucial to an adequate understanding of the functioning of elites in the public opinion-public policy process. But personal attributes are not the only forces to have an impact on elite opinion and behavior. Another set of influences can be found within the context of the elite establishment itself. In order to examine these forces, we will now turn our attention to the institutional setting in which the political elite operate.

NOTES

[1] See, for example, Irving Louis Horowitz, ed., *Power, Politics and People: The Collected Essays of C. Wright Mills* (New York: Oxford University Press, 1963).

[2] For excellent discussions of the social backgrounds of American political elites see Malcolm E. Jewell and Samuel C. Patterson, *The Legislative Process in the United States,* 2nd ed. (New York: Random House, 1973); John R. Schmidhauser, "The Justices of the Supreme Court: A Collective Portrait," *Midwest Journal of Political Science,* 3 (February 1959), 1–57; Kenneth Prewitt, *The Recruitment of Political Leaders* (Indianapolis: Bobbs-Merrill, 1970); and Charles W. Wiggins and William L. Turk, "State Party Chairman: A Profile," *Western Political Quarterly,* 23 (June 1970), 324.

[3] Donald R. Matthews, *The Social Backgrounds of Political Decision-Makers* (New York: Doubleday, 1954), p. 30.

[4] For an excellent treatment of this entire subject see Heinz Eulau and John D. Sprague, *Lawyers in Politics* (Indianapolis: Bobbs-Merrill, 1964). See also Joseph A. Schlesinger, "Lawyers and American Politics: A Clarified View," *Midwest Journal of Political Science,* 1 (May 1957), 26–39.

[5] 274 U.S. 200 (1927).

[6] Charles Beard, *An Economic Interpretation of the Constitution of the United States* (New York: Macmillan, 1913).

[7] See, for example, Jewell and Patterson, *The Legislative Process in the United States,* esp. ch. 17.

[8] See, for example, Stuart S. Nagel, "Political Party Affiliation and Judges' Decisions," *American Political Science Review,* 55 (December 1961), 844–50; S. Sidney Ulmer, "The Political Party Variable in the Michigan Supreme Court," *Journal of Public Law,* 11, No. 2 (1962), 352–62; and Glendon Schubert, *Quantitative Analysis of Judicial Behavior* (New York: The Free Press, 1959).

[9] See David Adamany, "The Party Variable in Judges' Voting: Conceptual Notes and a Case Study," *American Political Science Review,* 63 (March 1969), 57–73; Thomas G. Walker, "A Note Concerning Partisan Influences on Trial Judge Decision-Making," *Law and Society Review,* 6 (May 1972), 645–49.

[10] Charles F. Andrain, "Senators' Attitudes Toward Civil Rights," *Western Political Quarterly,* 17 (September 1964), 496.

[11] Eulau and Sprague, *Lawyers in Politics.*

[12] David R. Derge, "The Lawyer as Decision-Maker in the American State Legislature," *Journal of Politics,* 21 (August 1959), 408–33.

[13] Justin J. Green, John R. Schmidhauser, Larry L. Berg, and David Brady, "Lawyers in Congress: A New Look at Some Old Assumptions," *Western Political Quarterly,* 26 (September 1973), 440–52.

[14] Derge, "The Lawyer as Decision-Maker . . .".

[15] See Harold D. Lasswell, *Psychopathology and Politics* (Chicago: University of Chicago Press, 1930) and *Power and Personality* (New York: W. W. Norton & Company, 1948).

[16] See, for example, Gordon J. DiRenzo, *Personality, Power and Politics* (Notre Dame, Indiana: University of Notre Dame Press, 1967).

[17] See Robert A. Dahl, *Who Governs?* (New Haven: Yale University Press, 1961), esp. ch. 19.

[18] Lasswell, *Power and Personality,* p. 22.

[19] Ibid., p. 54.

[20] Alexander L. George, "Power as a Compensatory Value for Political Leaders," *Journal of Social Issues,* 24 (July 1968), 29–49; see also Alexander and Juliette George, *Woodrow Wilson and Colonel House* (New York: John Day, 1956).

[21] Rufus P. Browning and Herbert Jacob, "Power Motivation and the Political Personality," *Public Opinion Quarterly,* 28 (Spring 1964), 75–90.

[22] John B. McConaughy, "Certain Personality Factors of State Legislators in South Carolina," *American Political Science Review,* 44 (December 1950), 897–903.

[23] See, for example, Fred I. Greenstein, *Personality and Politics* (Chicago: Markham Publishing Company, 1969); and Gordon J. DiRenzo, ed., *Personality and Politics* (New York: Anchor Press, 1974).

[24] Herbert McClosky, "Conservatism and Personality," *American Political Science Review,* 52 (March 1958), 27–45.

[25] See, for example, R. A. Schoenberger, "Conservatism, Personality, and Political Extremism," *American Political Science Review,* 62 (September 1968), 868–77.

[26] See, for example, M. Rokeach, *The Open and Closed Mind* (New York: Basic Books, 1960); and DiRenzo, *Personality, Power and Politics.*

[27] For example, George and George, *Woodrow Wilson and Colonel House;* and Arnold Rogow, *James Forrestal: A Study of Personality, Politics and Policy* (New York: Macmillan, 1963).

[28] See Greenstein, *Personality and Politics.*

[29] Richard E. Neustadt, *Presidential Power* (New York: John Wiley & Sons, 1960).

[30] Erwin C. Hargrove, *Presidential Leadership: Personality and Political Style* (New York: Macmillan, 1960).

[31] James David Barber, *The Presidential Character: Predicting Performance in the White House* (Englewood Cliffs, N.J.: Prentice-Hall, 1972).

[32] Quoted in Barber, *The Presidential Character,* p. 191.

[33] See, for example, Richard E. Donley and David G. Winter, "Measuring the Motives of Public Officials at a Distance: An Exploratory Study of American Presidents," *Behavioral Science,* 15 (May 1970), 227–36.

[34] James David Barber, *The Lawmakers* (New Haven: Yale University Press, 1965).

[35] See, for example, Samuel A. Stouffer, *Communism, Conformity and Civil Liberties* (Gloucester, Mass.: Peter Smith, 1963); Herbert McClosky, "Consensus and Ideology in American Politics," *American Political Science Review,* 58 (June 1964), 361–82; Herbert McClosky, Paul J. Hoffman, and Rosemary O'Hara, "Issue Conflict and Consensus among Party Leaders and Followers," *American Political Science Review,* 54 (June 1960), 406–27.

[36] For a review of the various approaches to the concept of belief systems and related research see Roger W. Cobb, "The Belief-Systems Perspective: An Assessment of a Framework," *Journal of Politics,* 35 (February 1973), 121–53.

[37] Philip E. Converse, "The Nature of Belief Systems in Mass Publics," in *Ideology and Discontent,* ed. David Apter (New York: The Free Press, 1964), p. 207.

[38] Ibid., pp. 209–13.

[39] Ibid.

[40] Norman Luttbeg, "The Structure of Beliefs among Leaders and the Public," *Public Opinion Quarterly,* 32 (Fall 1968), 398–409.

[41] See John H. Kessel, "Cognitive Dimensions and Political Activity," *Public Opinion Quarterly,* 29 (Fall 1965), 377–89; Robert S. Hirschfield, Bert E. Swanson, and Blanche D. Blank, "A Profile of Political Activists in Manhattan," *Western Political Quarterly,* 15 (September 1962), 489–506.

[42] Bernard C. Hennessy, *Public Opinion,* 2nd ed. (Belmont, Calif.: Wadsworth Publishing Co., Inc., 1970), p. 386.

[43] Duncan MacRae, *Dimensions of Congressional Voting* (Berkeley: University of California Press, 1958); see also Lee Anderson, "Variability in the Unidimensionality of Legislative Voting," *Journal of Politics,* 26 (August 1964), 568–85; Warren E. Miller and Donald E. Stokes, "Constituency Influence in Congress," *American Political Science Review,* 57 (March 1963), 45–56; and Samuel C. Patterson, "Dimensions of Voting Behavior in a One-Party Legislature," *Public Opinion Quarterly,* 26 Summer 1962), 185–200.

[44] John L. Sullivan and Robert E. O'Connor, "Electoral Choice and Popular Control of Public Policy: The Case of the 1966 House Elections," *American Political Science Review,* 66 (December 1972), 1256–68.

[45] See, for example, Stuart S. Nagel, *The Legal Process from a Behavioral Perspective* (Homewood, Ill.: The Dorsey Press, 1969), ch. 16; S. Sidney Ulmer, "Supreme Court Behavior and Civil Rights," *Western Political Quarterly,* 13 (June 1960), 288–311.

[46] William O. Douglas, *Points of Rebellion* (New York: Vintage, 1970), pp. 88–89.

[47] See, for example, Glendon Schubert, *The Judicial Mind* (Evanston, Ill.: Northwestern University Press, 1965).

ELITE OPINION
AND POLITICAL
DECISION MAKING:
INSTITUTIONAL FACTORS

8

Research on the personal characteristics of political elites reveals a great deal about the opinions and behavior of governmental officials. If leaders acted alone or in a social vacuum, our knowledge of their personal attributes would be sufficient. But this, of course, is not the case. The policy making process is conducted in a social atmosphere. Elites must constantly interact with other elites as well as with members of the general population. The policy making process takes place within political institutions. These institutions are structured by law, tradition, and the various individuals holding political office. The many forces operative within these institutions have an impact on the opinions and behavior of political elites. These forces act at various times either to modify or to reinforce the previously existing propensities of elite incumbents. For these reasons we need to extend our study beyond the personal characteristics of elites and into the institutional context in which elites function.

In this chapter we will analyze the influence of the institutional setting on elite opinion and decision making by examining three basic institutional factors: roles, norms, and group interaction. A discussion of political roles will demonstrate the influence on the policy making process provided by expectations of how elites *should* behave. Knowledge of institutional norms will reveal the informal "rules of the game" which prescribe the manner in which politics is practiced within different governmental settings. From an analysis of the group interaction process we will gain an understanding of how relationships among political elites affect opinions and behavior.

Institutional roles

THE CONCEPT OF ROLE

Social scientists have occasionally developed theories of political behavior based upon the conceptualizations and language of other fields of human endeavor. Role theory is based upon such a hybrid of theoretical crossbreeding.[1] It uses the language of the theater to explain behavior in the political sphere.

In the theater an actor is assigned a part or role to portray. The final outcome of that role is determined by many individual expectations. In the first place, the words and actions of the actor are shaped by the playwright. It is he who initially creates the play itself and the interrelationships among the various roles therein. His play is written with the expectation that each of the parts will convey the message he intends. The portrayal of the role also depends upon the producer and director. These individuals guide the behavior of the actor in order to fulfill not only the perceived expectations of the playwright, but also their own expectations. The actor who is cast in a particular part also contributes to the final outcome of the role. We often speak of a certain actor's interpretation of a role. By this, of course, we mean that the actor's expectations of how the role should be played are translated into his characterization. Finally, it is important to consider the expectations of the public; or perhaps more accurately, the expectations of the theater-going public. If the portrayal of the role violates the expectations of these relevant publics the play will not be a success.

Because the expectations of all the participants in a play have an impact upon its presentation, each time the play is produced the quality of the drama changes. A variation in actor, producer, or director means a change in the manner in which the intentions of the playwright are portrayed by the characters. Although the script itself may not change, the expectations of the individuals controlling the play do.

In society we all assume roles similar in nature to those in the theater. These roles are shaped by the expectations of a host of individuals and institutions. For example, societies often have well-defined sex roles. Traditionally in the United States expectations of what constitutes proper behavior on the part of males and females have differed sharply. As children, boys play with toy guns, trucks, and athletic equipment whereas girls play with dolls. Boys are trained to be aggressive and rational; girls are expected to be submissive and emotional. Males are supposed to grow up to be lawyers and doctors and secondarily fathers; females are told to be mothers first and secondarily nurses and secretaries. Males are expected to be intelligent and females not so intelligent. Male students are supposed to excel in mathematics, females in language arts. Individuals respond to these pervasive if arbitrary societal expectations. Women, for example, have often concealed their intellectual abilities while playing the role of "available mate." Even though Americans have begun to reevaluate male and female roles, societal expectations remain a strong force.

A role, then, consists of a set of generally accepted normative expectations connected to a particular societal position. An essential element in the concept of role is that the expectations are associated with a position and not a person. All individuals who hold a given role position are subjected to similar expectations regardless of their differing personalities and backgrounds. For example, we have certain expectations of the role of physician which we ascribe to all medical doctors. If a given practitioner fails to live up to our expectations, we will probably respond by terminating our doctor-patient relationship. This, however, does not preclude the possibility of slightly differing expectations associated with individuals holding the same position.

Possible variations in the way in which persons define their roles are important to our understanding of political roles. We refer to the way in which an individual views his role as a *role perception* or *role orientation*. An implicit assumption in role theory is that individuals with differing role perceptions will behave differently. For example, we would expect a policeman who perceives the primary purpose of his job in terms of police-community relations to carry out his law enforcement duties much differently than an officer whose role orientation focuses on the apprehension of criminals. In applying role theory to political phenomena, we would anticipate that public officials would perform their functions in line with their perceptions of the way in which their offices should be conducted.

By a political role, then, we are referring to a coherent set of normative expectations which apply to all persons occupying a particular political position.[2] A given political role is constituted by the sum total of all expectations including those of the political actor himself.[3] For example, there are definite expectations in the United States relating to the position of judge. The public has expectations of how a judge should behave; the bar has certain expectations of judicial conduct; and the judges themselves provide definitions of the role. When all these expectations are combined we have the "role of judge," which includes the prescriptions and proscriptions to be followed by the occupants of that position.

Role theory is a useful means of understanding the opinions and behavior of political elites. It assists us in explaining how the political leader acts and reacts within his institutional milieu. Because political roles are tied to specific institutional positions, we should examine the applicability of role theory within particular institutional contexts. Specifically, we will analyze leadership, legislative, executive, and judicial roles.

LEADERSHIP ROLES

Carl Friedrich has argued that there are three primary functions of political leadership: to initiate, to maintain, and to protect.[4] Initiating leadership is innovative in character. It moves a society to accept new attitudes and ideals; it urges a nation to conquer new goals; and it promotes creative public policies to alleviate societal problems and improve existing conditions. Its primary emphasis is on progress and change. Maintaining leadership is essentially conservative in nature. It upholds the established order and uses avenues of political action which the people find familiar. Maintaining leadership, rather than urging acceptance of new values, stresses fundamental and traditional beliefs. Of utmost importance to maintaining leadership is the stabilization of political order. Protecting leadership sees as its goal the prevention of destruction, either physically or culturally. Rather than simply urging a conservative course, protecting leadership is willing to take severe action against any internal or external forces which threaten the destruction of a society or its way of life. In return for provided security the followers of this type of leadership offer passive allegiance and allow almost total discretion to the leadership.

The necessity of all three leadership functions should be apparent. In the best of all possible worlds political elites would provide each function in exactly the proper proportions: exerting creative leadership to solve problems, conserving the beneficial aspects of the political order, and insuring against physical and cultural violence. If this proper mixture were attained on a regular basis, we could declare the government a responsible one. But human leadership rarely works with perfection. In most instances one of the functions becomes clearly dominant and in many elections the voters must choose between candidates who emphasize differing leadership functions.

In performing their leadership duties, political officials will often conceptualize their obligations in terms of these three forms of leadership. How politicians perceive the leadership role at least partially determines the character of the campaigns they wage and the policy objectives they will pursue once in office.

An excellent example of this situation occurred during the 1968 presidential campaign. In this election the roles were played by Humphrey the Innovator, Nixon the Maintainer, and Wallace the Protector. Senator Hubert Humphrey, the Democratic nominee, proposed a reasonably innovative program to cope with the nation's ills. While many liberals claimed that Humphrey did not go far enough in calling for fundamental change, particularly in the area of foreign policy, the programs he supported were essentially initiating in character. This, of course, was in line with Humphrey's political history, built upon his long record as one of the most creative minds in the United States Senate. Republican Richard Nixon's proposals were basically conservative. His campaign speeches were often based upon the theme of bringing Americans together again. He deplored the preceding eight years of Democratic control of the Presidency as moving too far, too fast. In much the same vein as Warren Harding's 1920 campaign, Nixon urged a return to normalcy, stressing traditional basic values such as the sanctity of the family, free enterprise, and dependence on the deity. Alabama Governor George Wallace, nominee of the American Independent party, argued for increased governmental actions to provide for the security of Americans. He stressed law and order at home and urged support for military victories abroad. In the classic protector fashion he found the domestic scene replete with subversives and saw the nation's security endangered by external communism. The response of the electorate favored the Republican candidate, preferring the nation to slow down and re-secure its ties to traditional moorings before launching another round of rapid progress.

LEGISLATIVE ROLES

The role of legislator is one which is reasonably well defined in our society. The American political culture has provided long-enduring expectations regarding the legislative function. As far as the general public is concerned the prescriptions attached to the legislative role are somewhat vague, but nonetheless firmly established. A legislator is basically expected to fulfill two functions: to legislate and to represent. These functions, of course, entail a great many corollary expectations. A legislator is expected to listen to his constituents, keep abreast of constituency problems, vote for legislation that will be beneficial to the nation as well as the representative's own district, and to provide some sort of political leadership. The public is also in general accord as to legislative proscriptions. A member of Congress or a delegate to the state legislature is expected to refrain from corruption and immorality, to be relatively aloof from the pressures exerted by lobbyists, not to accept bribes, and not to become too rich too fast. If these normative expectations are violated the public will cease to accord its support to the legislator at reelection time. The reason for such an electoral rejection is that the citizenry has become convinced, either by the incumbent's own behavior or in response to the urgings of an opponent, that the expectations of the legislative role have not been fulfilled.

The loosely defined expectations of the electorate are in contrast with the sharply delineated expectations provided by the legislative institutions themselves. Each legislative chamber has its own code of informal rules or norms which governs behavior within that legislative assembly. These unwritten codes impose expectations as to the relationship between the legislator and his party, constituency, colleagues, lobbyists, and other governmental elites. They govern the content and frequency of participation in legislative deliberations and structure the representative's legislative work. While we will examine the specific impact of these legislative norms in subsequent sections of this chapter, it is important to note here that the general expectations of the public and the more specific norms of the relevant legislative institution combine to define the role of legislator in this society.

Occupants of the legislative position must give life to this particular political role by imposing their own perceptions of how a legislator should behave within the bounds set by the political culture and the relevant lawmaking body. The interpretation supplied by the political actor cannot be general in scope but must be sufficiently specific to meet the daily demands of the office. The legislator must reach a judgment as to what he considers to be proper behavior in each of the many aspects of his official life.

The legislative role, like many societal roles, is made up of several components. These components are known as *role sectors*. Each sector represents a specific dimension of the role; and in each role sector the individual may have a specific orientation. Several role sectors and corresponding role perceptions have been identified with respect to legislators.[5] For purposes of illustration we will briefly discuss four of these role sectors which have particular relevance to the public opinion process.[6] The first two deal with constituency relationships and the second two with organized political groups.

Areal roles. One of the more important role sectors involves the problem of what the legislator believes he should represent; that is, what comprises his constituency. This constituency or areal role is concerned with the question of representational focus. Usually this question has two possible alternatives: (1) does the legislator see his own district as the subject of his representational efforts; or (2) does he see the broader polity (i.e., the entire nation; or, in the case of a state legislator, the entire state) as his representational concern? It is a restatement of the perennial battle of representational theory between local and national interests. If a legislator sees his district as the primary focus of his representational activities, he will expend a great deal of effort attempting to determine the opinions of the people in his home district. On the other hand, a nation (or state) oriented representative will pay greater heed to the will of the entire citizenry rather than the feelings of his specific district. Some legislators may in fact attempt to mix the district–nation role perceptions. They may do this by giving a certain amount of weight to both interests or perhaps by switching roles from issue to issue. For example, a southern senator may follow a national constituency role on economic issues but switch to a district orientation on civil rights matters.

One of the most compelling factors in the legislator's selection of a constituency role orientation is the extent of political competition in his home district. Studies of both Congressmen [7] and state legislators [8] have found that the more competitive the district is the greater the tendency to select a district orientation. This, of course, makes intuitive sense. If a representative's reelection chances are marginal, he will undoubtedly respond by catering to the opinions of his home constituency. On the other hand, the legislator with reelection assured can afford to pursue the more statesmanlike national (or state) representational focus.

Representational roles. A role sector closely related to areal considerations is the representational role.[9] This aspect of legislative life encompasses the variations in representational style. The two polar positions on this dimension are those legislators who carry out their representational function by molding their behavior in close correspondence to the views of their constituents ("delegates") and those who conduct their representational activities by following their own consciences and beliefs ("trustees"). Between these two extremes is the "politico" who combines delegate and trustee representational traits. The delegate perceives his representational obligations in terms of expressing the views of his constituents and not his own opinions. The delegate downplays the possibility of discretion in his official behavior. Instead, he follows the instructions given him by the people he represents. He often will go to great lengths to determine the majority position in his district and he then will exactly follow that majority sentiment. The trustee, however, feels that his election was a mandate from his constituents to use his own judgment and to follow his own analysis of situations as they arise. His notion of representation is not to replicate majority public opinion, but to use his own evaluations of issues and bills, and then to stand on the strength of his record. The politico pursues the middle ground. He may weigh his own feelings against those of his constituents or he may alternate trustee and delegate positions from issue to issue.

The determinants of representational role orientations have received considerable attention, and several findings have emerged.[10] First, there is a clear relationship between constituency and representational roles. As might be expected, legislators who have a district representational focus have a tendency to adopt the delegate role. Legislators who view their constituency as the entire nation (or state) tend to accept the trustee role. Second, the more competitive the legislator's district the more frequently the representative will opt for the delegate role. Third, there is a slight tendency for Republicans to favor the delegate role and Democrats to accept the politico position. And finally, the greater a legislator's seniority, the more likely he is to adopt the trustee role. While most of these suggested determinants of representational role variations are far from proven, they do constitute interesting patterns and provide a general profile of trustees, delegates, and politicos.

Interest group roles.   A representative's relationship with lobbyists, termed his "interest group role," is often quite significant. The stance a legislator assumes here reveals his perceptions of the value of pressure group activity and the limits which should be placed on the behavior of lobbyists. Three basic role orientations emerge from this sector of legislative activity. They are based upon a legislator's response to two questions: (1) how much does the legislator actually know about lobbyists and pressure groups; and (2) are his attitudes toward such private interests favorable or hostile? The "facilitator" role is played by a representative who is knowledgeable about lobby groups and has a friendly attitude toward them. Generally he recognizes the beneficial effects of pressure group activity in providing information, legislative assistance, and functional representation. He works in cooperation with interest group representatives whenever such cooperation is mutually beneficial. The "resister" is knowledgeable about interest groups but harbors hostile attitudes toward them. He may view interest groups as dysfunctional, unrepresentative forces which impose their power in order to encourage the passage of legislation favorable to their membership at the expense of the public good. The "neutral" is characterized either as having little knowledge about pressure groups or as not possessing intense attitudes in any direction regarding the lobbying process.

A number of variables have been found to be associated with the choice of interest group role orientation. First, partisan differences tend to emerge.[11] Republicans are generally more favorable toward interest groups than Democrats. Republicans rarely fall into the resister category, whereas Democrats commonly do. Senior Democratic Congressmen from safe districts are the most hostile to interest groups. Second, educational level is related to interest group role orientation.[12] Increased educational attainment is associated with a propensity to select the facilitator role. Legislators with lower educational levels tend to opt for the neutral or resister positions. These differences may be attributable to the fact that increased education prompts a greater understanding of the complexities of modern societal and economic systems and the beneficial role interest groups may play in the governmental process. Increased education may also contribute to the breakdown of the stereotyped view of the lobbyist as a high pressure, frequently unethical evangelist for monied ·special interests.

Party roles.   Because of the pervasiveness of political party influences in American legislatures, a representative's activities with respect to his partisan colleagues is particularly significant. A legislator's party role orientation includes his perceptions of the extent to which partisan considerations should constitute criteria for his official behavior, the degree to which party is seen as a relevant reference group, and the status of party loyalty and unity in the legislator's value scheme. A "party man" is a legislator who has a high degree of attachment to his political party. He perceives his legislative duties in terms of supporting the programs and policies backed by his political party. He feels obliged to vote in favor of party sponsored bills with little interjection of his own opinions and despite possibly harmful consequences. To the "party indifferent," partisan considerations are unimportant. Just because a given issue position is supported by his political party does not mean that the party indifferent will assume that posture. In fact, party programs and platforms have little salience whatever. Instead, the party indifferent perceives his job as representing his constituency independent of party considerations. The "maverick" role orientation is centered on the belief that independence from party line behavior is not only acceptable but something of value. The maverick pursues his legislative tasks with total independence from party direction. He may often vote in line with party positions, but not because of party loyalty or partisan attachments. He does so only because he independently agrees with his party's position. Unlike the party man, the maverick has no qualms about voting with the opposition party and may do so on a regular basis.

The distribution of party role orientations varies widely. In fact, we can make few accurate generalizations about the frequency of each of these role orientations. This wide variation is caused by a number of factors. First, the general political culture existing in the several states contributes to the lack of uniformity. Some state cultures place a premium on political party attachments and, therefore, tend to produce a large number of party men. Other states, like Wisconsin and Oregon, have long traditions of supporting party mavericks. Second, the tradition and organization of the legislature itself is a significant factor in party role acquisition. The United States Congress, for example, has long stressed the importance of political parties. Research on Congress has discovered what might be expected from an institution with such a tradition—a large proportion of party men (60 percent), out of which a significant portion are "superloyalists" to their parties, and relatively few mavericks (19 percent).[13] Third, the legislator's district has an impact on the party role he selects. The more a district is atypical of party strongholds and the closer the legislator's election margin, the lesser the probability that he will adopt the party man role orientation. The legislator in such a situation naturally responds by becoming more concerned with constituency problems and placing less importance upon party matters. Finally, party status within the legislature affects party role orientations. A majority party is much more likely to intensify efforts to promote party unity, thus increasing the number of party men. The minority party, however, has relatively little to gain from strict unity and, therefore, may encompass larger numbers of party indifferents and mavericks.

EXECUTIVE ROLES

The important theoretical and empirical research that has been conducted on legislative roles has no counterpart in studies of the executive branch. Neither Presidents nor governors have easily yielded to role analysis. This is perhaps due to two important methodological considerations. First, the basic technique used in other role investigations has been the personal interview. Structured discussion with political elites is the best means yet developed to tap the role perceptions of political leaders. But as we have noted in earlier sections of this book, gaining scholarly access to chief executives is quite difficult. No President is likely to submit himself to a battery of opinion inventories administered by a political scientist. Second, the limited number of chief executives restricts comparative research efforts. While these factors have retarded the growth of role theory as applied to the executive branch, they do not discount the potential role theory may hold for understanding the behavior of Presidents and other political executives.

Specific executive role orientations may not be well defined or empirically verified, but the various role sectors of a chief executive's position can be stipulated. The President's perceptions and expectations about certain facets of his office are unquestionably important; e.g., the manner in which specified duties and obligations are to be fulfilled or powers to be exercised. Knowledge of these matters may provide a great deal of insight into a specific administration. In this section we will briefly discuss three such role sectors relevant to the Presidency.

Power roles. In our discussion of presidential personalities in Chapter Seven we noted that the President's personality has an impact on the entire executive branch. A similar point can be made about the chief executive's perception of the power of his office. How a President conceives the limitations and restraints on his power is translated into the way he exercises power both directly and indirectly through those agencies which come under his purview. A President's role orientation toward the power sector of his office has probably exhibited as many variations as there have been Presidents, but two general types tend to emerge. The first is the President who feels that the powers of his office extend to all actions not specifically denied him by the Constitution and the laws of the land. Presidents such as Andrew Jackson, Theodore Roosevelt, and Franklin Roosevelt generally conceived of presidential power in this way. It is Abraham Lincoln, however, who is often accorded the distinction of being a pure activist. Lincoln went so far as to argue that even unconstitutional measures could legitimately be taken by the President in order to preserve the nation.[14] President Richard Nixon's argument that electronic surveillance activities, ordinarily judged unconstitutional, might be justified on grounds of national security also expounds an expansionist view of presidential power. The second role orientation sees presidential power only in terms of that authority specifically granted by the nation's Constitution and laws. This of course, is a much more limited view of power. Examples of Presidents holding this more restricted view of their office would include James Buchanan, William Howard Taft, and Herbert Hoover.

Lawmaking roles. The lawmaker role orientation of the President has become increasingly important during this century. From a meager constitutional power to recommend and report to Congress and to veto congressional acts, history has thrust upon the chief executive increasingly significant legislative responsibilities. No longer is Congress considered the originator of significant social policy legislation. Instead, the executive has taken an ever-expanding grip on the legislative initiation process so that it is usually the President who proposes major laws and Congress who reacts to such initiatives. The people, and even Congress itself, recognize this growth in presidential authority and expect its continuance. How the President fulfills this responsibility obviously has a great impact on the legislative process. If the President can strike a cooperative working relationship with Congress, as Lyndon Johnson did, the results will be productive. If, however, the President assumes a competitive and hostile role relationship with the Congress, as did Richard Nixon, the outcome will be less than satisfying for all. Of course, the relationship between the President and Congress is also dependent on other factors, such as political party control of the two branches. But how the President sees the legislative responsibilities of his office remains an important variable.

Party roles. While the Constitution and laws of the United States make no mention of presidential activity in partisan politics, the chief executive has historically assumed a party role since the first Adams administration. As the highest officeholder among the members of his political party, the President is considered the leader of his partisan colleagues. His views become the party's views, his choices for party leadership positions normally are accepted without significant dissent, and his political strategy decisions are adopted by the party. He controls party machinery and through his patronage powers is able to reward the party faithful. Most Presidents assume an activist role as party leader, working to strengthen party control at all levels and supporting fellow party candidates from Capitol to courthouse. Lyndon Johnson's first few years in power are exemplary of an activist party leadership orientation. However, in the final months of his administration Johnson neglected party duties by concentrating on the Vietnam war effort and thus lost control to more liberal elements of the Democratic party. A prominent example of a negative party leadership role orientation was that of Richard Nixon. During his first administration Nixon was criticized by fellow Republicans for neglecting the party leadership role. In the 1970 congressional elections, Nixon actually worked for the defeat of liberal Republicans, notably Senator Charles Goodell of New York, who had not totally supported the President's policy positions. In the 1970 and 1972 elections, this negative role orientation manifested itself in administration pressure to keep Republican candidates from challenging certain conservative Democratic incumbents and even permitting Nixon-controlled campaign funds to find their way into the campaign chests of particular Democratic candidates. The impact of this negative party leadership orientation was disastrous for the Republican party. In 1972, while Nixon was amassing one of the largest presidential election margins in history, Republican congressional candidates were losing heavily to Democrats. Given this background, it is not surprising that the party's defense of Mr. Nixon during the Watergate investigations was far from enthusiastic.

We should make two precautionary statements about the preceding discussion. First, we have presented only brief sketches of three possible role sectors—one could hypothesize additional role orientations toward the President's administrative, military, and diplomatic duties, for example. And second, what we have said about presidential role orientations can be generalized, with certain modifications, to state and local executives.

JUDICIAL ROLES

The role expectations held by the public relating to the judicial branch are perhaps the most well defined of all. The American citizenry has definite views on what a good judge should be. We expect judges to be fair and objective, to temper justice with mercy, to follow the law, and to be learned and ethically sound. While executives and legislators can be forgiven for doing favors requested by interest groups or even having shady financial dealings, a jurist is not given this latitude. There is perhaps nothing lower in the public's estimation than a corrupt judge. Generally this is because we are taught that we are a nation of laws and not of men. We believe that justice should be blind and that laws should apply equally to presidents as well as paupers. The courtroom is supposed to be the political arena in which rich and poor, educated and illiterate, white and black are treated in identical ways with equal rights. Political clout and economic power are to have no place before the majesty of the law. While these ends are not always realized, the normative expectations of a judge remain.

This does not mean, however, that there is no room for interpretation of the judicial role. When we probe beneath the general expectations of the public, we find differentiated, well-defined role sectors. In this section we will discuss two basic role sectors applicable to courts at all levels of our judiciary.

Decision making criteria. One component of a judge's position involves what criteria he relies on in his decision making processes. Some judges perceive the judicial objectivity model of behavior as the correct manner by which to reach decisions. A judge whose standard model of behavior is judicial objectivity will simply examine the facts of the case as he sees them and apply the literal meaning of the law to these facts. By means of this rather mechanical approach the judge attempts to reduce the influence of his personal views, societal standards, and other "non-relevant factors" on his decisional processes. A judge who perceives the decision making role in terms of personal evaluations of law and justice may temper the strict application of the law with personal feelings of justice. While this role orientation may make legal processes more "human" and perhaps more workable, it also leaves the door wide open for the judge's personal attitudes and prejudices to subvert the intent of the law. Finally, a judge may see his decision making role in terms of interpreting community standards. Local customs, mores, and attitudes will be pervasive in such a judge's decisions. This orientation preserves community norms of justice. Each of these three role perceptions has advantages and disadvantages for the political system. The objectivity model provides uniformity and reliability in the law, but also imposes rigidity. The personal values model sacrifices uniformity for possibly more just rulings in specific cases. The community standards model upholds regional standards to the detriment of a nationwide system of legal rights and obligations. The first model is responsive to the law, the second to the judge's sense of justice, and the third to the community.

Decision making functions. How a judge perceives the functions of the judicial decision making process focuses on the relationship between the courts and the law.[15] The "law interpreter" orientation perceives the decision making process as simply a methodical application of the law to a specific set of circumstances. The law is interpreted literally, according to the intentions of those lawmaking bodies who created it, not according to the personal views of the judge. The law interpreter is likely to draw sharp distinctions between the traditional legal and interpretive function of the judiciary and the lawmaking functions of the legislature. Judges who subscribe to the "lawmaker" orientation feel that appellate decision making fills in the gaps in the law and extends the law to those circumstances not fully anticipated by the legislators who originally passed the statutes. The "lawmaker" generally believes that every time he hands down a decision he is changing the meaning of the law and therefore creating it. To believe otherwise, to the lawmaker, is to take an unrealistic position. Finally, there is the "pragmatist." A judge of this variety combines the lawmaking and interpreting functions as he sees fit from specific case to specific case. He is not ideologically wed to either position, but changes his orientations to suit the peculiar needs of the cases brought before him.

A knowledge of the role orientations of a judge provides us with considerable insight into his behavior in much the same manner as legislative and executive roles do. But like legislative and executive orientations, a judge's role perceptions are not the total answer to the questions surrounding his opinions and behavior. They do provide information as to how the judge relates to his official environment, but nothing more. Furthermore, they are not immutable truths about a political actor's philosophy of official behavior. There are few pure and absolutely consistent law interpreters, just as there are few pure and absolutely consistent trustees and facilitators. The utility of the role analysis of political elites is to provide general cognitive and behavioral categories for elite actions, but not definitive conclusions to the search for an understanding of political leaders.

Institutional norms

THE NORMS
OF POLITICAL INSTITUTIONS

Whenever individuals group together for more than a short period of time with the purpose of engaging in some endeavor or activity, norms tend to develop. A norm is a generally accepted standard defining the behavior of group members in particular circumstances. Norms are informal, unwritten rules of behavior governing the group membership, although over time they may become formalized and written. When one enters an established group he is expected to follow these customary modes of activity. Norms are perpetuated by the transmission of these values from established to new members through group socialization processes. Peer group pressure enforces norms on the membership and informal sanctions may be applied against those who fail to conform with established norms. For example, groups of prison inmates usually have certain codes of conduct governing relationships among themselves and with prison officials. College fraternities often have well-developed norms of behavior regulating how a pledge behaves vis-à-vis senior "brothers." Families may have unwritten rules regarding respectful attitudes toward parents. Specific norms may vary from human unit to human unit, but all are powerful forces commanding conformity to standards of conduct. Those who violate these norms may be dealt with severely. The noncon-forming inmate may find himself assaulted, the errant pledge may be eliminated from the ranks of the fraternity, and the misbehaving teenager may find his privileges of using the family automobile denied him.

Political institutions, like other groups, develop norms of behavior governing institutional activity. These political norms are important for several reasons. First, they have an impact on the behavior of political elites. Norms evoke certain types of behavior and prohibit others. They structure how a political leader carries out his duties. Secondly, norms shape the operations of the entire institution. When specific rules of con-duct are followed by almost all members of a political institution, the fabric of that institution is significantly molded. Third, because norms are usually informal and unwritten, they are largely hidden from the public's eye. This means that an important force shaping the way in which political actors behave is never evaluated by the citizenry and therefore never tested at the ballot box. And, finally, norms affect insti-tutional responsiveness. For the most part, institutional norms develop in response to the need for institutional preservation and for the survival of group members. They are not primarily designed to make an institu-tion more functional, efficient, or responsive to public needs. In fact, many norms have the opposite effect.

Research on congressional norms has isolated at least seven basic rules of conduct widely accepted by members of the Senate and House.[16] Historically the most important of these has been the *seniority* norm.[17] In Congress, seniority permeates almost every aspect of legislative life: each legislator is ranked by political party affiliation according to years of continuous service in the respective chamber. Legislative leaders are often selected at least partially on the basis of seniority and committee assignments also take this into account. Legislative rewards in terms of office space, invitations to social gatherings, and selection for foreign junkets are distributed according to seniority rankings. And, perhaps most important of all, until recently committee chairmanships and subcommittee assignments have been made almost exclusively on the basis of committee seniority.[18] There are few exceptions to the rule that when two Congressmen both desire the same thing, the one with the most seniority will obtain it.

Two congressional norms specifically pertain to the assimilation of new members—*apprenticeship* and *specialization.* Freshmen legislators are expected to serve a period of apprenticeship. The senior members of Congress do not appreciate newcomers who exhibit extreme activity— speaking on every issue, orating to the press corps, or attempting to run Congress. Instead, freshmen are advised to watch, work, and learn for their first year or two of service. Congress is a complex political and social system which takes considerable time to understand. New legislators are expected to learn the ropes before becoming too active. They are expected to refrain from speaking often, to carry much of the burden of routine and boring tasks, and to show respect to senior members.

During the apprenticeship period legislators are expected to begin specializing in specific areas of legislation and to maintain this specialization as they develop seniority.[19] Congress is saddled with an almost impossibly large and complex workload, ranging from flood control to immigration to foreign affairs. No Congressman can possess adequate knowledge about every piece of legislation on which he is required to vote. Congress has therefore found it necessary to develop a division of labor with experts in each area of legislative work. The norm of specialization, then, requires that each Congressman develop expertise so that he may be called upon to contribute his knowledge when bills in his domain are called before the chamber. Normally a Congressman's area of expertise is related to his committee and subcommittee assignments.

Related to the functional norm of specialization is the *legislative work* rule. Congress cannot function well unless its members devote time and resources to their legislative duties. A Congressman who performs his legislative tasks adequately will be respected by his colleagues and ultimately obtain substantial power. In fact, the most powerful men in Congress are probably those whose names would only be recognized by a very small segment of the population. They spend their time on legislative tasks and not on making headlines. Conversely the least respected members of Congress are often those whose attention-getting behavior indicates that they are more interested in running for higher office than in tending to their legislative chores.

Two norms are specifically designed to regulate interpersonal relationships. The first of these is the norm of *interpersonal courtesy.* Members of Congress are expected to treat each other with respect and dignity. Personal hostilities are to be hidden under a cloak of honor. No legislator would be easily excused from deriding another legislator's state or constituency or engaging in personal attacks—at least in public. Instead, debate is couched in very respectable language with references to colleagues made in terms such as "the senior senator from Utah" or "the gentleman from Alabama." The norm of interpersonal courtesy allows foes to battle in a friendly, respectful fashion; it suppresses acrimony and increases interpersonal harmony. The second norm regulating interpersonal relationships is the *reciprocity* norm. Members of Congress are expected to assist their colleagues whenever possible. This norm encourages vote trading, compromise, and mutual favors.

Finally, there is the norm of *institutional patriotism*. Members of both the House and Senate are expected to believe or at least claim to believe that their chamber is the greatest lawmaking body ever established and that their position is the most important and respected one possible. This emotional attachment contributes to the morale and functioning of the body and encourages public respect for it.

Similar norms can be found at the state legislative level.[20] However, in the American states there appears to be much less general agreement on legislative norms. One study of four state legislatures found no less than forty-two norms cited by the various lawmakers.[21] However, three general norms tended to be recognized by an overwhelming number of legislators: (1) legislative work; (2) respect for the rights of colleagues; and (3) interpersonal courtesy. The greater number of cited norms and the lower rate of agreement among the state legislators can probably be attributed to the fact that state legislatures are less stable, less professional, and have greater rates of turnover than does Congress.

Research on legislative norms has recently spilled over into the judicial domain. Our knowledge of the impact of norms on judicial decision making is quite minimal, but we do know that norms have some influence on court output and that judicial norms are not simply a duplication of legislative "rules of the game." Like other institutions, the judiciary has developed its own informal prescriptions native to its own purposes and environment.

The judicial research has indicated that the notions of apprenticeship, seniority, and so forth, characteristic of the legislative branch, have little applicability to the judiciary.[22] Furthermore, partisanship, so prevalent in legislative bodies, does not emerge as an important factor among judges. Judges tend to reject overt involvement in partisan politics, and with few exceptions prefer to engage in politics only to the extent of recommending a candidate to friends. Similarly, the majority of state judges find campaigning for office to be an undesirable requirement. The norm among judges, then, is to disengage from partisan activity as much as possible.

Like all decision making and deliberative bodies, courts must arrive at informal rules regarding decisional processes and conflict management if they are to remain functional and effective. Unless there is agreement on resolving differences within the court, divisions can cripple the workings of the institution. Judicial norms are intended to restrain the negative aspects of the dissenting privilege. Openly criticizing the majority may erode public respect for the court, lessen confidence in the definitiveness of the decision, and accentuate the disharmony existing on the court. For the most part, then, judicial norms dictate that the right to dissent should be used sparingly and only when the dissenting judge cannot in all good conscience accept the views of the majority or even allow them to pass without comment. The maintenance of orderly deliberation and institutional solidarity is imposed through adherence to these informal rules governing decision making and divisions of opinion within collegial tribunals.

Institutional norms at the executive level have yet to receive adequate scrutiny by political scientists. There is little doubt that certain "rules of the game" exist at the highest levels of the executive branch, but we have little systematic information about them. One reason for this is that norms existing around presidential or gubernatorial decision making processes are largely dependent upon the occupant of the chief executive position; and because the incumbents of these offices regularly change, so do the operative institutional norms. But we do know that executive norms exist and that they have an impact on the manner in which the business of government is transacted. We often know nothing about these norms until some unusual event brings the public spotlight to focus upon them. For example, the unwritten rules governing White House relationships during the Nixon administration were not uncovered until the Watergate investigations brought them to light. Only then was the public made aware of the fact that loyalty and obedience to superiors regulated the behavior of public officials even when such behavior was proscribed by federal statute. The zealous loyalty to Nixon exhibited by White House officials arose out of the "team player" norm. Each person holding a position within the White House was given a particular role to carry out in the team's effort to follow its "game plan." Officials who were not "team players" and who refused to execute orders were eliminated from the White House roster. When Secretary of the Interior Walter Hickel criticized the communications networks existing within the White House hierarchy, he was replaced. These particular institutional norms were generated, of course, from President Nixon's intense desire to impose order, eliminate confusion, and protect the presidential system he had created. The development of similar norms undoubtedly occurs in most presidential administrations, but what makes this example so prominent is the fact that charges of illegality and corruption within the White House lifted these informal rules from obscurity to public headlines.

NORM ACQUISITION, ENFORCEMENT, AND CONFORMITY

The perseverance of institutional norms depends upon three basic factors: (1) the transmission of norms from veteran to freshmen officials; (2) the enforcement of norms against deviant members; and (3) the conformity of the institutional membership to the standards set by these unwritten rules of behavior. The processes of norm learning, enforcement, and conformity have most often been studied within the legislative branch, and, therefore, it is to the subject of legislative norms that we again direct our attention.

The acquisition of norm information and the internalization of appropriate behavioral standards by freshmen legislators has recently been studied at both the state and congressional levels.[23]

For the most part, these studies have been unable to discern any significant point during a legislator's first year or two at which he tends to adopt the norms of the legislature as his own standards of conduct. Nor has there emerged any clear-cut agent within the legislature which transmits these institutional values to the neophytes. Instead, the greatest amount of norm learning appears to occur before legislative service begins. A study of California legislative candidates indicated that, prior to their election, representatives had a general understanding of the rules of legislative conduct.[24] This prior understanding focused on general rules regarding interpersonal relationships, integrity, and legislative work. When the same individuals were interviewed after completing a period of service, researchers found increased agreement on specific norms and reduced disagreement among the legislators as to what norms were operative within the legislature. In addition, there was increased concern with norms dealing with such legislative matters as committee decorum and management of bills. The results of this study indicate that representatives enter the legislature cognizant of the existence of norms and generally understanding the parameters of these norms. What occurs during the first months of service is the development of increased levels of sophistication and technical knowledge of the norms applicable to the representative's chamber.

A similar study of congressional norms lends even greater credence to the notion that the preponderance of norm learning occurs prior to legislative service.[25] Substantial agreement was discovered on congressional norms among entering freshman representatives and non-freshman Congressmen. These data indicate that little norm learning occurs after a legislator takes office. The newly elected representatives apparently come to Washington with relatively accurate information about the informal folkways of Congress. This may well be due to the fact that previous political experience, particularly in state legislatures, had already initiated these political elites into the ways of institutional norms.

We have stipulated that norms are those informal, unwritten rules of behavior generally accepted by the greatest portion of the members of an institution. In all large or complex organizations, however, not all members will readily espouse these normative standards. If the norms are to remain intact the institution must provide some form of enforcement process or sanction to be used against those reluctant to conform. Wahlke's study of four state legislatures found ample evidence to indicate the presence of such informal norm enforcement machinery.[26] One interviewed legislator revealed the wide variety of enforcement methods employed against nonconformists:

> There are all sorts of tricks of the trade. You give 'em false leads, run 'em around in circles, not vote for their bills, give them no place on sub-committees, don't get their bills out of . . . Committee. It happens much too frequently.[27]

The most common type of sanction used to punish deviant legislators and to convince them to mend their ways involved obstructing a legislator's bills. Over one-half of the respondents cited this as a frequent sanction. A deviating legislator would find his bills defeated, amended, or bottled up in committee—particularly if the bill was of special importance to the legislator or his district and not one affecting the general welfare. The second most common sanction involved social ostracism. The majority of the legislature will give the nonconforming member the "silent treatment," rejecting him personally and giving selective inattention to his speeches, suggestions, and wishes. Similar ostracism processes are operative in Congress.[28] Third, Wahlke found that deviating legislators were often treated with mistrust. The punished legislator would be constantly questioned and cross-examined on the floor and in committee; and he would rarely receive assignments authorizing him to exercise responsibility. The fourth common means of norm enforcement involved denying the erring representative political rewards—i.e., patronage, good committee assignments, etc. Other enforcement sanctions, including the more extreme measures of private or public ridicule, were not frequently cited as common vehicles for compelling conformity.

These enforcement penalties exacted against those members who refuse to live up to the legislature's standards of conduct are only applied against a small portion of the total membership. Most, of course, conform. Matthews' study of norms in the United States Senate cites four basic factors which have an impact on whether a legislator conforms with institutional norms.[29] The first factor is the previous training and experience of the legislator. Matthews found that former governors and federal executives conformed to Senate norms much less readily than Senators who had previously served in state legislatures or in the House. Furthermore, amateur politicians—i.e., those who entered politics late in life—had much more difficulty conforming than those who had been active in politics since an early age. Matthews concludes that the greater a man's pre-Senate accomplishments and the greater his age at election, the less likely it is that he will conform with the Senate norms. Second, the political ambitions of the Senator affect his degree of conformity. As might be expected, Senators with presidential ambitions had very low rates of conformity. Preparing for a presidential campaign requires a Senator to seek publicity and national recognition, often at the expense of legislative duties. Pursuing such activity runs directly against congressional norms. Third, constituency problems can have an impact on conformity with legislative norms. A Senator from a competitive state whose political future may be insecure will often become restless and impatient following the apprenticeship and specialization norms. He may feel that he must build a very strong image as an active and effective Senator among his constituents. He may well feel that violating the chamber's norms is a small price to pay for consolidating his political gains and securing his future. Finally, Matthews found political ideology to affect norm conformity. Liberals are much more likely to challenge the norms of the Senate than are conservatives. Since senatorial norms are biased against rapid action, a progressive legislator elected on a platform of reform and change will find these norms an obstacle to his mission. Conservatives will not often find themselves in this predicament.

. The deviant, of course, may undergo considerable difficulty living with his decision to buck the institutional powers and pursue an independent course of action.[30] In spite of the sanctions which will undoubtedly be imposed on the deviant, he has one consolation. The institutional "club" has no control over the legislator's reelection. If he can please his constituents and maintain his support back home, he will be returned regardless of his nonconforming behavior.

THE CONSEQUENCES
OF INSTITUTIONAL NORMS

The consequences of institutional norms are substantial for the interests of individual members serving in the institution as well as for the interests of the institution itself. For the individual, norms provide a behavioral guide. The individual knows that if he follows this guide he will profit in the long run. He will gain the respect of his colleagues and gradually gain power and influence. Following the norms of an institution will facilitate an officeholder's effectiveness. Matthews, for example, found that norm conformists in the United States Senate were much more effective than nonconformists.[31] But norms also place restrictions on public leaders. Conforming by necessity means that political elites are not able to exercise the freedom they might have anticipated. It also means that public officials must wait seemingly endless periods of time before they are able to engage in any really meaningful decision making.

For the institution, norms above all else promote institutional preservation. In all political institutions a good portion of the operative norms have no other purpose than self-maintenance and survival. This is accomplished through norms enforcing institutional loyalty, restricting the means and frequency of dissenting from institutional decisions, and controlling the political and personal conflicts which naturally arise. Another consequence of political norms is to place a conservative bias on institutional actions. Norms are generally status quo oriented rules of behavior which reduce the effectiveness of newly admitted members and maximize the influence of senior members. One of the goals of such informal rules is to create an ordered system of business and behavior within the institution; and a consequence of this is to erect roadblocks to rapid changes and quick actions. Finally, institutional norms tend to reduce the responsiveness of political agencies. Seniority, apprenticeships, institutional loyalty, restricted frequency of political dissent, and the failure to grant newly selected members of a political institution full powers of membership unmistakably reduce responsiveness capabilities. Norms are powerful forces governing the behavior of our political leaders. For the most part they are forces which have been beyond the purview of public opinion to modify or eliminate; but they are an intervening force which must be recognized before we can come to an adequate understanding of the public opinion/public policy process.

Collective behavior
in political institutions

The decisions made by political elites in the United States frequently occur after interaction and deliberation with other elites. The President reaches decisions after conferring with his White House staff, personal advisers, or Cabinet officials. Congressmen reach decisions on bills only after subcommittee, committee, and floor discussion. The Supreme Court hands down its rulings after meeting in collegial conference. Given the importance of collective behavior within our elite decision making institutions we need to discuss several aspects of group interaction. We will give particular emphasis to three topics: (1) subgroups within political institutions; (2) institutional integration; and (3) leadership within political institutions.

SUBGROUPS AND
POLITICAL INSTITUTIONS

The institutions in which political elites function do not exist exclusively as unitary collectivities. Within these decision making institutions can be found a myriad of formal and informal subgroups. The formation and operation of subgroups within larger collectivities can have a significant impact on the way in which political institutions function.

Subgroup formation tends to occur within elite institutions according to three basic patterns. The first is the formal development of subgroups for purposes of increasing the efficiency of the task completion function of the institution. Subgroup formation for this reason is initiated and preserved in order to reduce the workloads of the members of the institution, to create a division of labor, and often to facilitate the development of expertise among the members of the larger collectivity. Second, subgroups may form because of a concern for goal attainment or because of ideological brotherhood. Subgroups of this variety work to advance the policy or philosophical interests of their members and may have a significant impact on institutional outputs. The final subgroup formation pattern is informal. Members of institutions often divide into small subdivisions according to largely extraneous factors. These factors may include such things as friendship relations, commonality of geographical origin, and similarity of background characteristics. Such groupings may be spontaneous in nature and are rarely created by official action or formal recognition. They often function in a positive way by enhancing the social nature of the institution and increasing institutional cohesiveness.

Perhaps the most commonly understood variety of subgroup formation is that based upon efficiency considerations. Among political institutions the congressional committee system is the best example of subgroup formation of this nature. The fact that every member of Congress cannot study, investigate, draft, and amend every bill which is proposed should be relatively apparent. The sheer volume of suggested legislation dictates against this possibility. Similarly, the vast number of subject areas with which proposed legislation is concerned and the technical nature of many laws regulating our increasingly complex society mean that no one legislator can gather sufficient knowledge about all areas of congressional business to reach decisions intelligently. For this reason Congress has a well-developed system of standing committees. These committees, created according to substantive legislative areas, function as a surrogate for the entire chamber during the initial stages of the legislative process. They study, investigate, draft, amend, and make recommendations on proposed legislation. Only after this screening and modifying process is completed does the entire chamber act upon a bill. The committee process, then, reduces the workload of the membership and increases the efficiency of the legislative body. Furthermore, because of the substantive jurisdictions of the committees these formal subgroups become the seats of legislative expertise and specialization. For example, members of the House Ways and Means Committee become the legislative experts in the field of taxation. The committee system fosters the development of such pools of specialized knowledge upon which the remaining members of the institution can rely.

Similar forms of subgroup formation often take place within executive and judicial institutions. For example, the White House staff under President Kennedy was often organized into task forces and given responsibilities for various problem areas. President Eisenhower broke his staff into hierarchical groupings organized in a command chain fashion. Within the court system there are occasional examples of formal subgroup formation in order to increase judicial efficiency. The Washington and Missouri state supreme courts, for instance, have broken down into formal departments in order to handle court caseloads more efficiently. When a dispute is appealed to these courts it is usually referred to a subdivision of the full court for a decision rather than to the court's full membership.

Ideological or goal-oriented subgroup formation is also quite common within elite political institutions. In a representative democracy governmental institutions can be expected to house elites of widely differing views and interests. It is not uncommon for individuals with similar interests or attitudes to seek each other out within the larger institution. These individuals may organize and work together to accomplish their policy or ideological ends; or they may simply provide mutual reinforcement of philosophical positions. Such subgroups may be short lived coalitions of individuals whose commonality only extends to the accomplishment of a specific goal or may be more permanent, persistingly cohesive cliques which are based upon value consensus or agreement on long-range goals.[32] The latter is the most frequently occurring and the most significant for our purposes.

Legislative parties serve as the best example of subgroups based upon long-range policy goals and ideological fellowship. In the United States members of the same political party organize for the purposes of gaining the adoption of party policy objectives, controlling the government, and promoting the political careers of members of their ranks. They select leaders, develop legislative strategy, and carry out party policy in order to accomplish these long-range goals. Generally members of the same party hold similar, although not identical, ideological values. In addition, legislatures often contain less formal groupings based upon ideological consensus. The Democratic Study Group, founded in 1959 by young liberal

Democrats in the U.S. House of Representatives, serves as an example of an ideologically based subgroup of legislators. The Democratic Study Group works toward improving communications, providing information, and promoting a sense of identification among liberal Democratic members of the House.[33] The Wednesday Club made up of liberal Republicans serves as a counterpart, albeit less effective, to the Democratic Study Group. Ideological groupings may also exist in the complete absence of any formal structure whatever. The Conservative Republican/Southern Democratic coalition in Congress consists of conservative Congressmen of both political parties who vote similarly on particular types of issues such as civil rights, but the group has no organizational structure. Similarly, we have known for a long time that attitudinally based voting blocs exist within collegial courts. The split in the U.S. Supreme Court during the early 1970s between the last vestiges of the liberal Warren Court era and the conservative justices appointed by President Nixon is illustrative of such persistently cohering, philosophically based groups within the judiciary.

Finally, there are the purely informal groupings within elite institutions. While these are found at all levels of political bodies, they are most pronounced within legislatures.[34] Informal groups based upon geographical origin are quite common. Of particular significance are informal groups of Congressmen from the same state or state legislators representing the same county or urban area. The state or county delegations, often consisting of individuals with diverse party, ideological, or social background characteristics, come together because of their commonality of origin. Groups based upon friendship or social interests are also quite common at all institutional levels. These groups provide an important communications and socialization function. Unlike ideologically based subgroups these social groupings may only share outside interests—based perhaps upon church membership, recreational devotion to golf, or appreciation of similar forms of art or music. These friendship groupings often act as a catalyst by allowing officials with dissimilar political positions to have affective bonds with colleagues and thus to promote conflict management within the institution. An interesting example of such friendship relations has occurred in recent years on the Supreme Court. The High Court's two antagonists from an ideological standpoint, liberal William O. Douglas and conservative William H. Rehnquist, share perhaps the warmest personal relationship on the Court. This friendship is based in part on mutual respect of the outdoors and the natural environment. The friendship has even extended to the point of the Rehnquist and Douglas families vacationing together in Douglas' home in remote Gooseprairie, Washington. This friendship obviously allows the two to disagree vehemently on the Court without the personal animosity which could endanger the functioning of the Court as an institution.

Subgroups within political institutions, then, are of substantial importance in understanding the opinions and behavior of political elites. Sub-groups contribute to institutional operations by performing the following six functions:

1. Facilitating task completion by allowing a division of labor.
2. Promoting specialization and the development of expertise.
3. Providing a sense of identity and commonality among elites with similar interests and values.
4. Operating as socializing agents, providing newly invested elites with communications and information regarding institutional business.
5. Often providing voting and behavior cues for the members of the subgroups.
6. Promoting social and friendship relations which assist in the maintenance of conflict management.

POLITICAL INTEGRATION
AND INSTITUTIONAL EFFECTIVENESS

How well a collection of political elites is able to function within decision making institutions or within subgroups is largely dependent upon two exceptionally significant factors. The first is the degree of political integration existing within the collectivity and the second is the quality of leadership exercised within the group. Both variables are sufficiently important to discuss at this point.

In our treatment of political elites we have highlighted several attributes common to public officials in a representative democracy. We noted in Chapter Seven that political elites tend to be very different people from those who never become substantially involved in politics. They come from higher socioeconomic backgrounds and have reached higher levels of educational and professional attainment. Their personality attributes are accentuated by extroversion, ambition, and power-seeking behavior. They generally have stable attitudes and reasonably well-developed belief systems. And finally, because of the nature of our democratic government, they tend to represent diverse and often conflicting interests. These factors, of course, do not portend well for the probabilities of attaining efficiently running political decision making bodies. The seeds of conflict undoubtedly outnumber the seeds of cooperation. Clashes between personalities, interests, and ideologies are potentially disruptive to the responsible functioning of our governmental bodies. Yet somehow our elite institutions have traditionally functioned rather smoothly.

One of the basic factors behind this relative success has been the degree of political integration achieved within our decision making institutions. Somehow diverse and conflicting political orientations are blended together to avoid crippling internal dissension. Of course, political integration within elite institutions is relative—some institutional groupings have been far more successful at nurturing cooperation than others. And the long-term success of an elite institution is often directly related to the degree of integration attained. This point can best be illustrated by comparing two congressional committees—the House Appropriations Committee, which has demonstrated relatively high levels of political integration, and the House Agriculture Committee, which has been plagued by dissension.[35]

The House Appropriations Committee has enjoyed high levels of internal integration. Appropriations is an especially attractive committee since it controls the purse strings of the federal government. All spending legislation is reviewed by the Appropriations Committee, and membership on the committee is considered a political plum. Although appropriations matters are potentially partisan issues and can give rise to internal conflict and disharmony, the committee has responded to this danger by maintaining standards of operation designed to curtail the growth of internal cleavages. First, the committee membership maintains consensus regarding its essential mission. The committee regards itself as the guardian of the federal treasury and its primary duty is seen as the protection of that treasury from raids by federal agencies who wish to propagate unwise and excessive expenditures. This common mission of cutting the fat out of the federal budget usually enables committee members to transcend partisan cleavages that might otherwise emerge.

Second, the subject matter with which the committee deals facilitates cooperation and compromise. The committee is concerned with appropriations levels and not with appropriations authorizations. It is much easier to compromise when the question is how much to spend rather than whether funding should be authorized in the first place. When a deadlock occurs over funding levels, the dispute can always be resolved by splitting the difference—which is not only an easy way to compromise, but also a means for both sides to claim victory.

Third, Appropriations maintains high standards for service within its ranks. Only more senior, moderate, hard-working, cooperative Congressmen are selected for Appropriations Committee membership. The membership remains very stable due to the attractiveness of the committee and the internal feelings of camaraderie within its ranks. Fourth, the committee has worked hard to integrate its subcommittees. This has been achieved primarily through the development of the norm of subcommittee reciprocity. The subcommittees are given a great deal of latitude and authority. The full committee rarely challenges subcommittee decisions in any direct manner. Subcommittees are accorded respect due to the expertise they have developed over their given areas of jurisdiction. Each committee member, while sitting on as many as four subcommittees, will specialize in one, becoming an expert in that area. In sum, each of these modes of operation contributes to the general integration of the committee's membership. The consensus as to the task of the committee and the tight control over the types of individuals selected for membership give the committee a considerable edge in controlling the possibilities of conflict inherent in its jurisdiction. The subject matter of funding levels is amenable to compromise as a method of dispute settlement and the norms of specialization and reciprocity restrict the roles of challenging other members of the committee and attacking the work of the various subcommittees.

The House Agriculture Committee serves as a much different example of subgroup integration and cohesion. Unlike Appropriations, the Agriculture Committee has suffered a low level of internal harmony. The jurisdiction of the Agriculture Committee extends to all aspects of federal regulation of farm policy, including the important matters of agricultural price supports. As such the committee is only moderately attractive to members of the House at large. This moderate attraction classification is deceptive, however. The committee can be very important to Congressmen representing food-growing constituencies and yet relatively unimportant to representatives serving urban districts. The low level of committee integration is due primarily to two contributing factors. The first is partisanship. Agricultural policy has for a long time been a matter of debate between Democrats and Republicans. The second factor rests upon the interests of the individual Congressmen. Members of the committee are not only Democrats or Republicans but also representatives of various commodity interests. There are wheat representatives, tobacco representatives, and corn representatives, each reflecting the dominant agricultural interests in their respective constituencies. Party and commodity interests dominate almost every important issue brought before the committee. This situation is further aggravated by the development of subcommittees for cotton, peanuts, rice, dairy products, and for all other major agricultural interests. Unlike Appropriations, the Agriculture Committee has not had a well-developed sense of a committee mission or a reciprocity norm to inhibit the growth of conflict. Coupled with partisan differences, these commodity hostilities reduce the general level of political integration within the committee and decrease its effectiveness.

Before decision making bodies can function responsively, their members must be integrated into a well-coordinated whole. In this respect political institutions are no different from basketball teams, assembly lines, or most other forms of social activity. As we have seen from the above analysis of congressional committees, integration levels vary from group to group and have a substantial impact on institutional productivity. Integration can be dependent on several factors. A prime factor is the relative attractiveness of the group to political elites. A more highly favored group will be able to recruit high quality members and exact a high degree of participation from them. An individual who prizes group membership will naturally devote more effort to the obligations imposed by such a group. Second, high levels of integration can be achieved by recognizing the forces of potential disruption and taking steps to minimize the impact of these forces. One of the most effective means of accomplishing this goal is through the maintenance of group norms designed to reduce conflict. If partisanship is potentially disruptive within a group, a norm of nonpartisanship will be beneficial to the group's well being. Similarly, norms stressing cooperation, respect, and reciprocity facilitate internal integration. Third, consensus as to the group's raison d'etre promotes a sense of unity and lends perspective to the narrower interests of various subgroups. Finally, the tasks of the group influence its integration level. As we have seen, when a group deals with subject matter amenable to compromise and cooperation, integration is much easier to obtain.

POLITICAL LEADERSHIP AND INSTITUTIONAL EFFECTIVENESS

A second determining factor in the matter of group productivity and effectiveness is the quality of institutional leadership. Elite institutions are themselves made up of political leaders, so that institutional leadership really refers to leaders of leaders. This is important because there is a much lower probability of finding a natural leader/follower division within elite institutions than in other segments of social life. The leader of an elite institution must strive to guide effectively a group of persons who themselves are accustomed to playing leadership roles and who may not easily assume another role. For this reason leadership within elite institutions is a very special variety of leadership.

Within political groups two dimensions of leadership are necessary if the institution is to survive and function effectively: task leadership and social leadership.[36] Task leadership provides the achievement motivation for the group. A person who exercises task leadership initiates and suggests action, clarifies issues, focuses members' attention on group goals and productivity, and evaluates the quality of the group's work. The task leader, then, is the member who insures that the group's efforts are concentrated on the appropriate business and are not focused on tangential matters. The social leader devotes his efforts to maintaining or improving the harmony of the group. He concentrates on providing social–emotional rewards for group members. The social leader tries to make the group a pleasant, satisfying experience, to keep hostilities at a minimum, and to encourage a friendly atmosphere even during periods of high stress and conflict. These two dimensions of leadership accentuate productivity and social satisfaction. If both are exercised successfully the group will normally be effective.

While these two types of leadership illuminate the concept of political leadership, the discussion is incomplete without an examination of the sources of leadership power within collections of individuals. What types of factors are apparent as bases of leadership qualities? What makes a particular person emerge as a leader and be accepted by his colleagues as a leader? The answer to these questions lies in the five basic sources of leadership power.[37] The first basis of leadership power is *reward power*. This refers to the ability of a leader to distribute positive reinforcements to group members. An individual who is able to provide valued rewards to members of the group will naturally have a leadership edge over others. The second basis of leadership power is *coercive power*. This is the reverse side of reward power. The group member who is able to punish or otherwise coerce individuals through the application of negative sanctions has the potential for acting as the group's leader. The third basis of leadership power is *legitimate power*. A person who holds a position to which is accorded an assumption of leadership exercises legitimate power. The power is connected to the office or position which the individual rightfully holds. Along with this formal position often come established powers which are only to be exercised by the official occupying that position. The fourth category is *referent power*. A person who holds referent power does so because others wish to be identified with him. If members of a group desire to be identified with and share a feeling of oneness with a particular group member then that person will exercise leadership founded on a referent power base. Such desire for identification may be based upon the leader's status, position, popularity, power, or a host of other possible attractions. Finally, there is *expert power*. This basis of leadership hinges on superior knowledge. A group member who possesses superior amounts of expertise over the subject matter confronted by the group will be looked to for leadership by other members of the collectivity. Each of these five areas provides a source or basis of leadership power. The more sources of power upon which a leader can draw, the stronger and more effective his leadership potential will be.

Political scientists' attempts to explicate leadership within elite institutions have often relied on these power base classifications either directly or indirectly. One of the more direct applications of this schema was accomplished by John Manley's analysis of the leadership of former House Ways and Means Committee Chairman Wilbur Mills.[38] According to Manley, Mills maintained his position of influential leadership because he was able to exercise power based on four of these five sources. First, Mills' expertise over the legislative jurisdiction of Ways and Means was overpowering. Mills was considered the foremost expert on taxation matters both within the committee and in Congress generally. This command over a most difficult and technical legislative area gave Mills immense status and influence. Second, Mills exercised legitimate leadership power. Not only was he looked upon as a leader because of his position as committee chairman, but the legitimacy of his reign was enhanced because he exercised his influence by being fair and even-handed with his colleagues. Mills stressed bargaining and compromise. He was a formal leader and also a leader who behaved as good congressional leaders are expected to behave. For these reasons Mills was perceived by members of the committee as the legitimate seat of leadership within the group. Third, Mills used his reward power to solidify support for himself within the committee. While the rewards he had at his disposal were not great, he was always responsive to the committee's membership and was willing to do favors for his colleagues. Fourth, because of his high expertise, status, and competence, Mills was esteemed by his colleagues and was very attractive to them. This gave Mills referent power. Because committee members wanted to be like their chairman they followed his lead. The single power source which Mills left largely untapped was influence based upon coercion. Mills realized the drawbacks of applying negative sanctions as a means to accomplish his desired ends. Therefore, he relied on more positive leadership inducements rather than risking possible resentment and divisiveness within the committee. Manley found that in Mills' utilization of these four basic sources of leadership power he was able to maintain an exceptionally high degree of influence and control over the members of his committee. Of course, Mills was forced to step down from his chairmanship in January of 1975, but this was not due to a failure of his leadership techniques.

Examples provided by legislative leaders such as Wilbur Mills are illustrative of effective leadership strategies within elite institutions. There is little doubt that the quality of institutional leadership has a great bearing on the quality of political action and decision making. How well collections of political elites are able to govern, whether they are responsive to the legitimate demands of the public, and to what degree they are able to maintain internal cohesion is largely dependent on the nature of leadership within the institution. With creative and effective leadership that responds to the needs of the public, political institutions will operate successfully. Without effective leadership the probability of providing responsive government is severely reduced.

Summary

In this chapter we have examined three basic dimensions of elite behavior within institutions. These facets of institutional activity provide us with substantial knowledge crucial to an understanding of the public opinion–public policy process. An analysis of the manner in which public opinion is translated into governmental policies and programs would be incomplete without an examination of the impact of roles, norms, and group interaction on the opinions and behavior of political elites.

From our discussion of political roles we have noted that the expectations attached to a particular governmental position and the orientations of the occupant of that position may have a significant influence on how the officeholder carries out his functions. These role orientations apply to each segment of the elite's official responsibilities and to all levels and branches of political service.

Institutional norms impose rules of behavior upon political elites who are members of particular governmental organizations. These norms are powerful forces for determining the types of behavior deemed acceptable within institutions. They are substantially important for our purposes because they often obstruct efforts to achieve more responsive governmental institutions. As we found in the case of roles, institutional norms influence political elites at all levels of government and within each of the three branches of the polity.

Finally, we examined the process of group interaction within elite institutions. This was necessary because political officials rarely reach decisions on public policy issues without engaging in group deliberations of some variety. We discussed the fact that subgroups have a substantial impact on the way in which elite institutions operate, and that political integration and leadership affect the quality of institutional effectiveness.

This chapter concludes Part Two of this volume on public opinion and governmental responsiveness. In Part Two we have devoted our attention to three basic subjects: political elites and democratic government, the individual characteristics of political elites, and the institutional forces affecting elite opinion and behavior. When we couple this information with our knowledge of mass opinion discussed in Part One, we have the necessary basis for understanding two of the three elements of the public opinion–public policy process. Before our understanding of this process is complete, however, we need to examine the third basic component in the flow of the democratic process—the linkages between the masses and their political leaders. In Part Three this final aspect in the public opinion–public policy process will be discussed.

NOTES

[1] See Bruce J. Biddle and Edwin J. Thomas, eds., *Role Theory: Concepts and Research* (New York: John Wiley & Sons, 1966).

[2] John C. Wahlke, Heinz Eulau, William Buchanan, and LeRoy Ferguson, *The Legislative System* (New York: John Wiley & Sons, 1962), p. 8.

[3] Samuel C. Patterson, "The Role of the Deviant in the State Legislative System: The Wisconsin Assembly," *Western Political Quarterly,* 14 (June 1961), 461.

[4] Carl Joachim Friedrich, *Man and His Government* (New York: McGraw-Hill Book Company, 1963).

[5] See, for example, Wahlke, et al., *The Legislative System.*

[6] Malcolm E. Jewell and Samuel C. Patterson, *The Legislative Process in the United States,* 2nd ed. (New York: Random House, 1973); and Roger H. Davidson, *The Role of the Congressman* (New York: Pegasus, 1969).

[7] Davidson, *The Role of the Congressman,* p. 128.

[8] Wahlke, et al., *The Legislative System,* p. 292.

[9] Heinz Eulau, John C. Wahlke, William Buchanan, and LeRoy Ferguson, "The Role of the Representative," in *American Legislative Behavior,* ed. Samuel C. Patterson (Princeton, N.J.: Van Nostrand, 1968), pp. 235–49.

[10] Davidson, *The Role of the Congressman,* p. 126; Eulau, et al., "The Role of the Representative," p. 246.

[11] Davidson, *The Role of the Congressman,* p. 166 ff.

[12] Wahlke, et al., *The Legislative System,* pp. 330–31.

[13] Davidson, *The Role of the Congressman,* p. 150.

[14] See Lincoln's letter to A. G. Hodges in *The Complete Works of Abraham Lincoln,* eds. John Nicolay and John Hay (New York: Tandy, 1894), Vol. 10, pp. 65–68.

[15] See Henry Robert Glick, *Supreme Courts in State Politics* (New York: Basic Books, 1971), esp. pp. 38–51; and Kenneth N. Vines, "The Judicial Role in the American States: An Exploration," in *Frontiers of Judicial Research,* eds. Joel B. Grossman and Joseph Tanehaus (New York: John Wiley & Sons, 1969), pp. 461–85.

[16] For two excellent discussions of these norms see Donald R. Matthews, *U.S. Senators and Their World* (Chapel Hill, N.C.: University of North Carolina Press, 1960), ch. 5; and Jewell and Patterson, *The Legislative Process in the United States,* ch. 15.

[17] See Nelson W. Polsby, Miriam Gallaher, and Barry Spencer Rundquist, "The Growth of the Seniority System in the U.S. House of Representatives," *American Political Science Review,* 63 (September 1969), 787–807.

[18] See Barbara Hinckley, "Seniority in the Committee Leadership Selection of Congress," *Midwest Journal of Political Science,* 13 (November 1969), 613–30.

[19] See Lawrence V. Grant, "Specialization as a Strategy in Legislative Decision-Making," *American Journal of Political Science,* 17 (February 1973), 123–47.

[20] See Malcolm E. Jewell, *The State Legislature,* 2nd ed. (New York: Random House, 1969), esp. pp. 88–90; Jewell and Patterson, *The Legislative Process in the United States,* esp. pp. 397–401.

[21] Wahlke, et al., *The Legislative System,* ch. 7.

[22] Glick, *Supreme Courts in State Politics.*

[23] See, for example, Herbert B. Asher, "The Learning of Legislative Norms," *American Political Science Review,* 67 (June 1973), 499–513; Charles M. Price and Charles G. Bell, "The Rules of the Game: Political Fact or Academic Fancy?" *Journal of Politics,* 32 (November 1970), 839–55; Charles G. Bell and Charles M. Price, "Pre-Legislative Sources of Representational Roles," *Midwest Journal of Political Science,* 13 (May 1969), 254–70.

[24] Price and Bell, "The Rules of the Game . . .".

[25] Asher, "The Learning of Legislative Norms."

[26] Wahlke, et al., *The Legislative System,* pp. 152–55.

[27] Ibid., p. 153.

[28] Asher, "The Learning of Legislative Norms."

[29] Matthews, *U.S. Senators and Their World,* pp. 102–17.

[30] See, for example, Jerry Voorhis, *Confessions of a Congressman* (Garden City, N.Y.: Doubleday, 1947), pp. 28–29; and Ralph K. Huitt, "The Outsider in the Senate—An Alternative Role," *American Political Science Review,* 55 (September 1961), 569.

[31] Matthews, *U.S. Senators and Their World,* pp. 114–15.

[32] S. Sidney Ulmer, "Toward a Theory of Sub-Group Formation in the United States Supreme Court," *Journal of Politics,* 27 (February 1965), 133–52.

[33] Kenneth Kofmehl, "The Institutionalization of a Voting Bloc," *Western Political Quarterly,* 17 (June 1964), 256–72.

[34] For two studies of such informal groupings see Alan Fiellin, "The Functions of Informal Groups in Legislative Institutions," *Journal of Politics,* 24 (February 1962), 72–91; and Samuel C. Patterson, "Patterns of Interpersonal Relations in a State Legislative Group," *Public Opinion Quarterly,* 23 (Spring 1959), 101–9.

[35] What follows relies heavily on Richard F. Fenno, Jr., "The House Appropriations Committee as a Political System: The Problem of Integration," *American Political Science Review,* 56 (June 1962), 310–24; and Charles O. Jones, "Representation in Congress: The Case of the House Agriculture Committee," *American Political Science Review,* 55 (June 1961), 358–67. See also Richard F. Fenno, Jr., *Congressmen in Committees* (Boston: Little, Brown and Company, 1973).

[36] See, for example, David J. Danelski, "The Influence of the Chief Justice in the Decisional Process of the Supreme Court," in *The Federal Judicial System,* eds. Thomas P. Jahnige and Sheldon Goldman (New York: Holt, Rinehart and Winston, 1968), pp. 147–60.

[37] John R. P. French, Jr. and Bertram Raven, "The Bases of Social Power," in *Group Dynamics,* 3rd ed., eds. Dorwin Cartwright and Alvin Zander (New York: Harper & Row, Publishers, 1968), pp. 259–69.

[38] John F. Manley, "Wilbur D. Mills: A Study in Congressional Influence," *American Political Science Review,* 63 (June 1969), 442–64.

Part three
Opinion
and government

OPINION INFLUENCE:
ELECTIONS
AND
DIRECT ACTION

9

Having examined the characteristics and distribution of mass opinion and elite opinion, we now turn to the interaction between the public and political elites. In Part Three, we shall analyze the effects which political linkages—elections and direct action, political parties and interest groups, and representative institutions—have upon this interaction. These linkages have been institutionalized in democratic politics, and their effectiveness in "connecting" the public with political leaders is a crucial determinant of government responsiveness.

In this chapter, we shall examine elections and direct action. As discussed in Chapter One, elections and direct action provide the potential for direct popular control of public officials. For example, in order to gain reelection or to satisfy public pressures, officials may act in accordance with their perceptions of public preferences. If this is to occur, however, officials must be convinced that citizens are sufficiently informed, interested, and active to employ sanctions if their preferences are not heeded. Thus, the effectiveness of direct influence linkages depends in great part upon the nature of public participation in politics.

How the mass public participates in politics represents one facet of popular control. It is not the only influence which public opinion has or can have upon government, but it is an important reflection of the public's readiness and capability to affect government action. The public's readiness can be assessed by examining actual participation—for example, voter turnout or involvement in political activities beyond voting. The public's capability is considerably harder to evaluate. But by examining such factors as voter awareness of issues and the relationship between issue preferences and voting, we can provide at least a partial test of the electorate's competence to influence government policy.

Elections

While elections are among the most visible features of democratic politics, there is considerable disagreement about their significance.[1] One persistent concern is the extent to which elections facilitate popular control of government. Are elections mandates (that is, do they provide direct popular control of political elites and hence of government policy), or do elections have little or no discernible influence over policy? To put it another way, is the significance of elections primarily symbolic, or do they actually have a substantial impact upon policy? [2]

In order to assess the influence and hence the significance of elections, it is necessary to focus upon voter behavior. If elections are to facilitate popular control, they must present voters with policy choices. But equally important, the public must have the interest and information to respond intelligently to such alternatives. In effect, the public must be active, informed, and rational. From this perspective, then, we can approach voter behavior in terms of: (1) the extent of popular participation in elections; (2) the role of issues in voters' decisions; and (3) the types of control voters actually exercise.

PARTICIPATION IN ELECTIONS

Analysis of the linkage potential of elections must take into account the realities of participation. The electoral linkage is obviously weakened when substantial segments of the population either are intentionally excluded from voting or decide not to participate. During this century, significant progress has been made in eliminating blatant forms of group discrimination in voting. Women, blacks, and younger citizens have been incorporated into the eligible electorate, which now comprises more than 140 million persons.[3] Yet voter turnout in the United States remains a serious problem. It is relatively low when compared with other democracies. It varies considerably by type of election. And turnout differentials between racial and class groups persist.

Cross-national comparisons. Differences in registration and voting procedures as well as variations in methods of calculating turnout make turnout comparisons between the United States and other democracies subject to

Table 9.1
Voter Turnout in the United States and Selected Countries

COUNTRY	YEAR	VOTER TURNOUT
Australia	1972	97%
Italy	1972	93
West Germany	1972	91
New Zealand	1972	90
Netherlands	1972	83
France	1973	82
Ireland	1973	75
Canada	1972	74
Great Britain	1970	71
United States	1972	56

Source: Adapted from Richard L. Strout, "The Stunning Drop in U.S. Voters," *Christian Science Monitor* (April 20, 1973), p. 16. Reprinted by permission from *The Christian Science Monitor* © 1973 The Christian Science Publishing Society. All rights reserved.

serious qualifications.[4] Nevertheless, turnout in other democracies tends to be considerably above that recorded even for presidential elections in the United States. In Table 9.1, participation figures for recent elections in selected countries are provided. Several of these countries employ compulsory or automatic registration procedures, and the disparities in turnout suggest that the effect of registration requirements in the United States is considerable. In 1974, for example, only 62 percent of the eligible voters (approximately 87.9 million) registered to vote in the off-year election. And according to United States Census Bureau estimates, turnout was only 38 percent of the eligible electorate, the lowest figure in over three decades.[5]

Changing registration requirements have been linked to long-term variations in presidential election turnout.[6] During the latter half of the nineteenth century, for example, turnout of the eligible electorate was typically in the 75–85 percent range. Yet many areas did not have registration requirements during this period, and of those that did, many employed automatic registration. As the states adopted stringent registration laws, turnout steadily declined, reaching its lowest point during the 1920s. And while the liberalization of registration procedures over the past several decades has resulted in a gradual increase in turnout, a substantial proportion of the electorate remains unregistered.

What the cross-national comparisons suggest, therefore, is not that citizens in the United States are necessarily less interested in politics than citizens of other democracies, but rather that the amount of interest or effort required in the United States is somewhat greater. Automatic regis-

Figure 9.1
Participation in Elections for President and U.S. House of Representatives,
1952–1970

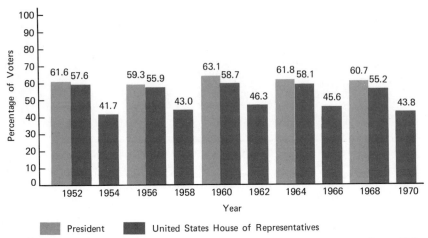

Source: Adapted from U. S. Bureau of the Census, *Statistical Abstract of the United States: 1972*, 93rd ed. (Washington, D.C., 1972), p. 373.

tration might increase turnout substantially and might make the electoral linkage *potentially* more effective. We say "potentially," because only an informed and rational electorate can achieve this goal.

Types of elections. While registration procedures might account for the relatively poor levels of participation in the United States as compared to other countries, it is also the case that turnout in presidential elections is considerably higher than in congressional or state and local elections. Given the number and types of elections in which Americans are asked to participate, it is understandable that they respond more readily to those elections having the highest visibility or salience. But even at the national level, there are considerable variations in turnout between presidential and midterm elections.

In presidential years, participation in elections for President and for the U.S. House of Representatives is roughly comparable. But in off-year elections, turnout in House elections declines by some 15–20 percent (see Figure 9.1). Differences of this magnitude cannot be attributed to registration procedures alone. They appear to reflect lesser interest in congressional as opposed to presidential elections. Again using the Census Bureau findings on the 1974 congressional election, 29 million persons said that they did not vote, because they disliked politics or were not interested.[7] Of those who were registered but did not vote, 7.7 million explained that they could not find candidates whom they liked or that they did not think that their votes would matter.

Correlates of voting participation. Registration and voting, along with other forms of political participation, are related to such factors as sex, race, and social class. As Table 9.2 indicates, there are important group-related differences in voting, and it is apparent that turnout increases along with socioeconomic status (as measured by education and income).

Participation in elections is also related, as might be expected, to differences in interest level and involvement. Those who are more interested in a campaign, who have a greater concern about the outcome of an election, who believe that their votes "matter," and who have a high sense of civic duty are more likely to participate.[8] And such interest, involvement, and commitment vary strongly as a function of education, for example. Thus, as education increases, we find that individuals follow politics more closely, are more aware of the impact of government, have more political information and opinions on a wider range of subjects, and are more likely to engage in political discussions.[9]

In sum, there are clear differences in voter turnout among socioeconomic groups, and these differences can be explained in part by variations

Table 9.2
Participation in National Elections, by Population Sub-groups, 1968 and 1970

	PERCENTAGES REPORTING NOT VOTING	
	1968	**1970**
SEX		
Men	27.6	43.2
Women	32.1	47.3
RACE		
Caucasian	28.9	44.0
Negro	38.5	56.5
EDUCATION		
8 years or less	45.5	56.6
9-11 years	38.7	52.9
12 years	27.5	41.6
More than 12 years	18.8	34.3
FAMILY INCOME		
Under $3,000	46.3	58.0
$3,000-$4,999	41.8	55.0
$5,000-$7,499	34.2	52.0
$7,500-$9,999	26.9	44.7
$10,000 and over	19.6	33.8

Source: Adapted from U.S. Bureau of the Census, *Statistical Abstract of the United States: 1972,* 93rd ed. (Washington, D.C., 1972), p. 374.

in political interest and involvement. But these differences also signal an important limitation of elections as political linkage mechanisms. To the extent that the electoral linkage depends upon an *active,* informed, and rational electorate, voting participation in the United States presents a problem. The absolute levels of turnout as compared with those of other countries are not especially distressing if procedural differences, such as registration requirements, are taken into account. But the differences in turnout by types of elections and between social groups indicate that citizens do not share an equal belief in the efficacy of the ballot. Moreover, the lower socioeconomic segments of the population (who presumably could benefit most from the rewards and sanctions involved in voting) are also least likely to participate. This abnegation not only reduces the immediate political influence of these groups but also renders electoral decisions less significant for the political system.

Despite the clear advances in extending and guaranteeing the vote, then, differential participation in elections persists. The number of elected officials and the frequency of elections in the United States may reflect a traditional belief in the efficacy of the ballot, but the utility of the election linkage as a transmitter of public opinion is greatly limited by the realities of participation. If elections provide popular control of government, such control will be exercised by those who participate.

In addition, the variations in turnout between types of elections suggest that citizens do not consider all elections equally important. That the electorate finds a presidential election more important than a mayoral election is not especially disconcerting. But the clear and consistent drop in turnout between presidential elections and congressional midterm elections is a more serious matter. Congress is obviously an important policy making institution, even when compared to the Presidency. But the possibility of popular control of Congress is reduced considerably by the fact that a majority of the electorate ignores midterm elections.

ISSUES AND VOTING

A second criterion for evaluating the electoral linkage is the accuracy and completeness of information citizens utilize in their voting decisions. If the public is to control political elites and to direct public policy through elections, it must be sufficiently well informed about issues to make rational judgments between competing candidates and parties. Similarly, if public officials are to seek accurate guidance from election returns, they must expect to deal with voters who are indeed capable of making such decisions and to whom they can appeal on the basis of issues.

The question of the electorate's competence to vote rationally has engaged considerable scholarly attention since the 1950s. Many early studies suggested that the electorate's competence was quite minimal. In particular, the electorate was found to be generally uninterested in politics, largely uninformed about political issues, and typically lacking ideological coherence in its views. Moreover, the links between party identification and issue preferences were found to be tenuous. In reaction to these findings, some concluded that voters could easily be manipulated, that limited public participation increased political stability, and that elections could not and should not serve as instruments of popular control.[10]

More recent studies, however, have suggested that these findings might have resulted from the relatively non-ideological politics of the 1950s. In effect, the major national elections did not stimulate ideological awareness within the electorate, and voters did not respond either to parties or candidates in terms of issue preferences.[11] According to this view, there is considerable variation in the impact of issues upon election outcomes, and the electorate is capable of taking issues into account in its voting decisions.[12] Thus, we now have additional evidence concerning the possibility of popular control through elections.

Time of decision.   When do voters make up their minds? Are they largely unaffected by campaigns, or are they able to sift through ideas and respond to issues and candidates during the campaign? Which voters are most likely to be affected by campaigns—the least interested and the most gullible, or the more interested and informed voters?

In presidential elections, most voters make up their minds before the campaign commences. Dividing the time of decision into three periods—before the conventions, during the conventions, or during the campaign— Table 9.3 indicates that a majority of voters have usually decided which candidate to support either prior to or during the conventions. Since 1960,

Table 9.3
Time of Decision on Vote Choice for President, 1948-1968

	1948	1952	1956	1960	1964	1968
Percentage who decided:						
before conventions	37	34	57	30	40	33
during conventions	28	31	18	30	25	22
during campaign	25	31	21	36	33	38
Don't remember, NA	10	4	4	4	3	7
Total	100	100	100	100	101	100

Source: Wílliam H. Flanigan, *Political Behavior of the American Electorate,* 2nd ed. (Boston: Allyn and Bacon, Inc., 1972), p. 109, © Copyright 1972 by Allan and Bacon, Inc. Used by permission.

however, there has been a definite increase in that portion of the electorate that has decided during the campaign.

The 1960 and 1968 elections, moreover, reflect the significance of this late decision group in close races. In 1960, Kennedy received an approximately 3 to 2 edge among that 35 percent of the electorate which entered the campaign undecided. This was enough to balance the margin Nixon had obtained among those who decided prior to and during the conventions, and gave Kennedy a slight popular majority in what turned out to be one of the closest presidential elections of this century. The 1968 election was nearly as close, but in this case, the Democratic candidate (Humphrey) was unable to gain a sufficient margin among the late deciders to overcome the lead which Nixon had established prior to the campaign.[13]

In addition to the variations in time of decision from election to election, there have been differences in the types of voters who put off their decision until during the campaign. In 1952 and 1956, the late deciders were disproportionately the least informed and least interested voters. But in 1960, this was reversed slightly, and in both 1964 and 1968, time of decision was unrelated to voter interest.[14]

Campaigns can make a difference, particularly in close contests where the late deciders may provide the margin of victory. Moreover, the impact of campaigns is not confined to the least interested and least informed voters. But it is also apparent that a very large segment of the electorate, indeed a majority, is committed by the time that the campaign begins.

Inter-party differences. Despite the increase in Independent identification over the past decade, a substantial majority of the electorate continues to identify with the Democratic and Republican parties. Moreover, the Democratic party's advantage in party identifiers—more than enough to overcome the higher turnout among Republican identifiers—has been reflected in Democratic congressional majorities for over two decades. Analysis of the congressional vote confirms the importance of party identification, especially during midterm elections. In these contests, some 80–90 percent of the Democratic and Republican identifiers have typically supported their party's candidates. And even in those cases where party identifiers have deserted their party at the presidential level, they have supported it in congressional contests. In 1972, for example, Richard Nixon obtained 42 percent of the votes of self-identified Democrats, but only 11 percent of all Democrats voting for Nixon also supported a Republican candidate for the U.S. House of Representatives.[15]

The relatively stable effects of party identification in congressional elections and the substantial albeit variable effects of party identification in presidential elections raise questions about the basis of party voting. Do voters perceive issue differences between the parties? Do they identify with the party which is closer to their issue preferences? Does the electorate perceive ideological distinctions between the parties?

Studies conducted during the 1950s found that voters generally were not aware of inter-party differences with respect to issues. While voters were strongly attached to traditional parties, many were not aware of or interested in specific policy issues and did not perceive the parties as being ideologically distinct. Moreover, the link between party identification and issue preference was tenuous or nonexistent for much of the electorate.[16]

Recent research has suggested that the electorate's response to the parties has changed. Perhaps in response to the more ideological politics of the 1960s, issue concerns among voters have become more apparent. And this change has been reflected in several ways. First, a growing segment of the population perceives inter-party differences in terms of specific issues. Comparing the electorate's perceptions of these differences in 1956, 1960, 1964, and 1968, Gerald Pomper found that over time the parties have come to be seen as more distinctive on issues involving federal domestic activities (see Table 9.4). With the exception of foreign aid, inter-party issue differences were perceived as markedly higher in 1964 and 1968 than in either 1956 or 1960.

Moreover, perceptions of party distinctiveness were linked to strength of identification. In general, strong partisans were more likely to see inter-party differences than were weak partisans. And weak partisans, in turn, were more likely to see differences in party positions than were Independents.[17]

Second, utilizing these same issues, Pomper found that issue preferences and party identification had become more strongly related by the

Table 9.4
Perceptions of Inter-Party Differences on Policy Issues, 1956 - 1968

ISSUE	PERCENTAGES OF THOSE WITH OPINIONS PERCEIVING DIFFERENCES			
	1956	1960	1964	1968
Aid to education	52	55	66	59
Medical care	54	58	82	71
Job guarantee	55	64	70	63
Fair employment	47	44	69	62
School integration	51	36	64	60
Foreign aid	49	39	56	46

Source: Adapted from Gerald M. Pomper, "From Confusion to Clarity: Issues and American Voters, 1956-1968," *American Political Science Review,* 66 (June 1972), 418.

Table 9.5

Consensus on Positions of Parties on Policy Issues, 1956 - 1968

ISSUE	PERCENTAGES OF THOSE PERCEIVING DIFFERENCES SELECTING DEMOCRATS AS LIBERAL			
	1956	1960	1964	1968
Aid to education	67	76	81	73
Medical care	77	81	92	87
Job guarantee	69	80	88	80
Fair employment	48	52	89	83
School integration	48	44	89	86
Foreign aid	43	49	88	85

Source: Adapted from Gerald M. Pomper, "From Confusion to Clarity: Issues and American Voters, 1956-1968," *American Political Science Review,* 66 (June 1972), 419.

middle 1960s. In 1956 and 1960, party identification and issue preferences were essentially unrelated—that is, Democratic identifiers did not differ appreciably from Republican identifiers on most issues. But this had changed considerably by 1964, as policy preferences and party identification became more congruent. As Pomper interpreted this change, "On five of the six issues—all but foreign aid—party identification meant something by 1968 other than a traditional reaffirmation: it was now related to the policy preferences of the voter." [18]

Third, the ideological identity of each of the parties was much clearer in 1964 and 1968 than previously. In particular, of those perceiving interparty differences in 1968, there was a clear consensus that the Democratic party was the more liberal party (see Table 9.5). Between 73 and 87 percent viewed the parties as ideologically distinctive on all issues.

In sum, the electorate accepted the liberal-conservative distinction as relevant to the policy orientations of the two parties, and there was impressive agreement as to the application of this distinction.

These changes in perceptions of responses to the parties occurred, moreover, within all segments of the population. While not necessarily uniform, they were evident in comparisons between different age groups, education groups, racial groups, and regional groups.[19] This suggests that the electorate in general has become more aware of and informed about interparty differences and that the link between party identification and issue preferences has been strengthened. And one interpretation of the reasons for these changes is that the politics of the 1960s—the events, campaigns, and political leaders of the period—developed an ideological awareness within the electorate and made issues more relevant for the mass public as well as for political elites.

Impact of issues.   The relative stability of congressional election results differs dramatically from party fortunes in presidential elections. The Democratic advantage in party identification within the electorate has consistently been reflected in Democratic congressional majorities, and midterm elections in particular have conformed fairly closely to what has been termed the normal vote. A normal vote assumes that most voters will vote consistent with their party identification, that "defections" between the parties will cancel out, and that Independents will split their votes between the parties.[20] A normal vote election, then, is one in which party identification is the major determinant of the vote. Correspondingly, the impact of short-term forces—such as candidates and issues—is minimal, so that the distribution of party identification nationally (with adjustments for higher turnout among Republican identifiers) has given the Democratic party a continuing congressional majority.

The variability in presidential election results, however, has been rather striking in recent years. Both the 1960 and the 1968 elections, of course, were extremely close (less than one percent of the popular vote separated the Democratic from the Republican candidates), with the Democrats winning in 1960 and the Republicans winning in 1968. But 1964 and 1972 were landslides, with the winner receiving over 60 percent of the two-party vote. And while the Democrats won the 1964 Goldwater-Johnson contest, the Republicans triumphed with Richard Nixon over George McGovern in 1972. If we take into account the presidential elections of the 1950s, the Democratic advantage in party identification has been translated into presidential victories in only two of the six presidential elections from 1952 to 1972. Thus the susceptibility of presidential elections to short-term forces (issues and candidates) provides a useful focus for examining the relative effects of party identification, issues, and candidates.

Here again, recent elections have indicated the increased tendency of voters to respond to issues. In 1968, for example, party identification was the major determinant of support for Richard Nixon and Hubert Humphrey. But the vote for George Wallace was linked very strongly to issue preferences. On such matters as race relations, law and order, and Vietnam, the Wallace voter was quite distinctive as compared to the Humphrey or Nixon voter, and the Wallace candidacy was interpreted as a clear issue candidacy.[21]

The 1972 election, moreover, provides an even clearer example of the importance of issues in a presidential campaign. According to a study issued by the Center for Political Studies at the University of Michigan, issue voting and ideology "provide a means for better explaining the unique elements of the contest than do social characteristics, the candidates, the events of the campaign, political alienation, cultural orientations or partisan identification." [22] Richard Nixon captured 94 percent of the Republican vote, 66 percent of the Independent vote, and an astonishing 42 percent of the Democratic vote.[23] According to a normal vote prediction, the Democratic party should have received 54 percent of the vote.[24] And differences between the expected and the observed Democratic vote were explained primarily by the impact of issues.

In comparing the issue preferences of Nixon and McGovern supporters, there were clear and consistent differences. Table 9.6 provides a comparison on several specific issues, on a five-issue policy orientation index, and on a liberal-conservative scale. While the degree of difference varies from issue to issue, it is clear that Nixon voters could be distinguished very sharply from McGovern voters. Table 9.6 also illustrates the ideological differences between loyal Democrats and defecting Democrats. These differences between Democrats are as striking as the differences between McGovern voters and Nixon voters generally.

The CPS study provided additional examples of the impact of issues in the 1972 election. For example, voters' perceptions of Nixon's position on specific issues placed him closer to the total electorate's position on 11 of 14 issues when compared to perceptions of McGovern's positions. And on each of these issues, McGovern was consistently placed to the left of where the Democratic party was placed and left of Democrats' self-perceptions.[25] Nixon also had a clear advantage on what were termed proximity measures—issue scales on which the respondent located his or her own position and then located the perceived position of the two candidates. It was found that regardless of their position, voters were likely to choose the candidate whose views they perceived as closest to their own. And since Nixon was perceived as closer than McGovern by a substantial majority of voters, his victory was based upon the electorate's perception that there were clear differences between the candidates.[26] The proximity measures, then, are especially useful in explaining the relationship between an individual's policy preferences and the vote decision. The voter's position on an issue becomes more meaningful to him if the candidates' positions on that issue differ appreciably. The concept of proximity can also be applied to the liberal-conservative distinction. Here again, the respondent locates himself or herself on a scale and then locates the candidates. In assessing the impact of the liberal-conservative proximity measure, the CPS study found that it was as strong a predictor of the vote as any single issue proximity measure.[27]

Analysis of the 1972 election, then, indicates that votes are actually cast because of issue preferences. Increased voter awareness of inter-party differences has been accompanied by the electorate's greater readiness to respond to candidates on the basis of issues and to interpret politics based upon a liberal-conservative distinction. But it is apparent that issues have a varying impact upon elections. For less visible and less highly publicized

Table 9.6
Issue Differences between McGovern and Nixon Voters, 1972

	ALL VOTERS		DEMOCRATIC VOTERS	
	McGovern voters	Nixon voters	McGovern voters	Nixon voters
N	566	1021	377	271
Vietnam				
Left	69%	29%	69%	30%
Center	19	29	19	31
Right	12	42	12	39
Amnesty				
Left	54	15	49	18
Right	46	85	51	82
Marijuana				
Left	37	17	30	10
Center	11	11	11	7
Right	52	72	59	83
Campus unrest				
Left	43	11	40	12
Center	20	23	18	24
Right	37	66	42	64
Minorities				
Left	52	25	50	25
Center	23	27	24	24
Right	25	48	26	51
Standard of living				
Left	50	18	53	21
Center	24	25	23	24
Right	26	57	24	55
Busing				
Left	22	3	23	2
Center	8	4	8	2
Right	70	93	69	96
Five issue				
Left	50	16	45	15
Center	29	34	30	33
Right	21	50	25	52
Liberal-Conservative				
Left	54	13	50	14
Center	32	37	36	44
Right	14	50	14	42

Source: Arthur H. Miller, et al., "A Majority Party in Disarray: Policy Polarization in the 1972 Election "
(Ann Arbor, Mich.: Center for Political Studies, 1973), p. 10. Portions of this paper will appear in
American Political Science Review, 70 (June 1976 forthcoming).

elections, such as midterm congressional elections, party identification tends to be the primary determinant of the vote. But the visibility and saliency of presidential elections, especially when the candidates are able to stake out issue positions that the voters can readily perceive, provide an opportunity for issues to have a much more substantial effect. In the 1964, 1968, and 1972 presidential elections, issues were important components of the electoral decision for large segments of the electorate. And candidates such as Goldwater, Wallace, and McGovern played a major role in encouraging the electorate to adopt an ideological perspective when responding to presidential politics. This does not necessarily mean that future presidential contests will evidence the same degree of issue impact that these recent elections have provided. It does mean, however, that the electorate is capable of making voting decisions based on issue preferences when candidacies become associated with these preferences.

The electorate has in recent years been more responsive to issues than was the electorate of the 1950s. This suggests a more balanced appraisal of the electorate's capabilities. We should, of course, continue to recognize that traditional party loyalties are important motivations for many voters, that a majority of the electorate has decided which presidential candidate to support before the campaign begins, and that perceptions of a candidate's position on issues may be distorted. The American electorate is not intensely interested in nor highly knowledgeable about politics, but it has shown an increased awareness of party differences and candidate positions on issues and an increasing tendency to vote on the basis of issues.

ELECTIONS AND POPULAR CONTROL

Studies of electoral behavior provide us with a voter whom Gerald Pomper has appropriately termed a "meddling partisan." [28] This description takes into account the considerable impact which party identification and social group membership have upon the electorate. Voters do not enter each campaign free of the references or biases that stem from party identification or social group membership. Indeed these directly affect their interpretations of political events, issues, and candidates.

Nevertheless, many voters are willing to desert their party when they believe that their interests are not being served. These voters need not respond to the entire range of issues discussed during a campaign but only to those issues which they perceive as being of direct and personal significance.[29] And, of course, different voters may be concerned about different issues. There are numerous issue publics within the electorate, and what is salient to one issue public may be a matter of indifference to others.

For the meddling partisan, voting is usually a retrospective judgment of past governmental performance rather than an attempt to prescribe future governmental initiatives. Election outcomes therefore represent responses to the incumbent party or to particular officials.[30] Voters might assess incumbent performance in terms of "the nature of the times" or of the success or failure of government in providing group benefits, or they might react to particular policies or programs. The sporadic intervention of the voter and the generalized response to governmental performance provide popular control, but this control is essentially indirect:

The quality of the American voter makes his direct control over policy unlikely. The American citizen largely reacts to the political world. His meddling is stimulated by external events; rarely is it an attempt to impose a coherent scheme on that world. Since voters are not ideological, and coherent majorities do not support specific and integrated programs, public officials are not severely restricted in their actions. Extensive "mandates" are improbable.[31]

Degrees of control.   If elections are not likely to represent extensive mandates, popular control as exerted through elections might best be understood by distinguishing between degrees of control.[32] In effect, popular control could be nonexistent on certain issues, present but not determinative on others, and direct and compelling on still others.

First, most governmental policies are not debated or discussed during campaigns, and they are consequently beyond immediate control by the electorate. Included among these are highly technical or extremely complex issues which are unlikely to engage the electorate's attention. Decision making on these issues is restricted to the few who have the necessary interest, information, and expertise. Accordingly, such matters as "foreign policies in peace time, strategic decisions, esoteric regulatory rules . . . are not likely to engage popular attention even though they may have a substantial impact on people's lives. . . ."[33] (Of course, policies can move in and out of this category. It appears, for example, that nuclear power plants may become a subject of serious political debate during the 1970s after almost three decades during which they were the sole concern of the "experts.") The electorate's attention is necessarily selective, and this reduces the likelihood of extensive programmatic constraints being imposed upon government.

Second, issues which are debated and discussed during a campaign and about which the voters have opinions need not result in the electorate's imposing specific policy alternatives. This is especially true when a new problem or issue is encountered—the voters may initially provide political leaders with a wide variety of options.[34] In subsequent elections, of course, the electorate can issue a retrospective judgment on how these options have been utilized. Voter influence in this context is indirect. Political officials are given initial discretion, but they must attempt to anticipate how voters will react to a given policy initiative in the future.

Several studies have concluded that this type of indirect influence characterized the electorate's response to Vietnam during the 1960s. Vietnam first emerged as a campaign issue in 1964, prior to the massive escalation of the war. Johnson's victory over Goldwater was interpreted by some analysts as being based upon the public's desire for military restraint; thus the policy which he pursued subsequent to the election was viewed as a violation of his mandate.[35] In fact, however, Johnson received majority support from "hawks," "doves," and "moderates." Among those who favored withdrawal, for example, Johnson received 63 percent of the vote. But he also obtained 52 percent of the vote from those who favored "a stronger stand even if it means invading North Vietnam," and he received 82 percent of the vote from those who advocated maintaining United States troops in Vietnam while trying to end the fighting.[36] As one study concluded: "What could the 1964 vote have told him (Johnson) about popular support for various war options? In brief, it could have told him anything he cared to believe." [37]

By early 1966, moreover, when a substantial United States commitment of troops and materiel had taken place, Johnson still retained much of his support. Among those who had voted for Johnson in 1964, for example, approval of his Vietnam policy exceeded disapproval by a margin greater than 2 to 1. And even among those who reported having voted for Goldwater, disapproval was only slightly higher than approval.[38]

Initially, then, the Johnson administration did not appear to be bound by any clear expression of public support for various Vietnam options. And even by 1968, when popular support for the war had diminished considerably, the public had not developed a clear consensus on what should be done to end the war. During the 1968 campaign, voters perceived little difference between the Vietnam policies of Humphrey and Nixon, although they did view George Wallace as being distinctive.[39] Moreover, the relationship between policy preference on Vietnam and the 1968 presidential vote was relatively weak. Advocates of withdrawal gave nearly equal support to Humphrey and Nixon. Those who favored keeping American troops in Vietnam while trying to end the fighting gave Humphrey a slight edge (50 percent vs. 45 percent for Nixon). It was only among the advocates of further escalation that Nixon far outdistanced Humphrey (51 percent vs. 31 percent, with 18 percent going to Wallace). Among Democratic party identifiers, however, Humphrey's support was considerably lower than Johnson's 1964 support in each of the opinion categories.[40] The impact of the Vietnam issue in 1968, then, can be interpreted as a retrospective judgment of the Democratic administration's performance since 1964. The 1968 election, like the 1964 election, did not prescribe particular policy options for Vietnam, but it resulted in a Republican administration being given the responsibility for dealing with the war.

Voters were no doubt deeply troubled by the war in 1968, but perhaps as a result of the relatively indistinguishable views which they perceived on the part of Humphrey and Nixon, their votes did not reflect any clear mandate for a specific policy.

We have thus far examined two categories of popular control—nonexistent and indirect—and it appears that governmental policies generally fall within these two categories. A third category involves direct popular control of public policy. For this to occur, several conditions must be satisfied: (1) a substantial segment of the electorate must have intense and stable opinions about specific policy alternatives; (2) the electorate must have accurate information about the views of competing candidates; and (3) the electoral verdict must clearly reflect majority policy preferences.[41] The obvious problem, of course, is the difficulty in ascertaining majority policy preferences for electoral verdicts. A winning candidate, for example, might be supported by those who agree with his position on a given issue, by others who are unaware of or uninterested in that issue, and by still others who disagree with his position but who support him for other reasons.

For direct control to occur, in fact, it would be necessary for a campaign to be so dominated by a particular issue that the electorate renders its judgment primarily on that issue and that the victorious party or candidate easily deduces its mandate. In presidential campaigns, domination by a single issue is exceptional, so interpretations of issue mandates are of necessity speculative. A study of constituency influence in Congress, however, suggests that direct control can occur on some issues, most notably civil rights.[42]

Miller and Stokes reported that in the typical congressional district, almost half of the voters had read or heard nothing about either candidate for the House. Of the remainder, about one-fourth reported having heard or read something about both candidates, and an additional one-fourth reported knowledge about the incumbent. In 1958, however, the Fifth District in Arkansas departed dramatically from this pattern. Brooks Hays, the incumbent, had served as intermediary between the Governor of Arkansas, Orval Faubus, and the Eisenhower administration during the school integration crisis in Little Rock. His constituents perceived his activities as reflecting a too moderate approach to civil rights, and Hays was defeated by a write-in candidate, Dale Alford, who campaigned on precisely this issue. According to Miller and Stokes, not a single voter in the Fifth District was unaware of either candidate. The entire sample reported having read or heard something about both candidates, and interviews showed that perceptions of Hays' moderation on civil rights brought about his defeat.

As we indicated in our case study of school busing in Chapter One, civil rights is an issue area which is susceptible to this type of direct control. The intensity and stability of popular opinion on civil rights issues, along with the public's willingness to support or to oppose candidates solely or predominantly on these issues, provide the potential for direct control. Incumbents who vote "correctly" may not gain any visibility, so direct, immediate control would not be obvious. But incumbents who vote "incorrectly," and are subsequently punished at the polls, provide a clear indication of direct control.[43]

Popular control of government through elections, therefore, can be usefully portrayed as the degree of control on specific issues. It is anticipated that most governmental policy will not be subject to control at the polls. Of policies which are subject to control, most will be controlled indirectly, particularly through wide discretion being initially conferred upon officials and through retrospective judgments rendered in succeeding elections. Electoral reactions to Vietnam appear to fit into this category. Finally, we have policies which are subject to direct control through elections and for which particular alternatives are either prescribed or proscribed. This type of control is exceptional, and to the extent that we can find examples of such issues, they would be typically related to civil rights and racial questions.

Direct action

In large part, the guidelines staked out by elections are tied to voters' evaluations of past performance rather than voters' insistence upon future policy initiatives. Yet for many citizens, future initiatives and government action in terms of specific policy are matters of concern. And this may require other forms of political activity. A broad variety of political acts—such as contacting governmental officials, working in campaigns, organizing ad hoc groups around a particular issue, participating in demonstrations—can be categorized as direct action; that is, attempts by individual citizens, acting alone or in groups, to influence government directly.

One useful way of looking at political actions of various sorts is to distinguish between them in terms of influence. Verba and Nie suggest, for example, that political acts differ in the type of influence they are likely to exert on governmental leaders:

They (political acts) can exert pressure or they can communicate information about the preferences of citizens, or both. Acts vary in how much pressure they exert—i.e., in how much the political leader is induced to comply in order to avoid some negative consequence. They also vary in how much information they convey about the preferences of citizens.[44]

Utilizing the factors of pressure and influence, Verba and Nie provide the following categorization of four types of political acts: [45]

Act	Type of influence
Voting	High pressure/low information
Campaign activity	High pressure/low to high information
Cooperative activity	Low to high pressure/high information
Citizen-initiated contacts	Low pressure/high information

To the extent that citizens wish to affect directly governmental action, their political activity must provide information about their specific preferences. As indicated, voting is not likely to provide such information. Other types of political activity may be more effective in communicating preferences, but they will vary in the degree of pressure they exert. Pressure varies directly with the number and status of the people involved. The low pressure characteristic of citizen-initiated contacts with governmental officials, for example, derives from the fact that only one citizen is involved. Cooperative activity (belonging to and/or working in groups or organizations which are active in community affairs) is likely to be tied to specific problems, and it is therefore useful in providing high information, but the pressure involved depends upon how many and which citizens are involved. Campaign activity, on the other hand, may have a pressure component similar to voting, but the greater interaction between candidates and campaign activists can produce a higher level of information about the participants' preferences.[46]

Viewed from this perspective, citizen participation beyond voting, in terms of the more traditional forms of direct action, can supplement the influence of elections. Campaign activity may provide candidates with better information about the broad policy concerns and preferences of at least one activist segment of the population. Cooperative activity can allow citizens to press officials about specific policies affecting them as groups. And citizen-initiated contacts may be particularly useful in allowing citizens to press officials about problems affecting them as individuals. But as with voting, the effectiveness of this linkage depends upon how many and what types of citizens utilize it. Does, for example, leadership responsiveness to public attitudes expressed through various forms of direct action make government more responsive to actual public opinion or simply to the opinion of those who participate?

PARTICIPATION

While a majority of citizens actually vote, only a small minority engage in other forms of political activity. According to data compiled by the Survey Research Center, only voting and giving political opinions involve substantial segments of the population. The more demanding and continuous activities (such as working for a political party or belonging to a political club) are confined to about 4 or 5 percent of the respondents.[47]

Some elaboration of this is provided by the 1964 election study. Respondents were asked whether or not they engaged in eight political activities other than voting. As Table 9.7 indicates, almost two-thirds engaged in none of the activities listed. It seems apparent that only a very

Table 9.7
Index of Political Activity among the Electorate, 1964

TYPES OF ACTIVITIES	ACTIVITIES ENGAGED IN BY RESPONDENTS	
Attendance at political meetings or rallies	No activities	63%
Work in behalf of a party or candidate	One activity	22
Membership in a political club or organization	Two activities	8
Use of a political button or campaign sticker	Three activities	3
Communication (via letter) with a public official	Four activities	2
Communication (via letter) with an editor of a newspaper or magazine	Five activities	1
Influence on others to contribute money to a party	Six or more activities	1
Contribution by self to a party or candidate	Total	100

Source: John P. Robinson, et al., *Measures of Political Attitudes* (Ann Arbor, Mich.: Survey Research Center, Institute for Social Research, 1968), p. 594.

small proportion of the population engages in substantial amounts of political activity beyond voting.

The small segment of the population to which extensive political activity is confined tends to be a very unrepresentative segment in terms of socioeconomic status. The politically active are generally drawn from among the better educated, higher income, and higher occupational status groups —"higher socioeconomic status (SES) is positively associated with increased likelihood of participation in many different political acts; higher SES persons are more likely to vote, attend meetings, join a party, campaign, and so forth." [48] The differences by education, moreover, are especially significant, since they tend to be greater than those associated with income or occupation, and since they tend to have similar effects in the United States and other democracies. In their five-nation study (United States, Great Britain, West Germany, Mexico, and Italy), Almond and Verba concluded that certain political orientations were affected strongly by education in each nation. Thus higher educational levels are generally concomitant with greater awareness of the impact of government on the individual; greater attention to and more information about politics; a wider focus of attention to politics; a greater likelihood of discussing politics with a wide range of people; and more efficacious feelings about the individual's ability to influence what government does.[49] The more educated person, in sum, is more likely to feel politically competent and to be politically active than is the individual with less education.

For our purposes, the importance of differentials in participation lies in two areas: (1) the possible bias in opinion transmitted to officials through the activities of the more activist segments of the population; and (2) the manner in which officials respond to such opinion. Insofar as officials are more sensitive or responsive to the opinions of those who are more active, in other words, then the differences between mass opinion and activist opinion assume significance.

An illuminating example of the potential bias in what might be termed activist opinion was provided by the Johnson-Goldwater election of 1964. In attempting to ascertain why Goldwater and his advisers continued to believe that he had a chance to win the election in the face of massive survey data to the contrary, Converse and his collaborators looked at the differences between mass opinion (the general public) and letter opinion (that segment of the public which reported having written letters to public officials).[50] First, only 15 percent of the respondents in the study reported ever having written a letter to an official, and about two-thirds of all such letters were accounted for by about 3 percent of the population. (Writing letters to newspapers or magazines, sometimes considered an indicator of grassroots opinion, is apparently even less prevalent. Less than .5 percent of the population accounted for about two-thirds of all such letters.)

In comparing mass opinion to "letter opinion," the Converse study found some striking differences in terms of voter preference and voter ideology. In particular, the massive Johnson edge in general opinion did not transfer to letter opinion, where Goldwater was heavily favored. And the basis for this was found in the ideological comparison between the two types of opinion. While mass opinion was essentially neutral on a liberal–conservative continuum, letter opinion was strongly conservative. It is not surprising that this more conservative public favored Goldwater, nor is it surprising that other analyses of activists and non-activists have found similar ideological differentiations. What is surprising, and what is potentially very important in dealing with official responses to public opinon, is the extent to which officials may indeed respond to a tiny segment of the population while assuming that this segment is somehow representative of the broader public. The authors of the 1964 election study, for example, concluded that the Goldwater campaign was addressed to a very limited public and that illusions about this public were not dissipated until the landslide Johnson victory was a reality.[51] Many of the same illusions, although at the other end of the ideological continuum, appeared to characterize the 1972 presidential election between Nixon and McGovern. Whatever other mistakes might be attributed to McGovern and his staff, it seemed apparent that the candidate and his advisers were assuming an ideological receptivity within the electorate which simply did not exist.

On the second point, leadership responsiveness, Verba and Nie have presented some interesting evidence. Utilizing a large national survey and supplementing it with information on citizens and leaders in 64 "target communities," the authors were able to investigate patterns of linkage between what we have termed masses and elites. They suggest that the effects of citizen participation are tied largely to differential responsiveness by leaders.[52] In communities with higher participation rates, in particular, leaders tend to pay attention to those who participate and to give less consideration to the opinions of nonparticipants—thus in the "more active communities, there is a wide gap between the responsiveness received by active and inactive citizens." [53]

The Verba and Nie study is encouraging in one respect. Participation does make a difference, and high levels of participation within a community encourage leader responsiveness to public opinion. At the same time, Verba and Nie found that participants and nonparticipants differed in their perceptions of important problems and in favoring solutions for those problems.[54]

For the individual citizen, it may well be that political participation beyond voting will have some positive effect upon governmental officials if enough like-minded persons are also participating. It also appears to be the case that nonelectoral types of participation can be effective in transmitting information about citizen preferences to officials. Thus electoral and nonelectoral participation may be complementary. But differential participation imposes a severe restraint upon the utility of nonelectoral forms of participation, since it makes it difficult for officials to have accurate information about general public opinion. Indeed, officials may assume that they have such information, when they are in fact dealing with a very unrepresentative group.

In sum, it appears that participation beyond voting is significant, particularly insofar as it does appear to affect officials' behavior. But the very limited and unrepresentative segment of the public which engages in such activities may actually make government less responsive. As Verba and Nie conclude, "[Participation] could work so that lower-status citizens were more effective politically and used that political effectiveness to improve their social and economic circumstances. Or it could work, as it appears to do in the United States, to benefit upper-status citizens more." [55] Thus the utility of various participatory activities depends upon who engages in such activities as well as upon the potential effectiveness of such activities.

PROTEST

Thus far, we have concentrated on the more conventional forms of political activity. While certainly not characteristic of most of the population, they are considered legitimate by the public and by officials, and they represent readily accessible and continuous forms of political participation. The more dramatic forms of direct action—protests and demonstrations—are also a part of American politics and must be taken into account as potentially effective means for influencing governmental policy.[56] Protest activity can be utilized by individuals or groups who feel that the normal political process is not responding to their needs or grievances. Conspicuous examples of this phenomenon have been the civil rights movement of the early 1960s and the peace movement that developed later in that decade.

Protest activity may be honored in an historical sense—the Boston Tea Party and the American Revolution occupy a prominent place in our political folklore—but it finds considerably less acceptance when people are actually confronted with it. If contemporary attitudes are any indication, the Tories would be a lot better off today than they were in 1776. Protest activity and similarly conspicuous forms of political dissent do not appear to enjoy much legitimacy, and there is a generally widespread opposition to strikes, demonstrations, and the like. In fact, "if there is any attribute that has consistently characterized public opinion in the United States, it is its opposition to protest demonstrations. . . ." [57]

The 1968 SRC election study provides some interesting evidence on this point.[58] Respondents were asked whether or not they approved of "taking part in protest meetings or marches that are permitted by the local authorities" as a way "for people to show their disapproval or disagreement with governmental policies and actions." Despite the fact that the question was confined to protest activities permitted by the authorities, a majority of respondents disapproved of such tactics, and less than one-fifth found them acceptable.[59] The remainder said that their reactions would depend upon the circumstances, presumably who was demonstrating, what they were demonstrating about, and how they went about demonstrating.

One manifestation of this public orientation was the response to the demonstrations surrounding the Chicago Democratic convention in 1968. It should not be surprising that significant majorities disapproved of the demonstrations and were sympathetic to Mayor Daley and the Chicago police.[60] What is surprising is the extent to which such opinions characterized both "hawks" and "doves" among the general public. While one might expect that those who favored the Vietnam involvement and could be classified as "hawks" would be opposed to the anti-war demonstrations and to the protestors in particular, it might be assumed that the segment of the public which agreed with the protestors about the war would be considerably more sympathetic. But among whites who could be clearly classified as "doves"—who thought the involvement in Vietnam a mistake and that the best course of action would be withdrawal—a clear majority took a very negative view of the protestors and nearly one-fourth were extremely hostile.[61] It is interesting to note that blacks who happened to be "doves" were much more in sympathy with the demonstrators.[62] This may reflect a more general acceptance of protest activity arising out of its use during the civil rights movement.

The attention accorded dramatic protest, moreover, should not obscure the fact that very few people participate in demonstrations. Even the Vietnam issue, which generated more protest activity than any issue in recent history, spurred only a minute segment of the population to demonstrate.[63] This in itself is not a critical drawback, but it underscores the extent to which protest, in order to have any chance for success, must have a positive effect upon the wider public. Officials who are out of sympathy with the aims of protestors, for example, may be unswayed in any case, but their position will undoubtedly be strengthened when public reaction to protest is negative. Similarly, officials who might be more sympathetic to the goals of protestors will find it difficult to lend support unless the public reaction indicates at least some support. Indeed, protests that produce a strongly negative public reaction may have the unintended and dysfunctional result of silencing whatever official support might exist.

As Michael Lipsky states, "Thus in successful protest activity the *reference publics* of protest *targets* may be conceived as explicitly or implicitly reacting to protest in such a way that target groups or individuals respond in ways favorable to the protestors." [64] The civil rights movement protests of the early 1960s, for example, were ultimately aimed at the federal government. Specifically, the protests sought action by the President and Congress to guarantee voting rights, to desegregate public facilities and accommodations, and to protect southern blacks against discriminatory action by state and local governments. But the success of these protests depended upon eliciting sympathy among the general public outside the South, and this in turn depended upon widespread and sympathetic media coverage.

There are several points to be noted here. First, the success of protest activities depends upon who the protestors are and the individuals against whom they are protesting. Relatively powerless groups, such as blacks and poor people, are extremely dependent upon "reference publics" for by definition they lack stable and significant political resources. For groups with such resources as numbers, status, and organization, protest can be aimed directly at officials. Thus protest activity which must appeal to a broad public base in order to influence officials is dependent upon the public's perception of the protestors. It was much easier to arouse public support for the plight of underprivileged southern blacks than for college demonstrators.

It is also apparent that protests are assisted by "villains." Segregationist southern governors and police officials undoubtedly, if unwittingly, assisted the civil rights movement, and it was relatively easy for the public outside the South to accept the view that these officials were "villains" without bringing strongly held beliefs into question. When the alleged "villain" is someone for whom there is great reverence, institutionally if not personally, then the results may be quite different. The Vietnam protests focused largely upon Presidents Johnson and Nixon, and many individuals who were not terribly enthusiastic about either found such assaults upon the Presidency unforgivable. If, in order to go along with a protest, people must compromise their strongly held beliefs about institutions or persons, it is much more difficult for such protest to succeed.

Second, the utility of protest depends upon the tactics employed. Again, the nonviolent tactics of the early civil rights movement and the brutal official response in places like Selma, Alabama, generated sympathy for the movement. The riots in northern cities such as Newark and Detroit, however, had quite the opposite effect. As the rhetoric or tactics of protest become increasingly militant, the effect may be to discourage potential public support.

The tactics of protest illustrate a particular difficulty. In order to keep the protest group together and to get media coverage, it may be necessary for protest leaders to adopt strident rhetoric and to encourage confrontations with officials. While this can provide some psychological gratification for the protestors and make sensational news, the end result can also be the disaffection of public support.[65] It is difficult, of course, for the public to separate tactics from who the protestors are. For groups toward which there is public antagonism, such as college anti-war demonstrators, even the most peaceful tactics can inspire public condemnation. But for groups toward which the public is mildly positive or even neutral, the choice of tactics (and the spokesmen and rhetoric associated with tactics) can be critical.

Third, the utility of protest depends upon the issues involved. The success of the civil rights movement with respect to voting, for example, has not been paralleled by progress in social and economic legislation. This disparity is no doubt accounted for by the fact that it is much more difficult and costly to legislate social and economic equality than it is to guarantee voting rights. With respect to foreign policy issues generally, some other difficulties obtain. In particular:

The general American public, like the general publics in most of the mass democracies, is usually rather indifferent to the details of our international problems and opportunities. And . . . that indifference is correlated with a rather low level of information and a rather easy (if variable) yielding to governmental justifications for current policies and international gambles and capers.[66]

To turn the public around on foreign policy actions taken by the government is likely to be extremely difficult. This is especially true when presidential initiatives are being challenged. The notion that "the President knows best" is very strongly related to the public's approach to foreign affairs, and the ability of the President to "propagandize" the public is difficult to overcome.

Summary

Governmental responsiveness to public opinion can be examined first by analyzing linkages which might provide direct popular control of government. Through elections and direct action, the public can attempt to influence not only the choice of governmental leaders but also the policies which these leaders pursue. The effectiveness of direct linkages, however, is dependent upon the public's readiness and capability to be politically active and politically knowledgeable. Direct linkages assume that government officials will respond to public preferences because of the sanctions (immediate and potential) which the public can employ. For officials to act in this fashion, the electorate must show itself willing and competent to impose these sanctions.

ELECTIONS

We have found that national elections cannot usually be interpreted as programmatic mandates but that elections do represent an important form of popular control. Our analysis has focused on: (1) the degree of public participation in elections; (2) the role which issues play in voters' decisions; and (3) the types of control the electorate typically exercises. As far as participation is concerned, turnout in national elections does not compare favorably with turnout in other democracies. Much of this differential can be accounted for by divergent methods of calculating turnout and by the more exacting registration procedures in the United States. More serious than absolute levels of turnout are the variations in turnout by type of election and the differential participation of various segments of the population. Both factors tend to limit the responsiveness which we can expect from elections.

Over the past decade, there has been an increased awareness among voters of issue differences between parties and candidates and a more pronounced tendency for the electorate to vote on the basis of these differences. Traditional party loyalties remain an important motivation for many voters, and a majority of the electorate enters political campaigns already committed. But the electorate has displayed a readiness to vote in accordance with its issue preferences. Elections do not provide clear popular majorities in favor of future policy initiatives, but the "meddling partisan" encourages public officials to act on issues in anticipation of judgments at the polls.

The degree of control exerted through elections varies considerably by the type of policy involved. On many issues, public control is nonexistent, since the public is not sufficiently interested or informed. This is especially true of issues which are highly technical or complex or which do not appear to have direct, personal significance for the individual voter. On those issues which are debated and discussed during campaigns, the public's judgment is usually retrospective. Leaders are initially granted considerable discretion in dealing with problems, but their performance is periodically reviewed at the polls. The public is interested in the performance of the parties or officials in power rather than in prescribing or proscribing particular policy initiatives. There are, however, certain issues, particularly those relating to race relations and civil rights, where the public has exerted direct and immediate control over leadership initiatives.

DIRECT ACTION

Direct action activities can be effective in transmitting information about citizens' preferences to officials, and this is particularly true concerning preferences about specific policy initiatives. But a very limited and highly unrepresentative segment of the public generally participates in such activities. Evidence indicates that, under certain circumstances, public officials are responsive to active citizens, but this is often accompanied by decreased responsiveness to the preferences of inactive citizens. Accordingly, direct action represents an opportunity for citizens to influence public officials on specific issues, but this opportunity has typically been taken advantage of by upper-status citizens.

Direct action, in the form of protest and demonstrations, can prove an effective means for influencing government, as, for example, in the civil rights movement. An important variable in this regard is the general public's response. Since protests and demonstrations are frequently aimed at influencing public opinion in order to affect official behavior, the public's generally low tolerance for protest activities, its views about the demonstrators and their tactics, and the types of issues upon which the protest activities focus must all be taken into account in evaluating the utility and potential success or failure of this form of direct action.

NOTES

[1] The most comprehensive treatment of this issue is provided in Gerald M. Pomper, *Elections in America* (New York: Dodd, Mead & Company, 1968).

[2] On the symbolic functions of elections, see Murray Edelman, *The Symbolic Uses of Politics* (Urbana: University of Illinois Press, 1964).

[3] *Congressional Quarterly Weekly Report,* 33, No. 5 (February 1, 1975), 246.

[4] See President's Commission on Registration and Voting Participation, *Report* (Washington, D.C.: U.S. Government Printing Office, 1963); and selected comparative data in Robert A. Dahl, ed., *Political Oppositions in Western Democracies* (New Haven: Yale University Press, 1966).

[5] *Congressional Quarterly Weekly Report,* 33, No. 5 (February 1 ,1975), 246.

[6] Stanley Kelley, Jr., Richard E. Ayres, and William G. Bowen, "Registration and Voting: Putting First Things First," *American Political Science Review,* 61 (June 1967), 374.

[7] *Congressional Quarterly Weekly Report,* 33, No. 5 (February 1, 1975), 246.

[8] See Angus Campbell, et al., *The American Voter* (New York: John Wiley & Sons, 1964), pp. 56–59.

[9] Lester Milbrath, *Political Participation* (Chicago: Rand McNally, 1965), pp. 122–23; also, Sidney Verba and Norman Nie, *Participation in America* (New York: Harper & Row, Publishers, 1972), pp. 125–37.

[10] See Gerald M. Pomper, "From Confusion to Clarity: Issues and American Voters, 1956–1968," *American Political Science Review,* 66 (June 1972), 415.

[11] On the view that political candidates can stimulate ideological awareness in the electorate, see Arthur H. Miller, et al., "A Majority Party in Disarray: Policy Polarization in the 1972 Election" (Ann Arbor, Mich.: Center for Political Studies, 1973). Portions of this paper will appear in the *American Political Science Review,* 70 (1976 forthcoming).

[12] Richard W. Boyd, "Popular Control of Public Policy: A Normal Vote Analysis

of the 1968 Election," *American Political Science Review,* 66 (June 1972), 429–49.

13 William H. Flanigan, *Political Behavior of the American Electorate,* 2nd ed. (Boston: Allyn and Bacon, 1972), pp. 109–10.

14 Ibid., p. 111.

15 Miller, et al., "A Majority Party in Disarray," p. 90.

16 Campbell, et al., *The American Voter,* ch. 7.

17 Pomper, "From Confusion to Clarity," p. 419.

18 Ibid., p. 418.

19 Ibid., pp. 420–25.

20 For a detailed description of the normal vote, see Philip E. Converse, "The Concept of a Normal Vote," in *Elections and the Political Order,* ed. Angus Campbell, et al. (New York: John Wiley & Sons, 1966), pp. 9–39.

21 Philip E. Converse, et al., "Continuity and Change in American Politics: Parties and Issues in the 1968 Election," *American Political Science Review,* 63 (December 1969), 1083–105.

22 Miller, et al., "A Majority Party in Disarray." p. 5.

23 Ibid., p. 38.

24 Ibid., at footnote 13.

25 Ibid., p. 18.

26 Ibid., p. 28.

27 Ibid., p. 31.

28 Pomper, *Elections in America,* p. 92.

29 Ibid.

30 See Gerald H. Kramer, "Short-Term Fluctuations in U.S. Voting Behavior, 1896–1964," *American Political Science Review,* 65 (March 1971), 140–41.

31 Pomper, *Elections in America,* p. 96.

32 Boyd, "Popular Control of Public Policy," pp. 441–42.

33 Ibid., p. 441.

34 Ibid., p. 442.

35 Pomper, *Elections in America,* p. 251.

36 Ibid.

37 Boyd, "Popular Control of Public Policy," p. 442.

38 Pomper, *Elections in America,* pp. 251–52.

39 See Milton J. Rosenberg, Sidney Verba, and Philip E. Converse, *Vietnam and the Silent Majority* (New York: Harper & Row, Publishers, 1970), pp. 50–51. The electorate perceived Humphrey and Nixon as having similar positions on Vietnam. Moreover, the "average American's" position on Vietnam was about the same as that perceived for Humphrey and Nixon.

40 Boyd, "Popular Control of Public Policy," p. 433.

41 Ibid., p. 443.

42 Warren E. Miller and Donald E. Stokes, "Constituency Influence in Congress," *American Political Science Review,* 57 (March 1963), pp. 45–56.

43 Ibid.

44 Verba and Nie, *Participation in America,* p. 47.

45 Ibid., p. 48.

46 Ibid., pp. 47–55.

47 John P. Robinson, et al., *Measures of Political Attitudes* (Ann Arbor, Mich.: Survey Research Center, Institute for Social Research of the University of Michigan, 1968), p. 594.

48 Milbrath, *Political Participation,* pp. 16–17.

49 Gabriel Almond and Sidney Verba, *The Civic Culture* (Princeton: Princeton University Press, 1963), pp. 379–87.

50 Philip E. Converse, et al., "Electoral Myth and Reality: The 1964 Election," *American Political Science Review,* 59 (June 1965), 332–35.

51 Ibid., p. 335.

52 Verba and Nie, *Participation in America,* p. 315.

53 Ibid., p. 333.

54 Ibid., pp. 267–85.

55 Ibid., p. 342.

56 The discussion which follows excludes violent or otherwise illegal forms of direct action.

57 Rosenberg, Verba, and Converse, *Vietnam and the Silent Majority,* p. 44.

58 Converse, et al., "Continuity and Change in American Politics," 1083–105.

59 Ibid., p. 1105.

60 Ibid., p. 1087. See also Richard M. Scammon and Ben J. Wattenberg, *The Real Majority* (New York: Coward, McCann & Geoghegan, Inc., 1971), p. 162.

61 Converse, et al., "Continuity and Change in American Politics," p. 1087.

62 Ibid.

63 Only 8 out of 1495 respondents in the survey reported in Sidney Verba and Richard Brody, "Participation, Policy Preferences, and the War in Vietnam," *Public Opinion Quarterly,* 34 (Fall 1970), 325–32.

64 Michael Lipsky, "Protest as a Political Resource," *American Political Science Review,* 62 (December 1968), 1146.

65 Ibid., 1151–53.

66 Rosenberg, Verba, and Converse, *Vietnam and the Silent Majority,* p. 126.

OPINION INFLUENCE: POLITICAL PARTIES AND INTEREST GROUPS

10

A second model of representation in American politics focuses on the activities of organized and stable groups. According to this model, political parties and interest groups promote popular control of government by serving as intermediaries between their members and government. Since public opinion may be too varied and dispersive to be effective unless it is organized, these intermediate institutions provide opportunities for individuals with common interests and opinions to join in a collective effort to influence government policy. And while political parties and interest groups typically differ in their composition and in their range of policy interests, both can serve as instruments through which the individual citizen can relate to the governing process.

Political parties

Most scholars are philosophically committed to the idea that political parties are essential to the conduct of democratic politics, but there continues to be considerable disagreement concerning the performance of the two major parties in the United States. As one analyst explains:

Although argument persists as to the type of parties we need, it is generally agreed that democracy requires groups such as parties to perform critical functions—to recruit leadership, formulate policy, organize decision-making, communicate upward and downward between leaders and public, promote consensus, enforce responsibility, and thus move the society forward toward the effective and expeditious resolution of its conflicts.[1]

One criticism of American parties is that consistency between their electoral appeals and their governing behavior is lacking. The major parties do dominate the electoral process, so that elected officials are invariably Republican or Democratic. But it is frequently charged that the parties do not present the electorate with sufficiently clear choices, that their appeals lack substance. Similarly, the ability of the parties to govern effectively has been challenged, particularly their ability to enact the policies which they advocate. It does seem that American parties are less interested in issue advocacy and less cohesive as governing bodies than their counterparts in some democracies. But the question remains as to whether or not such a linkage is in fact possible in the United States—that is, whether or not responsible parties can be developed.

In theory, at least, the political party offers an efficient mechanism for converting popular preferences into governmental action. First, the party can present the voters with a group of candidates who take similar positions on policy issues. In other words, the party advocates certain policy proposals through its candidates. Second, the voters take into account the differences between the parties and select the candidates of that party which best reflects their preferences. Third, the party which elects a number of its candidates sufficient to control the government proceeds to enact the policy proposals it has advocated. This is, of course, a simplistic conception, for it is apparent that the parties are neither so united nor the voters so perceptive as to render this conversion process automatic.

Nonetheless, the ability of the political party to advocate policy proposals and to provide voters with a readily available and relatively direct method for responding to these proposals—namely, the candidates who run under the party label—gives it a unique place in the political system. Therefore, the potential utility of political parties as linkage mechanisms involves considerations such as: (1) the differentiation between the parties in terms of policy; (2) the differentiation between candidates of the parties in terms of policies; (3) the ability of voters to perceive the inter-party differences and to make choices between candidates within this frame of reference; and (4) the ability of the party in power to achieve sufficient cohesion among its members to enact the policies it has advocated. We will examine, accordingly, inter-party differences, first at the elite level and then among the mass public.

INTER-PARTY DIFFERENCES: ELITE LEVEL

Any number of factors might be considered in assessing the existence of significant inter-party differences, but several seem most appropriate to the discussion here. First, the utility of parties as linkage mechanisms depends upon a real differentiation between them in terms of policy choices, one indication of which is provided by the platforms adopted every four years at national conventions. Second, candidates of the two parties must reflect these policy distinctions to some discernible extent. Third, incumbents must also evidence support for party positions.

Party platforms. Gerald Pomper has provided a useful assessment of an oft-derided document, the national party platform. As everyone is no doubt aware, the party platform often contains a multitude of meaningless statements, and the difficulties in comparing parties by means of platforms must lead to the realization that platforms are mainly campaign documents. If one does not expect a detailed plan for governmental action, however, there are certain general findings about platforms which may help to assess their genuineness as indicators of party advocacy.

Using a method known as "content analysis," Pomper analyzed the platforms of the Republican and Democratic parties during the period from 1944 to 1964.[2] Among his findings were the following:

A. "They [the platforms] include considerable discussion of policy questions, often with a meaningful degree of specificity."[3]
B. "The record of the incumbent party, the one more crucial to the voter, is roundly debated, and this debate is conducted principally in terms of policy actions."[4]
C. "The parties present rather full descriptions of their future policy objectives and intentions and tend to be relatively specific. Their future pledges are most explicit in those policy areas involving distributive benefits, of most interest to voters with limited time and knowledge."[5]

The party platforms do constitute a relatively meaningful statement of what each of the parties advocates. Moreover, they reflect inter-party differences to a significant degree. As Table 10.1 indicates, only a minority of platform pledges are similar or bipartisan, while the majority relate to distinctive pledges by one or the other party, and approximately one in ten pledges finds the parties taking conflicting positions. Despite the variation over time and by policy area, then, the platforms provide substantial differentiation between the parties.

Finally, the pledges contained within the platforms are fulfilled. As Pomper states, "Moreover, and contrary to the conventional wisdom, these platform pledges are redeemed. Legislative or executive action directly fulfills more than half of the planks, and some definite action is taken in nearly three-fourths of the cases. Achievement is even greater for the party in the White House."[6]

The platforms, in sum, provide a reasonable guide for the "rational" voter. Along with cloudy rhetoric and vague promises, there is enough issue specificity to suggest the course of action which each party is likely to pursue (or not to pursue), and there is a good likelihood that the party will act on its pledges, particularly if it is given control of the White House.

Party activists and leaders.   Inter-party differences are also clearly reflected in the policy preferences of activists and leaders within the two parties. Research comparing the ideological distinctiveness between Democratic and Republican identifiers in the general electorate with that evidenced by party officials, candidates, and officeholders indicates quite clearly that much of the ideological distinctiveness in American politics is contributed by party activists and leaders.

Among party officials in the Detroit metropolitan area, for example, Eldersveld found "major (ideological) differences between the two parties' leadership structures, at all leadership levels." [7] Thus, "while the leadership is again not completely congruent in positions on all issues, the party structure may be characterized as a group in ideological terms—the Republican structure predominantly conservative, the Democratic structure strongly liberal." [8] Among party followers in the electorate, however, this distinctiveness was not nearly so pronounced, and there was substantial confusion

Table 10.1
Similarity and Conflict in Platform Pledges

	N	ONE-PARTY PLEDGE ONLY	BIPARTISAN PLEDGES	CONFLICTING PLEDGES
ELECTION YEAR				
1944	102	70%	28%	2%
1948	124	51	42	7
1952	205	52	29	19
1956	302	61	34	5
1960	464	51	39	10
1964	202	70	19	11
POLICY TOPIC				
Foreign	216	47	47	6
Defense	84	65	33	2
Economic	177	62	22	16
Labor	84	42	33	25
Agriculture	150	56	33	11
Resources	185	63	26	11
Welfare	255	60	27	13
Government	136	76	24	0
Civil Rights	113	40	60	0
All pledges	1,399	57	33	10
Total N	1,399	799	464	136

Source: Reprinted by permission of Dodd, Mead & Company, Inc. from *Elections in America* by Gerald M. Pomper. Copyright © 1968 by Dodd, Mead & Company, Inc.

Note: Rows add horizontally to 100 percent for the three right-hand columns.

about the ideological positions of the parties.[9] A number of other studies provide similar evidence that ideological distinctiveness of party leaderships is a characteristic phenomenon, even at the local level.

A comparison of delegates to the 1956 Democratic and Republican national conventions with a national sample of party identifiers provides relevant data about the relative distinctiveness of party leaders and followers. Using twenty-four policy issues (which could be categorized into five general areas: public ownership of resources; government regulation of the economy; equalitarianism and human welfare; tax policy; and foreign policy), McClosky and his colleagues found the Democratic and Republican leaders "separated by large and important differences. . . . In addition, the disagreements are remarkably consistent, a function not of chance but of systematic points of view. . . ."[10] The rank and file members of the parties, however, were far less divided than the leaders, both in the number of issues on which they diverged and in the magnitude of their divergence on these issues. As the authors suggest, "These findings give little support to the claim that the 'natural divisions' of the electorate are being smothered by party leaders. Not only do the leaders disagree more sharply than their respective followers, but the level of consensus among the electorate (with or without regard to party) is fairly high."[11] A study of delegates to the 1968 conventions supported the earlier findings of substantial ideological differences between Democrats and Republicans.[12]

There is differentiation between the parties in terms of policy, and these differences characterize attitudes among party officials. For linkage purposes, however, it is important that party candidates also display these attitudinal differences. Recent studies have indicated that candidates do, in fact, present the electorate with ideologically relevant choices based on the orientations of their respective parties. Fishel's study of congressional challengers during the 1964 election, for example, suggests that congressional challengers by and large provide the voters with meaningful alternatives: "Congressional challengers, whether potential winners or doomed losers, are not simply an aggregate of individuals contesting in isolated constituencies on issues relevant only to their districts . . . these party candidates constitute groups in ideological terms."[13]

Fishel found that a majority of Democrats classified themselves as liberals (59 percent) and a majority of Republicans designated themselves as conservatives (53 percent). Thirty-seven percent of the Democrats and approximately one-third of the Republicans (34 percent) chose the "middle of the road" or moderate classification. When this subjective identification was compared with the positions which the challengers actually took on issues, the general accuracy of the liberal-conservative self-identification and the distinct inter-party differences were quite clear.[14] As Table 10.2 indicates, Democratic "liberals" differed very sharply from Republican "con-

Table 10.2
Issue Positions of Democratic and Republican Congressional Challengers, 1964

POLICY OR PROGRAM AREA	PERCENTAGES RESPONDING THAT FEDERAL GOVERNMENT SHOULD "DO MORE"			
	Democratic Liberals	Republican Conservatives	Democratic Moderates	Republican Moderates
N	83	83	57	56
Minority and Negro rights	57%	19%	27%	26%
Assist public education	79	8	73	19
Provide medical care for elderly	96	8	73	28
Help poverty-stricken generally	87	12	60	19
Regulate labor unions	9	60	12	56

Source: Adapted from Jeff Fishel, *Party and Opposition* (New York: David McKay Company, 1973), p. 70. Only the domestic policy issues are presented here, and Republican liberals (only 12 in number or 8 percent of all Republicans) have been dropped.

servatives" in each of the five domestic policy areas, and these differences were consistent with widely accepted definitions of liberal and conservative policy positions. Moreover, with only one exception (programs for minority and Negro rights), significant if somewhat less sharp differences characterized the Democratic and Republican "moderates."

We have argued that the party linkage depends upon party candidates faithfully reflecting inter-party policy differences. A study by John Sullivan and Robert O'Connor provides particularly good evidence relating to this point. Sullivan and O'Connor assert that, in addition to other necessary conditions, linkage depends upon opposing candidates for the same office differing in their attitudes toward the issues. They compared the attitudes of all candidates for the United States House in the 1966 election on a series of questions dealing with Vietnam policy, civil rights, and domestic welfare. The research design allowed comparisons between Republican and Democratic candidates within the same district, and the results complemented the findings discussed in the Fishel study. Sullivan and O'Connor concluded that: (1) "the electorate in the aggregate was offered a substantively significant choice in the congressional election of 1966"; (2) "the Democratic candidates were almost invariably more liberal than their intradistrict Republican competitors"; and (3) "if a voter in 1966 wanted to vote conservatively, he only had to know that the Republican party is generally more conservative than the Democratic party in order to cast his ballot correctly in light of his values." [15]

It should be noted, however, that the type of choice offered by the intradistrict candidates in the Sullivan and O'Connor study was restricted in two respects. First, relatively few House districts are in fact competitive. In only 73 of 435 districts studied was the policy choice between candidates matched by effective competition between the parties.[16] Second, the ordering of candidate attitudes along a liberal-conservative dimension was not matched by a similar ordering of mass attitudes.[17] Therefore, Sullivan and O'Connor found that in practical terms the intradistrict differences in policy attitudes between candidates provided the *opportunity* for the electorate to affect policy but that in fact the 1966 election did not significantly affect public policy. In terms of our discussion, however, this difference is important, for it indicates that the "relatively weak linkage between public opinion and policy outputs is . . . [not] a result of the party system's failure to provide choices on issue positions. . . ." [18]

Party officeholders.   The third requirement for a potentially strong party linkage is that party officials in public office reflect relevant inter-party differences. We have already noted that party officials and party candidates present the public with viable choices, but the "party in government" must display some cohesion among its members if it is to enact the policies it has advocated.

Congressional Quarterly's studies of congressional voting behavior provide a useful means for assessing inter-party differences. In recent years, approximately 30 to 40 percent of all recorded votes in Congress have been party unity votes—that is, a majority of voting Democrats opposing a majority of voting Republicans.[19] Despite the variations by year and the slightly higher figures for the Senate, it is clear that inter-party divisions account for a significant number of legislative votes (see Table 10.3). Moreover most members of Congress support their party more often than they oppose it. In 1974, for example, the average party unity scores for non-southern Democrats and for all Republicans were substantially higher than their party opposition scores (see Table 10.4). Democrats from the South constitute a peculiar case, since they vote more often with the Republicans on partisan votes than with their fellow Democrats. But the distinctiveness of southern Democrats is of long duration, and it can be explained in terms of their pronounced conservatism when compared to other Democrats.

Ideological differences between the parties and party cohesiveness are certainly less pronounced in America than in some parliamentary systems. And there is, particularly within the Democratic party, a significant group of legislators whose voting is not consistent with their party label. Neverthe-

Table 10.3
Party Unity Votes in Congress, 1971 - 1974 (92nd and 93rd Congresses)

	TOTAL RECORDED VOTES	PARTY UNITY RECORDED VOTES	PERCENTAGES OF TOTAL
1974			
Both chambers	1,081	399	37%
Senate	544	241	44
House	537	158	29
1973			
Both chambers	1,135	463	41
Senate	594	237	40
House	541	226	42
1972			
Both chambers	861	283	33
Senate	532	194	36
House	329	89	27
1971			
Both chambers	743	297	40
Senate	423	176	42
House	320	121	38

Source: *Congressional Quarterly Weekly Report,* 33, No. 4 (January 25, 1975), 199-200.

Table 10.4
Average Party Unity Scores in Congress, 1974

	SUPPORT	OPPOSITION
SENATE		
Northern Democrats	73%	15%
Southern Democrats	35	50
Northern Republicans	55	33
Southern Republicans	73	11
HOUSE		
Northern Democratics	72	14
Southern Democrats	44	42
Northern Republicans	60	28
Southern Republicans	74	15

'Source: *Congressional Quarterly Weekly Report,* 33, No. 4 (January 25, 1975), 200.
Note: Data are composites of individual scores within each group. Support is defined as *voting* in agreement with a majority of the individual's party. Opposition is defined as *voting* against a majority of the individual's party. Failures to vote account for the difference between support, opposition, and 100 percent.

less, partisan divisions in Congress affect a significant number of legislative issues, and most members of Congress go along with their respective parties on these divisions.

The inter-party division in Congress is also consistent with liberal-conservative distinctions. Each year, a number of pressure groups assign ratings for members of Congress which can be used as rough measures of liberalism-conservatism. The ratings are derived from support of each group's position on what it considers key votes. In Table 10.5, the average 1972 ratings for Democratic and Republican senators are shown for the ADA (Americans for Democratic Action), COPE (Committee on Political Education of the AFL-CIO), and the ACA (Americans for Constitutional Action). The ADA and COPE are "liberal" pressure groups; thus high support scores can be considered as indicators of liberalism. The ACA is

Table 10.5
Pressure Group Ratings of United States Senators, 1972

	AVERAGE SUPPORT SCORES		
	ADA	COPE	ACA
Democrat	50%	66%	33%
Republican	25	31	64

Note: ADA scores are lowered by non-voting. COPE and ACA scores are calculated on the basis of issues on which the individual voted, and failure to vote does not lower the scores.

a "conservative" group, so high ACA scores reflect conservative orientations. All Democrats have been considered together, so the inter-party differences are not as sharp as would be the case if southern Democrats had been considered separately. Nonetheless, the inter-party differences are substantial. The support score for Democrats is twice as high as the average Republican score in the liberal direction (ADA and COPE). And the Republican score is twice as high as the Democratic score in the conservative direction (ACA).

Assessment of these inter-party differences depends to a great extent upon one's perspective. For those who would like to see responsible and cohesive parties, the levels of partisanship indicated are not overwhelming. Conversely, Republicans and Democrats do, in general, display differing orientations. There are liberal Republicans, just as there are conservative Democrats. Yet the "average" Democrat is more liberal than his Republican counterpart.

The effect of party on voting, however, differs by policy area. On some issues, partisan differences are quite distinct, and party represents a good "predictor" of voting behavior. On other issues, partisan distinctions are less clear, and the effect of party on voting diminishes. Aage Clausen has examined issue voting behavior in Congress during the period from 1953 to 1964 by classifying specific issues into five policy dimensions and assessing the importance of party on each dimension. The policy dimensions used include civil rights, international involvement, agricultural assistance, social welfare, and government management (government management of the economy and resources, including regulatory policy).[20] In Figure 10.1, the results of Clausen's analysis are shown. Note that the level of prediction based on a coefficient of correlation known as the Pearson product moment r (where the predictive value increases as r approaches 1.0 and decreases as it approaches 0) is greatest for issues falling in the government management, agricultural assistance, and social welfare dimensions. There is some variation in party as a predictor, as indicated by the two outer bars within each dimension; the center bar represents the average for all six Congresses. But the effect of party is remarkably consistent in both the House and Senate within each policy dimension, and, as Clausen states, "This strongly suggests that the factors affecting the variations in party-as-predictor across the five policy dimensions originate in a political community that embraces both houses of Congress." [21]

One final point on this topic: in the aforementioned Sullivan and O'Connor study, data were collected on the roll-call votes of all winners in the 1966 election on the same issues which were used in the pre-election comparison of intradistrict candidates. This was done to test the proposition that winners voted in accordance with their pre-election attitudes. The

Figure 10.1
Party as a Predictor of Voting on Five Policy Dimensions

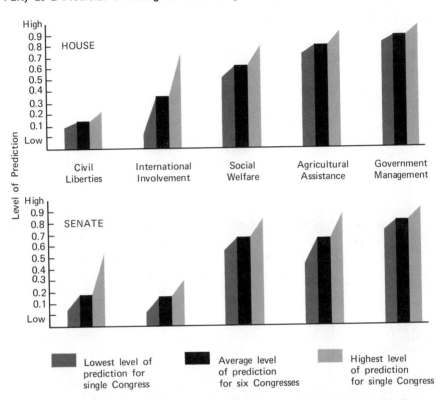

Source: Aage R. Clausen, *How Congressmen Decide: A Policy Focus* (New York: St. Martin's Press, 1973), p. 93.

results showed that "winning candidates in that election generally voted as their pre-election issue positions predicted. . . ."[22]

Three factors relating to inter-party policy differences among elites have been discussed. First, national party platforms have been utilized as indicators of the differing policies advocated by the parties. Second, party activists, party leaders, and party candidates have been considered as reflecting inter-party policy distinctions. Third, party groups in Congress have been examined in terms of the effects of inter-party differences on actual issue voting. In each instance, it appears that significant and consistent inter-party differences exist. Although ideological cohesion within both parties is imperfect, and despite inter-party agreement on some policies, there is enough differentiation to allow a "rational" voter to respond to the party label with some confidence. Parties do sustain and articulate a reasonably coherent partisan ideology. The question remains, however, of whether or not voters either respond or are capable of responding to such distinctions.

INTER-PARTY DIFFERENCES: VOTERS

The linkage provided by the political parties hinges on an additional and most important consideration, namely, whether voters are aware of inter-party differences and are able to make choices between candidates within this frame of reference. In other words, the voters must perceive the issue positions of the parties and vote for that party (or its candidates) which best represents their issue preferences. According to the responsible parties model, the voters must give the parties *programmatic* support.

Partisan voting. While the United States continues to be a two-party democracy, some important changes in partisan voting have occurred over the past two decades. In particular, partisan integration of voting behavior —that is, voter support of a party's entire ticket—has declined. The most apparent result of this decline at the national level has been divided party control of the Presidency and Congress. Since 1952, for example, the Republican party has won four of the last six presidential races and by 1977 will have controlled the Presidency for 16 of the past 24 years. The Democrats, on the other hand, have gained majority control of both houses of Congress in every election since 1954.

The decline in partisan integration can also be illustrated by examining "split results" and split-ticket voting in national results. Split results can be measured by comparing the party outcome of concurrent presidential and U.S. House election results at the congressional district level. Between 1900 and 1952, split results occurred in 15 percent or fewer congressional districts in 10 of 14 presidential elections. In only two elections during this period, 1912 and 1948, did split results occur in as many as 20 percent of congressional districts (25.2 percent in 1912 and 22.5 percent in 1948, with a substantial proportion of the splits involving third party candidates). From 1956 to 1968, however, split results occurred in from one-fourth to one-third of all congressional districts.[23] Moreover, the actual vote spread between a party's presidential and United States House candidate in congressional districts was substantial during this period. A spread of 10 percent or more between the Democratic share of the two-party vote for President and U.S. House occurred in nearly 40 percent of the congressional districts in elections from 1956 to 1968.[24]

As one might expect, this decline in partisan integration has been accompanied by an increase in split-ticket voting. Between 1952 and 1966, for example, the proportion of the electorate which reported having supported the same party in all presidential elections dropped from 68 percent to 46 percent.[25] (The same phenomenon occurred at the state and local level. The percentage reporting straight-ticket voting for state and local offices was in the low 70s from 1948 to 1960 but dropped to 50 percent by 1966.) [26]

This increasing tendency for partisans to support the other party in national elections is further evidenced by the growth in defection rates (the proportion of party identifiers supporting the opposite party) over the past decade (see Table 10.6). Among strong partisans, the defection rate nearly doubled, and the defections among weak identifiers, while less striking, were considerable.

Defections by party identifiers have had a very pronounced effect on presidential election results. While 42 percent of the Democratic identifiers supported Nixon in 1972, 84 percent supported a Democratic candidate for the United States House. Among Republican identifiers, 94 percent supported Nixon, and 82 percent supported the Republican congressional candidate.[27] Party loyalty among Democratic and Republican identifiers, then, was quite similar at the congressional level but very different at the presidential level.

Party identifiers who defect at the presidential level frequently return to their party at the congressional level, and this indicates that partisan support can be differentiated between presidential and congressional elections. Among party identifiers, for example, 85 percent voted consistent with their party identification in the 1958 midterm election; in 1970, 83 percent did so.[28] In assessing programmatic support for the parties, it is therefore necessary to examine two factors: (1) the effect of issues in

Table 10.6
Defection Rates for Party Identifiers in National Elections, 1952 - 1972

	1952 - 1960	1962 - 1972
Strong Democrats	4.3%	8.0%
Weak Democrats	18.2	22.4
Weak Republicans	16.2	19.6
Strong Republicans	3.7	7.2

Source: Arthur H. Miller, et al., "A Majority Party in Disarray: Policy Polarization in the 1972 Election" (Ann Arbor, Mich.: Center for Political Studies, 1973), p. 90. Portions of this paper will appear in *American Political Science Review*, 70 (June 1976 forthcoming).

producing defections at the presidential level; and (2) the effect of issues in maintaining the stability of partisan support at the congressional level.

Issues and presidential voting.   Our discussion of elections in Chapter Nine revealed that issue voting has become quite significant in presidential elections. And issue voting has been especially useful in explaining party defections in presidential voting. In a study of the 1960 and 1964 presidential elections, for example, David RePass found that defections from party were frequently explained by perceptions that the opposite party was better able to handle those problems the voter considered important.[29]

Rather than employing a predetermined set of issues, this study utilized open-ended questions to discover the voters' issue concerns and then ascertained their party preferences on those issues by asking respondents which party they felt was best able to deal with the issues. In allowing the respondent to define the salient issues for himself, RePass demonstrated the existence of a much higher level of issue awareness than had previously been assumed. Moreover, there was a pronounced tendency toward "issue alignment"—respondents generally chose one or the other party as being best able to handle all of the problems they considered salient. For respondents whose party identification and issue alignment was consistent (that is, Democratic identifiers who saw the Democratic party as best able to handle salient problems, or Republican identifiers who viewed the Republican party as correspondingly capable), party identification and voting choice were generally consistent. But for those whose party identification and issue alignment conflicted, issue alignment frequently overcame party identification in voting choice.[30]

This tendency to seek consistency between voting and "issue alignment" is also reported in V. O. Key's study, *The Responsible Electorate.* Key was especially interested in the forces which led people to switch party support in successive elections, and Table 10.7 is an illustration of the effect of issue alignment. For individuals who voted for the same party in 1956 and 1960 (D-D and R-R), there was, as expected, an overwhelming endorsement of that party as best able to handle what they considered the most important problem facing the country. Among switchers (R-D and D-R) voting choice in 1960 was consistent with issue alignment in 1960. And the same effect characterized new voters (O-D and O-R). Key suggests that these and related patterns of behavior indicate that "voters, or at least a large number of them, are moved by their perceptions and appraisals of policy and performance."[31]

It appears, then, that the saliency of presidential elections, the visibility of presidential candidates, and the relative clarity of issue differences between the parties' candidates in presidential elections have increased programmatic support for presidential candidates. At the same time, how-

Table 10.7
Patterns of Presidential Preference, 1956 - 1960

RESPONSE*	VOTING PATTERNS**					
	D-D	R-D	O-D	O-R	D-R	R-R
N (total = 2,993)	678	348	469	298	61	850
Republican	1%	5%	7%	56%	52%	81%
Democratic	79	63	65·	8	12	1
No difference	13	17	10	16	20	10
No opinion	5	12	14	17	3	7
No answer	2	3	4	3	13	1
Total	100	100	100	100	100	100

*Question: "Which political party to you think can do a better job of handling the problem (the *most* important problem facing this country) you have just mentioned—the Republican party or the Democratic party?"

**D-D and R-R include those who voted for the same party in 1956 and 1960; R-D and D-R include those who switched their party vote; O-D and O-R are those who did not vote in 1956 but who voted in 1960.

Source: V. O. Key, Jr., *The Responsible Electorate* (Cambridge: The Belknap Press of Harvard University Press, 1966), p. 134. The Belknap Press of Harvard University Press, © 1966 by the President and Fellows of Harvard College.

ever, voters have not transferred their perceptions of party differences (as evidenced by the presidential candidates) to the parties at the congressional level.

Issues and congressional voting. Since partisan support is generally significant and stable at the congressional level, we are interested in whether or not this support is based upon the voters' issue preferences. We have noted previously that the relationship between issue preferences and party identification has become stronger in recent years, and to this extent we might assume that partisan support at the congressional level has a programmatic basis. Programmatic support for one or the other party, however, would involve some knowledge about each party's past legislative record as well as consideration of future pledges or programs, and this type of information has not been evident in studies of congressional voting.

A study of the 1958 midterm election, for example, reported that few responses to the parties were related to legislative issues: "In 1958 . . . more than six thousand distinct positive or negative comments about the parties were made by a sample of 1,700 persons. Of these, less than 12 percent by the most generous count had to do with contemporary legislative issues." [32] An updating of the 1958 study utilizing data from the 1970 midterm election found that voter knowledge and perceptions had not changed substantially.[33] A majority of voters did not know which party controlled Congress. Over one-half of the 1970 respondents did not perceive inter-party issue differences on questions relating to Vietnam, integration, and government power. Among those respondents who did perceive inter-party issue differences and who supported their party, there was agreement between perceptions of the party's position on issues and the voter's position on issues. But among respondents where this agreement was lacking—that is, where a voter's own position on an issue differed from the position which he perceived his party as taking—partisan support was still quite strong. In effect, party loyalty tended to overcome issue differences between the voter and his party.

Both the 1958 and 1970 studies also examined voters' awareness of their own party's candidate and the opposition party's candidate. The largest group of voters in both years reported no knowledge about either candidate, and among these voters, party-line voting was quite strong (92 percent in 1958 and 84 percent in 1970). For voters who were aware only of their own party's candidate, party-line voting was almost perfect. As knowledge about the opposition party candidate increased, however, party-line voting decreased. This was especially true among voters who were aware only of the opposition party candidate. While this was a relatively small group—8 percent in 1958 and 11 percent in 1970—defections in 1958 occurred among 40 percent of these voters, and in 1970, a majority actually supported the opposition party candidate.

Programmatic support for parties in congressional elections is limited, particularly insofar as we define such support in terms of the parties' legislative records. The impact of particular candidates, moreover, is limited by the fact that approximately two-thirds of the voters are aware of neither candidate or only of their own party's candidate in congressional elections. And for many voters, party loyalties are sufficient to overcome issue disagreements with their parties at least in congressional elections.

Issues and the parties.   Among voters, inter-party differences are less significant than among elites. Party voting, for example, tends to be most pronounced during congressional elections, yet these elections appear to be less affected by issues than presidential elections. In fact, the level of party voting may be high, largely because issues intrude so little. In presidential elections, issue voting has been significant in recent elections, and issues have been useful in explaining the very considerable defections from party identification. Voter behavior consistent with the concept of responsible parties is difficult to discern. The effect of party loyalties, and the voters' willingness to abandon these loyalties when their positions differ from their party's, are quite different in presidential and congressional races. Programmatic differences do distinguish the major parties, but we find that programmatic support by the voters is limited.

Interest groups

The interest group may be regarded as another intermediate linkage between the citizen and government. Instead of citizens expressing their individual preferences directly to public officials, they join with others having common interests and similar preferences in private organizations. The leaders and activists of these private organizations, in turn, represent the interests and preferences of their memberships to government.

Interest group activities aimed at influencing government policy have been defended under the First Amendment guarantees of free speech and of the people's right "to petition the Government for a redress of grievances." In Washington, hundreds of diverse groups—including commercial and industrial interests, agricultural interests, labor unions, professional organizations, ethnic and racial groups, cause-oriented groups, state and local government associations, and the new citizen's lobbies—work with congressional committees, executive agencies, regulatory commissions, and occasionally with the courts in seeking to promote the interests of their members.

The level of interest group activity at the national level has increased substantially in recent decades, largely in response to the growth of federal government programs and budgets. Many issues which stimulate interest group activity do not engage the interest or attention of the mass public, while others may result in interest groups attempting overtly to influence or to mold public opinion. The broad variety of interest group activities can be illustrated by looking at some of the major lobbying campaigns during the first term of the Nixon administration:

A coalition of aerospace companies and labor unions pushing for government-financed development of a supersonic transport plane . . . battled in Congress by another coalition led by groups interested in environmental problems and in competing national priorities.

Temporary coalitions of groups which combined their pressure on policymakers in repeated campaigns to force an end to U.S. military involvement in the Vietnam war.

Bipartisan coalitions of labor, civil rights, and other groups sucessfully opposing confirmation by the Democratic-controlled Senate of two successive Supreme Court appointments by the Republican President.

A quietly successful effort by lobbyists for drug interests to block legislation to place two high-selling tranquilizers, Librium and Valium, under mandatory Government controls.

A bitter battle between United States manufacturing and labor interests who urged restrictions on certain foreign imports and a combination of free trade exponents, foreign interests, and American-based multi-national corporations who opposed import curbs.

A coalition of shipping companies, unions, and shipbuilders successfully culminating years of attempts to enact a Federal subsidy program to rebuild the aging United States merchant fleet. . . .

The American Petroleum Institute successfully pressing Congress and the Executive Branch for continued protective quotas on oil imports—and countered by groups which opposed import restraints.

The AFL-CIO speaking on a continuing basis, though with varying indications of unanimity, as the organized voice of 14 million labor union members, whose lobbyists listed an interest in "all bills affecting the welfare of the country generally"—and joined or opposed on specific issues by groups as different in general outlook as the business-oriented Chamber of Commerce.

Ideological pressure groups such as Americans for Democratic Action on the left and Americans for Constitutional Action on the right, working in opposing directions to influence the general trend of United States Government policy.[34]

The interest group, like the political party, is an intermediary institution. It represents a means by which individuals with common interests can organize and use their resources to make demands on government. Theoretically, the interest group is close enough to the concerns of the citizen to engage at least his limited participation and also to provide the stable organization and collective strength necessary to gain access to government decision makers. The assumption that interest groups increase governmental responsiveness, however, must be examined by looking at the representativeness, political salience, and responsiveness of the groups themselves. For example, in order for interest groups to provide popular control of government, membership in interest groups must be widespread and generally representative of the mass public, citizens must join interest groups for the purpose of gaining political representation, and the leadership of interest groups must faithfully represent the interests and preferences of their members.[35] If these conditions are not satisfied, interest groups cannot be expected to provide relatively equal access to the government for the variety of interests and groups constituting the mass public.

REPRESENTATIVENESS

Membership in organizations is more widespread in the United States than in other democracies (see Table 10.8). But while a majority of Americans report membership in at least one organization, only about one in four belongs to an organization which he or she perceives as involved in politics. Approximately one-half of the organizational memberships involve social, charitable, fraternal, and church-related groups.[36]

We find, moreover, that just as other forms of political participation reflect class or status differentials, membership in organizations varies according to socioeconomic status. Individuals in upper income, education, and occupational status groups are more likely to belong to organizations

Table 10.8
Organizational Membership—Voluntary Associations and
Organizations Perceived as Politically Involved

	PERCENTAGES OF RESPONDENTS REPORTING MEMBERSHIP IN:	
COUNTRY	All voluntary associations	Organizations they perceive as politically involved
United States	57	24
Great Britain	47	19
Germany	44	18
Italy	29	6
Mexico	25	11

Source: Excerpts from Gabriel A. Almond and Sidney Verba, *The Civic Culture: Political Attitudes and Democracy in Five Nations* (copyright © 1963 by Princeton University Press; Little Brown and Company, Inc. © 1965), pp. 304-474. Reprinted by permission of Princeton University Press.

than are those in the lower categories even when labor union membership is included.[37] As one study concluded, "whichever index of status is used, an appreciably higher percentage of persons in higher status positions belong to voluntary associations than do persons of lower status." [38] In addition, multiple organizational memberships are more characteristic of higher status individuals than of lower status individuals. Key reported, for example, that over one-half of the respondents in professional households claimed three or more group memberships, but only five percent of the respondents in households headed by unskilled workers claimed a similar level of group membership.[39] Activity within organizations also varies with social status. Those who participate most actively or who hold leadership positions are predominately the better educated.[40]

Substantial segments of the population are not organized into politically active organizations. The interest group system thus provides a clear differentiation in the types of opinion transmitted to government. Only a small portion of the public is politically active, and this stratum tends to be disproportionately upper status and to have a relatively high frequency of organizational memberships. This suggests that "the higher political strata may gain leverage in the political process by their participation in politically relevant private groups." [41] The political linkage provided by interest groups is perhaps quite effective, but it is a means of influence only for those who are organized. Even mass-membership organizations, such as farm groups and unions, typically fail to organize substantial numbers of potential members.[42] And while labor unions and various citizen groups have been extremely active in Washington, a majority of the groups in Washington reporting lobbying expenditures have been business associations. Dye and Zeigler report, for example, that "business associations are the single largest lobbying group at the state and national levels." [43]

POLITICAL REPRESENTATION

We have already seen that a minority of organization members consider their groups to be political. Even groups which are considered political, however, generally have nonpolitical functions, and these functions may even take priority over the political objectives of the group. There are, no doubt, individuals who join interest groups for purely political objectives. This would generally be the case for members of ideological or cause-oriented groups, such as Americans for Democratic Action or Americans for Constitutional Action. At the same time, many individuals join interest groups for basically nonpolitical reasons.

In fact, there is a good case for the theory that interest group membership is predicated upon nonpolitical benefits for some members.[44] Many associations functioning as interest groups also provide selective benefits to their members, such as social activities or bargaining efforts of unions, the professionally relevant activities of organizations like the AMA, or the recreational and educational activities sponsored by conservation groups. This does not mean that members of these organizations are uninterested in the political objectives of the organization (although they may not agree with the positions taken by the leadership on specific issues), but it does indicate that the motivations fostering group membership are varied.

The leaders of interest groups and their lobbying staffs, however, are directly and immediately concerned with the political objectives of their organizations. These persons necessarily define their organization's political agenda and take responsibility for developing and articulating it. In so doing, they are able to exercise considerable discretion. This is partially a result of the fact that many members of their organization are not primarily politically oriented, but also because many of the issues with which the leaders must deal are complex, detailed, and sometimes obscure matters of legislative or administrative policy.

The influence of many major interest groups is based partially upon their expertise in a given policy area. And this expertise must obviously be translated into positions on specific matters of law. Within the broad confines of an organization's political objectives, leaders and their staffs are responsible for this translation. On many of the issues with which they must deal, few members are likely to have much interest or information, much less an intense opinion.

Occasional issues may be politically relevant for the membership, however. To this extent, such organizations have political salience for their members. At the same time, the nonpolitical or selective benefits of membership represent important inducements. What this suggests is yet another stratification of political participation. Within interest groups, there is a small core of activists, intensely interested in the political goals and objectives of their organizations and willing to expend the time, energy, and resources necessary to achieve these goals and objectives. These individuals are likely to determine their organization's political stance. Most members, on the other hand, will not be very active, and their opinions and preferences may serve only to define very broad parameters within which the leaders and activists must operate.

This suggests that the distinctions which can be drawn between active and passive citizens among the general population—such as differences in political participation, political involvement, and sense of political efficiacy—might also apply to the membership of a given interest group.[45] Some members might identify more strongly with the group than others and be more interested in the group's political objectives. In comparing sense of union identification with level of political involvement, for example, V. O. Key found that those who identified most closely with the union were also likely to be more politically involved (see Table 10.9). For the "hard core" as opposed to the peripheral members, we might expect that the political salience of the union would be substantial.

We cannot assume, then, that interest groups are important sources of political representation for all their members. Many individuals may be drawn into joining a group by nonpolitical services or activities which they could not receive as nonmembers. For these individuals, the political

Table 10.9
Sense of Union Identification and Level of Political Involvement

POLITICAL INVOLVEMENT	LEAST IDENTIFIED (1)	(2)	(3)	MOST IDENTIFIED (4)
N	83	126	109	110
High (4)	17%	14%	26%	34%
(3)	19	29	24	23
(2)	36	33	26	31
Low (1)	28	24	24	12
Total	100	100	100	100

Source: V. O. Key, Jr., *Public Opinion and American Democracy* (New York: Knopf, 1965), p. 507. Reprinted by permission of Alfred A. Knopf, Inc.

salience of the interest group is likely to be limited or nonexistent. For those group members who identify strongly with their groups, and as a consequence are willing to invest the time and the attention necessary to keep informed about political activities, the political salience of the group is probably very high. To this extent the group helps to provide political representation for them.

LEADERS VS. FOLLOWERS

Although we cannot expect that interest group opinion will reflect public opinion, we would expect, however, that the positions taken by an interest group would conform to the preferences and opinions of its members. Several studies have indicated, though, that there exists an underlying lack of consensus between leaders and followers not only about issues but also about the activities and strategies an interest group pursues. Even though interest groups are presumably comprised of like-minded individuals, leaders have assumed positions about which their members are unaware or about which they disagree. We cannot realistically expect all members of an interest group to subscribe to the group's position on all issues, but we might expect the group's positions on issues to be in general accord with the preferences of a majority of members.

What limited evidence there is relating to opinion homogeneity within interest groups suggests that opinion differences between leaders and followers are sometimes substantial. One study of attitude consensus and conflict in an educational interest group found leaders more positive in their choice of political activities for the group. The leaders also attached more significance and influence to the group's activities than did the followers and displayed significant differences in issue opinions from the general membership.[46] This study also suggested that "the position of group leader contributes to the development of attitudes which differ from those of the followers." [47]

There are a number of factors which might account for the divergence between group positions and member opinions. First, as suggested above, there may be a "natural" division of opinion within an organization resulting from the leader-follower distinction. And even if leaders believe that they should represent what their members want, their perceptions of members' opinions can be inaccurate.

Second, members of an organization may be unaware of the organization's position. If the position is poorly communicated or equivocal, the resultant confusion or conflict can be expected to limit the group's influence over its members. For example, a group's endorsement of a presidential candidate may be clearly communicated to its members, in part because this endorsement is widely publicized and considered to be important. Its endorsement of a congressional candidate, on the other hand, may receive considerably less publicity, with the result that members are unaware of the endorsement. Lack of clarity in a position can also result from conflict within the leadership. In the Nixon-McGovern contest in 1972, the leadership of the AFL-CIO endorsed neither candidate. But the heads of some unions did endorse the Democratic candidate. While it can be argued that the AFL-CIO's neutrality did not have a crucial effect on the outcome, the fact remains that a union member who was looking for cues concerning labor's position would have been faced with patent ambiguity.

Even if a group can communicate its position effectively, however, its influence may still be limited. Members may be willing to accept the group's position on some questions but not on others, depending upon whether they perceive the issue in question to be a salient one for the group and/or a legitimate group concern.[48] Candidate endorsements, for example, may be accepted as appropriate by members of one group, while members of another might consider such endorsements to be inappropriate. Similarly, members of an organization might lend credence to their group's positions on certain types of issues, while dismissing other issues as outside the group's legitimate responsibility.

Finally, there exists among interest group members varying degrees of identification with the group.[49] For strong identifiers, including the leadership and activist echelons, the salience of group positions and the legitimacy of group activities will tend to be relatively high. This is a circumstance not unlike the effect of strong identification with a party. Strong identifiers tend to stick with the party, even when they are not particularly pleased with a candidate or when they disagree with the party's position on a particular issue. Weak identifiers, on the other hand, will be less inclined to follow the group's lead—possibly as a result of being unaware of what that lead is.

It is the nature of the opinion transmitted as well as the effectiveness of its transmission which represents an important question concerning interest group linkage. The distribution of interest group membership, the limited salience of interest group activity for group members, and the gaps between group positions and member opinions indicate that it is very selective opinion which is being transmitted. It is clear that the interest group "system" does not adequately represent mass opinion. It is also clear that even the more limited model of interest group action—in which the group's representatives, e.g., lobbyists, speak for a membership united on goals and means to achieve them—does not always fit reality.

Summary

Group influence in American politics can be assessed by examining the activities of political parties and interest groups. As intermediate institutions, these organizations aggregate the interests and opinions of individuals and attempt to influence government action in accordance with the common interests and goals of their members. Political parties and interest groups therefore represent stable linkages through which public opinion may be transmitted to government.

POLITICAL PARTIES

The transmission of popular preferences through the political party finds its clearest expression in the responsible party model. Responsible parties provide the electorate with clear-cut policy alternatives and with candidates committed to a common program. Accordingly, the voter is primarily interested in the legislative records and proposed programs of the competing parties and evaluates candidates based upon national party programs. Armed with programmatic support, the majority party then proceeds to enact its program.

We have found, however, that the responsible party model has not been fully achieved. At the elite level, the parties do provide policy alternatives. Their platforms are meaningful, and each party has managed to fulfill many of its promises. The activists, leaders, and candidates of the two parties are ideologically distinct, and the parties' legislative performance does reflect significant levels of party cohesion. The party elites are not, of course, similarly distinguishable in all policy areas, nor is party cohesion in the legislature as strong as it is in some parliamentary democracies. The programmatic alternatives provided by the Republican and Democratic parties are not as clear or as comprehensive as some critics would prefer, but the party labels cannot be dismissed as meaningless or irrelevant.

At the mass level, however, the American parties face formidable difficulties. Over the past decade, significant increases in Independent identification and the clear decline in the partisan integration of the vote indicate that many Americans no longer rely solely on the parties for their political cues. Much of the electorate's heightened issue sensitivity has been directed at presidential races, and the party coalitions have been unusually fluid and unstable as a result. Party has remained as a powerful reference symbol in congressional elections, but on this level and in these elections it has had a limited programmatic content. Whatever the objective differences between the parties, it appears that much of the electorate finds these differences boring or inconsequential. That we do not have disciplined governing parties capable of overcoming the separation of powers between the President and Congress is in great part a result of the electorate's perception that such parties are unnecessary or undesirable.

The representation of public opinion through the party linkage is an important component of opinion influence in American politics, but the effectiveness of the linkage is limited by the erosion of stable, long-term party loyalties. The parties have aggregated and mobilized political influence and have been active intermediaries in transmitting mass opinion, but they have not monopolized these functions in the past and are unlikely to do so in the future.

INTEREST GROUPS

Interest groups are effective participants in the political process, but they do not serve as mechanisms for transmitting mass opinion to government. In part, this is a result of the lack of representativeness characterizing interest groups. While voluntary association membership in the United States is relatively high in comparison to other democracies, only about one in four Americans belongs to a group which is perceived as politically involved. Moreover, there is a clear upper-status bias in the membership and leadership of interst groups. Much of the public remains outside the interest group system, and this is particularly true of those in the lower income, education, and occupational status groups.

In addition, the political representation provided by interest groups is not uniformly distributed among their members. Many members are interested in the selective, nonpolitical benefits of their organizations. Thus most organizations are characterized by a small group of activists who are intensely interested in political goals and who are willing to invest the time and resources necessary for effective participation in group decisions. As a result, cohesion and consensus within interest groups are frequently limited. Leaders and members may differ with respect to the position the group should take on particular issues and the kinds of political activities and strategies it should pursue. Leaders' perceptions of members' attitudes and opinions are not necessarily accurate, and the same misperceptions may characterize members' views of their organization's positions on given issues.

The opinions and interests of the mass public are more effectively aggregated and represented by political parties than by interest groups. For selected segments of the public, however, the interest group linkage has been an active device for collective pressure on government.

NOTES

[1] Samuel J. Eldersveld, *Political Parties* (Chicago: Rand McNally, 1964), p. 22.

[2] Reprinted by permission of Dodd, Mead & Company,· Inc. from *Elections in America* by Gerald M. Pomper. Copyright © 1968 by Dodd, Mead & Company, Inc. The technique is explained on pp. 149–78 and 274–79.

[3] Ibid., p. 175.

[4] Ibid., p. 176.

[5] Ibid.

[6] Ibid., p. 202.

[7] Eldersveld, *Political Parties*, p. 218.

[8] Ibid., p. 529.

[9] Ibid., pp. 190–202; 474–91.

[10] Herbert McClosky, et al., "Issue Conflict and Consensus among Party Leaders and Followers," *American Political Science Review*, 54 (June 1960), 410.

[11] Ibid., p. 419.

[12] John W. Soule and James W. Clarke, "Issue Conflict and Consensus: A Comparative Study of Democratic and Republic Delegates to the 1968 National Conventions," *Journal of Politics,* 33 (February 1971), 72–91.

[13] Jeff Fishel, *Party and Opposition* (New York: David McKay Company, Inc., 1973), p. 74.

[14] Ibid., pp. 69–74.

[15] John L. Sullivan and Robert E. O'Connor, "Electoral Choice and Popular Control of Public Policy: The Case of the 1966 House Elections," *American Political Science Review,* 66 (December 1972), 1264.

[16] Ibid., p. 1265.

[17] Ibid., pp. 1264–65.

[18] Ibid., p. 1264. A further discussion of constituency responses in relation to ideological distinctions between the parties can be found in Robert S. Erikson, "The Electoral Impact of Congressional Roll Call Voting," *American Political Science Review,* 65 (December 1971), 1018–32. Erikson concludes that ". . . the small portion of the voters who are most politically attentive are sufficiently influenced by what candidates do and say to have a measurable impact on election outcomes."

[19] Recorded votes include roll-call votes in the Senate and roll-call or recorded teller votes in the House.

[20] Aage R. Clausen, *How Congressmen Decide: A Policy Focus* (New York: St. Martin's Press, Inc., 1973), pp. 38–51.

[21] Ibid., p. 94.

[22] Sullivan and O'Connor, "Electoral Choice and Popular Control of Public Policy," p. 1264.

[23] Walter Dean Burnham, *Critical Elections and the Mainsprings of American Politics* (New York: W. W. Norton & Company, Inc., 1970), pp. 108–9.

[24] Ibid., p. 110.

[25] Ibid., p. 120.

[26] Ibid.

[27] Arthur H. Miller, et al., "A Majority Party in Disarray: Policy Polarization in the 1972 Election" (Ann Arbor, Mich.: Center for Political Studies, 1973), pp. 38, 90.

[28] Stanley R. Freedman, "The Salience of Party and Candidate in Congressional Elections: A Comparison of 1958 and 1970," in *Public Opinion and Public Policy,* rev. ed., ed. N. Luttbeg (Homewood, Ill.: The Dorsey Press, 1974), pp. 127–28.

[29] David RePass, "Issue Salience and Party Choice," *American Political Science Review,* 65 (June 1971), 389–400.

[30] Ibid.

[31] V. O. Key, Jr., *The Responsible Electorate* (Cambridge: Harvard University Press, 1966), p. 150.

[32] Donald E. Stokes and Warren E. Miller, "Party Government and the Saliency of Congress," *Public Opinion Quarterly,* 26 (Winter 1962), 535.

[33] Freedman, "The Salience of Party and Candidate in Congressional Elections," pp. 126–31.

[34] *The Washington Lobby* (Washington, D.C.: Congressional Quarterly Service, 1971), p. 1.

[35] Thomas R. Dye and L. Harmon Zeigler, *The Irony of Democracy,* 2nd ed. rev. (Belmont, Calif.: Wadsworth Publishing Co., Inc., 1972), p. 215.

[36] Gabriel A. Almond and Sidney Verba, *The Civic Culture* (Princeton: Princeton University Press, 1963), p. 302.

[37] Ibid., p. 429; see also Charles R. Wright and Herbert H. Hyman, "Voluntary Association Memberships of American Adults: Evidence from National Sample Survey," *American Sociological Review,* 23 (June 1958), 284–94.

[38] Wright and Hyman, "Voluntary Association Membership," 288.

[39] V. O. Key, Jr., *Public Opinion and American Democracy* (New York: Knopf, 1965), p. 502.

[40] Almond and Verba, *The Civic Culture,* p. 315.

[41] Key, *Public Opinion and American Democracy,* p. 508.

[42] Ibid., pp. 503–4.

[43] Dye and Zeigler, *The Irony of Democracy,* p. 217.

[44] See, for example, Mancur Olson, *The Logic of Collective Action: Public Goods and the Theory of Groups* (Cambridge: Harvard University Press, 1965).

[45] Key, *Public Opinion and American Democracy,* pp. 504–6.

[46] Norman R. Luttbeg and Harmon Zeigler, "Attitude Consensus and Conflict in an Interest Group: An Assessment of Cohesion," *American Political Science Review,* 60 (September 1966), 655–66.

[47] Ibid., p. 666.

[48] Angus Campbell, et al., *The American Voter* (New York: John Wiley & Sons, 1964), pp. 161–83.

[49] Ibid.

OPINION INFLUENCE: REPRESENTATIVE INSTITUTIONS

11

The influence of public opinion upon government depends in great part upon the responsiveness of political leaders, especially those entrusted with the responsibility for acting in the public's behalf. In national politics, this responsibility is associated most closely with the President and Congress. The manner in which Presidents and members of Congress approach public opinion is affected of course by the motives, attitudes, and values which they bring to the conduct of politics. The Watergate scandals, for example, indicate that the Nixon Presidency was characterized by a cynical disregard for democratic "rules of the game," democratic rights and liberties, and democratic goals. That public officials sometimes pursue personal or political gains in violation of ethics or law should be a constant reminder of the effects of character upon politics.

But the relationship between political leaders and the public is also tied to the institutional contexts within which Presidents and members of Congress operate. If, for example, the Watergate mentality can be traced primarily to the "inner circle" of the Nixon White House, does this simply reflect unfavorably upon the individuals involved or does it point to serious institutional defects in the contemporary Presidency? On a more general and less dramatic level, does public dissatisfaction with congressional performance lead to the mundane conclusion that we need better men and women in Congress or does it require a closer look at the institutional practices and capabilities of Congress?

Much of what can be said about the linkages provided by political leaders is bound to be speculative and inferential, but the importance of the Presidency and Congress in responding to and influencing public opinion is so clear and substantial as to justify some tentative theorizing. In examining the executive and legislative branches, then, we shall be interpreting their relationship to the public in terms of several factors: (1) public expectations and perceptions concerning their roles and responsibilities; (2) the major channels of influence and information between them and the public; (3) the resources and institutional mechanisms which they utilize in dealing with the public; and (4) the institutional strengths and weaknesses which each displays in attempting to perform the linkage function between the public and government.

The presidency

The overextension of governmental power has been a recurring source of concern in American political theory, and the Presidency has, in recent decades, represented one of the most important manifestations of that concern. More than three decades ago, a noted constitutional scholar warned against the "personalization" of presidential power and the possibility of undue presidential influence upon public opinion.[1] In its report issued in 1950, the Committee on Political Parties of the American Political Science Association asserted that the weakness and lack of responsibility of America's major political parties might lead the public to "go too far in compensating for this inadequacy by shifting excessive responsibility to the President." And this, in turn, would favor the kind of President "who exploits skillfully the arts of demagoguery, who uses the whole country as his political backyard, and who does not mind turning into the embodiment of personal government." [2] Several years ago, George Reedy, a former press secretary for Lyndon Johnson, gloomily analyzed the Presidency as the "American monarchy," an office filled by men increasingly isolated from reality and insulated from critical opinion.[3]

In early 1973, the dire warnings about presidential power and constitutional imbalance seemed to come to a head. The Nixon administration and Congress were embroiled in serious disputes about presidential powers and prerogatives—executive privilege; presidential impoundment of appropriated funds; independent executive war-making; and the accountability of executive officers and agencies to Congress. Citing its landslide victory of the previous November, the Nixon administration argued that it had a mandate which Congress was attempting to frustrate, and many members of Congress appeared reluctant to challenge what they considered to be an extremely popular President. As the Watergate crimes were uncovered, however, presidential popularity plummeted, and the administration lost a number of major battles in Congress and the courts. By the time that Richard Nixon was forced to resign in August, 1974, the threat of excessive presidential power had receded, and there was even some concern that the Presidency had in fact been crippled. But the aforementioned studies concurred that there were serious institutional defects in the Presidency and, in particular, that excessive presidential power rested on the relationship which had developed between the Presidency and the public. The question remains as to whether or not any serious alteration has occurred in this relationship.

PUBLIC EXPECTATIONS

Public attitudes toward the Presidency and toward Presidents have, at least until recently, been deferential and supportive. As one analyst has summarized this phenomenon, the Presidency has been characterized by public perceptions of omnipotence and benevolence, and the result has been expectations that the President provide personal and moral leadership.[4] There is, in other words, a climate of expectations surrounding the Presidency which differentiates it from other political institutions. This interpretation of the Presidency is generally based upon studies of political socialization, of the "psychological functions" which the Presidency performs for citizens, and upon popular attitudes toward presidential power.

Studies of political socialization indicate the President is the first public official of whom children become aware and develop feelings.[5] By the time that they reach the third and fourth grades, children have come to view high political office as being important, and their perceptions of the Presidency are overwhelmingly positive and correspondingly benevolent. That the Presidency receives such emphasis in children's early learning about politics is seen as a reflection of the visibility which the office commands within the political system. As children are eventually introduced to political partisanship, less positive and more partisan views of the Presidency emerge, but a high degree of confidence in the office remains. It has also been suggested that perhaps this early political learning shapes later learning about politics and affects assumptions about the importance of the Presidency as opposed to Congress or other political institutions.[6]

There has also been speculation that the relationship between the President and the public is affected by the psychological functions which this office performs for the citizenry. Greenstein, for example, has outlined "a number of ways in which citizens seem to make psychological use of their Chief Executive."[7] First, the President may serve to simplify perceptions of government and politics. As chief executive and head of state, the President occupies a central and highly visible role in the policy making process, and he can therefore provide the public with general guidelines or indications about what the government is doing.

Second, the President can serve as a symbol of unity. During periods of crisis, particularly those relating to foreign affairs, the President can be perceived as representing the nation, and the appropriate response for many citizens is to rally to his support. Third, the President might provide citizens with a means for emotional expression and identification. This can allow citizens to "identify" with the President, again especially during periods of crisis, and consequently to participate vicariously in politics. And finally, the President can serve as a symbol of social stability, someone who can be relied upon to provide direction and control in a threatening world. According to Greenstein:

> It is a great parody of the complex, sprawling, uncoordinated nature of the political system to think in terms of a ship of state, sailing on, with the President firmly at the rudder. But it is a comfort to be able to think in these terms, and the perceptually simple, easily personified nature of the presidential role enables a good many people to do precisely this.[8]

The public psychology is accompanied by a need for what the public considers to be strong and inspired presidential leadership. Sigel's study of the image of the American Presidency found that the public wants a man "who is strong, who has ideas of his own on how to solve problems, and who will make his ideas prevail even if Congress or the public should oppose him." [9] One cannot seriously object to a President who has ideas of his own. But the implications of the view that he should make his ideas *prevail* would seem to be far-reaching. This is reflected in the responses to one of the questions used in the Sigel study. Respondents were asked whether a President should send troops abroad even if he knew that most Americans were opposed to doing so. By better than 3 to 1 (75 percent vs. 20.8 percent), respondents felt that the President should send troops despite public opposition. This study was conducted prior to the major expansion in Vietnam, and it could well be that responses to this particular question would be quite different today. But what is indicated here is a tendency to grant the President carte blanche, particularly in the realm of foreign policy (although it should be noted that the Sigel study also found a majority of respondents who preferred decision making responsibility to rest exclusively with the President, as opposed to Congress and the public, even in domestic affairs.) The check on presidential authority is viewed by the public as coming primarily from the two-term limit on the office.[10] The attitudes toward authority and power reflected in the Sigel study suggest that the normal public opinion–government relationship does not pertain to the Presidency. The public apparently sees nothing wrong in asking members of Congress to do its bidding, but it grants considerably greater discretion—and in turn, expects much more—from its Presidents.

These studies suggest that the President's relationship with the public and, hence, his relationship to public opinion are unique. Public expectations appear to extend beyond the President's political responsibilities. People may look to the President for reassurance, and this "climate of expectations" may be difficult for any President to satisfy. Moreover, this could mean that Congress or other political institutions are at a serious disadvantage in competing with the President for public attention and public support.

PRESIDENTIAL "POPULARITY"

Public opinion is a matter of serious concern to presidential administrations. It appears, however, that this concern is not necessarily tied to public approval or disapproval of specific presidential policies. Rather, administrations often appear to be concerned with maintaining high levels of "prestige" or "popularity" which can be utilized in dealings with the rest of the government, particularly Congress. A President is dependent upon Congress for the passage of legislation, for appropriations to be used in carrying out programs, and for the confirmation of his appointees. High levels of popularity do not guarantee an administration success in any of these, but they do reduce its vulnerability to congressional harassment and may facilitate the passage of legislation and success of policies it considers of prime importance.

One of the ways of measuring presidential popularity is the approval-disapproval rating for an administration. Beginning with the Truman administration, the Gallup Poll (and other polling organizations) has regularly asked the question: "Do you approve or disapprove of the way [the incumbent] is handling his job as President?" While this question is obviously quite general and unfocused, Richard Neustadt asserts that it is a measure which is "very widely read in Washington" and "widely taken to approximate reality." [11] If Neustadt is correct, members of Congress, for example, are likely to rely heavily upon a President's popularity index in assessing the relative vulnerability of an administration.

The limitations of the question notwithstanding (it does not tell us, for example, why people approve or disapprove, and it certainly does not admit of any selectivity of response), the variations in the index show some interesting patterns. Harry Truman took office in 1945 after the death of Franklin Roosevelt, and his earliest ratings exceeded 85 percent. Throughout the remainder of his administration, the index never approached this figure. At one point in March 1952, Truman's rating dropped into the twenties, and by the end of his Presidency, he had lost some 50 points on the index. President Eisenhower's popularity was much more stable. It never exceeded 79 percent, but it never fell below 49 percent, and for most of his tenure, the index was comfortably above 50 percent. By 1961, however, Eisenhower had lost approximately 15 points from the level he enjoyed upon taking office eight years earlier.

The period covered by the Kennedy administration was relatively short, and the popularity ratings were generally 60 percent or higher. Yet his popularity was in decline at the time of his assassination and had dropped almost 15 percent below the high of 83 percent recorded during the first few months of his administration. With Lyndon Johnson, the decline was fairly steady, particularly after the first year of his administration. Indeed, Johnson's loss was almost 40 points over the course of his tenure. Richard Nixon never achieved the high levels of popularity enjoyed by his predecessors. His highest ratings came at the beginning of 1973, shortly after his reelection and coinciding with the peace settlement in Vietnam. By the middle of 1973, however, his ratings had declined by about 30 points below this high and by about 20 points below the level at the beginning of his administration. At the end of October, 1973, Nixon's ratings were the lowest recorded since the Truman administration. In 1974, the year of his resignation, Nixon's ratings were typically in the 20 to 30 percent range.

What this indicates is a seemingly inevitable decline over the course of a presidential administration. Even Eisenhower, who could justifiably be considered the most popular of recent chief executives, lost ground during his second term. And the declines registered by Truman and Johnson were remarkably similar. In an attempt to gain a better understanding of the changes in presidential popularity, John Mueller investigated the effects of several factors on the ratings of Presidents Truman, Eisenhower, Kennedy, and Johnson.[12]

Mueller's analysis took into account the following: (1) the coalition of minorities hypothesis, which asserts that an administration will lose popularity over time even when it usually acts with majority support, since the minorities on each issue may be cumulative; (2) the "rally round the flag" phenomenon generated by crisis; (3) the effect of economic conditions; and (4) the effect of wars, namely Korea and Vietnam.

The coalition of minorities variable is especially interesting, since it suggests that a President will inevitably suffer a decline in popularity over the course of his term. This is based upon a variety of assumptions. Presidential action on a number of issues may alienate specific groups in a serial effect. While each group may represent a distinct issue-oriented minority, the effect over time is to build a "coalition of minorities" which gradually increases into a sizable opposition. As Mueller puts it, "This could occur when the minority on each issue feels so intensely about its loss that it is unable to be placated by administration support on other policies it favors." [13] There may also be cases in which presidential action will alienate both sides, so that an administration "loses" regardless of what it does. Finally, there can be a gradual accumulation of disillusionment as an administration fails to deliver on its promises, something that often seems unavoidable. If an administration takes credit when things are going well, it is faced with being the target of resentment when the economy is in trouble or when the international situation deteriorates. Presidential popularity can therefore be subject to limiting factors about which little can be done; for example, certain actions can generate hostility and result in stubborn opposition to future actions, or a "what have you done for me lately" attitude, whereby an administration's accomplishments receive scant regard as people become upset about new problems.

Dramatic international events may have a "rally round the flag" effect which favors a President regardless of the course he chooses or the wisdom of the policies he adopts. Military interventions (the Eisenhower administration's actions in Lebanon or the Johnson administration's in the Dominican Republic), major diplomatic developments (such as summit meetings or major treaties), major developments in ongoing wars (stopping the bombing or extending it in Southeast Asia, for example), and even domestic events of great moment (such as Truman's or Johnson's coming into office upon the death of an incumbent President) can serve to unite much of the public behind the President, at least temporarily.

The effect of economic conditions on presidential popularity has been a source of considerable speculation. An administration is usually blamed, justly or not, for economic dislocations, such as inflation, high unemployment, or recession. It would appear that economic conditions are quite prone to the "what have you done for me lately" attitude. An administration which is characterized by booming economic conditions during its first two years and by a severe slump during its last two is unlikely to receive much credit for the boom, but it is almost certain to get much of the blame for the slump.

After operationalizing these variables and taking the presence or absence of a major war into account, Mueller speculated that presidential popularity would be affected as follows:

It is anticipated (1) that each President will experience in each term a general decline of popularity; (2) that this decline will be interrupted from time to time with temporary upsurges associated with international crises and similar events; (3) that the decline will be accelerated in direct relation to increases in unemployment rates over those prevailing when the President began his term, but that improvement in unemployment rates will not affect his popularity one way or the other; and (4) that the President will experience an additional loss of popularity if a war is on.[14]

The study provided general support for these assumptions but with some important qualifications. There are obvious differences of personality, style, and party and in the conditions under which an administration takes office. Unless these are taken into account, the variables discussed above have only a limited effect in explaining changes in presidential popularity over several administrations. Despite these qualifications, however, there were some interesting patterns. The coalition of minorities hypothesis worked very well for all but the Eisenhower administration. Perhaps most important, it was reported that "the important differences between administrations do not lie so much in different overall levels of popularity, but rather in the widely differing rates at which the coalition of minorities variable takes effect."

During international crises or similar events, the "rally round the flag" phenomenon resulted in short-term boosts in presidential popularity. These were, however, only temporary increases, and there was a steady decline over time after a given rally point. The economic slump variable was also instructive. Mueller found a decline of about three points in presidential popularity for every percentage point rise in the unemployment rate over the level prevailing at a changeover of administrations. Conversely, however, an improving economy did not help a President's rating. Finally, the war variable had a curious effect. While the Korean war had a substantial, negative, *independent* effect on Truman's popularity, the Vietnam war had no such independent impact on Johnson. Johnson's popularity, however, was declining anyway, so it may well have been that there was little additional room for the war to have an independent impact.

The Mueller study is analytically interesting in several respects. First, the ability of an administration to manipulate public opinion and thereby to maintain high levels of popularity appears to be limited by the coalition of minorities phenomenon and the effects of economic conditions. That Eisenhower was actually able to increase his popularity during his first four years in office seems to be an aberration, and it can be attributed in part at least to his personal appeal and to his substantial achievement in presiding over the end of the Korean war. But other administrations have evidenced a fairly consistent decline, and it would take a unique administration to escape this. Second, the major "weapon" an administration has in arresting this decline depends on fortuitous circumstances, that is, international crises. Improvements in the economy do not generate substantial increases in presidential popularity. Thus, the very visibility of the presidential office carries assets and liabilities. When dramatic events occur, the public tends to look to the White House for leadership, and the result is at least a short-term boost in prestige. But unless "good times" can be maintained throughout an administration (and this seems rather dubious), the President is likely to be the focal point for much of the blame.

CHANNELS OF INFLUENCE

The ability of a President to accomplish his goals requires the cooperation of others inside the government, such as members of Congress and bureaucrats, and of organized interests outside the government. Presidential influence with these groups, however, is conditioned by an administration's public standing. As Richard Neustadt explains:

The Washingtonians who watch a President have more to think about than his professional reputation. They also have to think about his standing with the public outside Washington. They have to gauge his popular prestige. Because they think about it, public standing is a source of influence for him, another factor bearing on their willingness to give him what he wants. Prestige, like reputation, is a subjective factor, a matter of judgment. It works on power just as reputation does through the mechanism of anticipated reactions. . . .[15]

During this century, developments in communications technology and in the presidential use of that technology have altered considerably the President's ability to deal with the public and to maintain or extend his public prestige. Modern communications, in particular, have given the Presidency a distinct advantage over other political institutions in the struggle to shape the news and to influence public opinion.[16]

The recent literature on the Presidency has emphasized three major points concerning presidential influence on public opinion. First, the President's access to the public through the media, most notably television, is unmatched by other branches of government, by the opposition party, or by other public figures. Second, the President's access is such that he largely determines the timing, format, and substance of what the public is to see and hear. Third, interpretations of public opinion are, for presidential purposes, highly subjective exercises.

Coverage and access. News coverage as an instrument of presidential leadership is a twentieth-century phenomenon that commenced with the development of mass circulation newspapers around the turn of the century. Theodore Roosevelt, for example, was the first President to provide the press with space in the White House, and he made very conscious efforts to achieve favorable press coverage and to assure continued press attention to presidential activities.[17] Beginning with the Roosevelt administration, moreover, there was a marked and more or less steady increase in the amount of presidential news coverage. During the first four decades of this century, for example, presidential news coverage increased more rapidly than congressional news coverage or national government news coverage generally.[18]

The Presidency's advantage in dominating news coverage has been further increased by the broadcast media, particularly television. The prime medium of political communication and political news today is, of course, television, and the President's access to television is unrivalled:

> Television is a personal medium, and no person looms so large on the television screens as the President. No one else can summon the cameras of all the networks simultaneously, in a setting and at a time of his own choosing, to address the massive national audience that the President can command; no one else has so great an ability to keep the cameras turned off or at a distance when he does not want them.[19]

During the first 18 months of the Nixon administration, for example, the President delivered 37 live nationwide television addresses. Fourteen of these were broadcast during prime time.[20] This use of television was unmatched by previous administrations, and since many of the addresses involved controversial policies relating to Vietnam and Cambodia, the lack of any guaranteed right to reply by the opposition represented a serious problem. On several occasions, Democratic leaders in Congress requested free and equal time to reply to presidential addresses, but the networks refused. Finally, the networks did make provisions for periodic "loyal opposition" reports, but neither the networks, the Federal Communications Commission, nor the courts have accepted a guaranteed right to reply for the President's opposition.

Format and timing. In utilizing the broadcast media, the President enjoys not only unrivalled access but also substantial control over the format, timing, and content of his presentation. Press conferences and direct addresses to the nation are the major vehicles through which Presidents can attempt to influence the public and to mobilize support behind their policies. But while the President clearly controls the direct address, his control over the press conference is somewhat more limited. Presidents have usually been able to dominate press conferences, but they have not been able to set the full agenda. And while most questions can be anticipated, the live, spontaneous news conference at least provides the possibility for introducing nonprogrammed questions and issues. It is perhaps this modest difference in control which has led to the relative deemphasis upon the press conference and the correspondingly greater use of direct addresses in recent administrations.

During the administration of Franklin Roosevelt, there was unprecedented use of both the press conference and the direct address. Roosevelt scheduled press conferences regularly and often, indeed as frequently as twice weekly. Dropping the previous practice of written questions submitted in advance, Roosevelt also introduced direct questioning by reporters. In addition, Roosevelt made direct appeals to the nation over radio. Through what became known as "fireside chats," he attempted to develop public support for administration policies and subsequently to utilize this support to counter congressional opposition. In many instances, Roosevelt's addresses dealt with specific pieces of legislation for which he was attempting to mobilize support.

Live broadcasts of presidential press conferences were inaugurated during the Eisenhower administration, and the practice has been continued by his successors. Especially under John Kennedy, the live press conference was an integral part of presidential news coverage. And, of course, both Eisenhower and Kennedy utilized television for nationwide addresses on specific administration policies. Up through the early 1960s, then, there was fairly regular utilization of the press conference, supplemented by direct addresses to the nation.

Both the Johnson and Nixon administrations, however, showed considerable ambivalence toward press conferences (and, indeed, toward the press generally). Relations between President Johnson and the press deteriorated as the war in Vietnam generated increasing opposition. And with Richard Nixon, hostility toward the press was obvious throughout his tenure. During the first two years of the Nixon administration, for example, fewer press conferences were held than during any comparable period since the Hoover administration.[21] And by the end of his administration, Nixon's press conferences had degenerated into tense and occasionally ugly affairs.

Johnson and especially Nixon, however, did utilize direct addresses quite frequently. And in both administrations, the reliance upon direct communication between the President and the public appeared to reflect the belief that the President was the rightful judge of what the public had a right to know (coupled with the belief that the media could not be depended upon to report the news accurately and fairly). A prime example of the President's attempt to control completely political communication with the public was the attack upon media "interpretations" of presidential addresses launched by the Nixon administration. In November, 1969, Nixon delivered a televised speech outlining his Vietnam policies and calling for the "silent majority" to support his administration (and to reject the "vocal minority" which had just mounted a Vietnam moratorium demonstration). Following the President's address, the networks presented their commentaries on the speech, and ABC interviewed former Ambassador W. Averell Harriman, a Democrat who had served under Johnson. These commentaries, and especially the Harriman interview, were immediately attacked by administration spokesmen as clear examples of the media's bias and hostility toward Nixon. Before long, a general assault on the press, spearheaded by Vice-President Agnew, had been launched.

To the extent that direct nationwide addresses dominate presidential communication with the public, it is apparent that there will be little two-way communication. Press conferences, on the other hand, need not be regarded as adversary proceedings. They are, in fact, to be viewed as one means for keeping the President in touch with reality by providing an opportunity for the media to bypass the White House staff and counter the isolation and insulation characterizing administrations such as Johnson's and Nixon's.[22]

Interpretations and feedback. In the President's dealings with the public, the responsibility for public relations has been firmly lodged within the White House staff. Since image building requires that favorable news be publicized and unfavorable news be suppressed, control must be centralized —the management of information has been a prime presidential resource.[23] Just as those closest to the President have come to dominate his interaction with the public, they have also become his chief interpreters of public opinion. And this creates another important channel of influence between the President and the public.[24]

In times past, a President who wanted to know what the public was thinking had many options. He could get indications from various newspapers. He could rely upon members of his cabinet, members of Congress, party officials, or private citizens to provide him with information. Much of the information he received was necessarily intuitive. One virtue of this type of decentralized procedure, however, was that at least some information was bound to come from people "whose salt," to use Edward Corwin's phrase, did not come from "the President's table."

Increasingly, recent Presidents have focused on the polls and on their staffs in order to interpret public opinion. The polls have an objective validity, although there has been a tendency in recent administrations to pay attention to polls only so long as they are supportive. Moreover, the polls can be "used." A President who addresses the nation on some major policy action can generally expect a favorable response reported in the polls, so long as he is not simply persisting in a course of action which the public has already found unacceptable.[25] And the favorable response may simply indicate the public's approval that the President is doing something, rather than an understanding of what he is actually doing or proposing. Despite these limitations, the polls can be helpful if a President is seriously concerned with what the public thinks and is willing to pay attention to negative opinion.

When one moves to more subjective interpretations of how an administration is doing with the public, however, who the interpreters are becomes quite important. And, as George Reedy has pointed out, these interpreters are predominantly the White House staff:

From the president's standpoint, the greatest staff problem is that of maintaining his contact with the world's reality that lies outside the White House walls. Very few have succeeded in doing so. They start their administrations fresh from the political wars, which have a tendency to keep men closely tied to the facts of life, but it is only a matter of time until the White House assistants close in like a pretorian guard. Since they are the only people a president sees on a day-to-day basis, they become to him the voice of the people. They represent the closest approximation that he has of outside contacts, and it is inevitable that he comes to regard them as humanity itself.[26]

The reciprocal channels of influence characterizing the President's relationship with the public do not seem in any way comparable. The Presidency is uniquely equipped to influence and to shape public opinion. Certainly its dependency upon public support necessitates that some attention be paid to public preferences. But whether this attention reflects a concern for the legitimate needs and desires of the public or simply an expeditious approach to the maintenance of presidential power is not at all clear. The public, on the other hand, is much more restricted in influencing presidential behavior. Public opinion, when it can be found, is rarely so uniform or unambiguous as to force action. And official contacts with public opinion are likely to be concerned with general support rather than with opinions on particular policies.

Ultimately, the influence of the public on the President is bound to be variable but skewed toward the modest end of the scale. There are many instances in which the public will be apathetic, others where it can be manipulated, and some in which the President acts in accordance with what he considers to be public preferences. In each case, however, the President and his advisers judge or predict what the public preferences are, whether or not they should be taken into account, and whether or not they can be countered.

Political opposition. The Presidency has an unusual advantage in political debate, for there is no clearly defined and continuous opposition. When what Reedy terms "crucial questions" arise, the public is inclined to look toward the President, and his "answers" are likely to be the only ones which are effectively communicated to the public. Thus, the debility of the opposition contributes to the already serious problems characterizing the President's relationship to public opinion.

The impotence of the opposition becomes more serious as presidential government becomes more powerful. No matter how benign a government may be, it will be tempted to manipulate public opinion, to try to dominate the flow of opinion, to cover up mistakes, and to cast doubt on the patriotism or a least the honesty of outside critics.[27]

The out-party faces serious obstacles in attempting to provide institutionalized opposition. Conflicts between congressional leaders and other party leaders, the differing interests of presidential aspirants and the party organization, and the difficulty of establishing a clear party "line" on issues all serve to work against the development of a collective leadership group for the opposition.

And even if these problems of divergent constituencies and institutional jealousies could be overcome, the opposition is still faced with the problem of overcoming a lack of public receptivity. For all practical purposes, the major public opinion forum for opposing an administration is television. Unless the public is willing to accept a designated spokesman for the out-party as a "legitimate" voice, the effectiveness of the opposition will be obviously quite limited.

If public opinion is to carry weight in the policy making process, the public cannot simply respond to authoritative answers. It must be able to acquire the information necessary to make sound judgments about what it wants, and this requires debate concerning political issues. To exclude the Presidency from this type of debate is to provide it with an unfair advantage with respect to Congress or the opposition party. That Presidents have seized this unfair advantage is not surprising, but that Congress has allowed it to persist reflects at least in part prevailing public attitudes toward the Presidency's unique role in American politics.

Within the space of 30 minutes, with full control over the timing and format of his presentation, and with the undeniable prestige of the office backing him up, a President should be able to generate additional public support, if not necessarily enthusiasm, for even the most misguided policies. And he is assisted in doing so by the circumstance that his facts, his reasoning, and his rendering of events are unlikely to be challenged by anyone except some television commentators after he has delivered his address. One would assume that both the public and the President would be better off if the opposition were provided with the right of reply. It would enlighten the public about what the President has said, and it would no doubt make the White House a bit more cautious about its pronouncements and follow-up actions.

There is no easy solution to the problem of presidential opposition. Suggestions for an institutionalized group with a highly visible and articulate leadership, for annual conventions to determine party policies, and for the necessary organization and staff have been made.[28] But even if Congress and the opposition party can somehow surmount the obstacles which have thus far prevented the development of an institutionalized opposition, there is still the problem of public attitudes. This is not something which can be dealt with in advance. As indicated earlier, the public response to past attempts does not provide a clear guide. There have been occasions on which an opposition spokesman has effectively challenged administration policy, but these have not generally been within the context of replies to presidential addresses to the nation. Political opposition can, of course, be carried on within Congress. But if, ideally, public opinion should serve as a kind of jury to which is submitted evidence about major policies, the present practice of one-way communication between the President and the public is undoubtedly harmful.

The impact of television on this aspect of the political process has been to provide the most powerful branch of the national government with the most effective communication medium, and this has had a significant impact on the opinion-government relationship. The opposition problem was certainly not created by television, but it has become more pronounced as Presidents have used the medium with increased frequency. Therefore, any serious resolution of the opposition problem must take into account the questions of access to television and the public legitimacy accorded to opposition spokesmen.

PRESIDENT AND PUBLIC

The relationship between the Presidency and public opinion represents one of the most important bases of presidential power. It also represents a potential source of presidential vulnerability. Since the Presidency is so dependent upon public opinion, incumbents and their staffs have devoted substantial efforts toward shaping that opinion. So long as an administration can maintain a favorable public image, it can pursue its legislative and administrative goals with at least some hope of success. Once that image has been compromised, however, an administration will be hard-pressed to act positively and to exercise initiative effectively.

In competing for the attention and interest of the public, the Presidency enjoys an overwhelming advantage over other political institutions. The Presidency is considered as more important and gains more public attention than, for example, Congress. It provides both the practical leadership and the psychological involvement which no other institution can.

At the same time, the preeminence of the Presidency in the public's political consciousness has encouraged both unrealistic expectations about what incumbents of the office can accomplish and a disturbing dependence upon presidential leadership. The precipitous drops in popularity which some administrations have suffered notwithstanding, it is unlikely that the general public will look elsewhere for direction or for alternatives to presidential leadership (except to presidential candidates during the campaigns).

The concept of a political leader who draws his authority not only from the Constitution but also from the people—what some call the democratized executive—may be appealing, for it seems to combine constitutionalism with popular sovereignty. But this concept is also troublesome, for it implies that it is possible and even wise to have a President of all the people. A President who draws authority from the people must necessarily be controlled by those people. Public opinion, however, does not appear to be an effective mechanism for controlling the Presidency. It is as un-discriminating in its support as it is in its rejection of a President and to that extent it is inappropriate in providing a stable and continuing check on the specfic exercises of presidential authority.

Congress

The relationship between Congress and public opinion involves one of the oldest and most basic questions relating to representative democracy: should a member of Congress depend upon his own judgment and con-science in deciding how to vote on an issue, or should he defer to the opinions of his constituents? If he decides to rely upon his own judgment, whose interests should he consider paramount—those of the nation or those of his immediate constituents? If he decides to defer to public opinion, should he act on the basis of national opinion or should he focus on opinion within his district or state?

There is limited evidence about how constituents stand on this ques-tion. In 1967, a Democratic Representative from Indiana, Lee H. Hamil-ton, conducted a constituent survey in which one of the questions dealt with how he should decide to vote on various issues. Some 69 percent of the 7,474 respondents agreed that a Representative should follow the majority wishes of his district as he interprets those wishes, while the re-mainder believed that a Representative should instead rely upon his own conscience and judgment.[29] While a constituency is likely to have discern-ible preferences on only a limited number of issues, and while it might be exceedingly difficult for a member of Congress to determine objectively what those preferences are, it is probable that Rep. Hamilton's constituents expressed a widely shared public attitude that members of Congress are obligated to pay serious attention to what their constituents want.

Roger Davidson's study of the U.S. House provides useful data re-lating to how members of Congress perceive their "style" of representa-tion.[30] As Davidson pointed out, a Representative's style reflects his attitude toward decision making: should he allow his own judgment to prevail during voting (the trustee style of representation); should he rely upon the preferences of his constituents (the delegate style); or should he shift between personal judgment and outside opinion, depending upon the issues and circumstances (the politico model)? In the Davidson study, forty-six percent of the House members characterized themselves as politicos, while twenty-eight percent adopted the trustee model, and only twenty-three per-cent chose the delegate model. According to Davidson, the "politico role is a natural response to the conflicting demands made upon legislators," and it fulfills the requirement that the legislator must not only avoid violating his constituents' preferences but must also act independently in their interests when their wishes are unclear because of lack of awareness or of information.[31]

It is difficult to assign a specific theory of representation to Congress. Members of Congress enjoy substantial discretion in choosing the issues to which they will devote their primary attention and the factors they will consider in deciding how to vote. What the findings relating to representation do indicate, however, is that many Representatives and Senators attach great weight to the normative requirements of representation, and the persistence of this attitude appears to go beyond the electoral sanctions which the constituency might employ.

CONSTITUENCY OPINION

Senators and Representatives cannot, of course, simply carry out the instructions of their constituents in making all their decisions. On the other hand, the wishes of the voters who elect them cannot be completely ignored. The relative importance of constituency influence in a given case is likely to depend upon a variety of factors—the type of issue involved, the nature and clarity of constituency opinion, the personal beliefs of the Representative or Senator involved, the extent of pressures from other sources, such as the White House or lobbies. Many congressional decisions take place within a grey area—constituency influence is not determinative nor can constituency opinion be completely ignored.

How Representatives respond to the opinions of their constituents has been illuminated in a study conducted by Warren Miller and Donald Stokes.[32] They interviewed the incumbent Representative, his opponent, and a sample of constituents in each of 116 congressional districts immediately after the 1958 congressional election. By supplementing these data with information about the roll-call votes of the incumbent Representatives, Miller and Stokes were able to examine the relationships between: (1) constituency attitudes; (2) the Representative's attitudes; (3) the Representative's perception of constituency attitudes; and (4) the Representative's roll-call behavior. The connections between these variables are depicted in Figure 11.1. They were examined by aggregating specific issues into three policy domains—social welfare, foreign involvement, and civil rights. As we noted previously, leadership responsiveness to constituency opinion may result from: (1) the district's choosing a Representative who so mirrors its views and attitudes that his decisions automatically conform to the constituency's will; or (2) the district's choosing a Representative who conforms to its will, because he believes that course to be necessary to his electoral survival. In the first instance, constituency influence operates through the Representative's own attitudes. In the second,

Figure 11.1
Model of Constituency Influence Upon Members of Congress

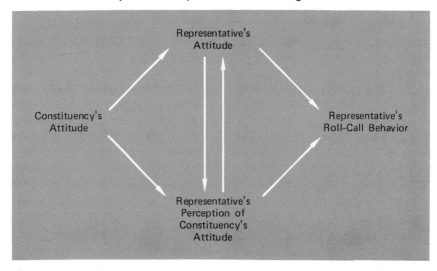

Source: Warren E. Miller and Donald E. Stokes, "Constituency Influence in Congress," *American Political Science Review*, 57 (March 1963), 50.

constituency influence operates through the Representative's perception of constituency attitudes.

Miller and Stokes found that the roll-call votes of Representatives could be "predicted" quite accurately by utilizing the Representative's attitudes *and* his perceptions of constituency attitudes. The multiple correlations for these factors, however, varied with the types of issues involved—.56 for the foreign involvement domain, .67 for social welfare, and .86 for civil rights. This study also indicates the importance of the style of representation by comparing Representatives who said they depended upon administrative advice on foreign policy matters with those who allegedly depended upon their own or their constituents' opinions on these issues. For Representatives who followed or looked toward the administration for guidance, the multiple correlation between the Representative's own views, his perceptions of constituency opinion, and his roll-call behavior was only .2 as compared to .56 for all Representatives. The variation in constituency influence, therefore, is dependent upon the types of issues involved, and it is also affected by Representatives' attitudes concerning the legitimacy of other "pressures" within a given policy sphere.

The actual extent of constituency influence depends upon the accuracy of perception of constituency attitudes as well as upon the similarity between Representatives' attitudes and constituency attitudes. As Table 11.1

Table 11.1
Correlations of Constituency Attitudes

POLICY DOMAIN	CORRELATION OF CONSTITUENCY ATTITUDE WITH:	
	Representative's perception of constituency attitude	Representative's own attitude
Social welfare	.17	.21
Foreign involvement	.19	.06
Civil rights	.63	.39

Source: Warren E. Miller and Donald E. Stokes, "Constituency Influence in Congress," *American Political Science Review,* 57 (March 1963), 52.

indicates, there are substantial differences by policy domain in the correlations between these variables. Perceptions of constituency attitudes were quite accurate and the similarity of attitudes quite high with respect to civil rights, but the accuracy of perceptions and the sharing of attitudes dropped off sharply for the foreign involvement and social welfare domains.

Also important was the existence of two major channels connecting constituent attitudes to roll call behavior: (1) the channel via a Representative's own attitudes; and (2) a second channel employing a Representative's perception of constituent attitudes as the catalyst. On civil rights, the influence path through the Representative's perception of constituency attitudes was more effective in connecting constituency attitudes to legislative behavior. On social welfare questions, however, the influence path through the Representative's own attitude provided the best connection between constituency attitudes and roll-call behavior.

The Miller and Stokes study underscores the twin factors of representational style and focus. The authors conclude that "no single tradition of representation fully accords with the realities of American legislative politics." In particular, "variations in the representative relation are most likely to occur as we move from one policy domain to the other." [33]

Charles Cnudde and Donald McCrone applied a different methodological analysis to the Miller-Stokes data on civil rights in order to investigate the relationship between Representatives' perceptions of constituency attitudes and their own attitudes.[34] According to Cnudde and McCrone, the shared attitudes between Representative and constituency result largely from the Representative's perception of constituency attitudes. Contrary to psychological theory which suggests that attitudes will, over time, distort perceptions (since attitudes are firmer and longer lasting), Cnudde and McCrone found that Representatives changed their attitudes to conform to their perceptions of constituency attitudes. The Cnudde-McCrone analysis confirms the importance of Representatives' perceptions in linking constituency attitudes to roll-call decision making. They state that "constituencies do not influence civil rights roll calls . . . by selecting Congressmen whose attitudes mirror their own." Rather, "Congressmen vote their constituencies' attitudes (as they perceive them) with a mind to the next election." [35]

The Miller-Stokes and Cnudde-McCrone studies provide useful models for assessing constituency influence in Congress. First, the extent of this influence varies by policy domain, as measured by the correlation between constituency attitudes and roll-call voting. Within a controversial and highly visible policy domain, the member of Congress is more likely to vote in accordance with generalized constituency attitudes than he is when the policies at stake are of less immediate concern to his constituents. Second, constituency influence is transmitted through both the sharing of attitudes between constituency and Representative and the Representative's perception of constituency attitudes. And here again, the differential importance of the attitude sharing or the attitude perception linkages is likely to vary by policy domain. Third, the motivational influences on congressional behavior include his own judgments *as well as* his perceptions of constituency attitudes.

A great deal of the congressional sensitivity to constituency attitudes can be attributed to pressures for reelection. One study of Representatives' evaluations of electoral factors reported that 85 percent believed that the electoral results in their districts had been strongly affected by their personal record and standing.[36] The watchful electorate, however, appeared to be largely a figment of the Representatives' imaginations, since few voters had any real information about their Representative. The low level of public knowledge about Congress seems to be characteristic. According to a Gallup poll conducted in 1965, members of the House had little visibility.[37] Some 57 percent of the adults polled did not know the name of their Representative; 41 percent did not know his party; 70 percent did not know when he stood for reelection; 81 percent did not know how he voted on any major legislation during the year; and 86 percent could not name anything he had done for the district. As might be expected, public knowledge varied by education. Of those who had attended college, almost two-thirds could name their Representative, while of those with a grade school education, less than one-third could do so. A Louis Harris poll conducted for *Newsweek* in the fall of 1973 produced quite similar findings.[38]

The discrepancy between what members of Congress believe about the visibility of their legislative actions and the extent of electorate knowledge about those actions can be explained, at least in part, by the following. First, members of Congress deal directly with only a small portion of the electorate, but that portion is likely to be the most informed and politically active segment. Accordingly, members of Congress could simply over-estimate their visibility and the salience of political matters. Second, those who are informed about congressional matters—such as local party leaders, interest group leaders, civic leaders, the media, and other local influentials and groups—may be able to influence those who are less informed. Stokes and Miller explain that a portion of the electorate "may get simple positive or negative cues about the Congressman which were provoked by his legis-lative actions but which no longer have a recognizable issue content." [39] Third, a member of Congress may be faced with potential opposition. His record could provide opponents with an opportunity to mount an effective campaign against him, either in the primary or in the general election. Fourth, electoral marginality in a district could depend upon a relatively small group of voters who *might* react to the incumbent's actions. And even in seemingly safe districts, national trends or regional or state dislocations might pose a potential electoral danger, thus making a Senator or Repre-sentative sensitive to voter alienation to a degree unwarranted by the normal electoral margins he has managed to acquire. Fifth, the odds on being re-turned are quite good, but there is still a risk. For many members, then, the cautious route might seem to be best—there is more to be lost by underestimating their constituents' attention than by overestimating it. [40]

A realistic portrayal of constituency influence must also take into account the factor of legislative discretion. Bauer, Pool, and Dexter, in their study of the politics of foreign trade legislation, suggested several ele-ments that allowed legislators some leeway: (1) the complexity of most districts permits some shifting in the base of a legislator's support; (2) the legislator can lead as well as change his electoral coalition, and his closest supporters may find it necessary and useful to follow this shift; (3) since few voters know exactly what they want, the legislator is relatively safe in simply showing that he is concerned with his constituents' problems and working in their behalf; (4) the opportunities for evasion in the legislative process are so many and diverse that most actions can be rationalized to all but the most knowledgeable; and (5) the pressures on a legislator are so extensive that they have the paradoxical effect of actually increasing his initiative—he must finally choose the pressures and problems to which he will respond. Faced with multiple demands from any number of groups, the member of Congress can artfully avoid too great a dependence upon any one of them. [41]

It is perhaps best to regard constituency influence as only one factor a member of Congress must consider—the influence of party leaders, the President, knowledgeable committee members, and colleagues must also be taken into account. And it is reasonable to expect that the relative influence of each of these factors depends in part upon the particular legislator. John Jackson's study of factors affecting voting in the Senate, for example, found that "senators develop standard routines for deciding how to vote on roll call votes. It does not appear that they are influenced by one person or one set of influences on one bill and an entirely different person or set on the next." [42] However, the models or routines developed by individual Senators differ, so that the relative weight accorded to particular factors will also vary. Thus, the influence accorded to constituency attitudes or interests by one Senator might be substantially greater than that accorded by another.

What emerges from the various studies of constituency influence suggests the rather limited nature of direct effects. For many legislators, the nature of the constituency might necessitate a particular attention to certain policy areas. They might seek committee positions which allow them to specialize in those policy areas most appropriate to their constituents' concerns. In a similar manner, the nature of a constituency may dictate rather clear voting limits. A legislator may thus feel compelled to desert his party colleagues on certain issues where he feels that his constituents' interests (and his own future) are at stake. If constituency interests are perceived as clear-cut, they can be compelling factors in legislative behavior, regardless of how these preferences are communicated to the legislator.

SOURCES OF INFORMATION

While many members of Congress agree with the view that "I seldom have to sound out my constituents because I think so much like them that I know how to react to almost any proposal," [43] effective representation often requires more tangible channels of communication to supplement the intuitive understanding which legislators have about their constituents. Among the more typical and important sources of information about constituency opinion and legislative action are constituency mail, congressional polls and newsletters, and direct contacts between constituents and legislators.

Constituency mail.   According to Lewis Dexter's analysis of constituency communications, "In the importance attached to it both by congressmen and by business constituents, mail outweighs every other form of communication." [44] There is no question that congressional offices devote a considerable amount of time to dealing with constituency mail. And while a great deal of this involves constituent requests for assistance in dealing with administrative agencies, a good portion consists of letters on legislative issues. Data gathered for the 89th Congress under the auspices of the

American Political Science Association's Study of Congress Project showed House offices receiving an average of over 500 letters per week.[45] Of these, some 30 percent were letters on issues or legislation, and an additional 10 percent were opinion ballots preprinted by an organization. The mail volume for Senate offices is generally much higher, with some offices receiving 10,000 or more communications per week. The quantity of Senate mail, as might be expected, is highly variable, depending upon the population of the state being served and the visibility of the individual Senator.

The amount of time devoted to the mail is usually paralleled by high assessments of its utility in discerning constituent views, at least as far as members of Congress are concerned (or at least as far as they are willing to admit publicly). But there are some obvious limitations on the utility of mail as an accurate reflection of constituency opinion. One of the most important of these is that letters are unlikely to originate within a valid cross-section of the constituency. Relatively few constituents ever write to their Senators or Representatives in Congress, and those who do write, particularly on a regular basis, are the more highly educated and politically involved.

Of course, the mail is quite useful in part because of these very biases. Since those who do write tend to be the more politically involved and not infrequently the more influential and organized, Senators and Representatives may find the mail to be a useful index of "articulate opinion." Moreover, those who write are more likely than the mass public to have intense or at least strong opinions on those issues about which they write, so that the mail might provide a gauge of the salience and potency of specific issues in particular states or districts.

Congressional polls.   National opinion poll results can often be far out of line with opinion distributions in certain states or congressional districts. The distribution of opinion nationwide on gun registration and control, for example, is very much out of line with opinion in many western and southern states. In addition, legislators who are interested in constituent attitudes might want information on a broader range of issues than those reported in the national polls. For these reasons and the obvious public relations benefits, a large number of legislators have begun to employ periodic questionnaires or polls.[46]

The weaknesses of congressional polls are substantial. Congressional offices typically conduct them (prepare the questionnaires, mail them out, and tabulate the responses) since the cost of using professional polling services would be prohibitive. Consequently, sampling techniques are generally poor.[47] Questionnaire construction is also a problem, with the wording of questions sometimes designed almost to force desired responses. And some questions are difficult to answer with a closed-ended format.

One Representative had a blank questionnaire returned by one of his constituents with a request that he fill it out himself and mail it back. He commented, "I guess I'm stupid. I don't know how to answer my own questionnaire. I mean you can't answer yes or no." [48] In addition, the response rate (averaging 16.7 percent) is so low as to encourage serious doubts about the validity of constituent polls. Those who do respond are unlikely to be a representative cross-section of the constituency.

Of course, those who employ such polls, particularly on a regular basis, may find them useful primarily as symbolic gestures, indicating to constituents that their legislators are concerned about their problems and interested in their opinions. And many constituents, in turn, might be satisfied with the opportunity to express their opinions, regardless of the weight those opinions carry.

Direct contacts.   In the study by Charles Jones of the House Agriculture Committee, members of the committee ranked personal contacts with their constituents as one of their most important methods of determining constituency attitudes.[49] Personal contacts can occur when constituents visit congressional offices, or when Senators and Representatives make periodic trips back to their constituencies.

The "fence-mending" trips legislators employ are considered effective electioneering devices. In particular, such trips appear to be necessary if an incumbent is to guard against possible campaign attacks that he has neglected the people who elected him and thereby lost touch with their opinions and interests. Members of Congress have also depended upon such trips to provide indications of public sentiment about important issues. Many legislators used the January recess in 1974, for example, to sound out constituent reactions to the various scandals surrounding the Nixon administration and to the impeachment proceedings initiated by the House Judiciary Committee. And for Republican members of Congress, especially those up for reelection in 1974, the recess provided an opportunity to determine the potential effects of the President's troubles upon the November elections.

Personal contacts with constituents can be useful in countering the insulation and isolation that often affects Washington officials. Separated from their districts or states and operating in the sheltered political atmosphere of the Capitol, contacts with the real world are an obvious benefit to legislators. The potential drawback lies in the perspective which individual legislators bring to these contacts. If efforts are made to go beyond the circle of friends and supporters, it is possible to get at least an idea of the variety of opinions, interests, and problems among constituents. But it is still virtually impossible to approximate anything close to a representative sampling of constituents.

Group contacts.   It is useful to remember that substantial and continuous communication occurs between members of Congress and the leaders and representatives of various groups—economic interests, civic associations, and the like. In recent years, a number of interest groups have increasingly employed what is called grassroots lobbying in an attempt to capitalize upon the constituent-legislator relationship. Complementing their traditional lobbying efforts, interest groups can encourage and direct constituent communication—letters, petitions, personal contacts, and so forth—with members of Congress. In addition to inspiring these communications, the lobbies can, in many cases, advise constituents on the most effective approaches.

The effectiveness of grassroots lobbying is variable. In some cases, sponsored or inspired grassroots campaigns (such as those in the form of standard letters or telegrams) are ignored or at least largely discounted. Yet by working through community influentials and by effectively organizing these persons, significant pressure can be brought to bear upon legislators. The National Rifle Association, the private utilities lobby, and certain of the new "citizen" lobbies, such as Common Cause, have used the grassroots approach regularly and, in some cases, effectively. This illustrates the efficacy of organized efforts in influencing legislators, but it also distorts the influence channels even further in the direction of the better organized, better educated, and more politically interested segments of the community.

Legislators' "reports."   Thus far, we have focused upon communications from the constituency to the legislature. Effective communication also necessitates, however, that members of Congress inform their constituents about their activities and about current legislative issues. Many congressional offices devote an impressive amount of work to this sort of project, but there is unfortunately little evidence by which the quality of these communication efforts or their impact can be assessed. The most widely used method of "reporting back" is the newsletter. The Study of Congress survey reported that 80 percent of the Representatives interviewed regularly sent out newsletters to their constituents. Approximately one-half of the newsletters had circulations of 30,000 or more, but most offices reported using mailing lists rather than blanket mailings to all postal patrons.[50]

In addition, many members reported giving regular radio or television presentations. The most popular type of presentation was the five-minute radio spot. And the use of radio was more frequent overall than the use of television.[51] A number of Representatives also used local newspapers as a forum, either by having their newsletters printed or by writing columns.

It is apparent that a great deal of effort is expended by some constituents and by many members of Congress in trying to communicate their interests, opinions, and concerns to each other. These various channels of communication cannot be dismissed as worthless, but they are all characterized by the sharp differences in political information and political participation evidenced by the American electorate. Most constituents never enter these channels of communication. The extent to which members of Congress are affected by any or all of these constituent contacts obviously varies. But more important, none of these channels is likely to provide accurate reflections of mass opinion. The unorganized, the uneducated, the politically unaware are not part of this influence system.

CONGRESSIONAL VISIBILITY

In what has been, by many accounts, an age of legislative decline, Congress has managed, unlike many national legislative bodies, to retain a great deal of its authority. Particularly in the use of its negative powers, Congress still is able to exercise the substantial authority formally granted by the Constitution. Despite the importance of Congress, there are significant limits upon its public visibility, and there is a clear tendency among citizens to underestimate Congress. In the words of D. W. Brogan, "A Senator or a Representative may well feel that his genuine services are disregarded by his countrymen, that the white light of publicity plays only on the White House, and that the general public regards Congress as at best something to laugh about and sometimes something to swear about." [52] The limits upon congressional visibility place Congress at a disadvantage in its more serious and public confrontations with the executive.

Congress is rarely capable of swift or dramatic action. The legislative process is complex and cumbersome, and it invariably requires a good deal of time for Congress to act upon major legislation. The Presidency, on the other hand, is uniquely equipped to convey at least the impression of bold and decisive action. Still another limitation on congressional visibility arises from the decentralization of power in Congress and the corresponding complexity of congressional operations. The responsibility for action or inaction in major fields of legislation is often difficult to pinpoint because of overlapping jurisdictions among committees, and the reasons for action or inaction are equally difficult to ascertain.

The limits on congressional visibility are distinct reflections of Congress' organization and method of operation. The decentralization of decision making authority to relatively autonomous committees and the dispersion of personal power among many members of the House and Senate minimize party responsibility and accountability. Consequently, it is difficult to pinpoint the responsibility for action or inaction in Congress.

Thus, even when there is substantial public dissatisfaction with Congress, the electorate cannot easily translate its frustration into sanctions against the parties or their more prominent members in Congress.[53]

It is unlikely that the visibility of Congress can be materially changed. So long as the energy in American politics is perceived as being provided largely by the executive branch, the public's interest in congressional operations will be confined to only a few issues with which Congress deals. The end result of the discontinuities and gaps in public knowledge about congressional activity is to maintain public dependence upon the Presidency.

Summary

An important linkage between the public and government is provided by representative institutions. In national politics, the responsibility for representing public opinion in government is now shared by the President and Congress. In this chapter, we have been concerned with the manner in which institutional characteristics of the Presidency and Congress have affected their representative functions and with the strengths and weaknesses which each of these institutions has displayed in its attempts to act in the public's behalf.

THE PRESIDENCY

A President's influence in dealing with the rest of the government and in attempting to accomplish his goals is affected not only by his professional reputation but also by his popular prestige or standing. Thus, the relationship between the Presidency and the public represents an important component of presidential power. In recent years, however, there has been considerable anxiety about this relationship, particularly insofar as its effects upon presidential accountability and responsibility are concerned.

First, the Presidency's relationship to the public differs markedly from that of any other political institution. The public's perceptions of the Presidency, the psychological functions which the office performs for many citizens, and the popular views of presidential power reflect unrealistic views about what the Presidency can or should be able to accomplish. The public's expectations about the Presidency go beyond its political responsibilities, and this suggests that Congress or other political institutions may be at a serious disadvantage in competing with the President for public attention and public support.

Second, presidential popularity has emerged as one of the most widely accepted indications of a President's popular standing. As it has been measured over the past three decades, however, presidential popularity has very severe limitations. It does not tell us why people approve or disapprove of presidential performance, and it is too general to provide an accurate view of how the public responds to particular presidential policies or actions. Having more serious implications for the future, however, are the efforts expended by some administrations to manipulate opinion in order to maintain popularity.

Third, the impact of modern communications, particularly television, upon the political process has been to provide the Presidency with an overwhelming advantage over other political institutions. The President's access to the media, his control over the timing and format of its use, and the relative debility of the political opposition in utilizing the media to challenge the President have not provided the public with the information and debate necessary to make sound judgments about competing policies.

If the President is to "represent" public opinion in a responsible and accountable manner, public perceptions and presidential practices must be altered. A more realistic public understanding of the Presidency, for example, requires that the Presidency be appreciated as a partisan office. A President is a partisan official—he is nominated by a party and runs as a representative of and spokesman for that party. To expect a President to function above his party is to personalize presidential power and to remove a primary restraint from that power. To recognize the partisan nature of the office, on the other hand, is to return the Presidency to the reality of politics—to make public expectations more realistic, to legitimize the political opposition, and to encourage meaningful public debate about presidential policies and the direction of presidential leadership.

CONGRESS

The relationship between Congress and the public is difficult to define precisely. Members of Congress enjoy substantial discretion in choosing the issues to which they will give attention and in weighing the factors they will consider in deciding how to vote. However, the models of congressional linkage—the legislator conforming to his constituents' will either because he shares their attitudes or because he believes it necessary for electoral survival—are clearly evident in certain policy areas. Thus we find that constituency interest is an important element of congressional representation, despite the fact that members of Congress do not communicate directly with their constituents on all questions.

In addition to the intuitive understanding legislators claim to have about their constituencies, effective representation often requires more tangible and direct channels of communication. Among these are constituency mail, congressional polls and newsletters, and direct contacts between legislators and constituents. While the amount of congressional time devoted to these types of communication is impressive, they are unlikely to provide accurate reflections of mass opinion. The reason is that each of these communication channels operates in favor of those who display more political knowledgeability and more frequent political participation; i.e., those of higher educational and social status.

Perhaps the most important problem affecting congressional representation, however, is the general lack of public interest in and knowledge about congressional politics. Congressional visibility is clearly less than executive visibility. One of the consequences of this inherent limitation is that it is difficult for the public to pinpoint the responsibility for congressional actions, and, in particular, to impose collective responsibility upon the parties for their performance in Congress. Congress' role as a representative institution, then, is frustrated in part, because the public lacks the knowledge and interest necessary to monitor and to judge congressional performance.

NOTES

[1] Edward S. Corwin, *The President: Office and Powers* (New York: New York University Press, 1940), pp. 255–316.

[2] Committee on Political Parties of the American Political Science Association, "Toward a More Responsible Two-Party System," *American Political Science Review*, 44, Supplement (September 1950), 93–95.

[3] George E. Reedy, *The Twilight of the Presidency* (New York: World Publishing Company, 1970).

[4] Thomas E. Cronin, "Superman, The Textbook Presidency," in *Inside the System*, 2nd ed., eds. Charles Peters and John Rothchild (New York: Praeger, 1973), pp. 10–11.

[5] Fred I. Greenstein, "The Psychological Functions of the Presidency for Citizens," in *The American Presidency*, ed. Elmer E. Cornwell (Chicago: Scott, Foresman and Company, 1966), p. 34.

[6] Ibid..

[7] Ibid., pp. 35–36.

[8] Ibid., p. 36.

[9] Roberta S. Sigel, "Image of the American Presidency—Part II of an Exploration into Popular Views of Presidential Power," *Midwest Journal of Political Science*, 10 (February 1966), 123–37.

[10] See Roberta S. Sigel and David Butler, "The Public and the No Third Term Tradition: Inquiry into Attitudes toward Power," *Midwest Journal of Political Science*, 8 (February 1964), 39–54.

[11] Richard E. Neustadt, *Presidential Power* (New York: Signet, 1964), p. 200.

[12] John E. Mueller, "Presidential Popularity from Truman to Johnson," *American Political Science Review*, 64 (March 1970), 18–34. A more detailed examination is provided in John E. Mueller, *War, Presidents and Public Opinion* (New York: John Wiley & Sons, 1973).

[13] Mueller, "Presidential Popularity," p. 20.

[14] Ibid., p. 25.

[15] Neustadt, *Presidential Power*, p. 88.

[16] See David S. Broder, "The Presidency and the Press," in *The Future of the American Presidency*, ed. Charles W. Dunn (Morristown, N.J.: General Learning Press, 1975).

[17] Dorothy Buckton James, *The Contemporary Presidency* (New York: Pegasus, 1969), p. 46.

[18] Elmer E. Cornwell, "Presidential News: The Expanding Public Image," *Journalism Quarterly*, 36 (Summer 1959), 275–83.

[19] Broder, "The Presidency and the Press," pp. 264–65.

[20] Testimony by Joseph Califano on "Television and the Loyal Opposition," United States Senate, Communications Subcommittee of the Committee on Commerce, *Public Service Time for the Legislative Branch*. Report No. 91–4, 91st Congress, 2nd Session, pp. 87–101.

[21] James David Barber, *The Presidential Character* (Englewood Cliffs, N.J.: Prentice-Hall, 1972), p. 425.

[22] Broder, "The Presidency and the Press," p. 266.

[23] See Barber, *The Presidential Character*, pp. 422–25.

[24] Reedy, *The Twilight of the Presidency*, pp. 85–98.

[25] This important qualification would apply to both Johnson and Nixon. Johnson's ability to affect public opinion relating to Vietnam declined as the war persisted during the end of his administration. And Nixon, of course, had little success in changing public opinion relating to Watergate after the firing of the special prosecutor in October 1973.

[26] Reedy, *Twilight of the Presidency*, p. 95.

[27] James MacGregor Burns, *Presidential Government* (Boston: Houghton Mifflin Company, 1965), pp. 342–43.

[28] Ibid., pp. 343–44.

[29] Quoted in Roger H. Davidson, *The Role of the Congressman* (New York: Pegasus, 1969), p. 115.

[30] Ibid., pp. 110–42.

[31] Ibid., p. 120.

[32] Warren E. Miller and Donald E. Stokes, "Constituency Influence in Congress," *American Political Science Review*, 57 (March 1963), 45–56.

[33] Ibid., 56.

[34] Charles F. Cnudde and Donald J. McCrone, "The Linkage between Constituency Attitudes and Congressional Voting Behavior: A Causal Model," *American Political Science Review*, 60 (March 1966), 66–72.

[35] Ibid., 69.

[36] Donald E. Stokes and Warren E. Miller, "Party Government and the Saliency of Congress," *Public Opinion Quarterly*, 26 (Winter 1962), 542.

[37] Cited in *Congressional Quarterly Weekly Report*, 23, No. 46 (November 12, 1965), 2320.

[38] *Newsweek*, 72 (December 10, 1973), pp. 40–48.

[39] Miller and Stokes, "Constituency Influence in Congress," p. 55.

[40] See David R. Mayhew, *Congress: The Electoral Connection* (New Haven: Yale University Press, 1974), pp. 33–38.

[41] Raymond A. Bauer, Ithiel de Sola Pool, and Lewis Anthony Dexter, *American Business and Public Policy*, 2nd ed. (Chicago: Aldine-Atherton, Inc., 1972), pp. 414–24.

[42] John E. Jackson, "Statistical Models of Senate Roll Call Voting," *American Political Science Review,* 65 (June 1971), 468.

[43] Davidson, *The Role of the Congressman,* p. 115.

[44] Lewis Anthony Dexter, "What Do Congressmen Hear?" in *Congressional Behavior,* ed. N. Polsby (New York: Random House, Inc., 1971), p. 28.

[45] Reported in Donald G. Tacheron and Morris K. Udall, *The Job of the Congressman,* 2nd ed. (Indianapolis: Bobbs-Merrill, 1970), pp. 305–6.

[46] In the 1965 Congress study, 91 of 152 Representatives reported the use of mail questionnaires. More than one-half of these had circulations greater than 30,000. John S. Saloma III, *Congress and the New Politics* (Boston: Little, Brown and Company, 1969), p. 175.

[47] See Leonard A. Marascuilo and Harriett Amster, "Survey of 1961–62 Congressional Polls," *Public Opinion Quarterly,* 28 (Fall 1964), 497–506.

[48] Quoted in *Congressional Quarterly's Guide to the Congress of the United States* (Washington, D.C.: Congressional Quarterly Service, 1971), p. 538.

[49] Charles O. Jones, "Representation in Congress: The Case of the House Agriculture Committee," *American Political Science Review,* 55 (June 1961), 366.

[50] Tacheron and Udall, *The Job of the Congressman,* p. 309.

[51] Saloma, *Congress and the New Politics,* p. 174.

[52] D. W. Brogan, Introduction to Joseph S. Clark, *Congress: The Sapless Branch* (New York: Harper & Row, Publishers, 1964), p. xii.

[53] See Mayhew, *Congress: The Electoral Connection,* pp. 164–65.

Part four
Overview

PUBLIC OPINION
AND
RESPONSIBLE DEMOCRACY

12

Throughout this volume we have concentrated on the role of public opinion in a democracy. Theoretically we expect citizen attitudes to hold a crucial position in the functioning of a democratic government. After all, the cornerstone of democracy is popular consent—expressed regularly and by a large segment of the population. Our government is built upon the assumption that the American people will select political leaders in a rational and informed manner and will regularly instruct them as to the policy preferences of the citizenry. Democracy is further built on the assumption that governmental elites will listen to the expressed will of the people and respond to it. Theoretically, then, a well functioning democracy is based on three important factors. First, the citizenry must acquire intelligent, well-informed attitudes. Second, these attitudes must be articulated to political leaders. Third, the political elite must respond. For these reasons we have approached the study of public opinion by examining the attitudes and behavior of the political masses, the opinions and behavior of governmental leaders, and finally the linkage between the citizenry and the political elite.

The people and their political leaders

The basic purpose of this text has been to conceptualize the flow of public opinion from its attitudinal formation stage through the incorporation of citizen attitudes into the public policy making stage. For a responsive democracy to result, each stage in this process must work efficiently. From our earlier discussions we know that the process works imperfectly—but it does work.

PUBLIC ATTITUDE FORMATION

No one seriously doubts the premise that for democracy to function the citizenry must hold some attitudes about issues of political concern. These attitudes may not be well informed or arrived at in an intelligent manner, but for the government to be responsive to the will of the people, such a public will must exist. Therefore, the first building block upon which democracy stands consists of the opinions and attitudes of the people. It is the political responsibility of citizens in a democratic society both individually and collectively to acquire meaningful attitudes on governmental affairs.

If for the moment we assume that governmental leaders and institutions are responsive to the will of the citizenry, then it becomes clear that the quality of governing will be directly related to the quality of public opinion. An educated, well-informed, interested, intelligent public can be expected to prompt sound, prudent, and effective governmental policy. Conversely, an ignorant, disinterested citizenry would prompt policy of a marginally acceptable standard at best. Thomas Jefferson expressed this position when he penned in a passage of dubious poetic quality that, "if a people expects to be both ignorant and free, it expects what never was and never will be."

While the United States measures well on this score in comparison to other nations, it does not fare well in absolute terms. We undoubtedly have one of the most literate and educated societies in history. Americans have more knowledge about their relatively complex government than most inhabitants of this planet, and they do take stands on the more important issues facing the nation. Yet the degree of their political information is surprisingly low. Few could name more than a handful of governmental officials; many become confused about the various levels and branches of government; and most fail to comprehend the basic processes through which the act of governing must pass. Not many American voters meet William Mitchell's description of a rational, well-informed citizen. Mitchell characterizes the rational voter as ". . . one who is sufficiently informed that he knows his own goals or preferences and can rank them in order, is aware of alternative public policies as they relate to his preferences, and has some grasp of the expected benefits and costs to himself and society of these alternatives."[1] While specific political information may not be well entrenched in the minds of the populace, Americans form definite attitudes on general public issues. The individual on the street can readily express his feelings about busing, abortion, crime, race relations, communism and war—often quite vociferously. Therefore, while the American citizen might be criticized for a lack of specific information, there is little questioning the fact that he possesses more than enough general knowledge to realize what he wants from his government.

PUBLIC ATTITUDE ARTICULATION

If we assume excellence in public attitude formation and the existence of responsive political leaders and institutions, the process of obtaining responsiveness in government would not result unless the linkage between the public and its leaders was effective. This is perhaps the most important aspect of the public opinion–public policy process. It is at this point the probabilities of responsive government rise or fall. Unless the opinions of the people are transmitted to and received by the nation's political leaders, public opinion has little significance. V. O. Key recognized this fact when he observed in his discussion of elites and masses that "it is in the dynamics of the system, the interactions between these strata, that the import of public opinion in democratic orders becomes manifest." [2]

This brings us to the crucial point of opinion articulation. For public opinion to have any impact it must be expressed. In Part Three we indicated two general forms of opinion articulation, individual and group related. Both forms leave a great deal to be desired in terms of adequately and accurately transmitting the will of the citizenry. The major weakness of each stems from a lack of citizen participation in those linkage avenues currently open.

The most common individual method of articulating citizen opinion is the act of voting. The United States conducts more free elections than any other nation in the world's history. We elect public officials from the high office of the President to the lowest county and municipal officials. This is the most important form of individual opinion articulation because in concert with millions of other Americans the individual has direct control over the selection of his governmental leaders. Citizen input in this form cannot be ignored by public officials. It is the direct act of the governed controlling the governors. Unfortunately it is an act in which relatively few participate. The highest voter turnout rate occurs in presidential elections, which attract roughly sixty percent of the eligible voters. In congressional election years the turnout drops to forty percent. State and local elections often have so few voters that their validity as an expression of the public will must be seriously questioned. Voting is obviously an excellent means of obtaining the views of the people on leader selection questions. But it is only a measure of the opinion of that segment of the population sufficiently attentive and interested to invest the cost of time and effort to arrive at the polls on election day. And as we have previously indicated, the attentive and interested public is not randomly drawn from the population as a whole, but disproportionately favors the higher socioeconomic classes.

Other forms of individual opinion articulation include such actions as writing letters to public officials, contributing time or funds to a political candidate or cause, displaying political bumper stickers or campaign buttons, attending public meetings, and a variety of other participatory acts. For the most part only a minuscule portion of the population expresses its opinion in any of these ways. And those who do are even more disproportionately drawn from the higher socioeconomic classes than the portion of the citizenry that votes regularly. These forms of activity, however, can be very important. Officeholders pay attention to letters from citizens and pay heed to those persons making campaign contributions or attending public meetings.

Group-related opinion articulation occurs primarily in the form of political party and interest group activity. While these two political phenomena fundamentally differ in many respects, they share the common feature of being collections of citizens banded together for the purposes of amplifying their individual opinion articulation through organizational activities. Political parties organize to control the government through electing individuals of their own membership to public office. Interest groups are composed of similarly situated individuals (usually on the basis of economic status) who hope to convince governmental officials to enact policies and programs favorable to the group's membership. Both are means by which the public is linked to the leadership echelon.

But as we have seen there exist severe weaknesses in these organizational efforts at opinion articulation. The first problem again is participation. Less than five percent of the public are active political party members, i.e., individuals who engage in party activities; most party membership is nominal only. Similarly, few people engage in any real interest group activity. Membership in an interest group is often an automatic result of occupational choice (e.g., a member of a labor union or professional association), and does not necessarily entail participation in interest group affairs. The second problem inherent in group-related opinion articulation as it exists today is the content of the opinion expressed. American political parties are essentially umbrella organizations whose positions are designed to be sufficiently broad to attract (or at least not offend) a majority of the voters. For this reason the content of party expressions is sometimes general, uncontroversial, and uncreative. But more important, voter knowledge of party positions and party performance is often insufficient to allow informed judgments about the parties' legislative records. Interest group opinion content suffers from the opposite malady. Interest groups are formed for the sole purpose of helping their membership. The messages sent to political leaders by such groups not surprisingly are narrow in scope and perhaps somewhat biased. This would be acceptable if each person in America were adequately represented by one or more such lobbying organizations, but this is not the case. There are powerful business lobbies and labor groups, but no consumer lobby of similar effectiveness. There is an American Medical Association, but no American Patients Association. There is a National Rifle Association, but no comparably organized group for gun control. Obviously, this absence of countervailing interest groups means that the opinion expressed by America's lobbies is not representative of the will of the entire citizenry.

While the limitations existing in the present means of public opinion articulation are substantial, we would be remiss in not mentioning some of the significant improvements that have occurred during the past fifteen years. These improvements have taken place primarily in the voting and interest group spheres of opinion articulation. First, voting rolls have been dramatically expanded. The Voting Rights Act of 1965 encouraged the registration of 1.5 million blacks in the South alone. The ratification of the 26th Amendment in 1971 made 11 million 18 to 20 year olds eligible to vote for the first time. Whether these new voters will actually vote, of course, is difficult to determine, but their very enfranchisement is an improvement. Second, new interest groups working in behalf of previously unrepresented citizens have blossomed. Poor peoples lobbies, welfare rights groups, consumer-oriented groups, and "good government" organizations such as Common Cause have been born. If such groups can survive and multiply, the days of the disproportionate influence of certain monied interests may be numbered.

POLITICAL LEADERSHIP

The final stage of the public opinion–public policy process involves action by the nation's political leadership. Even if mass opinion is sufficiently well informed and articulated, a government will not be responsive unless its political elite acknowledge expressed opinions and honestly attempt to meet the needs and interests of the people.

In our discussions of American political elites in Part Two of this volume, we discovered that the nation's leaders in many ways differ dramatically from the masses who selected them. In terms of socialization, social background characteristics, personality traits, and political attitudes there are significant distinctions between the citizenry and its leaders. This forces us to confront a question fundamental to the democratic process. Prewitt stated the problem well when he wrote:

Theorists interested in the workings of democracy spend considerable energy on the complex paradox of how public leaders can be both "different" and yet "representative," different in the sense that they are unlike the populace from which they are chosen and yet representative in the sense that they somehow act in accordance with the preferences of that populace.[3]

The answer to this question is that a political leader need not be a composite of whatever constitutes the "common man" in order to represent common people. The fact that leaders are disproportionately white, male, middle-aged, and from the higher socioeconomic classes does not necessarily mean that they exclusively represent white, male, middle-aged, high socioeconomic class citizens, although one's social background characteristics undoubtedly have an impact on political perceptions and attitudes. A President like the wealthy, Catholic, Harvard-educated John Kennedy represented more than his social class. He is remembered most for his humane compassion for the poor, uneducated, and unemployed.

In our attempts to make democratic rule more responsive and responsible we should strive for quality leadership and not for leaders who reflect the weaknesses as well as the strengths of the population. One example of thinking that confused representativeness with leadership occurred in the United States Senate in the spring of 1970. At that time the Senate was debating the confirmation of President Nixon's nomination of G. Harrold Carswell of Florida to be an Associate Justice of the United States Supreme Court. One of the charges against Carswell's confirmation was that the nominee was an inferior lower court judge with a mediocre record of accomplishment. In an attempt to defend Carswell, President Nixon's floor manager for the confirmation debate, Senator Roman Hruska of Nebraska, made the following statement:

Even if he is mediocre there are a lot of mediocre judges and people and lawyers. They are entitled to a little representation, aren't they, and a little chance? We can't have all Brandeises, Cardozos and Frankfurters, and stuff like that there.[4]

As if this statement was not damaging enough, another Carswell supporter, Senator Russell Long of Louisiana, added:

Does it not seem . . . that we have had enough of those upside down, corkscrew thinkers? Would it not appear that it might be well to take a B student or a C student who was able to think straight, compared to one of those A students who are capable of the kind of thinking that winds up getting us a 100-percent increase in crime in this country?[5]

The majority of the Senate did not accept this attempt at making mediocrity a democratic virtue and defeated the nomination, 51–45.

The reason that the Hruska-Long logic fails is that it miscomprehends the nature of leadership. Political elites, even in a democracy, are more than mere personifications of the public. If we wanted political leaders to respond in a litmus paper-like fashion to citizen input, it would make little difference who occupied official positions. In fact, we would not need leaders at all, but could create governments by public opinion poll. The "litmus paper leader" may be absolutely responsive, but he is not a leader. For all practical purposes he is a follower. A true political leader must be more than responsive in a simplistic sense. He must combine responsiveness with responsibility. He must respond to the needs of the people not only by articulating their feelings, attitudes, and biases, but also by developing creative solutions to the complex problems of modern society and directing governmental machinery for the purposes of improving the lives of the citizenry. Citizens should use their power to demand nothing short of excellence in their political leaders.

The conclusion of this discussion of political leadership is simple and straightforward. The probability of attaining effective, responsive, qualified leaders increases as the number of potential candidates and the openness of political competition increase. Once the leadership is selected, it is the duty of the electorate to demand responsive and responsible government. There is a bit of truth in the old saying that Americans get exactly the quality of government they deserve. When people do not vote, participate in the political process, or hold public leaders accountable for their actions, then they deserve little sympathy when control of the government slips away from them. But by improving mass opinion formation, making better use of opinion articulation channels, expanding the number of potential candidates, and holding leaders accountable, Americans can enhance the effectiveness and responsiveness of their government.

Responsiveness and governmental institutions

A final consideration we must accord to the subject of democratic responsiveness is the question of the quality of the nation's governmental institutions. To what extent are those governing bodies and agencies capable of responding to the needs and concerns of the people?

THE EXECUTIVE BRANCH

The executive branch in American politics has undergone a significant transformation. In the beginning the Presidency and its developing bureaucracy were considered of secondary importance to the Congress. The President was viewed primarily as the administrator of congressional policy, the executor of the law. Gradually, however, the Presidency grew until today it is the paramount agency of the federal political machine. A number of factors have contributed to this great expansion in the President's role. The withering away of the importance of the Electoral College has made the President a popular leader rather than a man chosen by a cadre of elite electors. The growth of the American military machine has given the commander-in-chief considerable power. The increased importance of foreign policy, over which the President has primary control, has boosted the prominence of the chief executive. The need for swift action caused by rapid technological advancement favors the President over the more deliberative Congress. And the growth of the bureaucracy has provided the President superior sources of information upon which intelligent actions can be taken and innovative programs developed. The Presidency has become the embodiment of the United States government. When the people credit or criticize the government they think of the President. He is the symbol and the seat of political power in this country.

This transformation of the Presidency from a relatively weak to a very strong governmental force has resulted in changing expectations about the office. We no longer view the President essentially in terms of following and executing the will of Congress. Instead, the President is perceived as the nation's primary leader. It is to him that the nation looks to receive guidance, hope, prosperity, and peace. We expect him to lead, create, propose, and administer. Given the monumental growth in expectations, there is danger that the Presidency has expanded beyond manageable limits. We must ask the question whether the office has become too powerful to be bound by our traditional values of responsiveness and accountability.

In recent years a number of developments in the Presidency have been significant enough to cause concern about the chief executive. Among these are several tendencies to restrict the information flow between the White House and the people. If public opinion is to have an impact it must be communicated and received by public officials. If the people are to perform their democratic responsibility of holding political leaders accountable, they must be given sufficient honest information about the activities of the governmental elite. Hopefully, this information will originate from multiple sources to insure its credibility. Three information developments are worthy of mention here. The first is the ever increasing isolation of the President. The President has lost considerable touch with the American people. Surrounded by a ring of political palace guards, known as the White House staff, the President receives only those communications which filter through the White House bureaucracy.[6] This, of course, blunts whatever opinion is articulated by the public. A second problem is the continuing antagonism between the chief executive and the press. When the President refuses to use the press regularly as a conduit for communication with the American people, the nation suffers. Third, the President's position of importance enables him to use the news media for his own purposes. At a moment's notice the President can appear on nationwide television or radio monopolizing the flow of information into American households. The people, agencies, or programs he might attack, even if given a chance to respond, have not the faintest chance of countering a presidential pronouncement.

The American republic is in need of increased openness among its political elite. This is particularly true with respect to what has become an isolated and unapproachable Presidency. During the 1968 presidential campaign, candidate Richard Nixon made this point clear when he stated over nationwide radio:

The President has a duty to decide, but the people have a right to know why. The President has a responsibility to tell them—to lay out all the facts, and to explain not only why he chose as he did but also what it means for the future. Only through an open, candid dialogue with the people can a President maintain his trust and leadership. . . .[7]

Ironically, Nixon's Watergate troubles are witness to the truth and the prophecy of his own words. When a President ceases to engage in an "open and candid dialogue with the people" he can indeed lose his trust and leadership.

THE LEGISLATIVE BRANCH

A good deal of what we have said about the executive branch has relevance to the legislature. The power accumulated by the President and the bureaucracy he commands has been accumulated largely at the expense of the legislative branch. Congress, which was originally designed by the framers to be the most important agency of the federal government, has gradually slipped in stature until today it runs a poor second to the Presidency.

This decrease in power has been associated with an alteration in function. Congress was originally intended to legislate, to be the creative, innovating force of the government. This function has gradually atrophied, until today the executive agencies of government have assumed the tasks of creating and drafting legislative proposals. The function of Congress has devolved into one of primarily reacting to these proposals. This is not to say that the Congress has reduced itself to a "rubber stamp" for the President. The national legislature does not always agree with the President's proposals and not uncommonly kills executive originated bills either through inaction or overt rejection. Congress, then, has not become an obsolete institution, but it has failed to live up to its potential in terms of creative, innovative leadership. As an institutional follower rather than a leader, Congress has not lost its independence as an institution, but has significantly abdicated its role as an architect of government policy.

In evaluating the role of the legislature in terms of responsiveness, we face a much different situation than confronted us in our analysis of the chief executive. There we were concerned with presidential power going too far—unchecked by either Congress or the people. The problem presented by the Congress, on the other hand, is how to make the legislature more active in behalf of the people.

Theoretically, Congress should be more subject to electoral account-ability than is the President. Members of the House must return to their districts every two years for reelection campaigns and Senators every six years. This gives the public ample opportunity to register its approval or disapproval of a Congressman's record. If the eighty to ninety percent re-election rate is any indication, the citizenry generally supports the way in which their legislators are conducting themselves. But the threat of defeat is a very real one, with 30 to 40 legislators suffering just such a fate every two years. This threat is sufficient to keep legislators busy attempting to deter-mine their constituents' attitudes. Therefore, the isolation problem plaguing the Presidency is not a crucial one with respect to Congress. The people possess the potential of easily controlling their legislators if they wish to do so. Unfortunately, the typical Congressman rarely receives any broadly based instructions from his district. Increases in the responsiveness of Congress, then, could result from improvements in mass opinion formation and articulation.

THE JUDICIAL BRANCH

Throughout those sections of this book dealing with governmental institutions, we have devoted the bulk of our attention to the legislative and executive branches. The reason for this emphasis has been that these political divisions of the government are directly tied to public opinion by the structure of their operations, by the intent of their creators, and by basic tenets of democratic theory. We expect the executive and legislative branches to respond to public opinion. Such is the nature of a democracy. Conversely, we have paid only passing attention to the judicial branch of government, since by their very nature the courts are designed to be insulated from public pressure. The framers of the federal Constitution structured the judiciary to be strong and independent. Toward this end direct popular control over the selection, retention and operations of federal judges was not permitted. The courts were designed so that judges would be responsive to the Constitution, law, and justice rather than to the popular will of the nation's majorities.

It would be a mistake to conclude, however, that public opinion has no effect on the behavior of a judge. As Justice Cardozo eloquently stated, "The great tides and currents which engulf the rest of mankind do not turn aside in their course and pass the judges idly by." [8] While the tie between public opinion and the courts is neither direct nor formal, it undoubtedly exists. No matter what constitutional restraints are imposed on political decision makers, no governmental leaders can be totally insulated from the force of public attitudes.

The federal courts have been particularly influenced by public opinion in times of war and national emergency. This is not surprising given the fact that in times of severe national stress the emotions of the nation are at their most intense level. During the Second World War, for example, when fears arose over a possible Japanese invasion of the Western coast of the United States, the Supreme Court bowed to the tenor of the times and upheld the constitutionality of governmental actions excluding all individuals of Japanese ancestry from the Pacific Coast and moving them to inland War Relocation Centers.[9] Quite obviously such a blatant denial of civil rights would not have been condoned at any time other than one of severe national stress. When the anti-communist hysteria overcame the nation during the Cold War of the 1940s and 1950s, the Court responded to public opinion by upholding restrictions on freedom of association and advocacy. Recognizing the linkage between public sentiment and the Court's decisions, Justice Hugo Black wrote in a dissenting opinion:

Public opinion being what it now is, few will protest the conviction of these Communist petitioners. There is hope, however, that in calmer times, when present pressures, passions and fears subside, this or some later Court will restore the First Amendment liberties to the high preferred place where they belong in a free society.[10]

Black's position was vindicated during the 1960s when pressures, passions, and fears did subside and the Supreme Court struck down much of the repressive legislation directed at unpopular political movements and groups.

There are, however, many incidents in which the judiciary has acted in the face of overwhelming public opposition. In some of these cases the Court failed to respond to public clamor for new interpretations of the law, such as when the pre-1937 Court struck down New Deal economic legislation. At other times, the courts have broken new legal ground when the people were generally critical of such moves. The school prayer cases, busing decisions, and criminal rights rulings are examples of judicial action in which the courts have assumed a leadership position despite adverse public reactions.

No other democratic society allows so much power to rest in the hands of its judiciary than does the United States. It is indeed ironic that a nation built on principles of democratic responsiveness has given non-elected officials, unaccountable to the will of the citizenry, such a great deal of authority. Because the courts ultimately have the final say regarding the validity of governmental actions and are capable of declaring the actions of the elected branches unconstitutional, the power of the judiciary cannot be underestimated. In creating the courts, this nation attempted to insulate the judiciary from the shifting forces of public opinion and political pressure. Judges were to be responsive to justice and the Constitution, not to the majority of the voters. But as we have seen, judges, being nothing more than humans in black robes, can be swayed by public opinion. This is inevitable. Yet the impact of public opinion on the federal judicial branch is significantly less than the effect of citizen attitudes on the more political branches.

Summary

The purpose of this book has been to explore the nature and importance of public opinion in the American democracy. In order to accomplish this task the volume has been divided into three parts dealing with mass opinion and behavior, elite opinion and behavior, and opinion linkages between the people and their political leaders. The real importance of public opinion lies in its long and precarious journey of transformation into public policy. To understand this process it was necessary to begin with the roots of public opinion formation, proceed through the articulation and reception of that opinion by the political elite, and evaluate the impact of such articulated opinion on the behavior of governmental officials.

Our aim, then, has been to show that public opinion is more than just percentage figures reflecting the results of an opinion survey, more than some undefined general will of the populace. Public opinion is a process. It is a process which links the governed to their governors; and a process which provides a portion of the energy upon which democratic regimes are run.

NOTES

[1] William C. Mitchell, *Public Choice in America* (Chicago: Markham Publishing Company, 1971), p. 369.

[2] V. O. Key, Jr., *Public Opinion and American Democracy* (New York: Knopf, 1964), p. 552.

[3] Kenneth Prewitt, *The Recruitment of Political Leaders* (Indianapolis: Bobbs-Merrill, 1970), pp. 205–6.

[4] Quoted in Henry J. Abraham, *Justices and Presidents* (New York: Oxford University Press, 1974), pp. 6–7.

[5] Ibid., p. 7.

[6] On this general problem see George E. Reedy, *The Twilight of the Presidency* (New York: World Publishing, 1970).

7 Richard M. Nixon, September 19, 1968, radio address. Quoted in L. Earl Shaw and John C. Pierce, *Readings on the American Political System* (Lexington, Mass.: D. C. Heath, 1970), p. 505.

8 Quoted in Abraham, *Justices and Presidents,* p. 270.

9 *Korematsu* v. *United States,* 323 U.S. 214 (1944).

10 See Justice Black's dissent in *Dennis* v. *United States,* 341 U.S. 494 (1951).

BIBLIOGRAPHY

Part one: Mass opinion

ALMOND, GABRIEL A., and SIDNEY VERBA. *The Civic Culture.* Princeton: Princeton University Press, 1963.

BERELSON, BERNARD, and GARY A. STEINER. *Human Behavior: An Inventory of Scientific Findings.* New York: Harcourt Brace Jovanovich, Inc., 1964.

BUCHANAN, WILLIAM. *Understanding Political Variables.* New York: Charles Scribner's Sons, 1969.

CAMPBELL, ANGUS; PHILIP E. CONVERSE; WARREN E. MILLER; and DONALD E. STOKES. *The American Voter.* New York: John Wiley & Sons, Inc., 1960.

————. *Elections and the Political Order.* New York: John Wiley & Sons, Inc., 1966.

CAMPBELL, ANGUS, and PHILIP E. CONVERSE, eds. *The Human Meaning of Social Change.* New York: Russell Sage Foundation, 1972.

CANTRIL, ALBERT H., and CHARLES W. ROLL, JR. *Hopes and Fears of the American People.* New York: Universe Books, 1971.

DAWSON, RICHARD E., *Public Opinion and Contemporary Disarray.* New York: Harper & Row Publishers, 1973.

DAWSON, RICHARD E., and KENNETH PREWITT. *Political Socialization.* Boston: Little, Brown and Company, 1969.

DEVINE, DONALD J., *The Political Culture of the United States.* Boston: Little, Brown and Company, 1972.

EASTON, DAVID, and JACK DENNIS. *Children in the Political System.* New York: McGraw-Hill Book Company, 1969.

FLANIGAN, WILLIAM H. *Political Behavior of the American Electorate.* Boston: Allyn & Bacon, Inc., 1972.

FREE, LLOYD A., and HADLEY CANTRIL. *The Political Beliefs of Americans.* New York: Simon & Schuster, Inc., 1968.

GREENSTEIN, FRED I. *Children and Politics.* New Haven: Yale University Press, 1965.

————. *Personality and Politics.* Chicago: Markham Publishing Company, 1969.

HARRIS, LOUIS. *The Anguish of Change.* New York: W. W. Norton & Company, Inc., 1973.

HESS, ROBERT D., and JUDITH V. TORNEY. *The Development of Political Attitudes in Children.* Chicago: Aldine-Atherton, Inc., 1967.

HYMAN, HERBERT. *Poltical Socialization.* New York: The Free Press, 1959.

LANE, ROBERT E. *Political Ideology.* New York: The Free Press, 1962.

————. *Political Life: Why People Get Involved in Politics.* New York: The Free Press, 1959.

LAZARSFELD, PAUL; BERNARD BERELSON; and HELEN GAUDET. *The People's Choice.* New York: Columbia University Press, 1948.

LIPSET, SEYMOUR MARTIN. *Political Man.* Garden City, N.Y.: Doubleday, 1960.

MATTHEWS, DONALD R., and JAMES W. PROTHRO. *Negroes and the New Southern Politics.* New York: Harcourt Brace Jovanovich, Inc., 1966.

McCLOSKY, HERBERT. "Consensus and Ideology in American Politics." *American Political Science Review,* 58 (June 1964), 361–82.

McCLOSKY, HERBERT; PAUL J. HOFFMAN; and ROSEMARY O'HARA. "Issue Conflict and Consensus among Party Leaders and Followers." *American Political Science Review,* 54 (June 1960), 406–27.

MILBRATH, LESTER W. *Political Participation.* Chicago: Rand McNally, 1965.

NEWCOMB, THEODORE M.; RALPH H. TURNER; and PHILIP E. CONVERSE. *Social Psychology.* New York: Holt, Rinehart & Winston, Inc., 1965.

NIEMI, RICHARD G., et al., *The Politics of Future Citizens.* San Francisco: Jossey-Bass, Inc., Publishers, 1974.

NIMMO, DAN. *The Political Persuaders.* Englewood Cliffs, N.J.: Prentice-Hall, 1970.

PROTHRO, JAMES W., and CHARLES M. GRIGG. "Fundamental Principles of Democracy: Bases of Agreement and Disagreement." *Journal of Politics,* 22 (May 1960), 276–94.

ROBINSON, JOHN P.; JERROLD G. RUSK; and KENDRA B. HEAD. *Measures of Political Attitudes.* Ann Arbor, Mich.: Survey Research Center, Institute of Social Research, 1968.

ROSENAU, JAMES N., ed. *Domestic Sources of Foreign Policy.* New York: The Free Press, 1967.

ROSENBERG, MILTON J.; SIDNEY VERBA; and PHILIP E. CONVERSE. *Vietnam and the Silent Majority.* New York: Harper & Row, Publishers, 1970.

SMITH, M. BREWSTER; JEROME S. BRUNER; and ROBERT W. WHITE. *Opinions and Personality.* New York: John Wiley & Sons, Inc., 1964.

STOUFFER, SAMUEL L., et al., *The American Soldier.* Princeton: Princeton University Press, 1949.

STOUFFER, SAMUEL L. *Communism, Conformity, and Civil Liberties.* Garden City, N.J.: Doubleday, 1955.

VERBA, SIDNEY, and NORMAN H. NIE. *Participation in America: Political Democracy and Social Equality.* New York: Harper & Row, Publishers, 1972.

WATTS, WILLIAM, and LLOYD A. FREE. *State of the Nation.* New York: Universe Books, 1973.

Part two: Elite opinion

ADAMANY, DAVID. "The Party Variable in Judges' Voting: Conceptual Notes and a Case Study." *American Political Science Review,* 63 (March 1969), 57–73.

ASHER, HERBERT B. "The Learning of Legislative Norms." *American Political Science Review,* 67 (June 1973), 499–513.

BACHRACH, PETER. *The Theory of Democratic Elitism: A Critique.* Boston: Little, Brown and Company, 1967.

BANFIELD, EDWARD. *Political Influence.* New York: The Free Press, 1961.

BARBER, JAMES DAVID. *The Lawmakers.* New Haven: Yale University Press, 1965.

————.*The Presidential Character.* Englewood Cliffs, N.J.: Prentice-Hall, 1972.

BEARD, CHARLES. *An Economic Interpretation of the Constitution of the United States.* New York: Macmillan, 1913.

BELL, CHARLES G., and CHARLES M. PRICE. "Pre-Legislative Sources of Representational Roles." *Midwest Journal of Political Science,* 13 (May 1969), 254–70.

BROWNING, RUFUS P., and HERBERT JACOB. "Power Motivation and the Political Personality." *Public Opinion Quarterly,* 28 (Spring 1964), 75–90.

COBB, ROGER. "The Belief Systems Perspective: An Assessment of a Framework." *Journal of Politics,* 35 (February 1973), 121–53.

CONVERSE, PHILIP E. "The Nature of Belief Systems in Mass Publics." In *Ideology and Discontent,* ed. David Apter. New York: The Free Press, 1964.

DAHL, ROBERT. *Who Governs?* New Haven: Yale University Press, 1961.

DAVIDSON, ROGER H. *The Role of the Congressman.* New York: Pegasus, 1969.

DIRENZO, GORDON J. *Personality, Power and Politics.* Notre Dame: University of Notre Dame Press, 1967.

EULAU, HEINZ, and JOHN D. SPRAGUE. *Lawyers in Politics.* Indianapolis: Bobbs-Merrill, 1964.

FENNO, RICHARD F. JR. *Congressmen in Committees.* Boston: Little, Brown and Company, 1973.

FIEDLER, FRED E. *Leadership.* New York: General Learning Press, 1971.

GEORGE, ALEXANDER, and JULIETTE GEORGE. *Woodrow Wilson and Colonel House.* New York: John Day, 1956.

GLICK, HENRY ROBERT. *Supreme Courts in State Politics.* New York: Basic Books, 1971.

HUCKSHORN, ROBERT J., and ROBERT C. SPENCER. *The Politics of Defeat.* Amherst: University of Massachusetts Press, 1971.

HUITT, RALPH K. "Democratic Party Leadership in the Senate." *American Political Science Review,* 55 (June 1961), 331–44.

JANIS, IRVING L. *Victims of Groupthink.* Boston: Houghton Mifflin Company, 1972.

JAROS, DEAN, and ROBERT I. MENDELSON. "The Judicial Role and Sentencing

Behavior." *Midwest Journal of Political Science,* 11 (November 1967), 471–88.

JEWELL, MALCOLM E. *The State Legislature.* 2nd ed. New York: Random House, Inc., 1969.

JEWELL, MALCOLM E., and SAMUEL C. PATTERSON. *The Legislative Process in the United States.* 2nd ed. New York: Random House, Inc., 1973.

JOYNER, CONRAD. *The American Politician.* Tucson: University of Arizona Press, 1971.

KELLER, SUZANNE. *Beyond the Ruling Class.* New York: Random House, Inc., 1963.

LASSWELL, HAROLD D. *Power and Personality.* New York: W.W. Norton & Company, Inc., 1948.

————. *Psychopathology and Politics.* Chicago: University of Chicago Press, 1930.

LUTTBEG, NORMAN. "The Structure of Beliefs among Leaders and the Public." *Public Opinion Quarterly,* 32 (Fall 1968), 398–409.

MADRON, THOMAS. *Small Group Methods and the Study of Politics.* Evanston, Ill.: Northwestern University Press, 1969.

MATTHEWS, DONALD R. *U.S. Senators and Their World.* Chapel Hill: University of North Carolina Press, 1960.

McCLOSKY, HERBERT. "Consensus and Ideology in American Politics." *American Political Review,* 58 (June 1964), 361–82.

————. "Conservatism and Personality." *American Political Science Review,* 52 (March 1958), 27–45.

MICHAELS, ROBERT. *Political Parties.* New York: The Free Press, 1949.

MOSCA, GAETANO. *The Ruling Class.* New York: McGraw-Hill Book Company, 1939.

NEUSTADT, RICHARD E. *Presidential Power: The Politics of Leadership.* New York: John Wiley & Sons, Inc., 1960.

PARRY, GERAINT. *Political Elites.* London: Allen and Unwin, 1969.

PREWITT, KENNETH. *The Recruitment of Political Leaders.* Indianapolis: Bobbs-Merrill, 1970.

PREWITT, KENNETH; HEINZ EULAU; and BETTY ZISK. "Political Socialization and Political Roles." *Public Opinion Quarterly,* 30 (Winter 1966), 569–82.

PREWITT, KENNETH and ALAN STONE. *The Ruling Elites.* New York: Harper & Row, Publishers, 1973.

SCHLESINGER, JOSEPH A. *Ambition and Politics.* Chicago: Random House, Inc., 1966.

SCHMIDHAUSER, JOHN R. "The Justices of the Supreme Court: A Collective Portrait." *Midwest Journal of Political Science,* 3 (February 1959), 1–57.

SCHUBERT, GLENDON. *The Judicial Mind.* Evanston, Ill.: Northwestern University Press, 1965.

SCHUMPETER, JOSEPH A. *Capitalism, Socialism and Democracy.* 3rd ed. New York: Harper & Row, Publishers, 1950.

SELIGMAN, LESTER; MICHAEL R. KING; CHONG LIM KIM; and ROLAND E. SMITH. *Patterns of Recruitment.* Chicago: Rand McNally, 1974.

WAHLKE, JOHN C.; HEINZ EULAU; WILLIAM BUCHANAN; and LEROY FERGUSON. *The Legislative System.* New York: John Wiley & Sons, Inc., 1962.

WALKER, JACK L. "A Critique of 'The Elitist Theory of Democracy.' " *American Political Science Review,* 60 (June 1966), 285–95.

Part three: Opinion and government

BARBER, JAMES DAVID., ed. *Choosing the President.* Englewood Cliffs, N.J.: Prentice-Hall, 1974.

BAUER, RAYMOND A.; ITHIEL DE SOLA POOL; and LEWIS A. DEXTER. *American Business and Public Policy: The Politics of Foreign Trade.* New York: Atherton Press, 1963.

BOYD, RICHARD W. "Popular Control of Public Policy: A Normal Vote Analysis of the 1968 Election." *American Political Science Review,* 66 (June 1972), 439–49.

BURNHAM, WALTER DEAN. *Critical Elections and the Mainsprings of American Politics.* New York: W. W. Norton & Company, Inc., 1970.

CLAPP, CHARLES L. *The Congressman.* Washington, D.C.: The Brookings Institution, 1963.

COHEN, BERNARD C. *The Public's Impact on Foreign Policy.* Boston: Little, Brown and Company, 1973.

CONVERSE, PHILIP E. "Change in the American Electorate." In *The Human Meaning of Social Change,* ed. Angus Campbell and Philip Converse. New York: Russell Sage Foundation, 1972.

CONVERSE, PHILIP E.; WARREN E. MILLER; JERROLD G. RUSK; and ARTHUR C. WOLFE. "Continuity and Change in American Politics: Parties and Issues in the 1968 Elections." *American Political Science Review,* 63 (December 1969), 1083–1105.

CNUDDE, CHARLES F., and DONALD J. McCRONE. "The Linkage between Constituency Attitudes and Congressional Voting Behavior: A Causal Model." *American Political Science Review,* 60 (March 1966), 66–72.

CRONIN, THOMAS E. *State of the Presidency.* Boston: Little, Brown and Company, 1975.

DREYER, EDWARD. "Change and Stability in Party Identifications." *Journal of Politics,* 35 (August 1973), 712–22.

ERICSON, ROBERT S. "The Electoral Impact of Congressional Roll Call Voting." *American Political Science Review,* 65 (December 1971), 1018-32.

FISHEL, JEFF. *Party and Opposition.* New York: David McKay Company, Inc., 1973.

GLENN, NORVAL D. "Class and Party Support in the United States: Recent and Emerging Trends." *Public Opinion Quarterly,* 37 (Spring 1973), 1–20.

GRABER, DORIS A. *Public Opinion, the President, and Foreign Policy: Four Case Studies from the Formative Years.* New York: Holt, Rinehart & Winston, Inc., 1968.

JACKSON, JOHN E. "Issues, Party Choices, and Presidential Votes." *American Journal of Political Science,* 19 (May 1975), 161–85.

KESSEL, JOHN H. "Comment: The Issues in Issue Voting." *American Political Science Review,* 66 (June 1972), 459–65.

KEY, V. O., JR. *Public Opinion and American Democracy.* New York: Knopf, 1964.

————. *The Responsible Electorate.* Cambridge: The Belknap Press of Harvard University Press, 1966.

KINGDON, JOHN W. *Congressmen's Voting Decisions.* New York: Harper & Row, Publishers, 1973.

KRAMER, GERALD H. "Short-Term Fluctuations in U.S. Voting Behavior, 1896–1964." *American Political Science Review,* 65 (March 1971), 131–43.

LADD, EVERETT CARLL, JR., and CHARLES D. HADLEY. "Party Definition and Party Differentiation." *Public Opinion Quarterly,* 37 (Spring 1973), 21–34.

LIPSKY, MICHAEL. "Protest as a Political Resource." *American Political Science Review,* 62 (December 1968) 1144–1158.

LUTTBEG, NORMAN R., ed. *Public Opinion and Public Policy.* Homewood, Ill.: The Dorsey Press, 1974.

LUTTBEG, NORMAN R., and HARMON ZEIGLER. "Attitude Consensus and Conflict in an Interest Group." *American Political Science Review,* 60 (September 1966), 655–66.

MAYHEW, DAVID R. *Congress: The Electoral Connection.* New Haven: Yale University Press, 1974.

McCLOSKY, HERBERT; PAUL J. HOFFMAN; and ROSEMARY O'HARA. "Issue Conflict and Consensus among Party Leaders and Followers." *American Political Science Review,* 54 (June 1960), 406–27.

MERELMAN, RICHARD M. "Electoral Instability and the American Party System." *Journal of Politics,* 32 (February 1970), 115–39.

MILLER, ARTHUR; WARREN MILLER; ALDEN RAINE; and THAD BROWN. "A Majority Party in Disarray: Policy Polarization in the 1972 Election." Ann Arbor, Mich.: Center for Political Studies, 1973.

MILLER, WARREN E., and DONALD E. STOKES. "Constituency Influence in Congress." *American Political Science Review,* 57 (March 1963), 45–56.

MUELLER, JOHN E. "Presidential Popularity from Truman to Johnson." *American Political Science Review,* 64 (March 1970), 18–34.

————. *War, Presidents and Public Opinion.* New York: John Wiley & Sons, Inc., 1973.

NIE, NORMAN, with KRISTI ANDERSON. "Mass Belief Systems Revisited: Political Change and Attitude Structure." *Journal of Politics,* 36 (August 1974), 547–54.

PAGE, BENJAMIN I., and RICHARD A. BRODY. "Policy Voting and the Electoral Process: The Vietnam War Issue." *American Political Science Review,* 66 (September 1972), 979–95.

POMPER, GERALD M. *Elections in America.* New York: Dodd, Mead & Company, 1968.

————. "From Confusion to Clarity: Issues and American Voters, 1965–

1968." *American Political Science Review,* 66 (June 1972), 415–28.

————. *Voters' Choice.* New York: Dodd, Mead & Company, 1975.

REEDY, GEORGE E. *The Twilight of the Presidency.* New York: World Publishing Company, 1970.

REPASS, DAVID E. "Issue Salience and Party Choice." *American Political Science Review,* 65 (June 1971), 389–400.

RIESELBACH, LEROY N. *People vs. Government: The Responsiveness of American Institutions.* Bloomington: Indiana University Press, 1975.

SCAMMON, RICHARD M., and BEN J. WATTENBERG. *The Real Majority.* New York: Coward, McCann & Geoghegan, Inc., 1971.

SIGEL, ROBERTA S. "Image of the American Presidency—Part II of an Exploration into Popular Views of Presidential Power." *Midwest Journal of Political Science,* 10 (February 1966), 123–37.

SIGEL, ROBERTA S., and DAVID BUTLER. "The Public and the No Third Term Tradition: Inquiry into Attitudes toward Power." *Midwest Journal of Political Science,* 8 (February 1964), 39–54.

SORAUF, FRANK J. *Party Politics in America.* Boston: Little, Brown and Company, 1972.

SOULE, JOHN W., and JAMES W. CLARKE. "Issue Conflict and Consensus: A Comparative Study of Democratic and Republican Candidates to the 1968 National Convention." *Journal of Politics,* 33 (February 1971), 72–91.

STOKES, DONALD E., and WARREN E. MILLER. "Party Government and the Saliency of Congress." *Public Opinion Quarterly,* 26 (Winter 1962), 531–46.

STROUSE, JAMES C. *The Mass Media, Public Opinion, and Public Policy Analysis: Linkage Explorations.* Columbus, Ohio: Charles E. Merrill Publishing Company, 1975.

SULLIVAN, DENNIS G.; JEFFREY L. PRESSMAN; BENJAMIN I. PAGE; and JOHN J. LYONS. *The Politics of Representation: The Democratic Convention of 1972.* New York: St. Martin's Press, Inc., 1974.

SULLIVAN JOHN L., and ROBERT E. O'CONNOR. "Electoral Choice and Popular Control of Public Policy: The Case of the 1966 House Elections." *American Political Science Review,* 66 (December 1972), 1256–68.

SUNDQUIST, JAMES L. *Dynamics of the Party System: Alignment and Realignment of Political Parties in the United States.* Washington, D.C.: The Brookings Institution, 1973.

TRUMAN, DAVID B. *The Governmental Process: Political Interests and Public Opinion.* 2nd ed. New York: Knopf, 1971.

VERBA, SIDNEY, and NORMAN NIE. *Participation in America.* New York: Harper & Row, Publishers, 1972.

WEISBERG, HAROLD, and JERROLD RUSK. "Perceptions of Presidential Candidates: Implications for Electoral Change." *Midwest Journal of Political Science,* 16 (August 1972), 1167–85.

WILCOX, WALTER. "The Congressional Poll—and Non-Poll," in *Political Opinion and Behavior,* ed. Edward Dreyer and Walter Rosenbaum. Belmont, Calif.: Wadsworth Publishing Co., Inc., 1970.

ZEIGLER, L. HARMON, and G. WAYNE PEAK. *Interest Groups in American Society.* Englewood Cliffs, N.J.: Prentice-Hall, 1972.

INDEX

Abortion reform, 92-99
  age differences over, 96
  educational differences and support for, 95
  party identification and, 99
  occupational differences over, 97
  race differences over, 94
  religious affiliation and opposition to, 87-88, 97
ACA (Americans for Constitutional Action), 249, 260
Accountability of political elite, 124, 132-35
Accumulation Model of socialization, 50-53
  family in, 53, 57
Acquisition norm, 193-95
Active-negative presidents, 159-60
Active-positive presidents, 159
ADA (Americans for Democratic Action), 249, 260
Adolescent rebellion, 56-57
Advertiser (legislative type), 162
AFL-CIO (American Federation of Labor–Congress of Industrial Organizations), 124, 263
Age
  of elite, 146-47
  impact of, on opinions of elite, 151
  liberalism-conservatism and differences in, 88-89
  in party identification, 79-81
  of presidents, 146
  public policy issues and differences in, 95-97
Agents in political socialization process, 53-65
Agnew, Spiro T., 278
Aggregate analysis of attitudinal data, 22-25
Alford, Dale, 227
Almond, Gabriel A., 54, 55, 112
AMA (American Medical Association), 260, 303
Ambition of elite, 137-38

American Federation of Labor–Congress of Industrial Organizations (AFL-CIO), 124, 263
American Institute of Public Opinion, see Gallup poll
American Medical Association (AMA), 260, 303
American participant citizen role, see Citizen roles
American Political Science Association, 269
American Voter, The (Campbell et al.), 80, 81
Americans for Constitutional Action (ACA), 249, 260
Americans for Democratic Action (ADA), 249, 260
Anticipatory socialization, defined, 66
Apprenticeship norm, 190
Areal roles, 180-81
Aristotle, 112
Attitudes, 19-118
  aggregate analysis of, 22-25
  attitude systems and attitude change, 37-40
  basic concepts about, 34-40
  collecting and analysing data on, 21-27
  defined as valenced cognition, 34
  about democracy, see Democracy
  elite behavior and political, 167-71
  elite-mass differences in, 163-67
  measurement of, 28-34
  political activity index, 31-33
  of political elite, 163-71
  political socialization as formation of, see Political socialization
  properties of, 35-37
  question wording in measuring, 28-29
  response set on, 33-34
  responsible democracy and articulation of, 301-3
  responsible democracy and formation of, 300-1
  status of attitude as concept, 20-21
  survey research on, 25-27

Attitudes (*cont.*)
types of measures of, 29-33
Authority
delegation of, 105-6
structure of, 45

Balance concept, 38-39
Bandura, Albert, 52
Banfield, Edward C., 65, 115, 124
Barber, James David, 159-63
Basic political orientations
five models of political socialization
in, 49-53
learning, 48-53
Bauer, Raymond A., 288
Beard, Charles, 150
Belief
distinguishing attitude from, 19
systems of, 164-67
Bennington study, 63, 64
Berelson, Bernard, 19
Black, Hugo, 309
Blacks
party identification among, 82
shift in partisan identification of, 73
See also Busing issue; Civil rights;
Race
Boarding schools, as socializing agents,
58
Brandeis, Louis, 147
Brennan, William, 169
Brogan, D. W., 293
Bronfenbrenner, Urie, 57, 64
Brown v. *Board of Education* (1954),
170
Buchanan, James, executive power under,
185
Buchanan, William, 23
Buck, Carrie, 149-50
Buck v. *Bell* (1927), 149
Buckley, William F., 65
Burger, Warren, 170
Burnham, Walter Dean, 24, 80
Busing issue
age differences over, 96
busing as case of direct influence, 5-7
educational differences over, 95
occupational differences over, 97
polls on (1970; 1971), 5-6
race differences over, 93
Butler, Pierce, 150

Cambodian war, 277
Capital punishment (issue)
age differences over, 96
educational differences over, 95
race differences over, 93, 94
Cardozo, Benjamin, 147, 309
Carswell, G. Harrold, 304
Catholics, *see* Religion
Censorship, 65
Census Bureau, 213, 214
Center for Political Studies (CPS; Uni-
versity of Michigan), 221, 222
Centrality, as property of attitude, 37

Change
elite attitude, 166-67
formed attitudes resistant to, 37-40
Chicago Democratic convention (1968),
234
Children
changing conceptions of democracy
among, 113
norm of participation encouraged in,
113-14
political socialization of, *see* Political
socialization
Citizen roles, 110-16
American participant, 112-16
nonpartisanship in American participant, 115-16
parochial, 111
participant, 112
public-regardingness in American participant, 114-15
subject, 111
movement for (1960s), 235
Civic duty, electoral participation and,
215
Civic man, defined, 152-53
Civil rights
constituency opinion and congressional
voting on, 286-87
Cleveland, Grover, 147
Clausen, Aage, 250
Cnudde, Charles, 286-87
Coefficients of correlation, defined, 23
Coercive power, 204
Cognition, defined, 34
Cognitive Development Model of politi-
cal socialization, 49-50
Cognitive learning, described, 34, 49-50
Collective behavior in political institu-
tions, 196-205
Committees, 197-202
comparison of, 201-2
legislative, 197-98
Common Cause, 292, 303
Competence of electorate, 216-17; *see*
also Issues
Conditioning Model of political sociali-
zation, 52-53
family in, 53
Conformity, norm, 193-95
Congress, *see* Legislative branch
Congressional polls, as source of information, 290-91
Congressional Quarterly (journal), 248
Conservatism
distribution of, 88-91
of judiciary, 170
of lawyers, 151
legislative norms and, 195
party, 164, 244-46
personality of conservatives, 156
use of term, defined, 88
Constituency
mail from, as source of information,
289-90
opinion of, 84-89

Constituency (*cont.*)
  survey of, on issues, 283
Coolidge, Calvin, personality type of, 160-61
COPE (Committee on Political Education; AFL-CIO), 249
Corwin, Edward, 279
Council for a Responsible Firearms Policy, 9
Court system, *see* Judicial branch
CPS (Center for Political Studies; University of Michigan), 221, 222
Cross-national comparisons of voter turnout, 212-14
Cuban missile crisis (1962), 37
Cumulative scale (Guttman scale), 32-33

Dahl, Robert, 105-6, 109, 152
Daley, Richard, 234
Davidson, Roger, 283
Day schools, as agents of political socialization, 58
Decision making
  judicial criteria for, 187
  as judicial function, 187-88
  social background and elite, 149-52
Defection, party, 253-54
Defense spending issue
  age differences over, 96
  occupational differences over, 97
Delegate (legislative type), 283
  defined, 181
Delegation of authority, 105-6
Democracy, 102-18
  the American participant in, 112-16
  citizen roles in, *see* Citizen roles
  direct, *see* Direct democracy
  distinguished from republic, 105
  Madisonian justification of representative, 106-7
  majoritarian justification of representative, 104-5, 107-9
  nonpartisanship of American participant in, 115-16
  problem of representation in, 109-10
  public-regardingness of American participant in, 114-15
  representative, 105-17
  responsible, *see* Responsible democracy
Democratic regimes, legitimacy of, 2
Democratic Study Group, 198-99
Democratic theory, political elite and, 125-26; *see also* Ideology
Dennis, Jack, 48, 113
Desegregation, school busing for, 5-7; *see also* Busing issue
Dexter, Lewis Anthony, 288, 289
Direct action, 211, 228-38
  participation in, 229-33
  protest as, 233-36
Direct contact, as congressional source of information, 291
Direct control
  clear indication of, 227-28
  issues and, 227

Direct democracy
  described, 103-5
  as ideal, 110
  natural limit of, 109
  representative democracy as superior to, 106, 107
Direct influence, 4-7
  school busing as case of, 5-7
Direction, as property of attitude, 35
Douglas, William O., 169, 170, 199
Dulles, John Foster, 38
Dye, Thomas R., 260

Easton, David, 48, 49, 113, 115
Ecological fallacy, in working with aggregate data, 24
Economic conditions, presidential popularity and, 273, 274
Economic Interpretation of the Constitution, An (Beard), 150
Education
  direct action and, 231
  of elite, 147
  liberalism and level of, 90-91
  and party identification, 79
  public policy issues and differences in, 94-95
Eisenhower, Dwight D.
  news media used by, 278
  popularity of, 273-75
  as President of restraint, 158
  school integration crisis and, 227
  Secretary of State under, 38
  subgroups under, 198
Eldersveld, Samuel J., 244
Elections, 211-28, 237
  direct action and, 228-29
  issues and, 216-24, 25-56
  participation in, 212-16
  popular control and, 224-28
  See also Presidential elections; Voter turnout; Voters; Voting patterns; *and specific presidents and candidates*
Enforcement, norm, 193-95
Equal Rights Amendment (1974), 92-93
  age differences over, 96
  educational differences and support for, 95
  occupational differences over, 97
  religious affiliation and, 97
Executive branch in responsible democracy, 305-7; *see also* Presidents
Expert power, 204

Family
  party identification and low and high income, 77, 79
  in political socialization process, 53-57
Faubus, Orval, 227
Federal Communications Commission (FCC), 277
Federalist, 105, 106
First Amendment (1790), 8, 257, 309
Fishel, Jeff, 245, 246

Flags, preferences in, among children, 43-44
Ford, Gerald, 29
Fortas, Abe, 147
Fourteenth Amendment (1868), 150
Frankfurter, Felix, 147
Freud, Sigmund, 51, 149, 152
Friedrich, Carl, 178

Gallup poll (American Institute of Public Opinion), 25
  on busing (1970; 1971), 5-6
  on constituency opinion, 287
  on political careers, 115
  on popularity of presidents, 272
  sampling questions and, 28
Goldberg, Arthur, 147
Goldwater, Barry, in 1964 elections, 37, 170, 221, 224
  black Republicanism erased by, 82
  potential bias of activist opinion and, 231-32
  Vietnam war and, 225, 226
Goodell, Charles, 186
Government, 45-48
  defined, 45
  responsiveness and institutions of, 305-10
Greenstein, Fred I., 52, 67-68, 270, 271
Group contacts, as congressional source of information, 292
Group differences, see Ideology; Issues; Party identification
Group influence, 7-10
  gun control as case of, 9-10
  of interest groups, 8-9
  responsible parties and, 7-8
Groups, see Interest groups; Peer groups
Gun control, 30
  age differences over, 96
  as case of group influence, 9-10
  occupational differences over, 97
  religious affiliation and, 97
Guttman scale (cumulative scale), 32-33

Hamilton, Lee H., 283
Harding, Warren G.
  1920 campaign of, 179
  personality type, 160
Hargrove, Erwin C., 158, 159, 161
Harriman, W. Averell, 278
Harris, Louis
  on 1972 Nixon victory, 27
  view of, on public opposition to SST, 12-13
Harris poll, 25
  on constituency opinion, 287
  on gun control (1968), 10
  sampling questions and, 28
Hays, Brooks, 227
Health, Education and Welfare, Department of (HEW)
  busing and, 5
  educational differences and spending reductions by, 95

Health, Education and Welfare, Department of (HEW) (cont.)
  occupational differences and spending reductions by, 97
  race similarities over spending issues in, 94
Hess, Robert D., 49
  definition of democracy and, 113
  nonpartisanship and, 115
  personal clout illusion and, 114
  political socialization and, 44, 50, 60-63, 67, 68
HEW, see Health, Education and Welfare, Department of
Hickel, Walter, 192
Higher Education Act (1971), 6
Hirsch, Herbert, 65
Hitler, Adolf, 156
Holmes, Oliver Wendell, 150
Holsti, Ole, 38
Hoover, Herbert
  executive power under, 185
  personality type, 160
  as President of restraint, 158
Hruska, Roman, 304
Hughes, Charles Evans, 160
Human Behavior: An Inventory of Scientific Findings (Berelson and Steiner), 19
Humphrey, Hubert, in 1968 elections, 36, 178-79, 218, 221
  black evaluations of, 83
  Vietnam war and, 226
Hyman, Herbert, 5

Identification Model of socialization, 52
  family in, 57
Ideology
  democratic theory, 125-26
  issues and, 88-91
  lack of tradition of diversified, 156-57
  major differences in, between two parties, 220, 244-45
  and potential bias of activist opinion, 231-32
  public policy issues and, 91-99
  subgroup according to, 198-99
  voting patterns and partisan, 248-52
  See also Conservatism; Liberalism
Impeachment, 11
Inclusiveness, as property of attitude, 36-37
Indirect influence, 10-13
  SST as case of, 11-13
Industry and Labor for the SST, 12
Institutional norms, 188-96
  acquisition, enforcement and conformity with, 193-95
  consequences of, 195-96
Institutional patriotism, 191
Institutional setting, 175-208
  collective behavior in, 196-205
  concept of role in, 176-78
  consequences of institutional norms in, 195-96

Institutional setting (*cont.*)
  executive roles in, 184-86
  judicial roles in, 186-88
  leadership roles in, 178-79
  legislative roles in, 179-84
  norm acquisition, enforcement and conformity in, 193-95
  norms of, 188-96
  political integration and effectiveness of, 200-3
  political leadership and effectiveness of, 203-5
  roles in, 176-88
  subgroups in, 197-200
Instructed delegate (congressional type), 10
Integration
  institutional effectiveness and political, 300-3
  school, under Eisenhower, 227
  school busing for, *see* Busing issue
Intensity, as property of attitude, 35
Interest groups, 8-10
  gun control as case of influence of, 9-10
  as intermediaries, 257-63, 265
  leaders vs. followers of, 261-63
  political representation and, 260-61
  representativeness of, 258-60
  in responsible democracy, 302-3
  roles of, 182-83
Intermediate institutions, *see* Group influence; Interest groups
International Telephone & Telegraph (ITT), 124
Inter-party differences in elections, 218-20; *see also* Party identification
Interpersonal courtesy, 190
Interpersonal Transfer Model of political socialization, 51-52
  family in, 53, 54
Issues
  elections and, 216-34, 255-56
  ideology and, 86-99
  impact of, 220-24
  inter-party differences and, 218-19
  as mandates, 212, 225-26
  presidential elections and, 220-21, 254-55
  presidential popularity and, 273-74
  and voting in congressional elections, 255-56
ITT (International Telephone & Telegraph), 124

Jackson, Andrew, executive power as viewed by, 185
Jackson, John, 289
Jackson, Robert H., 170
Jefferson, Thomas
  on informed public, 300
  and Rousseau's views, 104
  yeoman farmer and, 108
Jennings, M. Kent, 48, 63
Jews, *see* Religion

Johnson, Lyndon B., 269
  black evaluations of, 83
  court appointments by, 147
  executive roles under, 185, 186
  and gun control, 9, 10
  landslide victory of, 221
  news media used by, 278, 279
  1968 elections and, 36
  personality type, 160
  popularity of, 273-75
  potential bias of activist opinion and, 231-32
  Vietnam war and, 225, 235
Jones, Charles, 291
Judicial branch
  attitudes influence behavior of, 169-70
  busing issue and, 7
  conservatism of, 170
  members of, 146, 147
  in responsible democracy, 308-10
Judicial roles, 186-88
  judicial subgroups, 199-200
  partisan influences on judges, 151

Keniston, Kenneth, 57
Kennedy, John F.
  as active-positive President, 159
  anti-Catholic attitudes threatening candidacy of, 85
  black Republicanism erased under, 82
  gun control issue and, 9
  as leader, 304
  news media used by, 278
  1960 victory of, 218
  and political socialization of children, 113
  popularity of, 273
  religion of, 147
  subgroups under, 198
  voting for, 22-24, 35
Kennedy, Robert F., 9
Key, V. O., 254, 259, 261, 301
Khrushchev, Nikita, 37
King, Martin Luther, Jr., 9
Korean war (1949–1953)
  polls on, 29
  presidential popularity and, 273, 275

Labor-management differences, 87
Landon, Alf, 25
Lane, Robert E., 54
Langton, Kenneth P., 63
Lasswell, Harold, 152-54
Lawgiver (legislative type), 162-63
Lawmaking roles, executive, 185
Lawson, Edwin D., 43
Lawyers, as elite, 149, 151-52
Leadership, *see* Political elite
Learning
  of basic political orientations as political socialization process, 48-53
  cognitive, described, 34, 49-50
Legislative branch, 268-69, 283-96
  attitudes influencing behavior in, 168-69

Legislative branch (*cont.*)
 and constituency opinion, 284-89
 elections for, *see* Elections
 institutional legislative roles, 179-84
 inter-party differences in voting in, 248-50
 legislative work rule in, 190
 party identification and legislative voting behavior in, 150-51
 in responsible democracy, 307-8
 sources of information for, 389-93
 visibility of, 293-94
Legislative Reorganization Act (1946), 38
Legislative types (personality types)
 the advertiser, 162
 the lawgiver, 162-63
 the reluctant, 162
 the spectator, 161-62
Legitimate power, 204
Legislators' "reports," as source of information, 292-93
Liberalism
 distribution of, 88-91
 of judiciary, 169
 legislative norms and, 195
 liberal-conservative distinction between parties, 220
 party, 244-46
 personality of liberals, 156
 use of term, defined, 88
Lincoln, Abraham
 executive power under, 185
 social background of, 146
Lipsky, Michael, 234-35
Literary Digest poll on 1936 elections, 25
Litt, Edgar, 67
Long, Russell, 304

McCarthy, Joseph, 156
McClosky, Herbert, 156, 245
McConaughy, John, 154-55
McCrone, Donald, 286-87
McGovern, George, in 1972 elections, 21, 26, 221, 222
 issues and, 224
 Jewish support for, 85
 nongovernmental elite support for, 124
 potential bias of activist opinion and, 232
 union endorsement and, 263
Madison, James
 and conflict in politics, 114
 representative government defended by, 105-9
Majority rule principle, 104-5, 107-9; *see also* Democracy
Makarenko (Soviet educator), 57
Mandates, elections as, 212, 225-26
Manley, John, 204, 205
Marshall, Thurgood, 147, 169
Mass media
 in political socialization, 64-65

Mass media (*cont.*)
 and presidential channels of influence, 276-77
 presidential use of, 276-79
Masses, power of, 2
Matthews, Donald R., 65, 194-96
Meany, George, 124
Measures of association, defined, 23
Military intervention, presidential popularity and, 273, 274
Miller, Warren E., 227, 284-88
Mills, C. Wright, 146
Mills, Wilbur, 204-5
Minority rights, majority rule and, 104-5; *see also* Democracy
Mitchell, William, 300
Modeling, defined, 52
Monsma, Stephen V., 115
Motivation, elite, 137-38
Mueller, John E., 29, 273-75

National Committee for the SST, 12
National Opinion Research Center, 25, 28
National Review (magazine), 65
National Rifle Association (NRA), 9-10, 292, 303
National Shooting Sports Foundation, 9
Nationalism, 43
"Nationalization" of politics, 86
Neustadt, Richard, 272, 276
New Haven study (1965), 67
Newcomb, Theodore M., 37, 63
News media
 and presidential channels of influence, 276-77
 presidential use of, 276-79
Newsweek (magazine), 25, 287
Nie, Norman, 228, 232, 233
Niemi, Richard G., 48
1984 (Orwell), 104
Nixon, Richard M.
 busing opposed by, 6
 court appointments by, 170, 199, 304
 disregard for rules of the game under, 268
 executive role under, 185, 186
 "Jewish seat" on Supreme Court and, 147
 Jewish support for, 85
 lobbying campaigns during first term of, 257-58
 loyalty to, 192
 news media used by, 277-79
 in 1960 elections, 35, 218
 1972 victory of, 221-22
 nongovernmental elite support for, 124
 party identification and support for, 221
 popularity of, 273
 potential bias of activist opinion and, 232
 on presidential accessibility, 307
 presidential power under, 269-70
 resignation of, 11, 270

Nixon, Richard M. (*cont*)
  role of, in 1968 elections, 178-79
  and SST case, 12
  union endorsement and, 263
  Vietnam war and, 226, 227, 235
  voting for, 20, 21, 24, 26-27, 218
Norms, *see* Institutional norms
NRA (National Rifle Association), 9-10, 292, 303

Occupations
  background in, of elite, 148
  differences in, reflected in public policy issues, 97
  impact of, on opinions of elite, 151
O'Connor, Robert, 246, 250-51
O'Hara, James G., 6
Omnibus Crime Control and Safe Streets Act, 10
Opinions, distinguishing attitudes from, 19; *see also specific opinions*
Opportunity, 140-42
Orwell, George, 104
Ostracism, 194

Pareto, Vilfredo, 122
Parochial school aid
  age differences over, 96
  educational differences over, 95
  occupational differences over, 97
  race differences over, 94
  religious affiliation and, 97
Participation
  in direct action, 229-33
  in elections, 212-16
  See also Citizen roles
Party identification, 72-86
  age in, 79-81
  in elections, 218-20
  general trends in, 73-76
  independent identification, 73-75, 79
  legislative voting behavior and, 150-51
  legislator party roles and, 183-84
  public policy issues and, 99
  race in, 82-83
  region and urban-rural differences in, 85-86
  religion in, 83-85
  social class differences in, 77-79
Party platforms, 243-44
Party roles, 183-84
  executive, 185-86
Passive-negative presidents, 160-61
Passive-positive presidents, 160
Patriotism, institutional, 191
Pavlov, Ivan, 52
Peer groups, 189
  in political socialization, 63-64
  See also Institutional norms
Perception, defined, 34
Personality factors
  elite, 152-63
  elite behavior and, 157-59
  elite opinion and, 155-63

Personality factors (*cont.*)
  political beliefs and, 156
  politics and, 152-55
Piaget, Jean, 49, 50
Political activity index, 31-33
Political community, described, 43-44
Political culture, *see* Democracy; Responsible democracy
Political elite, 121-208
  attitudinal factors in, 163-71
  accountability of, 132-35
  concept of, 122-25
  democratic theory and, 125-26
  direct influence on, 4-5
  elite-mass attitude differences, 163-67
  institutional effectiveness and leadership of, 203-5
  institutional leadership roles of, 178-79
  institutional setting and, *see* Institutional setting
  inter-party differences at level of, 242-52
  leadership and power of, 126-29
  opportunity for becoming part of, 140-42
  people and their political leadership, in responsible democracy, 299-305
  personalities and opinions of, 155-63
  personality factors among, 152-63
  personality and politics among, 152-55
  political attitude and behavior of, 167-71
  political interest and socialization of, 136-37
  political motivation and ambition of, 137-38
  power of, 2-3
  recruiting, 135-42
  resources needed by, 139-40
  responsible democracy and political leadership of, 303-5
  responsibility of, 131-32
  responsiveness of, 129-31
  social background of, 146-52
  social background theory and decision making by, 149-52
Political man, 152, 153
Political opposition, presidents and, 280-82
Political parties
  activists and leaders of, 244-47
  attitude influence on, 168
  conservatism in, 164, 244-46
  group influence in, 7-8; *see also* Group influence
  as intermediaries, 241-56, 264-65
  inter-party differences at elite level in, 242-52
  inter-party differences at voter level in, 252-56
  party officeholders and, 247-52
  platforms of, 243-44
  socialization into, 55
  See also Party identification

Political Parties, Committee on, 269
Political philosophy, 88-91
  as not "theoretical," 102-3; *see also*
    Democracy; Ideology
Political socialization, 42-71
  agents in process of, 53-65
  discontinuities and differential, 66-69
  of elite, 136-37
  family in process of, 53-57
  five models of, 49-53
  government and, 45-48
  learning basic political orientations as,
    48-53
  mass media in process of, 64-65
  peer groups in process of, 63-64
  political community in, 43-44
  political system and, 43-48
  public school in process of, 57-63
  regime and, 44-45
Politicos
  defined, 181
  example of, 283-84
Politics, as term with bad connotations,
    115-16
Polls, *see* Survey research; *and specific
    poll takers; for example:* Gallup poll;
    Harris poll
Pomper, Gerald, 219-20, 224, 243
Pool, Ithiel de Sola, 288
Popular control
  elections and, 224-28
  promoters of, *see* Interest groups; Po-
    litical parties
  public participation in politics as facet
    of, 211
Power
  executive, 184-85, 269-70
  need for, as personality factor in elite,
    153-54
  types of, 204
Presidential Character, The (Barber),
    159
Presidential elections
  black vote in 1964 and 1968, 82
  disappearance of Solid South from, 73,
    85
  electorate's time of decision in, 217-18
  impact of issues on, 220-21, 254-55
  study of 1964, 229-30
  study of 1968, 232-34
  *See also specific candidates and presi-
    dents*
Presidents, 268-83, 294-95
  active-negative, 159-60
  active-positive, 159
  age, sex, race of, 146
  channels of influence for, 276-82
  children's view of, 51
  coverage and access to, 276-77
  executive roles, 184-86
  executive subgroups and, 197-98
  format and timing in use of news
    media by, 277-79
  idealized, 51-52

Presidents (*cont.*)
  institutional role of, 184-86
  interpretations and feedback of public
    opinion to, 279-80
  overextension of power of, 269
  party control by (1952-present), 252-53
  passive-negative, 160-61
  passive-positive, 160
  personality and behavior of, 157-58
  political opposition and, 280-82
  popularity of, 272-75
  protest and, 235-36
  public expectations from, 270-72, 282-
    83
  religion and, 147
  in responsible democracy, 305-7
Press conferences, presidential, 277-79
Prewitt, Kenneth, 303-4
Programmatic support, 252-56
Protestants, *see* Religion
Protests, as direct action, 233-36
Prothro, James W., 65
Public, types of influence available to, 3
Public opinion, influence of, 1-14; *see also*
    Survey research
Public policy issues, *see* Issues
Public relations, presidential, 279-80
Public schools, political socialization in,
    57-63; *see also* Busing issue; Paro-
    chial school aid

Race
  changes in attitudes toward, 38
  of elite, 146-47
  liberalism-conservatism and, 88-89
  in party identification, 82-83
  of presidents, 146
  public policy issues and differences in,
    93-94
Rebellion, adolescent, 56-57
Reciprocity norm, 191
Recruiting of political elite, 135-42
Redundancy effect, 63
Reedy, George, 269, 279-80
Referent power, 204
Regime, defined, 44-45
Regional differences
  liberalism-conservatism and, 88-90
  in party identification, 85-86
Registration requirements, 213-14
Rehnquist, William H., 170, 199
Religion
  abortion reform and, 87-88, 97
  of elite, 147
  impact of, on opinions of elite, 151
  and party identification, 83-85
  public policy issues and different, 96-97
Reluctant (legislative type), 162
RePass, David, 254
Representational roles, 181-82
Representational style, constituency opin-
    ion and, 284-89

Representative democracy, *see* Democracy
Representative institutions, *see* Legislative branch; Presidents
Representative samples, 26
Republic
  defined, 106-7
  distinguished from democracy, 105
Resources needed by political elite, 139-40
Response set, 33-34
Responsibility of political elite, 131-32
Responsible democracy, 299-310
  executive branch in, 305-7
  judicial branch in, 308-10
  legislative branch in, 307-8
  people and their political leaders in, 299-305
  public attitude articulation in, 301-3
  public attitude formation in, 300-1
  political leadership in, 303-5
  responsiveness and governmental institutions in, 305-10
Responsible Electorate, The (Key), 254
Responsiveness of political elite, 129-31
Reward power, 204
Right, the, personality characteristics of elites on, 156
Riots, 87
  banning reporting of, 65
Role sectors, defined, 180
Role theory, 176-78
Roles
  concept of, 176-78
  executive power, 184-85
  institutional, 176-88
  representational, 181-82
  See also specific roles; for example:
    Citizen roles; Judicial roles; Party roles
Rolling Stone (periodical), 65
Roosevelt, Franklin D.
  as active-positive President, 159
  executive power under, 185
  New Deal of, 77
  news media used by, 277-78
  1936 election of, 25
  party identification during administration of, 72, 79
  popularity of, 272
  as President of Action, 158
Roosevelt, Theodore
  executive power under, 185
  news media used by, 276
  as President of Action, 158
Roper poll, 25
Rousseau, Jean-Jacques, 103-4

Sampling
  as basic to survey research, 25-26
  question wording in, 28-29
  sample error in, example of, 25
Scammon, Richard M., 36
Schaatschneider, E. E., 108-9, 112

Schools, political socialization in, 57-63;
  see also Busing issue; Parochial school aid
Second phase, defined, 44
Selective perception, defined, 34
Senority norm, 189-90
Sex
  of elite, 146-47
  of presidents, 146
Sex differences over public policy issues, 92-93
Sigel, Roberta S., 271
Sirica, John, 169
Skinner, B. F., 20
Smith, Al, in 1928 elections, 39-40
Social background of political elite, 146-52
Social background theory, elite decision making and, 149-52
Social class
  belief systems and, 165-66
  public-regardingness and, 115
  See also Political elite
Social class differences
  importance of, 67
  in party identification, 77-79
  political socialization and, 63
Socialization, *see* Political socialization
Socioeconomic conflicts, party identification and, 86-87
Socioeconomic status
  direct action and, 231
  membership in organizations and, 258-59
  voter turnout and, 215
  See also Social class; Social class differences
Specialization norm, 190
Spectator (legislative type), 161-62
Split ticket voting, 252-53
Sporting Arms and Ammunition Manufacturers Institute, 9
Spuriousness concept, 23
SRS (Survey Research Center; University of Michigan), 28, 82, 229, 233-34
SST (supersonic transport), as case of indirect influence, 11-13
Steiner, Gary A., 19
Sterilization, compulsory, 149-50
Stokes, Donald E., 227, 284-88
Structure of authority, 45
Study of Congress survey, 292
Subgroups, political institutions and, 197-200
Sullivan, John, 246, 250-51
Supersonic transport (SST), as case of indirect influence, 11-13
Survey research (opinion polling)
  attitude measurement in, 28-34
  on attitudes, 25-27
  bandwagon psychology created by, 28
  of constituents, on voting issues, 283
  on presidential popularity, 272-73
  question wording in, 28-29

Survey research (opinion polling) (*cont.*)
  response set in, 33-34
  on trends in liberalism and conservatism, 88
  *See also specific survey researchers;
    for example:* Gallup poll; Harris poll
Survey Research Center (SRC; University of Michigan), 28, 82, 229, 233-34

Taft, Robert, 164
Taft, William Howard
  executive power under, 185
  personality type, 160
  as President of Restraint, 158
Television, presidential use of, 277; *see also* Mass media
Time (magazine), 25
Torney, Judith V.
  and definition of democracy, 113
  nonpartisanship and, 115
  personal clout illusion and, 114
  and political socialization, 44, 50, 60-63, 67, 68
Town meeting, 103, 104, 112
Truman, Harry S.
  as active-positive President, 159
  party identification during administration of, 79
  popularity of, 272-75
Trustee (legislative type), 283
  defined, 181

Unions, political involvement and identification with labor, 261
Urban-rural differences in party identification, 85-86

Verba, Sidney, 54, 55, 112, 228, 232, 233
Vietnam amnesty issue
  age differences over, 96
  educational differences and support for, 95
  occupational differences over, 97
  race differences over, 93, 94
  religious affiliation and, 97
Vietnam war
  black opposition to, 82
  as campaign issue (1964), 225-26
  Chicago Democratic convention (1968) and, 234
  Nixon and, 226, 227, 235
  polls on, 29
  presidential popularity and, 273, 275
  presidential use of news media and, 278

Violence, Douglas on, 169
Visibility, congressional, 293-94
Voter turnout
  cross-national comparisons of, 212-14
  low, 212
  registration of, 303
  socioeconomic status and, 215-16
  by type of election, 214-15
Voters
  correlates of participation of, 215-16
  expression of attitudes through voting, 301-2; *see also* Attitudes
  inter-party differences at level of, 252-56
  party identification and age of, 79-81
  party platforms as guides for, 243-44
  rational, 300
Voting patterns
  analyzing, 22-23
  in 1896 elections, 24
  and political activity index, 31-32
  voting discrimination, elimination of, 212
Voting Rights Act (1965), 303

Wahlke, John C., 194
Wallace, George, in 1968 elections, 75, 81, 178-79, 221
  as candidate, 224
  union member support for, 166
  Vietnam war and, 226
War
  legislation in time of, 309
  presidential popularity and, 273-75
  See also Cambodian war; Korean war; Vietnam war
Washington, George, 113
Watergate (scandal), 66, 169, 186, 268-70, 307
Wattenberg, Ben J., 36
Wednesday Club, 199
White, Edward, 147
White, Ralph K., 38
Whitten amendment, 6
Wilkinson, Rupert, 58
Wilson, James Q., 115
Wilson, Woodrow, 147
  personality type, 160
  as President of Action, 158
Woodward and Roper Political Activity Index, 31-32
Wylie, Laurence, 48

Zeigler, Harmon, 260